In Her Own Image

In Her Own Image

Women's Self-Representation in Twentieth-Century Art

Danielle Knafo

Madison • Teaneck
Fairleigh Dickinson University Press

Associated University Presses
2010 Eastpark Boulevard
Cranbury, NJ 08512

The paper used in this publication meets the requirements of the American National Standard for Permanence of Paper for Printed Library Materials Z39.48-1984.

Library of Congress Cataloging-in-Publication Data

Knafo, Danielle.
In her own image : women's self-representation in twentieth-century art / Danielle Knafo.
p. cm.
Includes bibliographical references and index.
ISBN 978-0-8386-4210-8 (alk. paper)
1. Women artists—Psychology. 2. Self-representation in art. 3. Women in art. 4. Art, Modern—20th century. I. Title.
N8354.K58 2009
704′.042—dc22

2009002460

PRINTED IN THE UNITED STATES OF AMERICA

Contents

List of Illustrations 7

Acknowledgments 11

Introduction: By Herself 15

1. Käthe Kollwitz: The Dead Mother 24
2. Claude Cahun: The Third Sex 37
3. Charlotte Salomon: The Art of Trauma 58
4. Frida Kahlo: Mirror and Mask 73
5. Carolee Schneemann: Feminine Erotics 89
6. Hannah Wilke: The Naked Truth 102
7. Ana Mendieta: Goddess in Exile 118
8. Adrian Piper: Plain as Black and White 133
9. Cindy Sherman: Dressing Up and Make-Believe 144
10. Orlan: Monster Beauty 157

Epilogue: In Her Own Image 171

Notes 175

Bibliography 186

Index 193

Illustrations

Black-and-White

Fig. 1: Edouard Manet, *Olympia, 1863*. . . . 16

Fig. 2: Countess de Castiglioni, 1863–66, Mayer and Pierson Studio 17

Fig. 3: Cindy Sherman, *Untitled #82*, 1979 20

Fig. 4: Käthe Kollwitz, *Self-Portrait*, 1924 26

Fig. 5: Käthe Kollwitz, *Woman with Dead Child*, 1903 29

Fig. 6: Käthe Kollwitz, *Death and Woman/Self-Portrait*, 1910. 32

Fig. 7: Käthe Kollwitz, *Self-Portrait*, 1934 34

Fig. 8: Käthe Kollwitz, *Self-Portrait Seated at Table*, c. 1892. 35

Fig. 9: Käthe Kollwitz, *Self-Portrait in Profile Facing Right*, 1938 35

Fig. 10: Claude Cahun, *Self-Portrait*, c. 1929 38

Fig. 11: Claude Cahun and Marcel Moore, *Self-Pride* (I.O.U.), 1929–30 40

Fig. 12 : Claude Cahun, *Self-Portrait*, 1928 43

Fig. 13: Claude Cahun, *Self-Portrait*, c. 1927 44

Fig. 14: Claude Cahun, *Self-Portrait*, c. 1921 47

Fig. 15: Claude Cahun, *Self-Portrait*, 1928 49

Fig. 16 : Claude Cahun, *Self-Portrait*, c. 1932 50

Fig. 17: Claude Cahun, *Self-Portrait*, c. 1927 52

Fig. 18: Charlotte Salomon, *Self-Portrait*, 1940 59

Fig. 19: Charlotte Salomon, from *Life? or Theater?* 1940–42 62

Fig. 20: Charlotte Salomon, from *Life? or Theater?* 1940–42 64

Fig. 21: Charlotte Salomon, from *Life? or Theater?* 1940–42 65

Fig. 22: Frida Kahlo, *My Nurse and I* (Mi Nana y yo), 1937 75

Fig. 23: Frida Kahlo, *The Two Fridas*, 1939 77

Fig. 24: Frida Kahlo, *The Broken Column*, 1944 81

Fig. 25: Frida Kahlo, *What the Water Gave Me*, (Lo que el agua me dio) 1939 82

Fig. 26: Carolee Schneemann, *Meat Joy*, 1964 90

Fig. 27: Carolee Schneemann, *Meat Joy*, 1964 91

Fig. 28: Carolee Schneemann, *Meat Joy*, 1964 92

Fig. 29: Carolee Schneemann, *Interior Scroll*, 1975 97

Fig. 30: Carolee Schneemann, *Interior Scroll*, 1975 98

Fig. 31: Carolee Schneemann, *Vulva's Morphia*, 1995 99

Fig. 32: Hannah Wilke, *Pink Champagne*, 1975 103

Fig. 33: Hannah Wilke, *What Does This Represent? What Do You Represent? (Ad Reinhart)*, 1978, from *So Help Me Hannah* Series 105

Fig. 34: Hannah Wilke, *So Help Me Hannah*, 1979–85 106

Fig. 35: Hannah Wilke, *S.O.S. Starification Object Series*, 1975 108

Fig. 36: Hannah Wilke, *STAND UP*, 1982 110

Fig. 37: Hannah Wilke, Performalist Self-Portrait with Donald Goddard from *Intra-Venus #3*, August 17, 1992, February 15, 1992, August 9, 1992 115

Fig. 38: Hannah Wilke, Performalist Self-Portrait with Donald Goddard from *Intra-Venus Series #1*, January 30, 1992/June 15, 1992 116

Fig. 39: Ana Mendieta, *Untitled* (Fetish Series), 1977 119

Fig. 40: Ana Mendieta, *On Giving Life*, 1975 123

Fig. 41: Ana Mendieta, *Untitled* (Silueta Works in Iowa), c. 1976–78 124

Fig. 42: Ana Mendieta, *Untitled* (Silueta Series, Iowa), 1977 127

Fig. 43: Ana Mendieta, *Untitled*, 1980 . . . 129

Fig. 44: Cindy Sherman, *Untitled #56*, 1980 145

Fig. 45: Cindy Sherman, *Untitled #15*, 1978 146

Fig. 46: Orlan, *Orlan Accouche d'elle M'aime [Orlan gives birth to her loved self]*, 1964 159

Fig. 47: Orlan, *Femme Avec Tête, no. 8: Close-up of hand on cheek*, 1996. 166

Fig. 48: Orlan, *The Reincarnation of Saint Orlan, or Pic new[s] Pics*, the "unicorn" operation with transparent sheets and grimacing lips, 1990 168

Color Plates

Between pages 96 and 97

Plate #1: Charlotte Salomon, from *Life? or Theater?* 1940–42

Plate #2: Charlotte Salomon, from *Life? or Theater?* 1940–42

Plate #3: Frida Kahlo, *Self-Portrait as Tehuana*, 1943

Plate #4: Frida Kahlo, *The Love Embrace of the Universe, the Earth (Mexico), Diego, Me, and Señor Xolotl*, 1949

Plate #5: Hannah Wilke, *So Help Me Hannah Series: Portrait of the Artist with her Mother, Selma Butter*, 1978–81

Plate #6: Hannah Wilke, Performalist Self-Portrait with Donald Goddard from *Intra-Venus Series # 4*, July 26, 1992/ February 19, 1992

Plate #7: Frida Kahlo, *My Birth*, 1932

Plate #8: Gustav Courbet, *L'Origine du Monde*, [Origin of the World], 1866

Plate #9: Orlan, *L'Origine de la Guerre* [Origin of War], 1989

Plate #10 : Marcel Duchamp, *Etants Donnés*, 1946–66

Plate #11: Ana Mendieta, *Untitled* (Rape Performance), 1973

Plate #12: Hannah Wilke, *I Object: Memoirs of a Sugargiver*, 1977–78

Plate #13: Ana Mendieta, *Silueta* Works in Mexico, 1976

Plate #14: Ana Mendieta, *Imagen de Yagul*, 1973

Plate #15: Ana Mendieta, *Rastros Corporales* (Body Tracks), 1982 (detail)

Plate #16: Ana Mendieta, *Ánima, Silueta de Cohetes* [Soul, Silhouette of Fireworks), 1976

Plate #17: Cindy Sherman, *Untitled #146*, 1985

Plate #18: Cindy Sherman, *Untitled #216*, 1989

Plate #19: Cindy Sherman, *Untitled #250*, 1992

Plate #20: Cindy Sherman, *Untitled #413*, 2003–4

Plate #21: Orlan, *Entre-Deux* [Between the Two], *No. 7*, 1994

Plate #22: Orlan, *Refiguration/Self-Hybridation, no. 27*, 1998

Acknowledgments

THIS BOOK IS DEDICATED TO ROCCO LO BOSCO whose presence and help have been invaluable to the completion of this book. He read and reread numerous versions of the chapters and edited them with extreme care, talent, and insight many times over. In addition, his emotional support throughout the writing and publishing process was unconditional and is appreciated beyond words.

My sister, Ruth Setton, and my friend and colleague, Janice Lieberman, also read early versions of the manuscript and offered many valuable suggestions. Others who read and commented on various chapters along the way were Kiki Elefant, Seymour Moscovitz, Jack Spector, Ariel Orr Jordan, John Ransom Phillips, and Maryellen LoBosco.

Daniel Dervin's comments and guidance helped me to find the book's guiding spirit and to state and elaborate on its major themes throughout.

Gratitude goes to Harry Keyishian for believing in this book from the start and to Julien Yoseloff and Christine Retz for getting it off the ground.

Thanks, too, to Diana Pepe for her beautiful jacket design and to Bill Allured for taking the author's photo.

Jacob Rossmer was available at all times to help me find obscure references and to make uniform the many references and footnotes found in these pages. Elisa Reich and Eva Leven helped prepared the index.

My mother, Rosine Knafo, informed me, through her life and our relationship, about what it means to be an immigrant woman, mother and grandmother. Her belief in this book was unwavering.

My son, Gavriel Matan Knafo, has given me one of the greatest gifts: the ability to look at the world and art with awe and a sense of wonder.

I thank the living artists who granted me interviews: Adrian Piper, Carolee Schneemann, and Orlan, as well as relatives and partners of the artists who spoke with me and shared valuable information that allowed me to know the artists better. Special thanks go to Donald Goddard, Hans Breder, and Raquelin Mendieta. I am also indebted to all of the institutions, museums, galleries, and societies that provided permission to use the wonderful images found in these pages. I am very thankful for the support of the CW Post Campus Faculty Research Committee.

Last but not least, I am especially grateful to the ten women artists on whom this book is based. Over the years, these women artists stepped off the page and out of my research. They walked and talked to me until I saw the world through their eyes. They taught me so much, deepening my understanding of and appreciation for the female experience and its creative possibilities. My wish is to share this knowledge with others and have it touch them the way it has touched me.

I am grateful for permission to reprint the following earlier versions of four chapters: "The Mirror, the Mask, and the Masquerade in the Art and Life of Frida Kahlo," *The Annual of Psychoanalysis* 21 (1993): 277–300.

Dressing Up and Other Games of Make-Believe: The Function of Play in the Art of Cindy Sherman, *American Imago* 53 (2) 1996: 139–164. @ The Johns Hopkins University Press. Reprinted with permission of The Johns Hopkins University Press.

Claude Cahun: The Third Sex, *Studies in Gender and Sexuality*, 2 (1) 2001: 29–61. *http://www.informaworld.com.*

Art on the Cutting Edge: Orlan's Medusan Female. In *Unconscious Fantasies and the Relational World*, 2005, the Analytic Press: 171–201.

"Castration and Medusa: Orlan's Art on the Cutting Edge" Copyright © 2009 from Studies in Gender and Sexuality 10(3) by Danielle Knafo. Reproduced by permission of Taylor and Francis Group, LLC, a division of Informa plc.

In Her Own Image

Introduction: By Herself

FACE THE FEMALE BODY AND YOU STAND NOT only before the body from which you first emerged, but also before a form whose manifestations are multiple, a form that has captivated the human imagination since people began fashioning goddess statues some thirty thousand years before the common era. Her body has been central to us from the very beginning, our beginning and the beginning of our civilization, so it is no wonder she has been represented countless times and in countless ways as goddess, mother, nymph, angel, demon, temptress, harlot, virgin, enigma and solution, origin and terminus, life and death, carved in stone, painted on canvas, formed in sand and rock, and frozen in photographs, on billboards and the glossy covers of magazines. Idealized versions of her are used to sell everything from cars to computers, land masses to toaster ovens. Pornographic images of her entice and excite, transmogrify her into a fetish, a dehumanized object, a thing to be managed, controlled, and consumed. Yet, however revealed she remains mysterious, however naked still unknown.

The image of the female body fascinates us like no other; we are soaking in the history of her unfoldment, innumerable poses and renderings in a myriad of contexts, the evolution of her cultural form, her body on the historical move as she speaks to us from the dark places of appropriation. Yet, although she has been held captive by the structures and dictates of patriarchal culture, controlled by presuppositions both spoken and unspoken, and even wounded by the violence and rage directed against her body and self, her power to captivate, inspire, frighten, and interrogate has not been diminished.

When we study the history of Western art, it is easy to observe that female representation has been the nearly exclusive province of male artists. Until very recently, the standard art history texts, such as Kenneth Clark's *The Nude* and H. W. Janson's *The History of Art*, have women appear as subjects, rarely as creators. If the female nude is not the image most often encountered in Western art, it is perhaps what we remember most and what is most clearly identified with high art and culture.[1] As an icon of Western culture, the female body in art has come to represent, among other things, the male's idealization of that body while simultaneously revealing its placement by him within the restrictive and secure boundaries of an aesthetic discourse that has excluded female self-representation. Women did not or could not speak for themselves, their bodies, or their experiences. Consequently, many writers, of whom I will mention only a few, have expounded on the "male gaze." John Berger famously stated that "Men act and women appear," and Laura Mulvey spoke of the male camera which captures the female quality of "to-be-looked-at-ness" in film. Luce Irigaray has noted that "the look" which appropriates is not as privileged in women as it is in men, and Griselda Pollack has referred to the late nineteenth-century *flâneur* as an exclusively male prototype of a stroller whose gaze is both "covetous and erotic."[2]

Self-portraiture as a genre is a relatively late phenomenon in Western art. It is usually connected to the Renaissance, a time when artists achieved social stature and became as worthy of representation as their wealthy portrait subjects. When one thinks of famous early self-portraits, those of Dürer and Rembrandt immediately come to mind. Although some wealthy, well-born, and educated women artists are also known to have painted self-portraits prior to the twentieth century, only a handful produced self-portrait series: sixteenth-century Italian artist, Sofinisba Anguissola, and eighteenth-century artists, Angelica Kauffman and Elisabeth Vigée-Lebrun. These

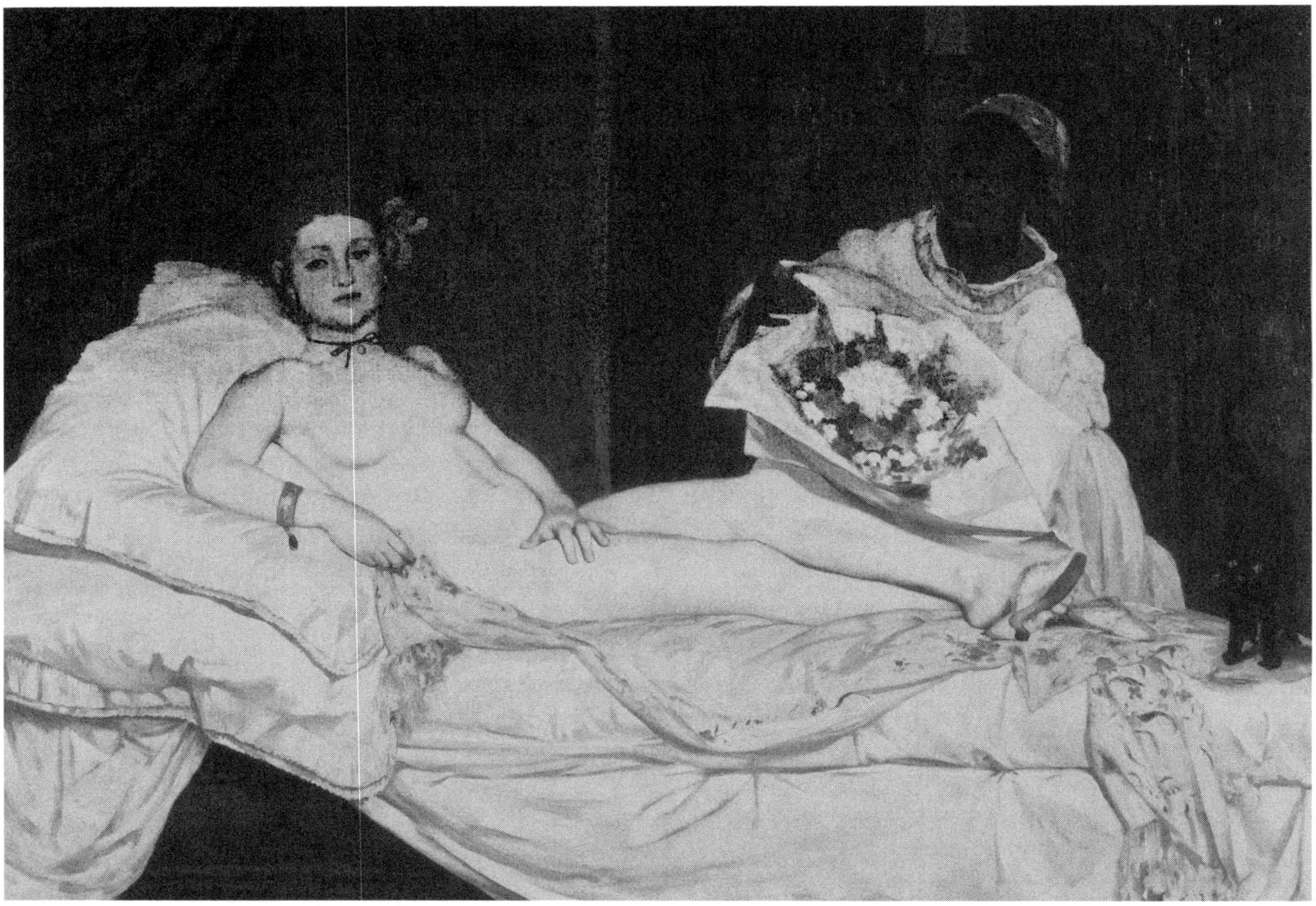

1. Edouard Manet (1832–1883), *Olympia,* 1863. Oil on canvas, 130.5 × 190.0 cm. Inv. RF 2772. Photo: Hervé Lewandowski. Musée d'Orsay, Paris, France. Réunion des Musées Nationaux/Art Resource, NY.

artists were careful to present flattering, feminine, respectable, and innocent renderings of themselves. Whereas no taboos were broken and no one was threatened by the artistic rendering of these self-conscious "ladies," self-representation itself can be considered a revolutionary act for that time.[3] Most impressive are the over four hundred portraits of the Countess de Castiglione, done in collaboration with photographer Pierre-Louis Pierson, from the nineteenth century. The countess's self-portrait photographs chronicled her attendance at soirées and masked balls, and depict her donned in the extravagant couture of the theater and opera, as well as costumes inspired solely from her imagination. Some of her poses were risqué for the era as they revealed her bare legs and feet.

Beside this handful of women artists who made serial self-representational art, it was not until the modern age that such art became an identifiable genre. Not coincidentally this finding corresponds with the artist's personality becoming important with the inception of modern art. Part of the change evident in Western art of the last hundred years is, of course, attributable to the long awaited inclusion of women into art academies.[4] As a result, twentieth-century women artists at last turned their gaze upon themselves, making their own image the subject of art. In so doing, they overcame gender and ethnic clichés and stereotypes and spearheaded the creation of a new feminine aesthetic.

In women's self-representational art, the individual woman's body is no longer offered primarily as an object for male contemplation or consumption, but as a physical and psychological presence seen through her own eyes. As they became artist and model, subject and object, seer and seen, women did far more than show their faces and bodies; they mapped their incarnate landscapes, revealing deeper dimensions of the feminine absent

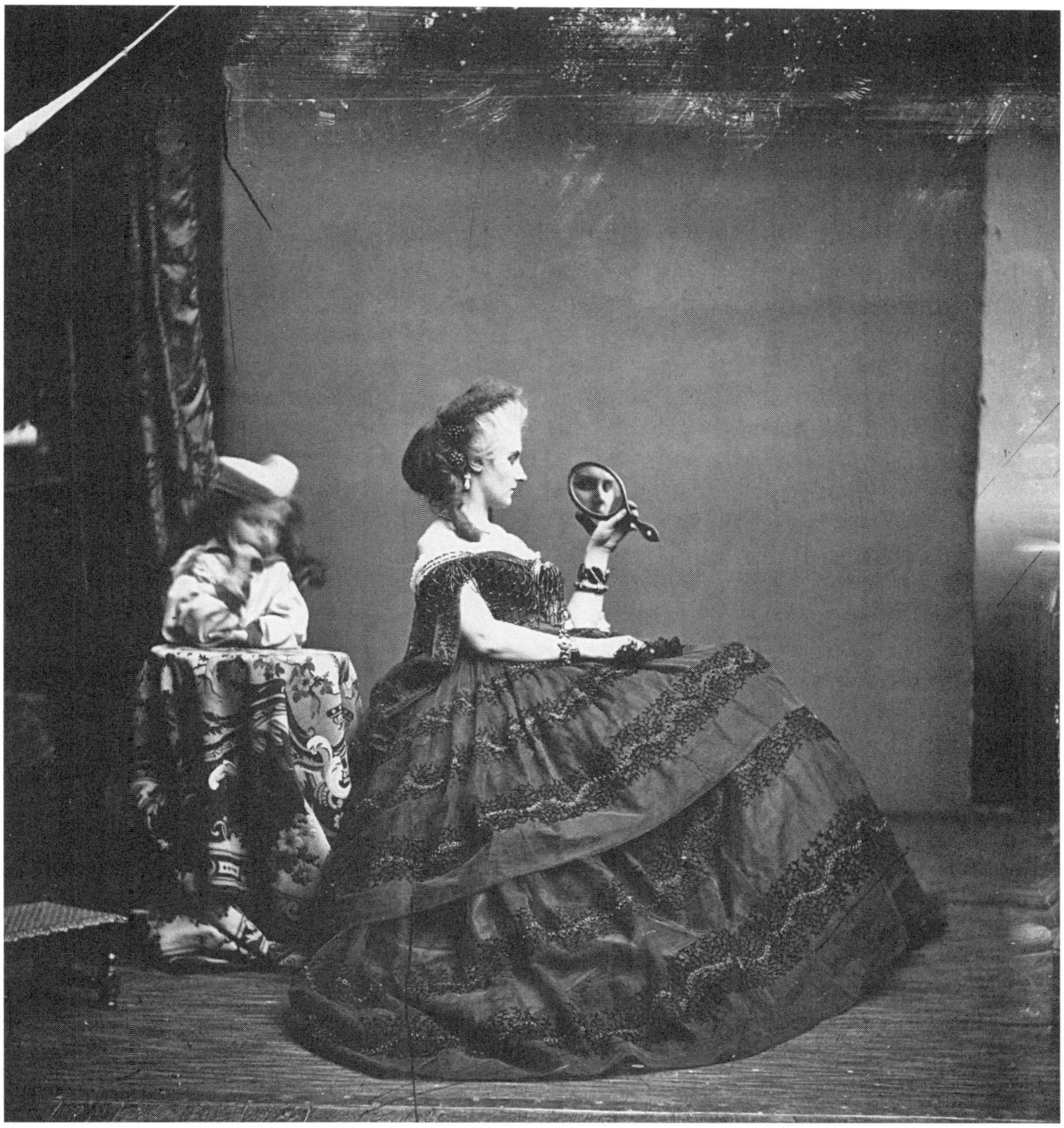

2. Mayer and Pierson studio (19th cen.). Virginia Oldoini, Countess de Castiglioni (1837–1899). Adoc-photos/Art Resource, NY.

from art until their time. They challenged dominant images of women within the Western tradition, creating art that reflects a profound dialogue between the female artist and her culture as she speaks to us with images, figures, memories, and dreams, and we answer her with delight and astonishment, or perhaps anger and shame. This playful, profound, and sometimes disturbing transformation takes place on and through the woman's body, a body which today is represented by a plurality of images that have no specific end or purpose except to continue to evolve.[5]

Let us not overlook or minimize the magnitude of this daring subversion; it literally opposes and interrogates centuries of cultural appropriation of the female form and self. The woman artist takes back what has always belonged to her, by altering the very context of traditional artistic representation of the female body and female life. In this artistic outpouring, she is at last by herself—voicing with paintings, photographs, sculpture, and cosmetic surgery a unique creative response to narrow and subservient confines; redefining her identity and place in the world, using everything at her disposal, including the assumptions and the psychological structures that still restrict her. And, indeed, she has something entirely new to tell us.

Feminism and feminist critique have been instrumental in recounting this story. That discourse, brilliantly exemplified in the writings of Linda Nochlin, Whitney Chadwick, Lucy Lippard, and Griselda Pollack, among others, is indispensable to the historicizing of women and art.[6] At times, however, certain limitations remain, such as the need to create a feminine mythology that romanticizes particular artistic figures or subjects, leaving insufficient room for multiple interpretations. Also, most criticism to date has focused almost exclusively on the white heterosexual female, neglecting women artists of color and lesbians whose art centers on self-representation and difference.[7]

This book examines women's art from the early twentieth century through today, incorporating feminism as well as additional thematic and methodological perspectives. In studying the work and lives of Käthe Kollwitz, Claude Cahun, Charlotte Salomon, Frida Kahlo, Carolee Schneemann, Hannah Wilke, Adrian Piper, Ana Mendieta, Cindy Sherman, and Orlan, I ask and attempt to answer the following questions: How does psychology shed light on the internal dynamics of creativity and experience, particularly the female experience of her body? How does women's self-representational art clarify, and at times challenge, certain psychoanalytic assumptions about female development and identity? How do the changes in women's self-representation over the last century reflect changes in their evolving psychological awareness? How does the art of these women express the transcendent possibilities of the female psyche? Which new perspectives do we bring to the sight of the female body as a result of viewing these works, and what do they make us see about ourselves?

In Her Own Image extends the dialogue between feminism and art history, while developing a psychoanalytic examination of women's self-representation. I will draw from a variety of psychoanalytic theories and concepts, all the while maintaining that feminism and psychoanalysis need not be at odds, even though their aims and methods are different. In fact, I hope to demonstrate ways that they inform and enhance each other. I join the collective effort of psychoanalytic feminist thinkers (Dinnerstein, Chodorow, Benjamin, Dimen, Harris, and Goldner) who write and practice at the intersection of psychoanalysis, feminism, and other disciplines.[8] The challenge as well as the excitement in this union stems, in part, from the tension that exists between "theoretical gender" as it has been constructed in the academy and the "psychological gender" of lived experience explicated in the clinic. Part of the purpose of my writing is to continue to extricate the enduring and still relevant elements of Freud's vision from the normative phallic structures in which they were fixed and to position gender in an object-relational matrix of mothering instead.[9]

Indeed, at the heart of my examination is the central concept of identification with the mother. Feminism has laid a great deal of emphasis on countering the male gaze without sufficiently taking into consideration what I believe to be an equally fundamental psychological dynamic: the mother's role in the construction of female identity.[10] As I will demonstrate, there are various ways in which women artists have captured the preverbal and nonverbal relationship with the mother in their work. Since she shares the female body with her mother, the woman artist who depicts herself, of necessity, portrays her internalization of and identification with the mother. Also, the procreative power of the mother figure is a major aspect of the work of the artists I address. In fact, the most crucial identification the woman artist has with her mother is in her power to create. Furthermore, in painting a self-portrait or creating body art, one necessarily treats oneself as both subject and object. Relating to the self as an object, I believe, represents the manner in which one was first treated as an object by one's primary caretaker. Therefore, artists who employ self-representation in their work can be thought of as transferring their original maternal care onto and into their art. By recreating the early mother-child relationship, the artist now identifies with both passive and active roles.

The way the mother-child relationship is expressed in women's art has contributed to the uniqueness of female self-representation and explains some of its special features. This art emphasizes nature, birth imagery, symbiotic merger, containment, inner space, doubling, the uncanny, and mirroring, all features that allude to the early tie with the mother. More importantly, relating to the self as an Other, like the mother once did, entitles the artist to take over the transformative function of the mother. The artist not only represents what might have gone awry in this highly charged and multilayered relationship, but also makes attempts at reparation through her art. I will show how most of these women strove to link their art to the theme of motherhood despite the fact that only one of them actually bore children of her own. Kollwitz repeatedly drew mothers with infants as a way of recapturing the mother of her childhood, a mother who was depressed and withdrawn due to the loss of three children. Cahun, whose mother was institutionalized when she was a child of four, endeavored to take her mother's place by becoming her own creator. Salomon's mother, aunt, and grandmother committed suicide, and she used her art to resist a similar fate. The infant Kahlo was neglected by her histrionic mother and, as a result, transformed her canvas into a mirror while filling her art with images of childbirth and nurturance. Schneemann was fascinated by her mother's pregnant body and later found a way, through her art, to explore and expose the mysteries of that body. Wilke believed her mother loved her sister more than herself and sought, through her art, to gain the attention she felt deprived of. Mendieta was torn from her mother as a child and produced earth art through which she symbolically reunited with her mother. Orlan's mother paid attention to her only when she was sick, so the artist developed an art form that converted the operating room into her studio and employed medical technology and surgical intervention as her implements. In all, most of the women had less than "good enough mothering" which left each one of them *by herself* to mother herself and to establish her own sense of femininity, sexuality, and identity.[11]

The father is also very relevant to the woman artist, though in a different way. In her classic paper, "Why Have There Been No Great Women Artists?" Linda Nochlin points out that nearly all successful women artists were either daughters of artist fathers or had a close relationship with a "stronger, . . . more dominant" male artist.[12] The daughters identify with the father's creativity, freedom, autonomy, and power, while garnering the encouragement and support of the father. Indeed, Kollwitz's father was very supportive of his daughter's artistic aspirations; he even wanted her to avoid marriage in order to focus exclusively on an artistic career. She did marry Karl Kollwitz, a man who, like her father, became a staunch supporter of her work. His profession as a medical doctor, who served the poor and disadvantaged, offered her subjects from which to make her socially inspired art. Kahlo is known to have held her photographer father in high esteem. As a girl, she worked as his assistant and later emulated him by becoming an artist herself. Her husband, Diego Rivera, was old enough to be Kahlo's father and replaced her father as her male model/artist. He not only praised his wife's art, but also influenced its Mexican content and bright colors. Likewise, Mendieta's father made wood carvings in a studio attached to the family home.[13] In adulthood, Mendieta found a supportive father figure in the person of Hans Breder, an art professor at the University of Iowa. Breder exposed Mendieta to a wide variety of performance artists and those who used their bodies in their work.[14] The influence of Breder's multimedia oeuvre is evident in the evolution of Mendieta's artistic idiom.

One important theme that runs through this study of women artists is the complex way in which the male gaze has been incorporated in the art of these women, many of whom conceive of their audience in terms of the Father. Kahlo, for instance, illustrates her awareness of Rivera as her designated audience when she writes, "I began to paint things that he [Diego] liked. From that time on he admired me and loved me."[15] Throughout the 1970s, Breder joined Mendieta in her annual sojourns to Mexico, and it was he who not only watched approvingly as she joined her body with Mother Earth, but also filmed her during the creation of her works.[16] Similarly, Wilke continuously disrobed before the men in her life, men like Richard Hamilton and Donald Goddard, who became her hidden co-collaborators and photographers. Sherman, too, had a boyfriend, Robert Longo, photograph her in her *Untitled Film Stills Series.* In the final analysis, Kahlo, Mendieta, Wilke, and Sherman created works of art that possess multilayered meanings revealing the complexity of their relationships to each individual parent as well as the parental couple.

This triangular relationship beautifully captures the oedipal tableau, the primal scene in which the child witnesses or fantasizes about what her parents are doing behind closed doors. The child, as excluded outsider, must come to terms with the difference between the sexes and the generations and cope with the narcissistic injury that ensues: one cannot be everything nor have everything one wants. The women artists in this book, by taking charge of their primal scene configurations, reverse their position as outsiders and become instead the ones who both look and are looked at. By incorporating the male gaze in their work, they look out from it at the audience, *at the father,* whose power they have co-opted. By additionally working out the relationship with the mother—merging with her, differentiating from her, taking select images of themselves from her magic mirror—they then became rulers of the oedipal triangle.

Cindy Sherman, for example, takes center stage and has her father, a man who collected cameras and enjoyed shooting family pictures, photograph her in a sexy nightgown as he peers down a long hallway separated by several doors. It is he, not she, who is now relegated to the role of outsider and voyeur. In this manner, Sherman and others incorporate the male gaze as well as their ambivalence about it: they desire the gaze but they wish to control its meaning and especially what it sees. The art in this book expresses this central ambivalence; it is the creation of a kind of body, a living vessel, that can incorporate the father in a way that contains the freedom and power he represents [both implied in the male gaze] while controlling the threat of violence and appropriation.

The psychological understanding of the female creative personality is accomplished by bringing together art and biography and by carefully analyzing the self-portraits of these ten compelling women artists. I will present a close reading of each artist whose primary subject matter is her own body and self. Each woman literally transforms herself into a work of art, thereby illustrating not only the close relationship between artist and artwork, but also the intimate connection between the self and creativity, self and other, private and public, image and medium. As such, the oeuvres of these artists have been selected to illustrate the mutually illuminating processes that take place among body, psyche, creativity, and audience.

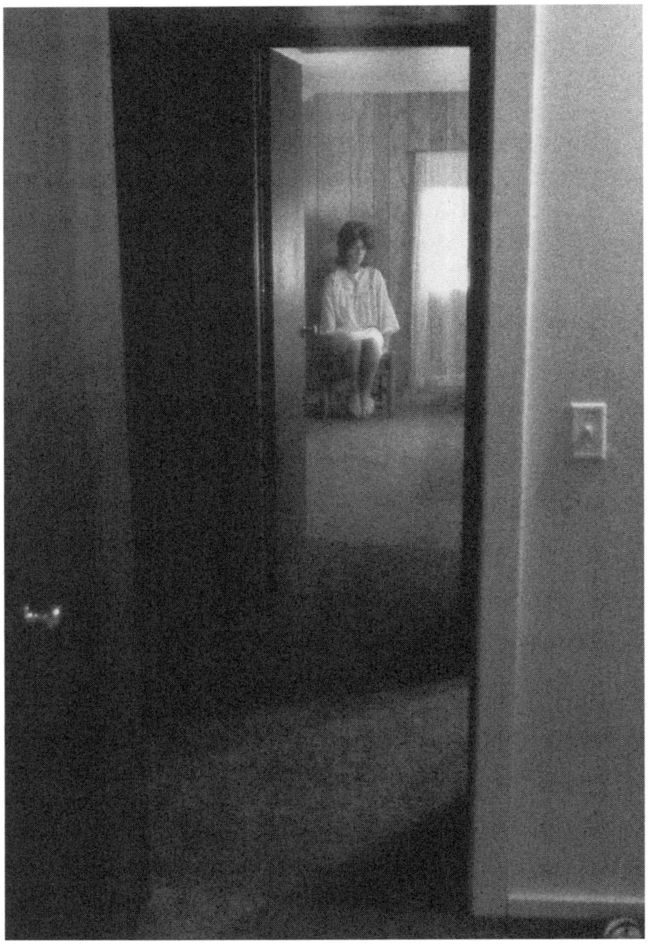

3. Cindy Sherman, *Untitled #82*, 1979. 10 × 8 inches. Courtesy of the artist and Metro Pictures, New York.

As a psychoanalyst with an expertise in art, I am in a privileged position to trace the connections between art and psychopathology and to show how they inform each other. While I indicate some problems in these women's lives that may have led to the particular form their art has taken, my intention is not to pathologize them. In fact, I oppose the psychoanalytic approach called "pathography" in which artists are diagnosed and their works equated with symptoms. Although it is true that many of the women in this book have experienced trauma, artists are not necessarily more traumatized than the general population. Rather than being destroyed by trauma, or passively accepting its deleterious consequences, these artists became adept at finding ways to combine reality and fantasy in a playful and profound engagement with their pasts. Thus, they create transformational objects of art that synthesize loss and attempt to repair it at the same time, while giving us something new and wondrous.[17] The reinvention of self through art has served them, as well as us, in its empowered expression of transformation and its challenge to traditional and cultural definitions of femininity, beauty, sexuality, health, aging, loss, and death.

When speaking of psychopathology, the temptation exists to attribute self-representation to female narcissism or exhibitionism. In fact, with few exceptions, all of the artists discussed here have been labeled narcissistic at one time or another. This charge truly misses the point, for once the female artist undertakes the challenge of responding to the objectification and control of her body, what else can she do except use her own body to regain herself? To equate this act of reappropriation with narcissism is like accusing someone of being vain for seeking a mirror to see herself for the very first time. Nonetheless, narcissistic and exhibitionistic factors do exist in female self-representation because women artists use their own bodies to represent their subjectivity. And, certainly, art-making and representation can serve a narcissistic function that is reparative.

Unsurprisingly, femininity and narcissism have been linked for ages and traditionally viewed in pejorative terms. This view became solidified through Catholicism, which dominated Europe for over one thousand years, and which had a profound effect on the evolution of representation in Western art: *vanity is a cardinal sin and woman, in her vanity and self-importance, caused the expulsion from paradise.* Freud, too, considered most women capable only of a narcissistic type of love, a love that places greater importance on being the object of love than the lover of another.[18] Furthermore, since male artists have most often portrayed women as objects to gratify their own narcissistic needs, it is sometimes assumed that women who depict themselves in their art do so in order to serve a similar (i.e., narcissistic) function. But this is not true for even if a woman makes of herself an object, her intentional relationship to herself-as-object must be different from a man's for she is the deciding subject, knowing herself as "object" from *inside.*

Perhaps what is most pernicious about the charge of narcissism is that it ignores the paradoxical message women receive regarding their external appearance. On the one hand, women have been valued and admired for their beauty and expected to exemplify popular standards of glamour and fashion, lest they suffer rejection and alienation.[19] On the other hand, they have risked being considered vain, superficial, or morbidly self-absorbed if they pay too much attention to their appearance. My study of various women artists will show how they have employed their art to both express and come to terms with this dilemma.

Self-representation, itself a paradoxical and iterative structure, is as much a psychological act as an aesthetic one. The artist transforms her body into a work of art, and her art into a means of self-revelation as well as a symbol of gender and identity polemics. As a creative subject who enters into a dialogue with herself as an art object and the outer world as an oppositional field of possibilities and encounters, she becomes the *femme impossible,* concealing as much as she is revealing, her angst on full display yet hidden as the vascularity that nourishes the meaning and the message of her work. Within the dynamic of that work she alternates between self and other, and intimacy and alienation, while generating multiple perspectives of herself and the world in which she lives. For an artist, the self-portrait gives rise to self-revelation and self-comprehension, but for the psychoanalyst (or the viewer), the self-portrait creates a special opportunity to examine the artist's psyche, its relationship to the creative process, and its potential for self-healing.

Although I focus on the individual dynamics in the art of these women, I do not ignore social influences. Their self-representational work portrays them anew and yet, by doing so, indicates and incorporates what it opposes

—the narrow and restricted ways they have been seen. These artists present their wish to be seen differently, and yet this difference rests upon the necessity of being incorrectly seen. Playing with this dyad, the artist engages us, provokes us, and at times even shames us. We are moved because we have already entered into both possibilities—the constriction of her being and her attempts to transcend it.

The ten artists discussed in this book represent a cross section of historical periods, cultural and ethnic backgrounds, and aesthetic styles. Each woman has struggled with her identity as woman and as woman artist, and each has employed her art to express and resolve these struggles. Each has been innovative both in the choice of subject matter (e.g., sexuality, beauty and the grotesque, illness, aging, exile, loss, mourning, and death) and in the artistic techniques and materials employed (mediums as varied as body art, earth art, performance art, video art, photography, painting, sculpture, and cosmetic surgery). Through their art, these women have stepped beyond socially defined marginalization and boldly confronted issues that have remained largely taboo in our culture. The art therefore is often raw and confrontational; it reaches out with a sense of urgency and invokes a visceral involvement in the viewer. Although highly personal and responsive to a particular social context, it also extends beyond the autobiographical, as metaphor for the female experience, to a universality that transcends each individual.

The careers of several of these artists were truncated by premature death; some were overshadowed during their lifetimes by their (at the time) more famous artist-husbands; and several are alive today and continue to produce fascinating work. Each has left her mark on the world, and the time has come to listen to these unique voices and to pay attention to their visions. I will make clear how these women are largely responsible for changing the face of art —certainly the way women appear in art—as well as the way spectators perceive and respond to art. They also address important questions regarding gender and creativity, female identity, essentialism vs. constructionism, narcissism and exhibitionism, the relationship between external appearance and inner reality, ritual and healing in art and, most importantly, the ways women become creators of their own meaning.

The female gaze is only beginning to receive the attention it deserves. Determined to overcome gender and ethnic stereotypes, women artists now own their gaze and direct it toward themselves as well as others. Thus, Kollwitz has us gaze into her aging face and consider her inner experiences as well as her physical presence. Cahun makes us contemplate her shifts from male to female, mask to masquerade. Salomon shows us how to come of age in the midst of personal and political tragedy. Kahlo has us watch what women undergo with their bodies, from birth to death, by nature and by accident. Schneemann insists that we both acknowledge and enjoy woman's erotic being, her dreams, her play. Wilke wants us to take pleasure in the beauty and sexuality of her body but to not avert our gaze when that same body becomes diseased. Piper forces us to be simultaneously aware of her visibility as a black woman and our own racism. Mendieta informs us about separation, loss, reunion, and regeneration. Sherman shows us how easily the beautiful can be turned into the ugly, the sane into the insane, the sexual into the perverse. And Orlan sears us with her multiple metamorphoses to show us the fate of embodiment in a post-human age. In sum, these artists demand, through their work, a gaze which does not limit what woman is or appears to be. They encourage us to accept and validate the many sides of female experience. They move us to change.

It will become clear, from the analysis of female self-representation over the last hundred years, that women have created an iconography that empowers the female, at the very least because of its insistence on self-definition. The diversity in women's self-representations reflects the multiplicity of female identities. Although woman's identity is still viewed as a puzzle, it is one that now contains many more pieces. As they continue to put together the pieces of their identity, women recombine in new ways what has been distorted, fragmented, or omitted to communicate the varied experiences of their bodies and selves in a changing world and a world they change. Each artist encountered in this book brought something fresh and daring into the world of art and culture. Each challenged and changed the aesthetic sensibility of her society by engaging in a vital dialogue with society and its history. Taken together they have opened up a new world of possibilities for women and for art.

1
Käthe Kollwitz: The Dead Mother

> The dead mother, contrary to what one might think, is a mother who remains alive but who is, so to speak, psychically dead in the eyes of the young child in her care.
>
> —André Green

HANS, KÄTHE KOLLWITZ'S OLDER SON, REPEATedly asked his mother to write her memoirs because she withheld the story of her life, even from her children. When at last she relented to his request, the first memory Kollwitz narrated with strong sensory intensity involved a dead girl who washed onto the raft in a neighboring yard from the Pregel River in Koenigsberg where they lived. Recalling Freud's concept of screen memory, a memory that "screens" other, hidden, and more important, memories, the central importance of this intense recollection may nestle in what it conceals. Although the screen memory can be a recollection of something real, its primary function lies in its power to organize and symbolize a number of unconscious impressions.[1]

The dead child is probably the central organizing theme in German born Käthe Kollwitz's (1867–1945) life and art. Three of her siblings died. Her mother became distant and reserved as a result of these deaths—unavailable—an emotionally "dead mother." And Kollwitz became the dead mother/child who internalized and identified with both her "dead" mother and her dead siblings. Later, she was forced to cope with the deaths of her own son and grandson, agonizing losses which intensified these early identifications. In fact, hers was a lifelong struggle with the forces of death. She warred with depression throughout her life and struggled to transcend death by giving birth to images of humanity in the face of grief, sorrow, and irrevocable loss. Kollwitz's oeuvre beautifully captures the tragic whose quintessential image is the mother grieving over the corpse of her precious child, the life expected completely undone, the monstrous, the unthinkable, held up for us to see and grapple with. She thus openly challenged the power of death, the threat of inevitable annihilation that casts its crepuscular shadow across our brightest hopes. Kollowitz's art stamps death with an immortal beauty, reducing its unconscious power by imbuing the tragedy of loss and destruction with a transcendent luminescence.

EXPRESSIONISM

The work of Kollwitz is steeped in the changing ambience surrounding the art of her age, a change greatly influenced by the Expressionist movement and by psychoanalysis, whose discoveries helped liberate the artist from the nineteenth-century notion that art was to represent external reality. In fact, twentieth-century art is characterized by a growing disbelief in an objective reality coupled with an increased emphasis on inner experience.[2] Expressionist artists, such as Egon Schiele, E. L. Kirchner, and Oskar Kokoshka, concerned themselves with the artistic rendering of the internal life, the world embodied in the human psyche. It is not surprising therefore that this movement generated a proliferation of portraiture, or that the most psychological of art forms, the self-portrait, became popular in this era. Whereas self-portraiture had always been a known form of artistic expression, from Rembrandt to Van Gogh, the genre regained prominence at the turn of the century, though with a twist. Kollwitz naturally felt the influence of Expressionist discoveries, and although she never joined either of the two German Expressionist groups, *Der Blaue Reiter* and *Die Brücke*, she shared both Expressionism's strong German graphic tradition and its propensity to express psychological and social reality through the human figure.

Coincidental with the expansion of psychoanalysis's sphere of influence in the early part of the century, artists began to focus upon, and employ as their artistic means, the individual, the subjective, and the psychological.[3] Kollwitz's art revealed the face of woman in a modern world. Hers is a deeply honest and personal account of her life in one hundred drawings, lithographs, and sculptures of her own image informed by encounters with the psychoanalytic model and its applications of introspection and self-reflection. Kollwitz's art documents her own self-analysis, an analysis as deep as Freud's analysis of his personality, for she employed self-portraiture as a means of arriving at emotional truths for the purpose of healing. She believed that "For work, one must be hard and thrust outside oneself what one has lived through."[4] Her art, and especially her self-portraits, can therefore best be understood as a therapeutic handling of the traumatic events in her life and her journey in self-discovery. The unique focus on the expressiveness of her facial features and the centrality of her steady, resolute gaze was therefore meant not merely for the viewer's consideration but, also, for Kollwitz's as well. Through the body of her self-portraits, Kollwitz charted the painful and moving adventures of her psychological and emotional development.

Among significant departures from traditional female depictions in art is Kollwitz's technique of shifting the viewer's focus from a woman's body to her mind by focusing on the face of woman—in poverty, despair, beset by social injustice, bearing tragic loss, reflecting in intense complexity the sheer weight of existence and the oppression of an era. She avoided the usual pose and detail associated with female representation, thereby thwarting voyeuristic access to the female body as a thing of beauty or signifier of sexual difference. In Kollwitz's depictions, the image of woman moved away from being viewed as object to being appreciated as subject. She was among the first to strip away the externals of male-donated idealistic feminine iconography by showing how woman could take her image into her own hands. She was not alone in this. Marianne von Werefkin and Gabriele Münter were two painters who were involved in *Blaue Reiter*, the only Expressionist group that allowed women to participate as full members. Although both of these women played key roles in the group, the male artists with whom they were personally involved overshadowed them.[5]

Neither idealized for their seductive physical charms nor assessed solely according to their external features, Kollwitz's images broadened the idea of female beauty by rejecting the reductive representation of woman as young, passive, and belonging to the middle or upper class. We do not find them basking in bourgeois repose or exuding sexual radiance; they are working women, women in the muck and not hearing about it from a distance, women suffering need, grief and loss, social activists, mothers oppressed by violence and war, women who trace the tragic trajectory of the feminine side of human experience. Kollwitz's style of unadorned realism represents the true plight of proletarian women by using aesthetic standards that differed from the norm: "My real motive for choosing my subjects almost exclusively from the life of the workers was that only such subjects gave me in a simple and unqualified way what I felt to be beautiful. . . . the broad freedom of movement in the gestures of the common people had beauty."[6] Interestingly, although many of her subjects were recruited from patients in her husband's medical practice, most of the women's features bear a striking resemblance to those of the artist. In the end, Kollwitz's portraits of working women and her self-portraits merge in the portrayal of suffering and transcendence.

Social Realism

Expressionism's overt rebellion against bourgeois aesthetic standards suggested an implicit rejection of the political status quo. However, after Germany's socialist revolution in 1918, the avant-garde adopted an expressly political stance. It is interesting to note that whereas male artists, like George Grosz or Otto Dix, are usually given credit for this shift in art, women had been producing

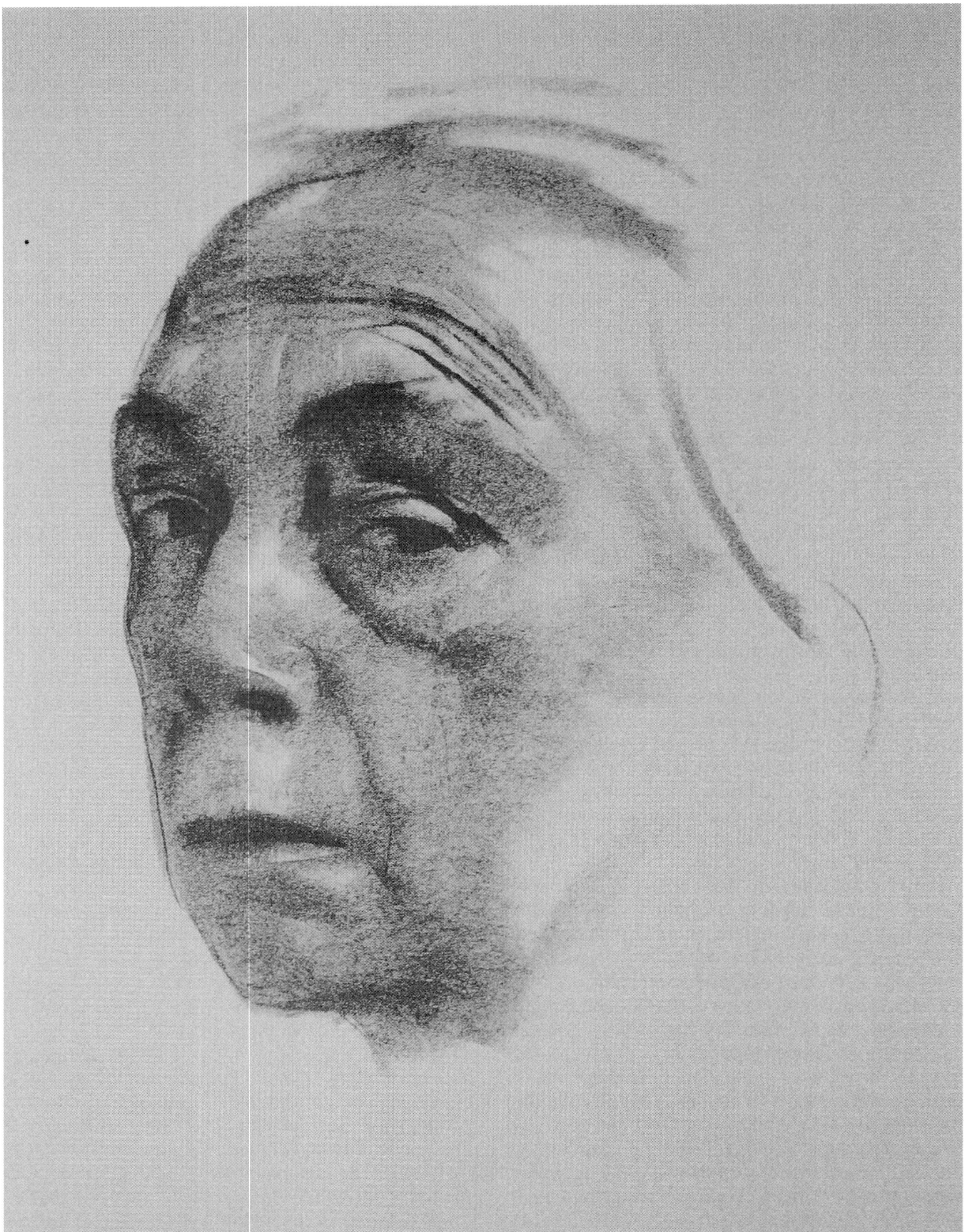

4. Käthe Kollwitz, *Self-Portrait,* 1924. Crayon lithograph. © Artists Rights Society (ARS), New York/VG Bild-Kunst, Bonn. Photo: Courtesy Spaightwood Galleries, Upton, MA.

socially engaging art for several decades prior. Kollowitz's first major work and one of the first of its kind, *Weaver's Revolt,* begun in 1893, was exhibited in 1898. The series of six prints based on a play by Gerhart Hauptmann, *The Weavers,* concerned a group of Silesian peasants turned linen weavers who, in 1844, revolted because of low factory wages and miserable living conditions. Kollwitz employed her evocative graphic genius to articulate a tragic vision of working class life. The first print, entitled *Poverty,* recalls Edvard Munch's *The Sick Child* (1894), and portrays a mother clutching her head in despair over the illness and imminent death of her tiny, emaciated child. Father and another child sit anxiously in the background while a spiraling movement created by diagonal forms in the room evokes the atmosphere of a situation veering out of control. Indeed, the event of the child's death motivates the workers to revolt, captured in the following lithographs.

The theme of grieving mothers is the most central in Kollwitz's oeuvre and one to which she returned periodically throughout her life. Kollwitz dedicated *Weaver's Revolt* to her father, the person who had most encouraged her artistic career, on his seventieth birthday, the year before his death. Although it was so well received that it immediately established Kollwitz as one of the foremost artists in Germany, it was denied the gold medal at the Great Berlin Art Exhibition of 1898 due to its political content. It is possible that Kaiser Wilhelm II's chauvinism was responsible for Kollwitz not receiving the prize. He is said to have remarked: "I beg you gentlemen, a medal for a woman, that would really be going too far. . . . Orders and medals of honor belong on the breasts of worthy men!"[7] Her acclaim notwithstanding, Kollwitz, too, suffered doubts and insecurities about her art, comparing it to the work of male artists whom she regarded as more talented and possessing something she lacked. In one diary entry, when discussing a similarity between herself and Thomas Mann, she concluded: "A genius and a Mann could do it. I probably cannot."[8]

Throughout her long and productive artistic career, Kollwitz repeatedly transformed her personal pain into potent social messages. Her maternal grandfather Rupp, a preacher of morality who founded his own Free Congregation, taught her that "every gift is a responsibility."[9] Kollwitz thus proved the personal to be political many years before the motto became the battle cry of feminists. As the most prominent woman to integrate the personal and political in art, Kollwitz championed the representation of social activism in real, as well as allegorical, women (see *Attack,* 1897; *Carmagnole,* 1901). The proletarian woman became the true heroine of her oeuvre.

During the Weimar era (1918–33), German women won the right to vote and hold office. The "new woman" worked and smoked cigarettes, had bobbed hair and wore stylish clothes (including male-style tailored suits, ties, and monocles), and practiced social independence. Although the media widely promoted this image, it was an ideal realized by few. Unlike her contemporary, Jeanne Mammen, whose stylish watercolors often depicted Germany's "new women," Kollwitz focused on the everyday heroines of physical abuse, unwanted pregnancies, tuberculosis, and poverty, working women struggling daily with life-and-death dramas. Kollwitz thus illuminated the duality of women: brave and socially active, warriors endowed with strength and fury, they were also unwitting victims and survivors of social and political misfortune.

A social activist and mother like many of her subjects, Kollwitz's incisive social realism is evident in her recurring themes: poverty, disease, famine, unemployment, war, and death. It is also magnified by her choice of stark black-and-white charcoal drawings, woodcuts, etchings, and lithographs over the more conventional European tradition of painting. Following the example of the brilliant printmaker, Max Klinger, Kollwitz believed that graphic arts best expressed the darker side of life, a subject she knew intimately from her lifelong struggle with depression. She also held that the technique of lithography allowed her to "seize the essential."[10] The severity of chiarascuro stresses the painful gestures and heartfelt expressions of her figures, who become illuminated against a surrounding darkness.

Motherhood

Kollwitz's social realistic style helped to distinguish her art from the sexual objectification of women. It also resulted in the creation of androgynous and desexualized female figures, including herself, though the traditionally feminine theme of maternity remained central to her work. That this theme has captured the attention of many women artists is not surprising since motherhood remains a primary life experience for most women. Maternity represents a unique female experience in which women's body egos are profoundly influenced by the fact that they are biologically structured for, and potentially taken over completely by, the procreative process.[11] By representing maternity in art, Kollwitz replaced phallic power with the power of the womb. This is not to say that male artists had not been interested in the theme of motherhood (e.g., Gustav Klimt). However, as with their idealized female nude portraits, most male artists tended to depict motherhood as naive glorification of femininity.

Paula Modersohn-Becker, a contemporary of Kollwitz, was also known for her depictions of pregnant women and mothers with infants. However, her portrayals of motherhood involve mythic women (although she often used herself as model) who resemble Gauguin's native Tahitian beauties. They seem to live out their instinctual female destiny in a natural paradise-like surrounding from which they emerge. Kollwitz, on the other hand, overturns the usual tender, even sentimental, portrayal of mothers and children that characterized turn-of-the century art.[12] Her mothers are often compelled to confront disease and death in their infants due to social conditions, malnourishment, or war (e.g., *Poverty,* 1893–94; *Woman with Dead Child,* 1903; *Unemployment,* 1909; *Run Over,* 1910; *Death, Mother and Child,* 1910; *Mothers,* 1919).

Kollwitz's depictions of mothers grieving for their dead babies are arguably the most poignant images in her oeuvre. In *Woman with Dead Child* (1903), reminiscent of Munch's *Vampire* (1895/1902) in its positioning of two figures, a mother hunches over as she cradles her dead child between her naked thighs and arms. Like an animal, she looks as if she is swallowing the child as if to return it to its source. In her early version of this work, *Pietà* (1903), Kollwitz borrowed from traditional Christian iconography associated with the Madonna mourning the dead Christ. Her later versions are much more powerful because she rejects the earlier frontal depiction of the figures and replaces it with a more dramatic, angled one. In the earlier ones, mother's and infant's heads are separated, the mother's in the center of the work and the child's on the side. In the later works, the mother's head merges with that of the child, as her body envelops his. Body parts are also drawn in segments to express the psychological fragmentation attending the loss of a child. Furthermore, the two figures are devoid of all narrative and social context, thereby rendering a universal rather than religious meaning: the primal maternal pathos aroused in grief and loss. These renderings offer no illusion of comfort, religious or social.

Dead Mother

Kollwitz's preoccupation with grieving mothers had personal as well as social sources. Some critics attribute Kollwitz's mother and dead child series to the loss of her son and grandson. An earlier origin is indicated, however, since she made several of these prints prior to her son's death. In fact, it is sadly ironic that Kollwitz used her son Peter as a model in her *Woman with Dead Child* series, thus eerily foreshadowing his death by many years.

Kollwitz admitted, in her diary, having felt responsible for the death of her younger brother Benjamin, and she blamed her unwillingness to believe in Christ for the tragedy. From the morbid atmosphere of her childhood, she also developed an inordinate fear that her mother would die or go mad.[13] As a child, Kollwitz experienced violent, screaming panic attacks that often lasted for hours. Possibly, the tantrums may have been the only way of obtaining attention from her otherwise undemonstrative mother. She also suffered from stomachaches of a self-admitted psychosomatic nature: "These stomach aches were a surrogate for all physical and mental pains . . . My mother knew that my stomach aches concealed small sorrows, and at such times she would let me snuggle close to her."[14] Nevertheless, most of Kollwitz's descriptions of her mother were of an aloof, unavailable woman with a "distant look"[15] and a "remote air of a Madonna."[16] Young Käthe was alarmed by her mother's unavailability and developed convulsion-like symptoms that had her parents fearing she was epileptic. She was also haunted by

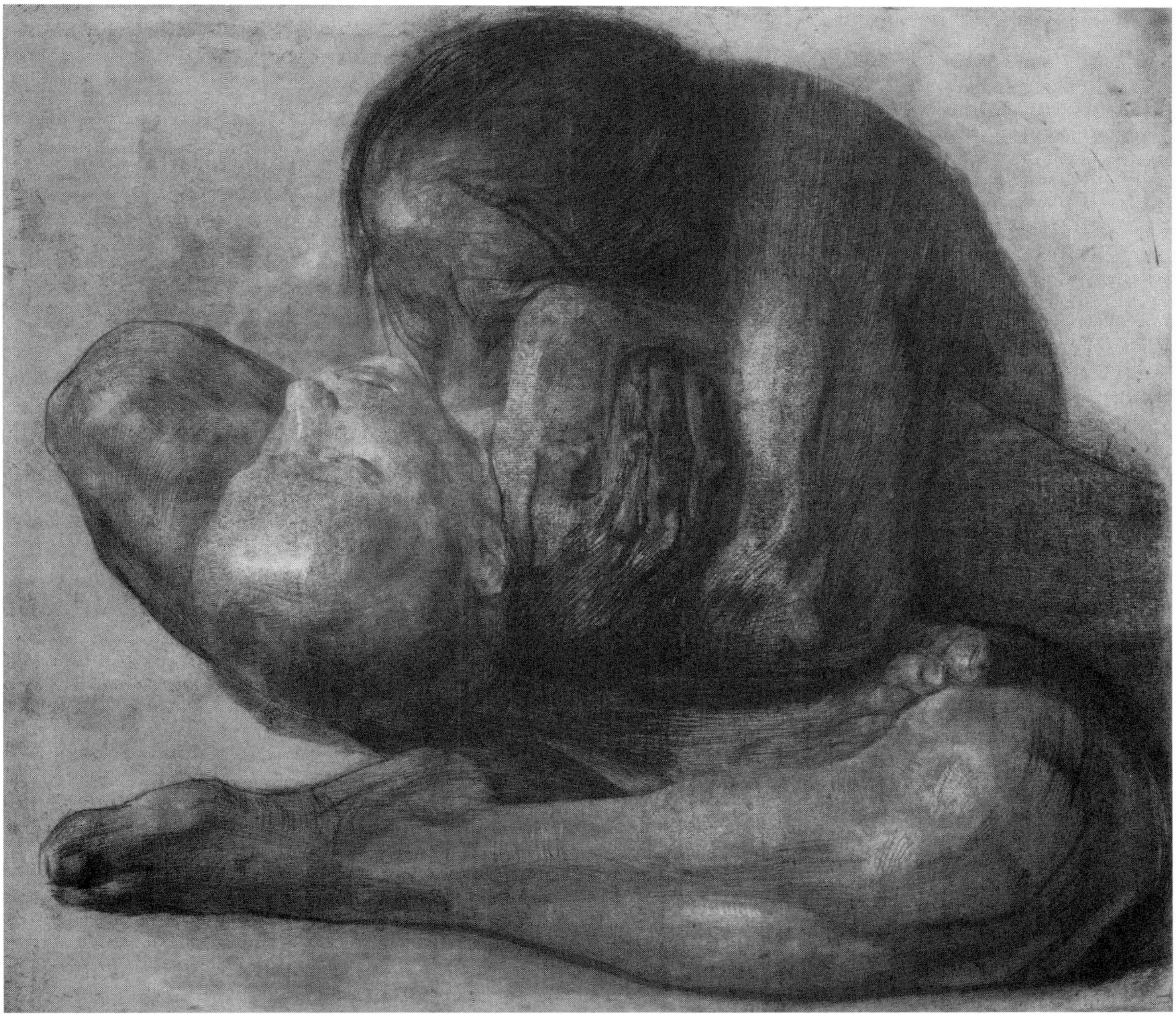

5. Käthe Kollwitz, *Woman with Dead Child,* 1903. Etching. Kunsthalle, Bremen, Germany. Photo Credit: Erich Lessing/Art Resource, NY. © Artists Rights Society (ARS), New York/VG Bild-Kunst, Bonn.

nightmares, many of which expressed her terror of losing her mother. The one she recalls as "the worst" follows: "I am lying in my bed in the semidarkness of the nursery. In the next room Mother is sitting in the chair under the hanging lamp, reading. I can see only her back through the half-open door. In one corner of the nursery lies a large coil of rope such as is used on ships. The rope begins to stretch out and unroll, silently filling the whole room. I want to call Mother and cannot. The grey cable blots out everything."[17] Rather than the rope —symbol of the umbilical cord—connecting mother and child, it obliterates connection and leaves a dark void.

In one of several anecdotes in her memoir, Kollwitz poignantly described her frustrated need for her mother's attention: "I needed to confide in my mother, to confess to her. . . . I decided to give my mother a daily report on what I had done and felt that day. I imagined that her sharing the knowledge would be of help to me. But she said nothing at all, and so I too fell silent."[18] Many years later, Kollwitz described how, having identified with her mother, she became withdrawn and silent: "One turns more and more to silence. All is still. I sit in Mother's chair by the stove, evenings, when I am alone."[19] Indeed, Kollwitz executed many of her works of grieving mothers during a period in which her mother, suffering from senility, came to live with her. In her diary entry of July 8, 1916, she wrote: "When I am here with Mother, I often feel like her."[20]

André Green, among others, has written about the devastating effects of maternal depression on the child. In his paper "The Dead Mother," he describes a type of mother who, while mourning the loss of one child, loses interest in a living child, leaving an indelible scar on the child's affection for her mother whom she perceives as psychically dead, transmogrified from a source of vitality into "a distant figure, toneless, practically inanimate."[21] Through identification, the child consequently renounces her own connection to life forces. Kollwitz's early psychosomatic symptoms transformed into lifelong depression which she chronicled not only in the bleak and darkly beautiful visions she depicted in her art but, also, in her diary entries. In April 1921, she wrote: "Now my work disgusts me so that I cannot look at it. At the same time total failure as a human being. I no longer love Karl, nor Mother, scarcely even the children. I am stupid and without any thoughts. I see only unpleasant things. The spring days pass and I do not respond. . . . So there is *nothingness* in me, neither thoughts nor feelings, no challenge to action, no participation."[22]

Unable to find maternal affection in her mother, the young Kollwitz turned to her father. Karl Schmidt, a progressive man trained in law but working in masonry, did not believe in public schools and schooled his children at home. He strongly encouraged his daughter's talent, providing for her art training by sending her to Berlin and Munich. Nonetheless, his act had an ulterior motive for he wished to prevent her marriage to Karl Kollwitz, a promising young doctor to whom Kollwitz had become engaged. Her father believed she would not be able to combine marriage and a career, but Kollwitz proved him wrong. Her husband, Karl, not only continued to provide her with the support her father had begun to give—he loved her unconditionally and became her anchor in life. Kollwitz's diary attests to her growing love and appreciation for this man with whom she lived for forty-nine years. Over time, she realized the extent of her attachment and dependence on Karl who she came to refer to as her "lifelong companion." In fact, Kollwitz used a cane to walk from the day her husband died until her own death five years later.[23]

The growing appreciation of her husband in her life is witnessed in her inclusion of him in several self-portraits. In the first, an 1893/1904 etching, *Young Couple,* she is seated and faces front, self-absorbed; Karl is seen from behind. There is no physical or apparent emotional connection between the two. Years later, in her sculpture (1924–32) honoring the memory of fallen soldiers in the war, we witness two figures, Karl and herself, who join together in the mourning of their son's death. Finally, a 1942 charcoal drawing, *Self-Portrait with Karl Kollwitz,* depicts the elderly pair seated side by side, an inseparable unit, looking off in one direction, sharing a single fate.

According to psychoanalyst Melanie Klein, the reparative working through of destructive fantasies against the mother for having lost the state of oneness with her is *the* source of artistic creativity.[24] Kollwitz's early symptoms and tantrums unleashed the pent-up fury she harbored toward her mother's inability to openly express her feelings about the death of her children; they were also reactions to her mother's emotional distance caused by the children's deaths. Kollwitz, too, had trouble expressing her own feelings about the death of her siblings. Later her art continued to express this fury. For example, in 1912, Kollwitz described her struggles with a sculpture of mother with child: "It still has a *dead* side that I do not know how to *attack*"[25] (italics mine). Her adoption of the woodcut technique around 1920 furnished a way to "attack" this deadness. Not only is woodcutting a more aggressive technique, it also results in simplification and distortion of figures. Kollwitz used the gouge as her primary cutting tool, rather than the knife, which created white lines on a black background. Like E. L. Kirchner, she adopted Expressionist effects that resulted in powerful images of primitive facial expressions and strong grasping hands that possess a sculptural character. The "dead mother" here functioned as a defense against her rage.

War, her series of seven woodcuts, added to those by many artists who took the subject as their theme (e.g., Ludwig Meidner, Max Pechstein, and Otto Dix). Unlike these male artists who typically depicted destruction in combat scenes, Kollwitz's *War* series illustrates the impact and horror of war from the perspective of those who stay home: mothers and children. Once again, the first of the series, *The Sacrifice* (1922), shows a nude woman who closes her eyes as she lifts up her child in sacrifice. On a conscious level, this work represents Kollwitz's ironic reply to the nationalistic and propagandistic call on German mothers to urge their sons to fight in the war. On an unconscious level, it is another attempt to deal with the dread of death that can, at any moment, sever the relationship between mother and child. It is this underside—the haunting refrain of death—that makes the work bristle with tragic resonance. Although scenes of combat are absent in Kollwitz's woodcuts, her use of stark black and white colors, along with powerful expressions and gestures, clearly addresses the presence of destructive forces. Unlike her male contemporaries, like George Grosz, who employed satire and acerbity to this end, Kollwitz did so with tender humanity.

Despite her efforts to express anger and resistance, Kollwitz's identification with her psychically dead mother emerged strongly in later years. When she lost a son and grandson, she, too, adopted a stoic attitude toward life's miseries. In fact, her older son, Hans, described her undemonstrative conduct: "Along with this reserve in talking about or showing love went a disinclination to speak about feelings at all, or about any personal matters."[26] Kollwitz's emotional muteness in her daily life was not reflected in her artistic endeavors, however, and her feelings certainly speak in her work, imbuing it with stark and compelling power. Again and again, she shows us something real and terrible, yet strangely beautiful and evocative, pulling us not only into her brooding visions, but also into what we wish to avoid and deny. She looked at and uniquely rendered what most would rather look away from.

Kollwitz's "Mother" works thus provide the most important insight into the conflictive relationship with her own mother. The "mothers" in her art represent both her mother and herself. The children are her dead siblings, son, and grandson. The mother, source of life, is therefore tied to every death including, and perhaps most importantly, the inner death of the artist. In these works, the artist repeatedly depicts the tragedy that robbed her mother from her. As a result of her mother's grief and unresponsiveness, something died in Kollwitz as a child. Her fascination with sickness and death, especially as it concerns babies, was most certainly related to the deaths of her siblings. As a child who survived, Kollwitz's sense of herself included the notion that she too should have died.[27] She identified with her dead siblings and returned again and again to the source of her greatest pain.

Yet, despite her lifelong struggle with her suffering, Kollwitz mobilized and channeled pain and mourning through her creativity. One way she accomplished this was to counter the separation and loss caused by family deaths and depression in her "Mother" drawings and sculptures. Whereas her earlier mother works depict a cycle of sacrifice, loss, and grief, her later works show mothers who refuse to allow their children to be harmed by malignant forces. In these works, mothers merge with their children to create an inseparable union. For example, sculptures *Tower of Mothers* (1937–38) and *Protecting Mother;* woodcut *The Mothers* (1922–23); and her final lithograph, named after a Goethe quote, "*Seed for the Planting Must not be Ground*" (1942), all depict mothers who form a tight, impenetrable circle that safeguards their young ones who huddle to be sheltered beneath their limbs. The large, powerful, and expressive hands of the mothers became a Kollwitz trademark, hands that hold their children tightly, hands that hold the seed so it would not be ground, hands that form a barrier between the precious and the pernicious. She described the mother's emotions in *Seed for the Planting* in a letter: ". . . the old mother who is holding them [the children] together says, No! You stay here!"[28]

Kollwitz's art, then, became a vehicle for mourning through which she gave shape to and attempted to overcome her losses. Although she did not always use herself in these works, the faces of her mothers and workers eventually became indistinguishable from her own. In this manner, she joined the countless images in her art of mothers who despair over the loss of their children. Kollwitz identified with their grief and sorrow, and also shared their inner resolve. Struggling with severe bouts of depression throughout her life,

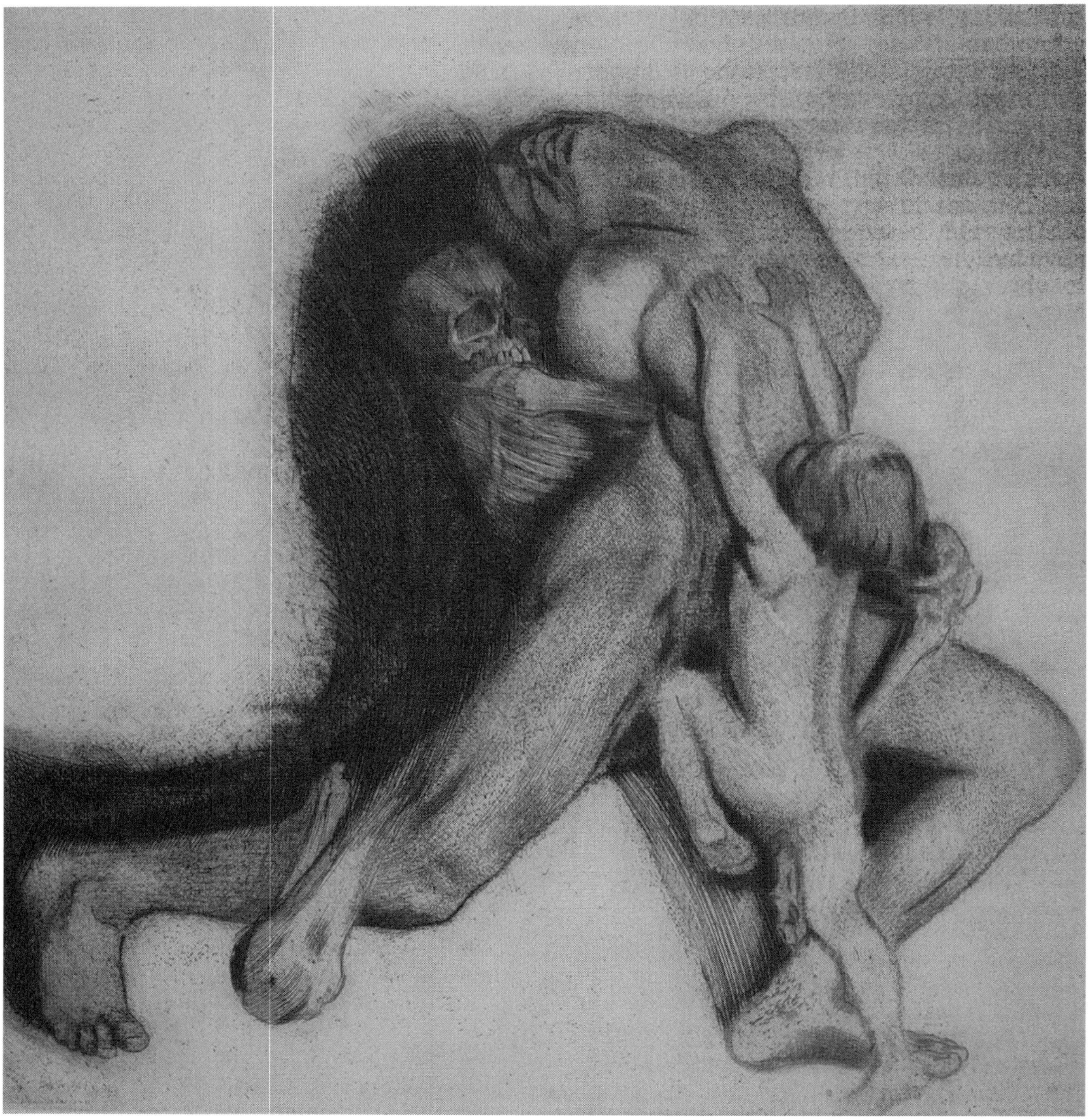

6. Käthe Kollwitz, *Death and Woman/Self-Portrait,* 1910. Line etching, drypoint, sandpaper, soft ground. © Artists Rights Society (ARS), New York/VG Bild-Kunst, Bonn. Photo: Courtesy Spaightwood Galleries, Upton, MA.

she depicted with stark realism the effort to retain a sense of dignity in the face of adversity. The deaths in her family of origin and those of her son in World War I and grandson in World War II were central to her creative/therapeutic struggle. In her diary, she wrote to her deceased son, Peter: "I pray that I can feel you so close to me that I will be able to make your spirit live in my work."[29]

Indeed, Kollwitz labored for seventeen years over a monument at the war cemetery in Roggevelde, Belgium, where Peter was buried. This was perhaps the most ambitious project of her life, certainly the largest and the most psychologically challenging, beginning as a monument for Peter and becoming a memorial to all victims of the war, thus transforming her intensely personal pain into a testimony to the universal suffering of war loss. Rather than sculpt the fallen hero, who was killed in the first weeks of World War I, as was her original plan, she sculpted the figures of his mourning parents—her husband Karl and herself—kneeling, arms pressed to their chests, huddled in agony. Part of the delay clearly had to do with her treatment of the parental figures. Kollwitz claimed she was afraid of the mother figure whereas the father figure, ". . . I expect to master more quickly."[30] Some of her fear was related to the realization that she could use her own head on the figure of the mother. Becoming one with the grieving mother—with *her* grieving mother—clearly frightened her and resulted in creative inhibition. Such a process was nevertheless necessary for her own mourning and creativity. She therefore continued to rework the theme of the grieving mother throughout the last third of her life, all the while claiming that she was "a mother who will not give up her sorrow."[31] At the same time, Kollwitz became the child-mother grieving for her own mother who was "dead" to her. Her depictions of motherhood are among the most powerful in the history of art; they paved the way for artists to portray maternity in all of its complexity.

The Aging Woman: Dialogues with Death

The Weimar era came to an end with Hitler's rise to power in 1933. So did Kollwitz's career. Because she had signed an appeal for left-wing parties to form a coalition to resist the National Socialists, Kollwitz was forced to resign her position as professor at the Prussian Academy of Art. (She was the first woman appointed to such a position.) She was forbidden to publish and to exhibit. Although her studio was closed and her work was banned by the Nazis who classified it as "degenerate," she continued to make sculptures privately. Kollwitz died shortly before the end of World War II. Much of her work was deliberately destroyed and her home and studio were bombed and burned.

Before her death, Kollwitz overturned another barrier in the artistic representation of women. She broke the spell of invisibility associated with older women and entered uncharted territory by portraying her own aging process in a fascinating series of late self-portraits.[32] These final drawings, mostly lithographs, also reveal Kollwitz's mature combination of a simple idea with an economy of means. She does not prettify or conceal the inevitable changes that accompany aging. Rather, she stares at us with courage and dignity, as she must have done in her mirror, and forces us to face and accept the reality of an aging woman. Her lined, weary face fills the entire frame; it demands its place; there is no avoiding it (see *Self-Portrait*, lithograph, 1934).

Kollwitz's earliest self-portraits indicate confidence and self-assurance. In fact, her first, *Self-Portrait en face, Laughing* (1888–89), is the only one that portrays her laughing. Another, *Self-Portrait on the Balcony* (1892), shows her looking out to the world, skirt lifted and leg exposed. Her early self-portraits are also the only ones in which she used color as several were done with pastel. As she entered middle age, her visage became filled with doubt and fatigue, even depression. In her diary, she complains of menopause and expresses longing for the years when her sons were babies. After Peter's death, many self-portraits, like *Woman Lost in Thought*, portray Kollwitz's anguish and grief as well as her valiant attempts to master sadness. Self-knowledge became the goal of these more mature works. With increasing age, Kollwitz's need for external experience and knowledge further diminished: "I am no longer expanding outward; I am contracting into myself. I mean that I am noticeably growing old."[33] Assuming the pose of Rodin's *The Thinker* in one self-portrait, Kollwitz contemplates her inner world. Her self-portraits represent a major psychological shift, as well as a formalistic one. In her own words, she went from being a "revolutionary to being an evolutionary."[34] Whereas early depictions are of an ideological fighter, albeit one who is often forced to surrender to powerful external forces, later works focus on acceptance rooted in inner strength and faith. Having shown compassion for others, she now turns to herself and comes to terms with her lost mother in herself. Although

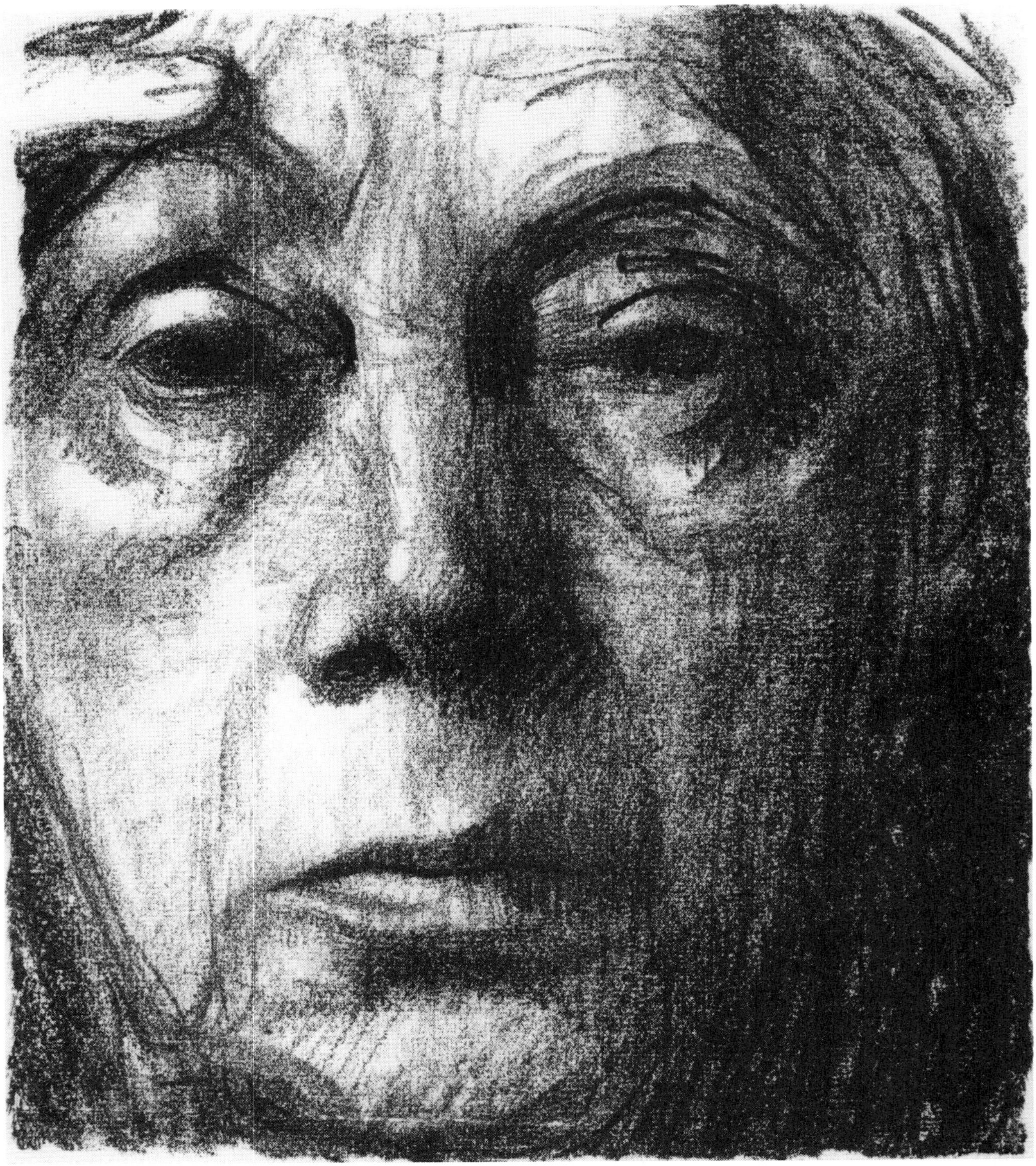

7. Käthe Kollwitz, *Self-Portrait,* lithograph, 1934. © 2009 Artists Rights Society (ARS), New York/VG Bild-Kunst, Bonn. Photo Credit: Art Resource, NY.

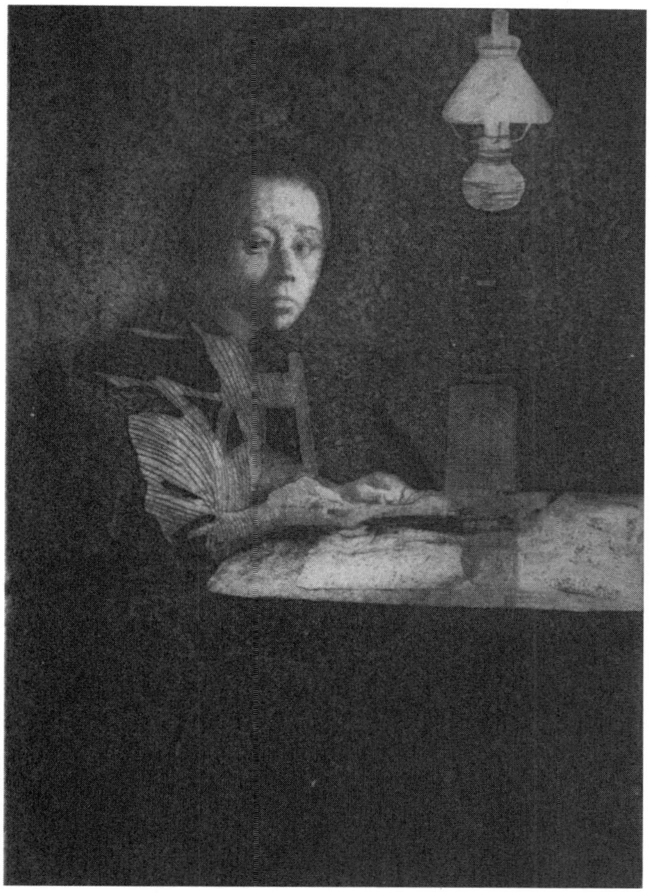

8. Käthe Kollwitz, *Self-Portrait Seated at Table,* c. 1892. Etching with aquatint. © Artists Rights Society (ARS), New York/VG Bild-Kunst, Bonn. Photo: Courtesy Spaightwood Galleries, Upton, MA.

the art changes over time, and we witness the deepening signature of experience on her face, one constant remains: the iron will, honesty, and intelligence in the face of a woman who "sees the suffering of the world."[35]

Kollwitz carried on a dialogue with death throughout her life. Whereas her early drawings show her struggle with the forces of death, later versions reveal her making peace with death. For Kollwitz, this meant making peace with the "dead" mother with whom she had so strongly identified. In her final self-portraits, her gaze remains steady, but has become more internalized, turning away from the viewer as if directed beyond this life. A good example is *Call of Death* (1934–35), the last in her final eight-lithograph series entitled *Death.* Kollwitz's face glances up toward the recognizable figure of Death, whose hands we see tapping her shoulder to beckon her beyond. She appears to accept her fate with quiet resignation. The aged artist makes only the necessary strokes with her black lithographic crayon to create this powerful final image.

Kollwitz's aging self-portraits represent one of the first artistic acknowledgments of the essentially historical nature of the female body[36] Like Rembrandt, who also produced a series of aging self-portraits, Kollwitz was captivated by the inscriptions of life etched on one's face over time. Her late self-portraits led the way for women artists to reevaluate the conventions of female beauty in the fine arts and to challenge viewers' expectations regarding the kind of woman who is "fit to be seen." One thinks of artists like Mary Kelly,

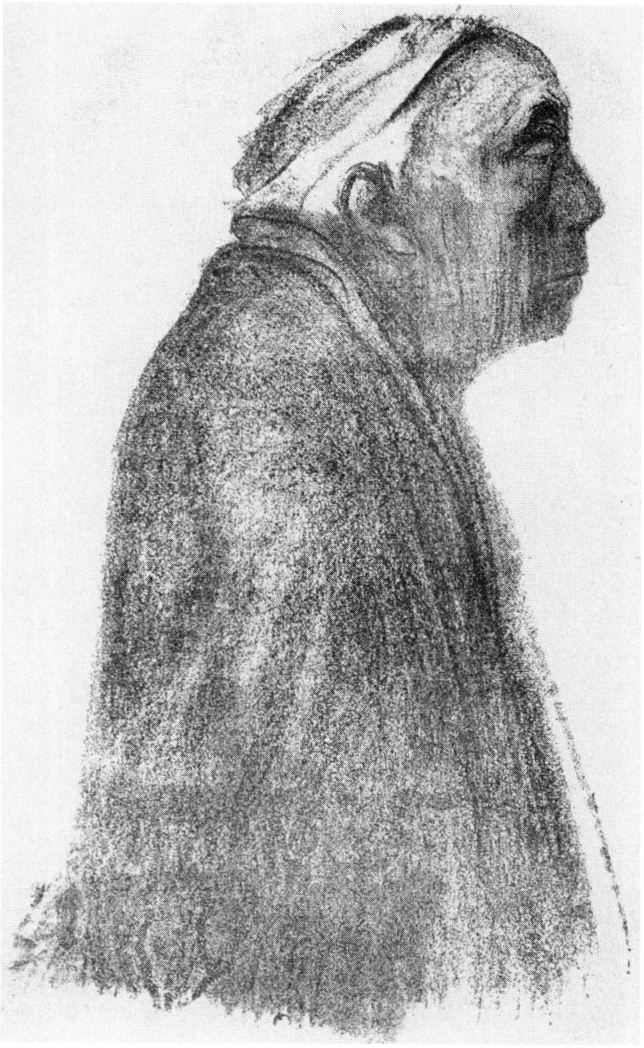

9. Käthe Kollwitz, *Self-Portrait in Profile Facing Right,* 1938. Lithograph. © Artists Rights Society (ARS), New York/VG Bild-Kunst, Bonn. Photo: Courtesy Spaightwood Galleries, Upton, MA.

whose *Interim* (1983–85) presents her meditations on middle age, or Ann Noggle, whose *Face Lift* series (1975) looks unabashedly at aging, or Alice Neel who, like Kollwitz, became known for her images of poverty and disease. In a striking nude self-portrait (1980) painted at the ripe age of eighty, Neel stares the spectator directly in the eyes as if to state that she, with her sagging breasts and flabby belly, has every right to be the subject of a work of art. The artist not only claims the right of subject, it is she who also controls the image. She grips her paintbrush in hand as a conductor holds a wand and unquestionably decides what the viewer will see. These artists, taking their cues from Kollwitz's pioneering efforts, refuse to be invisible or to represent the usual negative stereotypes of older women as ugly or obscene, hags, grannies or witches.

Kollwitz's struggle with the sadness and aggression she felt toward her own "dead mother" resulted in the processes of personal growth, social confrontation and the creation of groundbreaking art. Her stunning breadth of perspective from the personal to the political, from the individual to the universal, becomes apparent when one views her self-portraits as parts of a greater whole rather than as single pieces. As a whole they form a continuum that expresses the tragic nature of human life, seen through feminine eyes. Indeed, all the artists who followed her life and work are indebted to her courageous and creative project.

2
Claude Cahun: The Third Sex

Masculine? Feminine? But it depends on the situation.
Neuter is the only gender that always suits me.
—Claude Cahun

Sometimes she is dressed like a man in a suit, a debonair dandy, and a sassy sailor. At others, she is a heavily made-up doll or poupée. Here, she is a vamp, a fairy, a third-sexed youth lifting barbells and there a yogi seated cross-legged, or a young child curled up in a cupboard. Her head is shaved or her hair cut short—dyed pink, gold, and silver. She gazes from behind bars, masks, from the mirror's reflection, or beneath a glass jar. Who is this androgyne flaunting her Jewishness by wearing an oversized Star of David or showing off her majestic beak-nosed profile?

She is Lucy Schwob, born in 1894 in Nantes; she is Claude Courlis, a lesbian whose lifelong partner was her stepsister; she is Daniel Douglas, named after Oscar Wilde's lover, Lord Alfred Douglas; she is "the unnamed soldier," veteran of The Jersey Resistance sentenced to death for urging occupying German troops to mutiny and desertion.

She is Claude Cahun, a little-known Surrealist photographer, writer, actor, artist, and political activist. At a time when anti-Semitism and homophobia reigned rampant in Europe, Cahun's daring self-portraits issued a revolutionary challenge to conventional notions of gender, sexuality, and identity.

Cahun's art prompts a number of questions on two sides of a critical issue: When an artist assumes multiple roles in her work, is it because a sense of security allows her to play with her boundaries of identity, or is it because she has no clear sense of self and, therefore, through disguise, searches for one? Is such an artist merely exaggerating the traditionally feminine connection between artifice and self-image? Does she rather foreshadow the postmodernist claim that there is no such thing as a stable, cohesive self and that the self is a mutable perceptual construction, a "text" with innumerable interpretations? Or is she indirectly telling us that without a sense of coherent selfhood, however much an illusion, we are far more vulnerable to inner chaos and dissolution, and must resist such forces through artifice and contrivance?

While these questions themselves may be relevant to the psychology of Cahun's art, the art itself seems to exist in the divide between them and defy either/or answers. She was an extremely prescient artist whose remarkable series of photographic self-portraits was the first of its kind, and her work reflected a provocative stance eluding simple categorization.[1] Offering no clue that it was created almost a century ago, her art appears to make her a woman of our time. Yet, history had nearly forgotten her. Despite the fact that Cahun was the only woman photographer to have remained loyal to the Surrealist movement, she is absent from many anthologies on Surrealist art. Even otherwise comprehensive books on women surrealist artists do not mention her.[2] When included, she is often assumed to be a man or killed off by the Nazis in World War II.

Only recently has Cahun begun to achieve a small but notable degree of recognition and celebrity among select art connoisseurs. This may be attributable to the fact that Cahun seems to perfectly illustrate Judith Butler's popular conception of identity—particularly gender identity—as a performative and fluid construct."[3] Cahun represents her psychological complexity through a compelling series

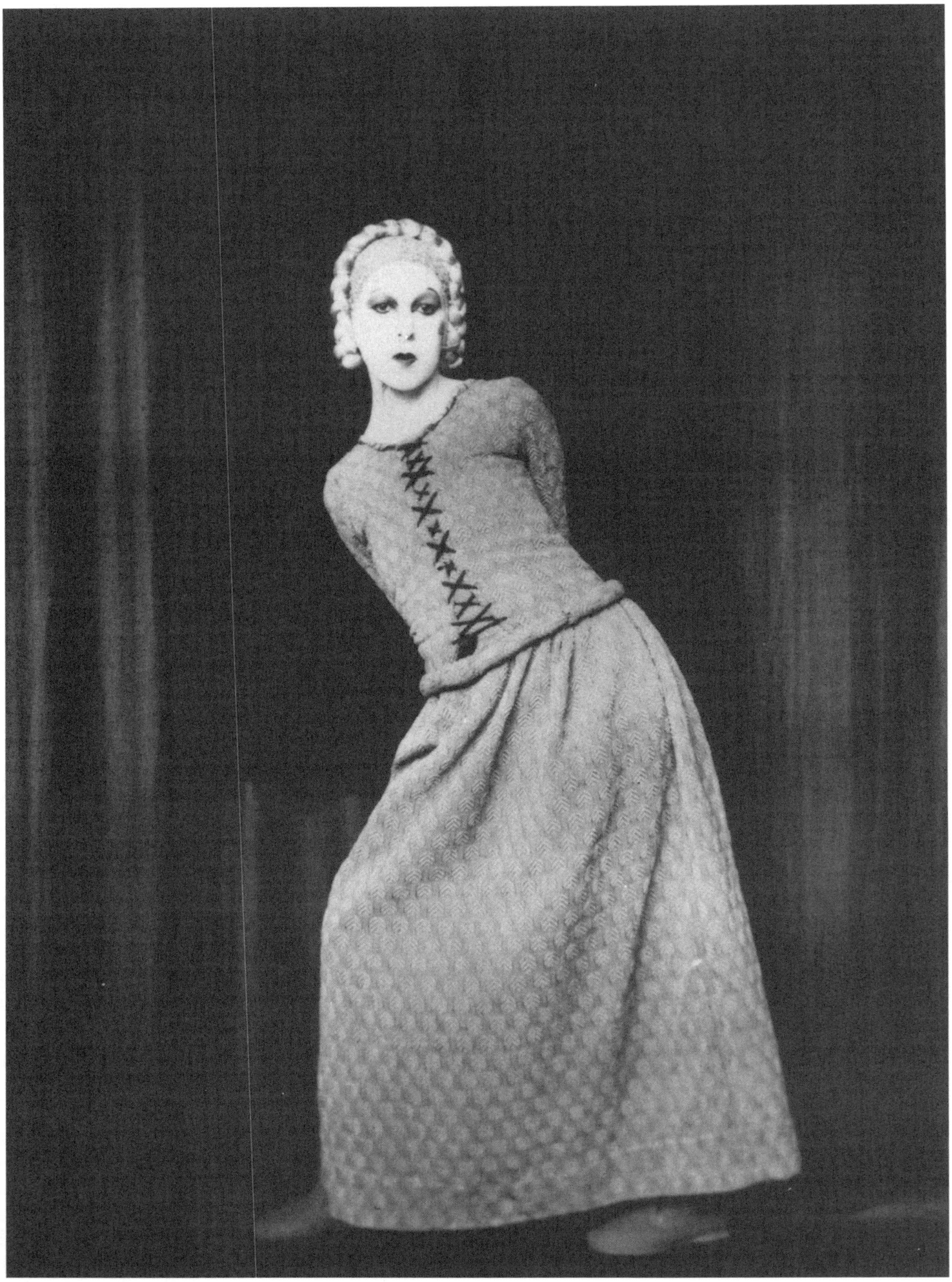

10. Claude Cahun, *Self-Portrait,* c. 1929. Courtesy Musée des Beaux Arts, Nantes.

of self-studies in which she dons costumes and disguises, engaging in games of masquerade and gender-bending. Though ostensibly her art may seem to anticipate Butler's theory, Cahun's theatricality, evident in many of the poses she assumes and costumes she wears, derives also from several theater productions in which she acted. Her dramatic flair had deeper roots too. She once exclaimed, "The happiest moment of my life?—The dream. Imagining that I am someone else. Acting my favorite role."[4]

Cahun performed numerous roles and is frequently compared to contemporary postmodern artist, Cindy Sherman, precisely because both women engaged in many games of mask and masquerade, playing with identity and gender, stretching and blurring boundaries, expressing existence as a continuum of change rather than as a set of fixed relations among entities and objects. Cahun's photographs, small and intimate, most the size of a snapshot (3.25 x 4.25 inches), prefigure Sherman's early black-and-white film-inspired stills. Nevertheless, the differences between the two artists are perhaps greater than the similarities. While Sherman's true self and identity are not meant to be part of her work, as she is all appearance with no hint of an inner self, Cahun imbues her photographs with a unique individuality despite her ever-changing roles. "Put on some makeup, apply a false nose—scrape away, the grimace reappears, the woman is always underneath,"[5] she wrote early on in life. Sherman's images are adopted primarily from external feminine stereotypes, film, and historical figures. Most of Cahun's transformations emerge from theatrical sources and from her pre- and unconscious fantasies and dream life. In many ways, it is the work of Francesca Woodman, whose oeuvre fits into the surrealist genre, that bears the greatest resemblance to Cahun's photographs. Woodman, apparently cognizant of Cahun's art, even posed in a cupboard just as Cahun had before her, in one of her many mysterious black-and-white self-portrait photographs.[6]

La Sainte Famille

Although little biographical information exists on her early life, it is known that Cahun came from a wealthy, literary Jewish family on her father's side.[7] She was influenced by, and strongly identified with, the prestigious men in her family: her father, Maurice Schwob, owned a successful liberal newspaper, *Le Phare et la Loire*, and her uncle, Marcel Schwob, was a well-known Symbolist writer. In a striking early self-portrait photograph, Cahun assumed the exact pose taken by her father in a photograph of him; each is depicted in stark profile emphasizing a duplicate beak nose. The nearly identical, even eerie, likeness between father and daughter is deliberate and reveals Cahun's conscious object of identification.

Cahun's mother is noticeably nonexistent in nearly all accounts of her life. Marie-Antoinette Courbelaise came from a Catholic, anti-Semitic family, and her marriage with Maurice Schwob was troubled from the start. Cahun was a mere four years old when her mother suffered a severe mental breakdown and was subsequently institutionalized in a psychiatric clinic where she remained indefinitely. Cahun recalled: "My memory of her was the expression of a half-childish nonchalant gaiety . . . laughing through her tears even during a crisis."[8] Cahun perhaps referred to her mother's illness and the absence of nurturing in her life when she avowed, "Before I was born, I was condemned to death. Executed by default."[9]

The photomontage, *Self Pride* (1929–30), is crucial in its depiction of Cahun's family romance. *La Sainte Famille* (Holy Family), as she ironically called it, consists of an oedipal drama, set in a triangle, containing mother, father, and child, all attached to each other in a grotesque symbiosis. Although the girl is directly merged to the mother at the abdomen, it is the father who holds the child aloft by clutching her hair. The child, in the middle of this rather violent scene, tightly grasps her dove, a bird of peace. Another image shows a beheaded, castrated male statue from whose abdomen sprouts a tree, like a giant umbilical cord:[10] the father *sans* head and penis as mother, the father depersonalized so as to be more of a cosmic principle, the beheaded and castrated father as the root source of her "inner" tree of life. Penis and face are the appropriated energy that nurtures the tree. Indeed, the tree's branches grow disembodied parts of Cahun's body and her sense

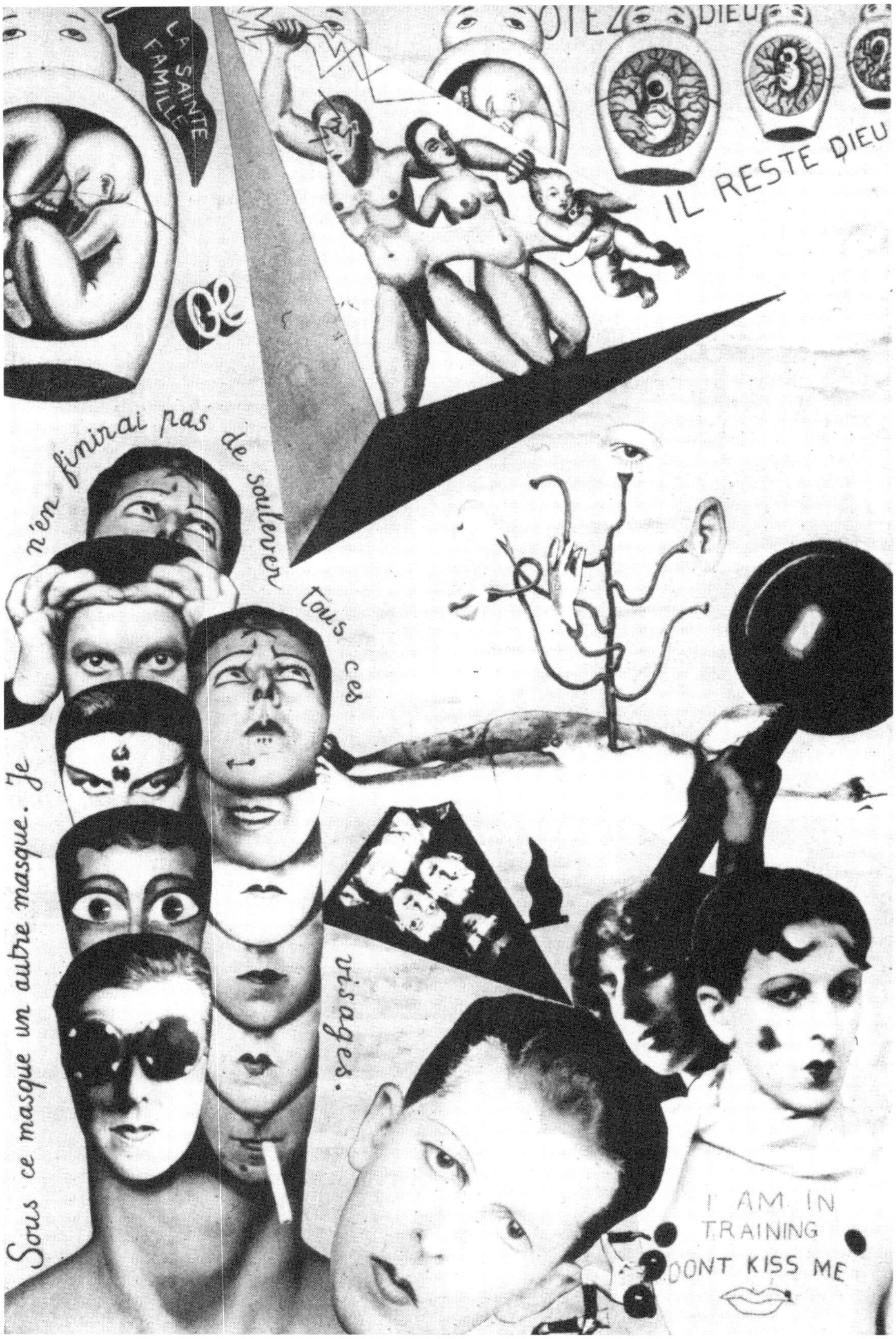

11. Claude Cahun and Marcel Moore, *Self-Pride* (I.O.U.), 1929–30. Photomontage. Courtesy Jersey Heritage Trust.

organs. Many pictures of a developing embryo are also displayed. In the final and largest one, there are two embryos rather than one. The idea of twinship as a replacement for a defective symbiosis is one of Cahun's solutions to her detrimental upbringing and recurs throughout her art. The eleven stacked self-portrait heads and the barbells and directive that she is in training and is not to be kissed are also repetitive motifs that relay the message that she is constantly trying to build a self the way one builds a body (bodybuilding). The implication is that when she succeeds, which is doubtful considering her second message ("I will never finish removing all these masks . . ."), she will be ready to be kissed (i.e., attain real intimacy).

This photomontage, in its brilliant juxtaposition of fractured images, therefore, represents a reconstruction of the familial origins of Cahun's developmental struggles. As a result of a violent situation with her parents, she preferred to recreate her birth situation in accordance with her will—she is reborn as a twin (with her stepsister?) and she is born from her father (rather than her mother). These alterations result in a disembodied self with fragmented senses, primarily male identified and, moreover, fictitious. *I.O.U.*, the subtitle Cahun gave to this photomontage, reveals the score she kept with her family. She "owes" them for the masks she wears, masks that require her to remain in a state of "training," a transitory prison from which there is no escape. It is not altogether clear who she owes her masks to more—Mother for going mad, or Father for helping Mother to get there, or perhaps both because they put her in the middle of their awfulness. Also, masks notwithstanding, she "owes" them for her brokenness—the pieces of herself that grow from a broken tree. Other self-portrait photographs depict Cahun behind bars, with hands outstretched, and face covered with a veil or enclosed in a glass jar. Still others show her strangled and beheaded. Her self-made prison is the outcome of the family of her childhood, a childhood destroyed by the violence of madness.

Naturally she was a troubled youth and her father feared she was prone to mental illness like her mother. When classmates during the Dreyfus affair[11] teased her, he sent her away to school. She first attended Oxford and later returned to France to study at the Sorbonne, where she took a degree in literature and philosophy.

Cahun had an older brother, George, about whom nothing is known, perhaps because both she and her father, for unknown reasons, broke off relations with him. After obtaining a divorce from her mother, Cahun's father remarried Mme Malherbe, a widow who had a daughter, Suzanne. Fifteen-year-old Cahun soon fell madly in love with her new stepsister, comparing her encounter with Suzanne to being struck by lightning and having inspired "a jealous and exclusive passion . . . Soon nothing existed for me except for my relationship with Suzanne."[12] This relationship consumed the adolescent Cahun and caused considerable distress to her family who attempted to curtail it. Cahun reacted with anorexia and suicidality, but refused to give up her first and only love. Indeed, this was a love that satisfied Cahun's need for symbiosis (the two girls referred to themselves as Siamese twins) as well as her incestuous homoerotic desires (that found no outlet due to her mother's absence). This was a love that precluded separation and loss, a love whose constancy and loyalty would accompany her throughout her life.

Paris and Surrealism

Cahun's intellectual, sexual, and financial independence attracted her to Paris where she moved in 1920 with Malherbe. At the dawn of the twentieth century, they joined an extraordinary group of talented lesbian women. Gertrude Stein and Alice B. Toklas, Sylvia Beach and Adrienne Monnier, Djuna Barnes and Thelma Wood all contributed to Paris's international avant-garde culture and lesbian subculture.

Cahun was drawn to the tenets of Surrealism, a movement that reached mythic status after its Parisian début in the 1920s. André Breton, the father of Surrealism, was deeply influenced by psychoanalytic discoveries and repeatedly paid tribute to Freud for the privileged place he accorded the substratum of consciousness as manifested in his *Interpretation of Dreams.* As an art movement, Surrealism aimed to access and reveal the reality underlying the world of appearances—the unconscious, the irrational, the realm of dreams. For the Surrealists, the dream was believed to be superior to the waking state, fantasy more potent than reality, and the unconscious mind representative of a more profound dimension of the human psyche than reason and logic.

Because of its emphasis on deeper areas of consciousness, Surrealism, promised the possibility of more complex, multidimensional attitudes toward women. The truth is that by very virtue of the unconscious embodiment lauded by Surrealists, their relationship to women was complicated, ambivalent, and even quite hostile. On the one hand, they admitted several brilliant women to their inner circle and admired and even exalted feminine qualities, like emotionality, intuition, and irrationality, which they thought superior to the emotionally flawed, overly rational thinking of men. On the other hand, these very qualities were associated with insanity, weakness, lack, sexuality, Otherness, and in Bataille's theory of the *informe*, chaotic baseness.[13]

The function and image of women in the Surrealist circle therefore frequently assumed the conventional mythological or allegorical roles of muse, child, or femme fatale. In addition, although Surrealists insisted on transgression against bourgeois boundaries, through revolution and emancipation, their homophobia and advocacy of heterosexuality was well-known. It is said that Breton avoided Cahun because he disliked her unconventional (unfeminine?) appearance and behavior, and he even abandoned his favorite café when he saw Cahun and Malherbe enter arm in arm.[14] He nonetheless encouraged her efforts and claimed she was one of the most singular spirits of the time.

The majority of Surrealist representations of women reflect a strong, traditional masculine bias. Women are exalted, feared, or degraded in the photographs of Man Ray, Jacques-André Boiffard, Raoul Ubac, Maurice Tabard, and Hans Bellmer. (This is also true of the paintings of René Magritte, Salvador Dali, Max Ernst, and Paul Delvaux.) The female torso, for instance, frequently stands by itself—faceless, headless—a fantasy dream site of male desire. When the face is present, it is often veiled, caged (e.g., Ubac, *Mannequin*, 1937), distorted, or hidden in shadows (e.g., Ubac, *Portrait in a Mirror*, 1938). Hans Bellmer's photographs of dolls—*La Poupée* or his *Unica* series—also assault woman's physical integrity and wholeness by depicting the female body as a headless conglomeration of parts often tied together and bruised. It is interesting in this context to mention the French proverb: *Femme sans tête tout en est bon* (A headless woman is all to the good).

Like her male counterparts, Cahun wished to elevate the unconscious, the irrational, and the dream in her work whose focus was also the female body. Unlike most Surrealist photographic works of women subjects, Cahun's self-studies are not castrative or fetishistic, nor do they jettison selfhood. Rather, they consist mostly of close-ups of her impressive face, drawing the viewer into its powerful expression. She thus demonstrated that a woman's gaze is commanding and autonomous, challenging and uncompromising. In a 1928 self-portrait, for instance, she stands next to her mirror as she stares at the viewer rather than at her reflection, thereby subverting the traditional notion of woman's relationship with her mirror as an expression of female vanity and narcissism. More importantly, she disrupts the fixed polarities of gender difference and the privilege of the male gaze by showing that she is not simply the object of a gaze. Her eyes in this portrait, as in most of her oeuvre, are unwavering, strong, and confrontational; they stare *us* straight in the eye. This image therefore indicates both self-reflection and the interplay between Cahun's and the spectator's gaze. *A woman looks at the viewer who looks at her.* Whether the viewer is a male or female, he or she cannot help but be struck by the questioning eye/I of Cahun. It must be added that Cahun replaced the male gaze with the female gaze in this photograph, as her photographer was none other than her lover. Thus, Cahun posed with her mirror yet chose to avert her eyes from it in order to meet the gaze of her mirror-self, her sister and lover, Suzanne, renamed Marcel Moore. By staring at the camera, her partner, and us all at once, Cahun seduces us into the role of mirror and lover as well.[15]

Cahun's art depicted a new vision of woman, a vision often tinged with humor and irony. She ridiculed, parodied, and took even the most serious of subjects—her identity—with a grain of salt. In a series of photographs she produced in 1927, she gazes coyly at her viewers as she lifts a set of toy barbells with her

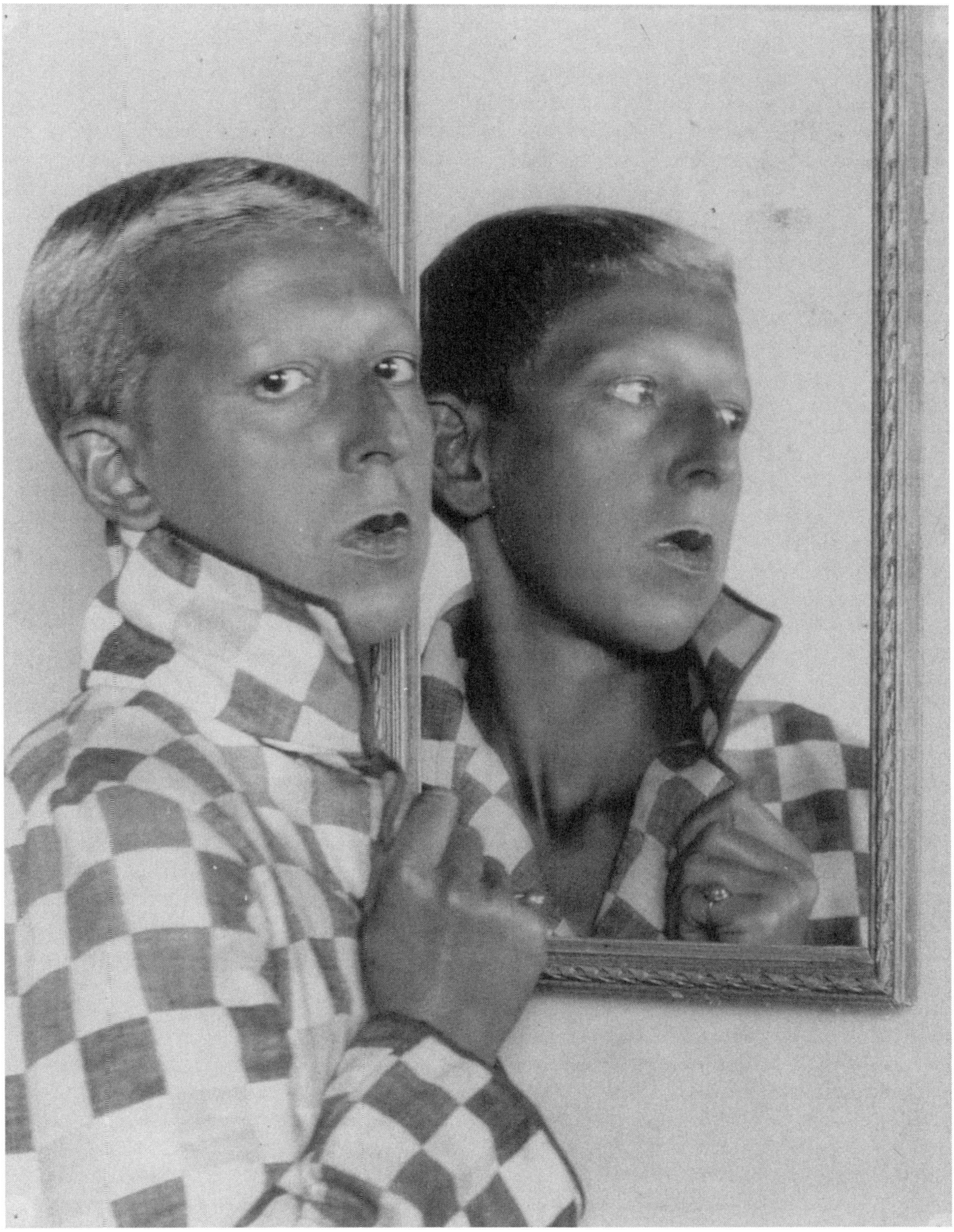

12. Claude Cahun, *Self-Portrait,* 1928. Musée des Beaux Arts, Nantes. Photo credit: Réunion des Musées Nationaux/Art Resource, NY. Courtesy Zabriskie Gallery.

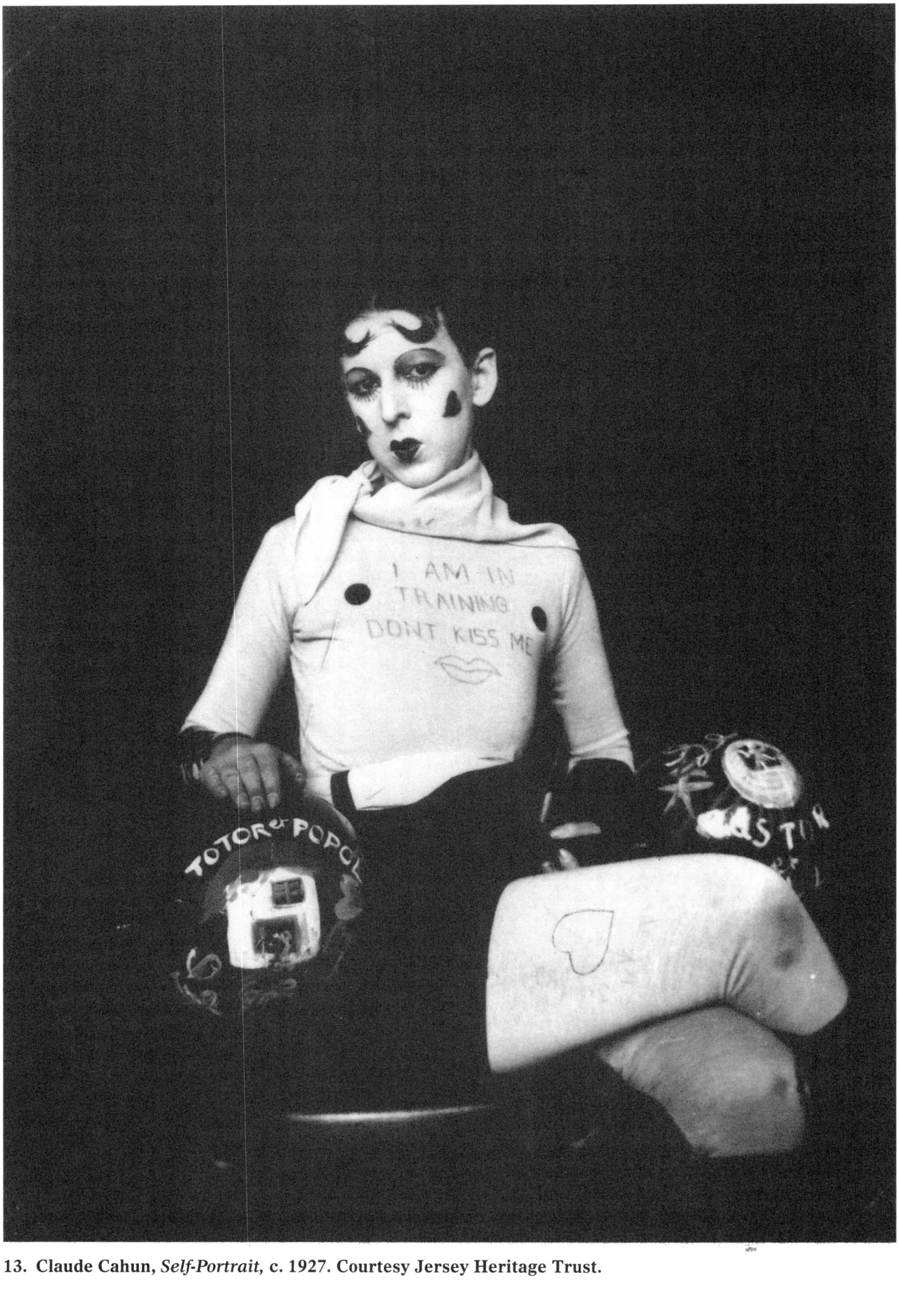

13. Claude Cahun, *Self-Portrait,* c. 1927. Courtesy Jersey Heritage Trust.

face made up and her nipples and cheeks accentuated. Her hair is slicked and curled. Who is this person and how can we categorize her along gender lines? The T-shirt she wears offers a humorous and enigmatic reply: "I AM IN TRAINING: DON'T KISS ME." All we can say for sure is that Cahun regarded identity as an ongoing process of becoming.

Like Duchamp's creation of his alter ego Rrose Sélavy in 1920, Cahun changed her name and staged a drama of the opposite sex, but her alterations of identity surpassed that of a drag performance. More than simply appropriating masculine features, she *created* a third sex, a hybrid cultural identity, a creature who was both and yet neither, an entity transcending sexual dualism. No wonder she grew fascinated with the writings of Havelock Ellis, an early sexologist, whose controversial theories allowed for precisely such a possibility. Cahun translated Ellis who wrote: "We may not know exactly what sex is; but we do know that it is mutable, with the possibility of one sex being changed into the other sex, that its frontiers are often uncertain, and that there are many stages between a complete male and a complete female."[16]

Continuing Ellis's line of thought, Marjorie Garber argues that we entertain a third space of possibility and desire when considering gender.[17] This third space calls to mind child psychiatrist and psychoanalyst D. W. Winnicott's "potential space," a space in which the child attempts to separate from and stay connected to the mother at one and the same time. This is a critical space where the child acts to develop autonomy while retaining the power to draw on needed maternal energies. It is Winnicott who coined the term, *transitional object* when referring to the young child's teddy bear or baby blanket to which it attributes maternal qualities of nurturing and soothing. The illusion of the mother's crucial functions takes place in a third space that exists between the child and mother, and between inner and outer reality. The ambiguity of such a space, its alternating poles of connection and separation, unity and differentiation, known and unknown, provides the child the opportunity for self-direction and safety in its creative possibilities, therefore encouraging a freer play of cognitive, emotional, and intuitive faculties. According to Winnicott, potential space is the location in which creativity originates.[18] Thomas Ogden has adopted Winnicott's notion of an intermediate area as that which best describes the intersubjective playing field in psychoanalysis. Ogden calls this space between therapist and patient a "third analytic space."[19] The third space is where boundaries are uncertain and definitions incomplete, a place of flux and a field of creation. Here, too, is the very space where profound personal issues may get worked out, where the artist, for instance, may address inadequate relationships to the mother by transferring maternal care into her art while simultaneously creating a work that transcends monolithic analysis and makes us stand before it in awe and appreciation. I believe that Cahun employed her art as a space that permitted exploration of the possibilities inherent in indeterminacy, the spontaneity and unexpectedness of creation, and the existence of unresolved paradoxes, a space in which she gave birth to a third sex.

Self-Creation

Cahun appears to have developed a conscious hatred for everything maternal as a result of her chaotic early years. With irony, she wrote: "The mother was so unappetizing that the infant was offered an aperitif before being served the breast."[20] It is as if she wished to "vomit the mother"[21] in her efforts to deny her matrilineage. She changed her name from Lucy Schwob, chosen by her mother, to a purposely ambiguously gendered pseudonym taken from her paternal grandmother's brother, Léon Cahun, an eminent orientalist. (Cahun adopted other pseudonyms, including Claude Corlis and Daniel Douglas, an homage to Oscar Wilde's lover.) As with Duchamp (Sélavy/Levy), Cahun's choice of a name that is a close relative of Cohen, the appellation of Jewish Priests, clearly emphasized her Jewish affinity at a time when anti-Semitism was on the rise in France.

Yet, in her driven urge to self-create, Cahun also rejected her father's family name. The ambivalence toward her father is expressed in two 1932 photographs, the first of which she titled *Le Père* (The Father). In it, a figure with a bird's head lies on the sand with a shovel in hand and a thin metal stick impaling its abdomen. The figure lies as if dead, stabbed by the rod. Although the stick suggests an erect phallus, a vulva-shaped crevice is dug in the sand between its spread legs, thereby creating an ambiguous implication of gender.

In a second photograph with this figure, the shovel that was placed in its hand is now stuck between its legs. Cahun stands adjacent to it with only her stomach and legs visible. She presses a skirt made of seaweed to her hips and four strips dangle along the length of her legs. Two of the strips hang between her legs, echoing the vagina-phallus motif. Cahun's shadow, also originating from between her legs, plays with light and dark elements. The bird/father image is superimposed on that of Cahun's. The photograph therefore blurs the boundaries between the two figures and the two genders all within a dream-like ambience.

Both photographs brilliantly and quite aggressively appropriate and play with her father's manhood, and proffer a third possibility combining femininity (skirt) and masculinity (phallus). The latter photograph may therefore additionally represent a statement to Breton, the père/father of Surrealism, in that it echoes numerous photographs by male Surrealist artists depicting headless bodies that conflate gender distinctions.

Despite Cahun's rejection of her mother, a powerful unconscious identification with the maternal can be gleaned from her art. For example, in a daring photomontage, she places her arms around an inverted photograph of her shaved head to create the impression of a newborn emerging from the uterus. Indeed, her oeuvre is replete with images in which she gives birth to herself, thus defiantly replacing her mother and appropriating the maternal function. Alluding to the enormous significance that the maternal had in shaping her identity, Cahun sometimes signed her name with a small c contained within a larger C.

Cahun's conscious rejection of her maternal identification led to the creation of a fictitious self that may have been artistically innovative but was, at times, alienated from her deeper orientation and sensibilities, a self far less contrived. At age thirty-three, in a moment of reflection, she perceptively noted: "I spent my life passionately, blindly desiring that things be other than what they are. I have only accumulated fictitious values."[22]

Though she vehemently attacked motherhood, Cahun's attendance at lectures on mental illness in Parisian hospitals, as well as her numerous self-portraits, might reveal her never-ending search for her mad, lost mother. Cahun clearly had personal reasons to both pursue and flee from the madwoman. In her autobiographical book, *Aveux non Avenus*, she questions: "Maman! Why are boats in the water, maman?" and replies to herself, "But the mother is elsewhere, out of the water, out of the boat, out of her mind."[23]

Surrealists, too, possessed a fascination with madness in women. Woman embodied the mad Other—at once powerful, perilous, endowed with strange talent, the primitive, and the visionary—who inspired both awe and fear. They sought to mime "convulsive beauty" in their art, which they associated directly to the infamous displays of hysterics in Jean-Martin Charcot's Salpetrière. Argon and Breton exclaimed: "We Surrealists are anxious to celebrate . . . hysteria, the greatest poetic discovery of the end of the 19th century."[24]

Cahun even adopted the face of a "mad woman" in some of her photographs. In one disturbing and hauntingly beautiful self-portrait, in which she resembles a psychiatric patient, Cahun's shaved head is unnaturally elongated and her gaze confused and lost. The eroticism, suggested by Cahun's décolletage in this photograph, provides an additional locus of tension in its odd conjunction with the stark portrayal of insanity. This self-portrait, probably the most bizarre in her oeuvre, resembles an otherworldly extraterrestrial, a cone-headed alien, and therefore accentuates her difference. It prefigures the subject of women portraying themselves in terms of monster beauty, a theme taken up much later by artists like Cindy Sherman and Orlan. Cahun's protracted skull can also be interpreted as a type of "erection of the head," which transforms her into a phallic woman.

The Uncanny Double

As Cahun incorporated the identity of her "mad" mother, her self-portraits evoked the uncanny, that particular category of experience Freud called *unheimlich*. Simultaneously familiar and unfamiliar, the uncanny is "in reality nothing new or alien, but something which is familiar and old-established in the mind and which has become alienated

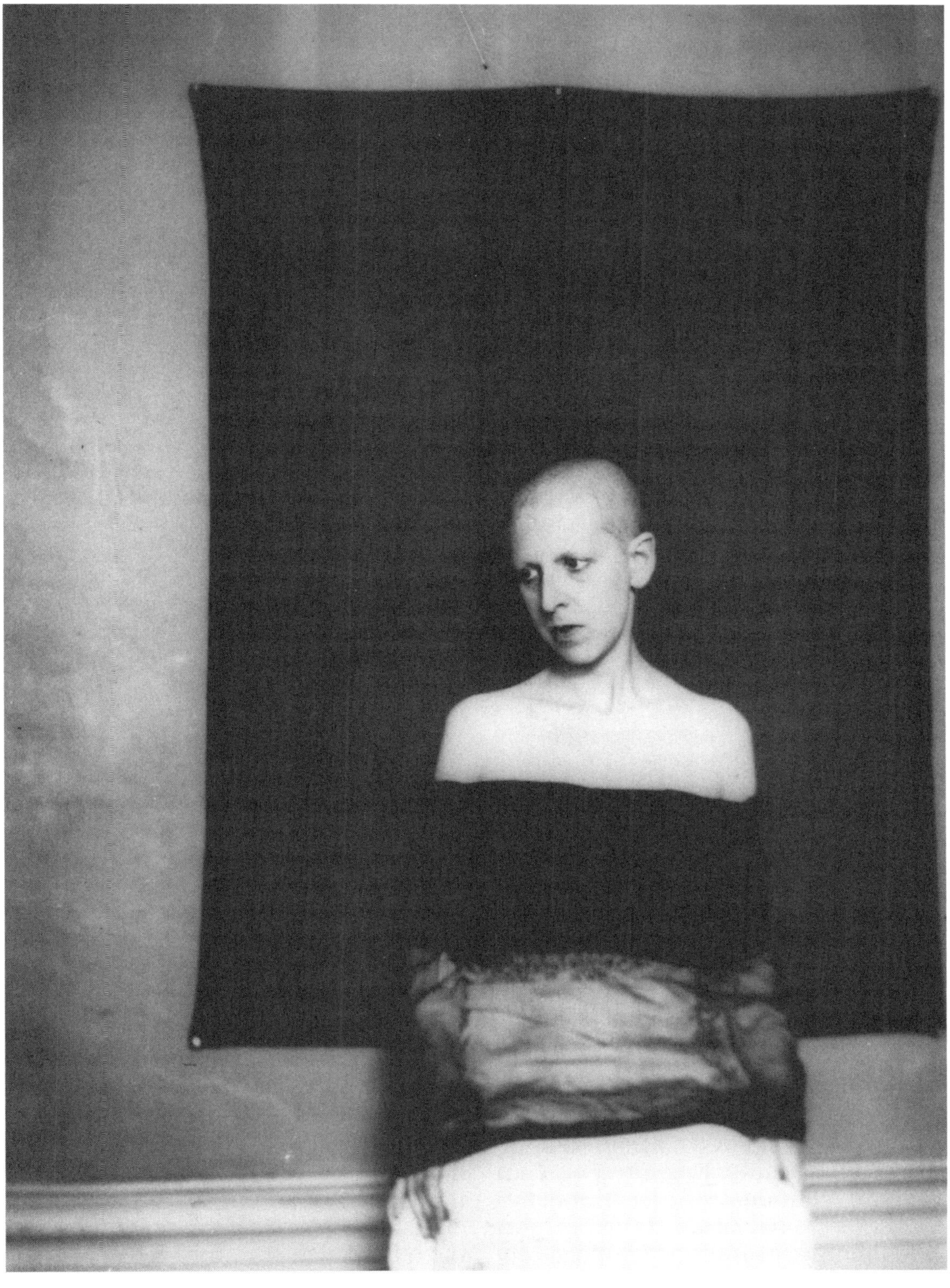

14. Claude Cahun, *Self-Portrait,* c. 1921. Courtesy Jersey Heritage Trust.

from it through the process of repression."[25] As a result, uncanny experiences, people, or objects create confusion between the symbolic and the real due, at least in part, to the widening chasm between the real and the remembered. The double, a figure that is somehow identical to, or interchangeable with, the self, is one of the most disconcerting examples of the uncanny. Freud explained that the double is uncanny because it brings us back to our infancy when we were identified with someone else: the mother.[26] Unsurprisingly, then, the way Cahun's mother appeared to her is steeped in the aura of the uncanny.

Freud's recognition that the maternal body can easily serve as the prototype for the uncanny double is illustrated in Cahun's double self-portrait photographs, arguably the most enigmatic in her oeuvre. Furthermore, the photograph, which undoes separation by preventing the past from being erased, represents an ingenious way to maintain one's tie to the mother. On one level, Cahun's double self-portraits, of which there are several, can be interpreted as representing the manner she found to reunite with her lost mother and the fear of that symbiosis all at once. A striking example of Cahun's attempt to unite with the maternal body is a 1928 double self-portrait depicting a set of her profiles, one facing to the left and one to the right, superimposed on a rock-like edifice. The entire picture is symmetrical; it has been folded in half to resemble a Rorschach blot. In fact, several inkblots stamp the photograph as a direct allusion to the psychological projective technique aimed at uncovering unconscious personality traits. Closer scrutiny reveals the outline of a human torso on the stone formation. Cahun's placement of her twin heads at the center of this body accordingly creates the image of a heart. In her art, Cahun reunites with her mother and becomes the heart of the body from which she was once separated. That one photograph includes so many layers of conscious and unconscious meaning showcases Surrealist art at its best. Two additional self-portraits exist with the same rock backdrop. In one, she is depicted swimming, as if in the womb, in opposite directions. Like the earth sculptures in Ana Mendieta's *Silueta* Series, these works in Cahun's oeuvre concern the reunion with the mother through a merger with Mother Earth.

Photographs of this kind can thus be viewed as Cahun's solution for her separation from and loss of her mother. As such, her work takes place in the third Winnicottian space of both creation and reparation. She transferred her original maternal care onto her art by merging symbolic elements of mother and child. In recreating the early mother-child relationship in her work, in both form and content, she now identified with both passive and active roles, child and mother. Her unconscious wish to return to the comfort of the womb, (or the post birth undifferentation between mother and child), is additionally depicted in one 1932 photograph in which she resembles a true *femme-enfant;* in pigtails and bobby socks, with bow in hair, she literally curls up in a fetal position and dozes on a shelf inside a womb-like cupboard. As a child, she was known to have hidden under the kitchen table to seek refuge from family turmoil, a unique self-imposed primal scene.

In 1996, I proposed the term *artistic transference* for the representation of this early mother-child dyad and its simultaneous attempts at reparation that take place in the creation of artworks. One purpose of Cahun's art, I suggest here, was to come to terms with her early maternal loss. Cahun fused her image with that of her mother, as did Kollwitz before her, to restore the broken tie she had with her mother as well as to create a new image of woman in art.

Cahun's double images recur throughout her oeuvre and additionally allude to an emphasis on self-perception and self-awareness. Like her mirror reflection, the double suggests narcissistic struggles that found a suitable stage in her art. She once wrote "Narcissism? Of course. It is my best feature."[27] Cahun's double self-portraits reverse the concept of the "selfobject," coined by the father of Self Psychology, Heinz Kohut, as one connoting the narcissistic use of an Other to function as part of the self structure. According to Kohut, the mother as mirror and father as idealized object initially serve to enhance a child's healthy narcissism. When this process fails, he postulated the emergence of a damaged sense of self and a self that uses others to fill in for self-esteem regulation that is lacking.[28] Although Cahun clearly used her mirror, camera, and Moore as selfobjects, she also showed how the self can

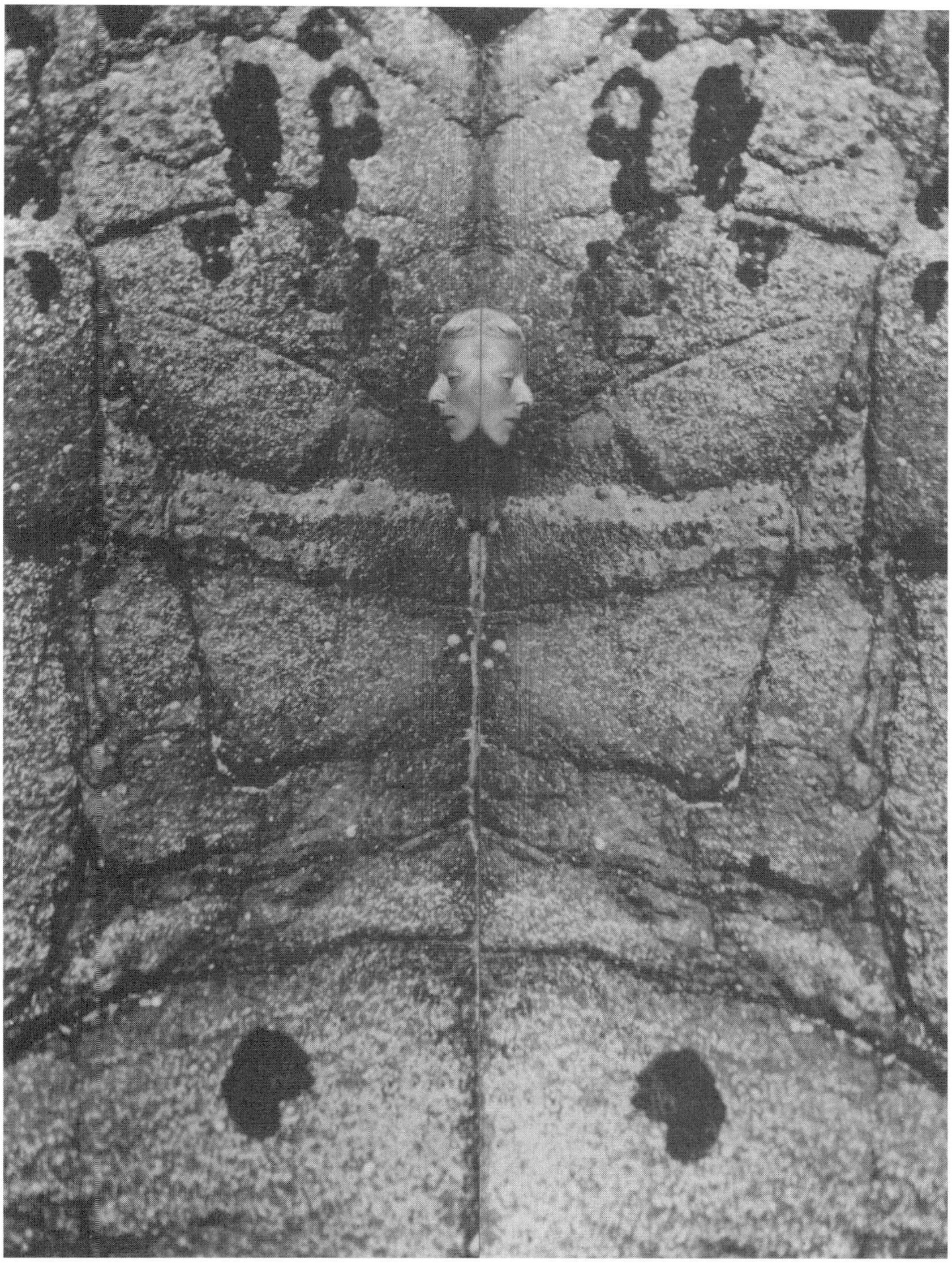

15. Claude Cahun, *Self-Portrait,* 1928. Courtesy Musée des Beaux Arts, Nantes.

become the Other. Her double self-portraits created a new type of relating to the self, a *self-othering,* as it were.

In a rarely titled 1928 double self-portrait, *Que me veux-tu?* (What do you want from me?), Cahun depicted two shots of her head, one in profile and one in three-quarter view. The heads are joined at the neck and resemble Siamese twins. Both are bald like newborns, revealing the forceful shape of her skull. In this powerful double self-portrait, Cahun is symbiotically tied to herself rather

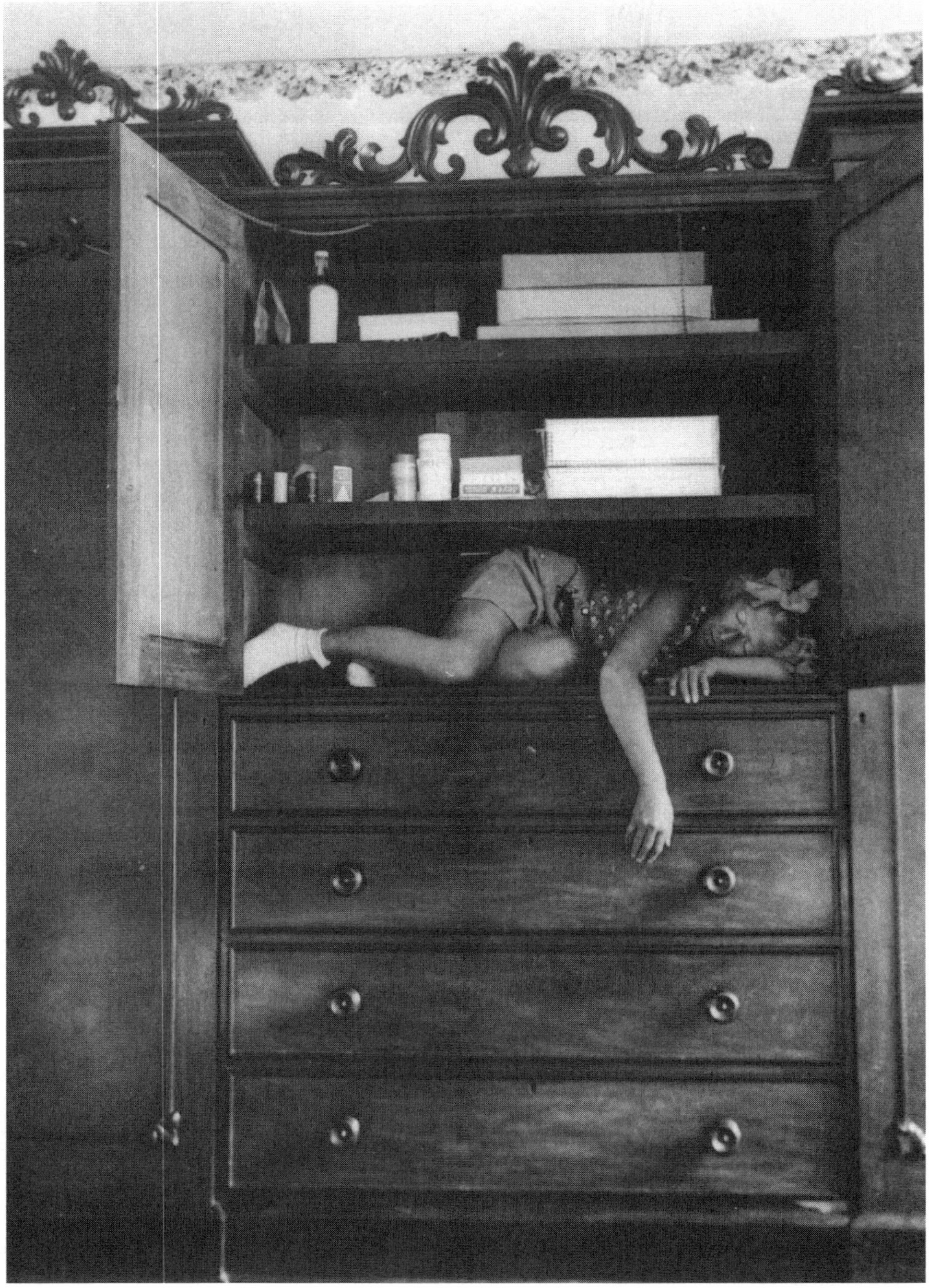

16. Claude Cahun, *Self-Portrait,* c. 1932. Courtesy Jersey Heritage Trust.

than to her mother and searches, through a process of twinship, for answers to questions about her identity.[29] Who or what is asking the question? To whom is the question addressed? Can one (half of) Cahun obtain what is needed from the other (half of) Cahun? Is the question doomed to repeat itself forever in her heart and her art? Is it a question she asks her mother? Or one her mother asks her? It may also be a question she asks her audience. The indeterminate context of the question within the artwork makes simultaneous all these possibilities. As with much of her art this question maintains an open dialogue with the artist and the viewer, an open process wherein training, self-work, and continual creation is always necessary. Creation and especially self-creation *is* repair.

Interestingly, Cahun used this same photograph as a model for a drawing that graced the cover of a novel, *Frontières Humaines,* in 1929. There too the image was accompanied by a text: *N'ayez pas peur d'etre dévorés* (Do not fear being devoured). The drawing, as opposed to its photograph version, creates sharper boundaries around the figures as if to counteract the verbal message of being swallowed alive. On some level, she alludes to the inevitability of death because death is, after all, the final "frontier." Cahun's preoccupation with the theme of the double, then, also concerns its protective function against loss of self. Otto Rank, who lived in Paris from 1926 to 1935, explored the double motif in anthropology and literature and stated that "The idea of death . . . is denied by a duplication of the self."[30] If Cahun, through inevitable identification with her mother, were to die or go mad, her second (created) self would no doubt survive. Perhaps sensing that she was in danger of losing her self, Cahun defensively and instinctively created a second self, an imaginary companion—at times even a Doppelgänger.

Strange that she needed a Doppelgänger since Malherbe had been in her life since she was fifteen and had permanently changed it. The artist regarded Malherbe as her alter ego and even referred to her as "*l'autre moi,*" the other me, her ultimate and tangible double. Cahun developed a sense of security from this woman who, unlike her mother, remained completely devoted to her and never left her side. Like Cahun, Malherbe adopted an ambiguously gendered pseudonym, Marcel Moore. Cahun, who regarded herself as one of a pair, had Moore photograph her before a mirror and vice versa, each portrait producing a double image of the woman: the real visages face front and the profiles are reflected in the mirror. When placed side by side, the two photographs show the mirror images of both women facing each other and thus uncannily meeting in gaze to become the mirror image of the other.[31]

Cahun was not entirely unambivalent about her relationship with Moore however. In 1930, she compared happy lovers to a hermaphroditic monster or Siamese twins whose entanglement she likened to a serpent or Gordian knot that ought to be severed. Thus, Cahun's double contained so many meanings related to symbiosis and autonomy, freedom and death. On the one hand, she needed the double to protect herself from loss and, on the other, she feared the loss of being devoured by the other. The greatness of her art derives from the elegant beauty of her images as well as the density of meaning she was able to pack into a single shot: the double, boundaries and their loss, the conflict between the self and other, the driven need to be someone and the impossibility of static identity.

The Mirror

In an arresting androgynous 1927 self-portrait, Cahun, clad in a black turtleneck, is surrounded by a black background, her whitened face emerging from it like a ghost. She has a painted widow's peak; one penciled eyebrow, and heavily tinted lips. Beyond male and female, human and inhuman, beautiful and ugly, she becomes a figure suggesting an amalgam of dualities and transcends them all. A circle is created by her arms that wrap around and grip a reflecting object resembling a crystal ball. Most striking is the cutting glare she casts at us. We are compelled, as if hypnotized, to take part in a visual showdown, to stare back and forth between her powerful eyes and the ball meant to reflect our own.

Any artist whose oeuvre consists primarily of self-portraits has a potent and complex relationship to her mirror. On one level, Cahun's attention to eyes and mirrors in her art indicates her self-perception as seer and visionary. On another level, it reveals a deep yearning for the mirroring of which she was most likely deprived during her early years. The mirroring experience provides the child with the primal sense of identity, which initially means body identity.[32] Lacan first articulated the "mirror phase" and referred to the infant's initial discovery of self in the mirror.[33] From Winnicott's view, the infant looks into the mother's eyes and experiences the first awakenings of identity; Winnicott emphasized "the mother's role of giving back to the baby the baby's own self" in early visual contacts."[34] Spitz considered the child's perception of the mother's face-Gestalt a psychic organizer and a forerunner of object relations.[35] Sustained eye-to-eye contact, he believed, provides stability for the child. Mahler

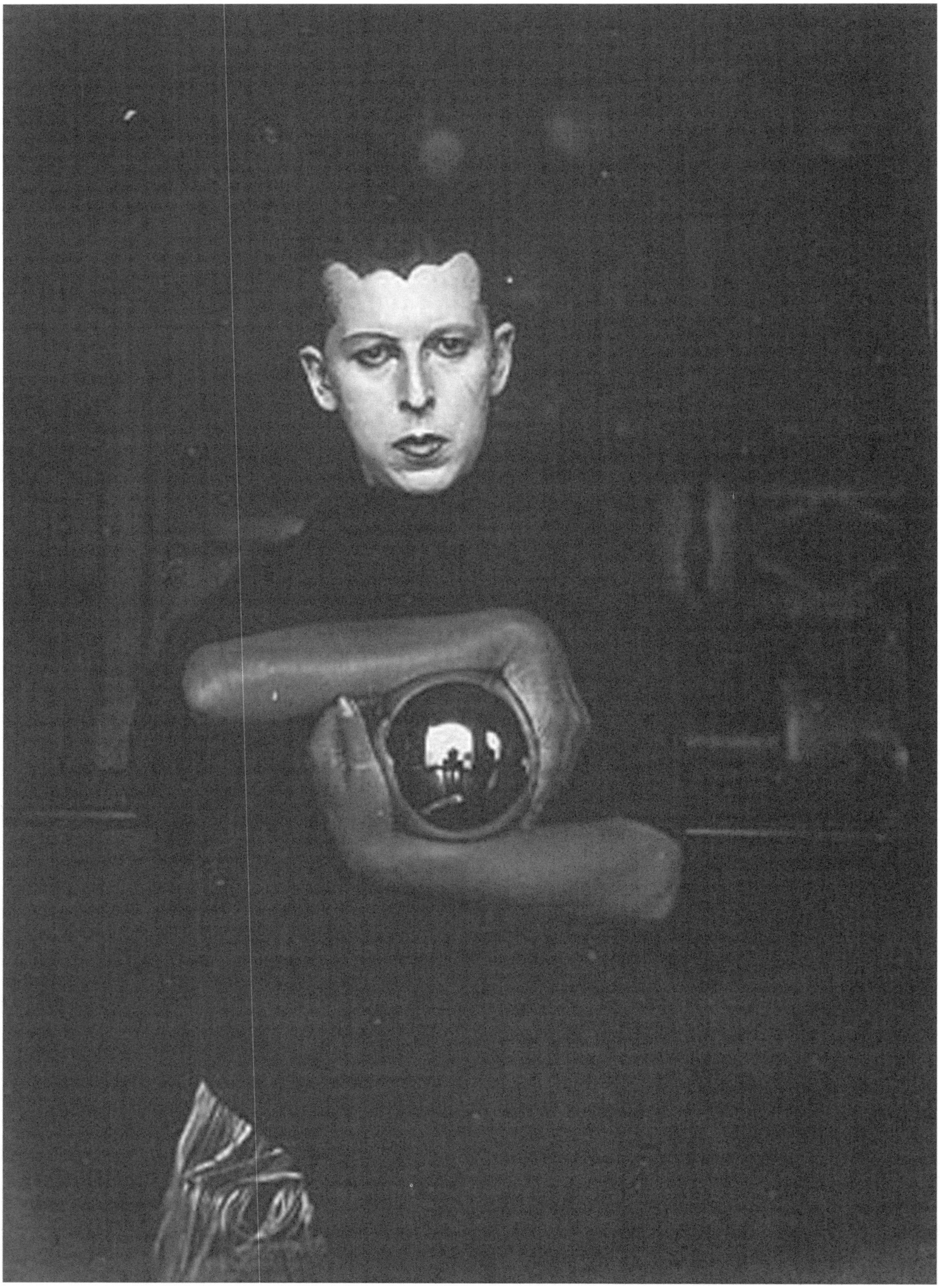

17. Claude Cahun, *Self-Portrait,* c. 1927. Founders Society Purchase, Albert and Peggy de Salle Charitable Trust and the DeRoy Photographic Acquisition Endowment Fund. Photograph © 1996 The Detroit Institute of Arts.

called "the human face in motion" the child's first meaningful percept. She delineated a stage, "the mirror frame of reference," in which the child alters his or her behavior in reaction to the mother's selective responses.[36] Analysts like Freud, Winnicott, and Kohut have emphasized the importance of mirroring in the psychoanalytic relationship.

Elsewhere, I have shown how the same search that takes place between mother and infant, and between analyst and patient, is also undertaken by artists in the creation of their works.[37] In particular, the self-portrait is an apt, self-evident means by which an artist acts as a mirror to herself, simultaneously reflecting her need for self-definition and her attempt to achieve it. Indeed, Cahun's diffuse wide stare in her "mad" self-portrait resembles that observed in the infantile gaze and contrasts with the direct, narrowly focused look in her more "masculine" identified self-portraits.

I suggest here that the self-portrait photograph in Cahun's oeuvre became a surrogate for the reciprocal encounter with the mother's face. Lacking the beneficial, identity-feeding mirroring responses from her mother at a crucial time in her development, Cahun hungered to provide herself with that which her mother could not: a mirror image. She wrote:

> A sheet of glass. Where shall I put the reflective silver? On this side or the other: in front or behind the pane?
>
> Before. I imprison myself. I blind myself. What does it matter to me, Passer-by, to offer myself a mirror in which you recognize yourself, even if it is a deforming mirror and signed by my own hand? . . .
>
> Behind, I am equally enclosed. I will not know anything of outside. At least I will recognize my own face—and maybe it will suffice enough to please me.[38]

The mirror served not only to reassure Cahun of her very existence; it was a reminder of the pain of individuality, the loss of her reflection in her mother's eyes. Cahun's solution to her denial of the pain of separation and loss was accomplished partly through a symbolic merger with her mother and partly by providing herself with a substitute mirror/mother in her art. No less important was Cahun's relationship with Moore as her double and mirror. It is perhaps no accident that several works include the shadow from Moore's head in the lower right corner, the location where artist's signatures are most often added. Thus, Moore secretly and silently made her presence known and brought her behind-the-scenes involvement onto the stage.

In Cahun's self-portrait photographs, she looks out at her audience, yet her gaze is directed toward the camera, a camera held by her lover; it is a female gaze responded to by another female gaze. We are not watching a woman pose for a camera held by a man, as we shall see later with Wilke, Mendieta, and Sherman; we are observing a woman looking at the closest person in her life, the woman she called her other self, her mirror and double, sister and soul. The camera held by Moore gave Cahun the gaze and the love, the containment for her scattered self, that her mother never could.

Cahun's autobiographical book, *Aveux non Avenus (Disavowed Confessions),* includes ten black-and-white héliogravures of brilliant photomontages created with Moore. Like the dream, the photomontage is composed of multiple visual images; it uses symbols and is not bound by a sequential construction of time. Frankfurt School theorist, Walter Benjamin, argued that the photomontage was a radical political art form because of its engagement with mass media and subversion through recontextualization.[39] As with German Dada artist, Hannah Höch, Cahun's photomontages represent some of her strongest works. In them, she opened up the Pandora's box of her unconscious and essentially gathered bits and pieces of photographic self-portraits, cut them up like paper dolls, and arranged them to form images of birth, wombs, mirrors, disembodied lips and eyes. It is significant that Cahun charged Moore with the task of assembling the many images in her photomontages. It was Moore who served as a container for the many parts of Cahun's personality; it was she who kept her tied to reality. Latimer describes the complementary functions of the pair as follows: "If [Cahun] reaches for the sky, [Moore] endeavors . . . to the ground."[40] The collaborative nature of the art produced by Cahun and Moore additionally prefigured feminist art projects initiated in the 1970s (e.g., Womanhouse).

The Mask

Related to the theme of the mirror and the double is that of the mask. Cahun's masks are often uncanny in their combination of Eastern and Western, doll and human, living and nonliving, child and adult features. At times their purpose is to simply hide her eyes, the bearers of her soul.

The mask enables an ambiguous and equivocal metamorphosis: wearing it one remains oneself while becoming other/more than oneself. Yet, the gap between one's presumed identity and its representation raises a question. Which face is the truer and more authentic—the mask or what it conceals? Wearing masks also underlines the burden of alienation carried in a woman like Cahun who dared to play with conventional codes of femininity.[41] In *Aveux non Avenus,* she exclaimed: "I wish to change skins, to tear mine off."[42] Indeed, in her time, a woman who did not fit into the rigidly circumscribed gender roles had little leeway to define herself. Whereas Cahun's masks offered her some freedom from societal roles, she confessed to having paid a heavy price for them:

> In front of the mirror, on a day full of enthusiasm, you put your mask on too heavily; it bites your skin. After the party, you lift up a corner to see . . . a failed decal. With horror you see that the flesh and its mask have become inseparable. Quickly, with a little saliva, you regulate the bandage on the wound.
>
> I remember, it was Carnival time. I had spent many solitary hours disguising my soul. Its masks were so perfect that when they happened to run into each other on the plaza of my consciousness, they didn't recognize one another. . . . But the facepaints that I'd used seemed indelible. To clean them off, I rubbed so hard that I took off the skin. And my soul, like a face galled to the quick, no longer resembled human form.[43]

For Cahun, artifice became fused and often indistinguishable from the rest of her self. In one mysterious self-portrait, one wonders whether she is even present behind a mask bearing a dazed expression attached to a limp body slumped into a chair. Similarly, the photomontage enigmatically titled *Self Pride* displays a text that winds around a string of seemingly endless images of Cahun and states: "Sous ce masque un autre masque. Je n'en finirai pas de soulever tous ses visages" (Under this mask is another. I will never finish carrying all these faces).

Is Cahun expressing the contemporary view that the self is a mask with no original? Is she illustrating Lacan's opinion that the encounter with one's mirror image is inherently an act of *méconnaisance* (misrecognition)? As in her "unavowed confessions" (*Aveux non Avenus*), Cahun's self-portraits promise revelation yet, quite frequently, flaunt disguise.

Masquerade

Masks therefore become masquerades as Cahun theatrically dressed in men's suits, a swami's costume, or a rag doll's attire. Whereas masks create tension between artifice (surface) and reality (depth), masquerades imply that the role or the performance is all there is.

Cahun performed in a short-lived symbolist-influenced experimental theater, Pierre Albert-Birot's *Le Plateau.* Her transgendered identities were probably inspired by theater models such as Sarah Bernhardt, Ida Rubenstein, and Beatrice Wanger. Nevertheless, nearly all the roles Cahun played involved some form of pretense.

Interestingly, during the years Cahun masqueraded, psychoanalyst Joan Rivière wrote the classic paper, "Womanliness as Masquerade."[44] In it she described the tendency found in some intellectual women to use masquerade to reduce the anxiety of striving to succeed in a masculine world: "Womanliness could be assumed and worn as a mask, both to hide the possession of masculinity and to avert the reprisals expected if she was found to possess it . . . The reader may now ask how I define womanliness or where I draw the line between genuine womanliness and 'masquerade.' My suggestion is not, however, that there is any such difference; whether radical or superficial, they are the same thing."[45] It is significant that both Rivière and Cahun were ahead of their time in their conceptions of femininity as a problematic construction rather than a simple essence.

Indeed, Cahun wished to construct a personal narrative, to stage a *mise en scène,* which involved borrowing from such mythological figures as Judith, Salomé, Sappho, Satan, Janus, and Narcissus.[46] Some of her heroes are masculine, some feminine, some androgynous, some ambiguous, some unreal, and some absurd. Not to be left out of anything, she makes sure to play all roles in her primal scene enactments. Her physical distortions, fragmentations, and rearrangements often result in a sideshow verging on the grotesque. At times, it seems she plays with the notion of woman making a spectacle of herself as she dramatically transforms herself into either a monstrous beauty or a person possessing sublime ugliness. Playing with seduction and repulsion, she tries to be all characters at once, but is sometimes left with none that feels real. Her numerous identities seem to ultimately cancel each other out in the final analysis. On the next to last page of *Aveux non Avenus*, she wrote: "In vain I try to put my body back in its place (my body with its dependencies), to see myself in the third person."[47]

Rebellion and Death

Cahun acknowledged that she wished to do everything in the extreme—to provoke, scandalize—as long as she could have an effect. An example is a 1925 self-portrait in which she ostentatiously displays her Jewishness by defiantly wearing a large, knit Star of David around her neck. Coincidental with Cocteau's alienated *enfants terribles*, Cahun was a rebel in life as well as art. She joined *L'Association des Ecrivains et Artistes Révolutionnaires* in 1933. In 1934, she published a pamphlet, *Les Paris sont Ouverts* (Place your bets), a fierce attack on the propagandist cultural policies of the Communist Party. In 1935, along with Breton and Bataille, she cofounded *Contre-Attaque*, a group organized by the Surrealists in response to the rise of Hitler and the spread of Fascism in France.

During these years, Cahun made many art objects in which she does not figure except by implication. *Poupée* (1936), a body of work for which exists the largest number of variations and photographs, involves a strange doll covered with newspaper clippings. Its torso is the masthead of the organ of the French Communist Party, *L'Humanité;* its arms are formed from headlines about "Hitlerian fascism" and the Spanish Civil War. A set of false teeth are pasted onto its head and held open in a perpetual Munchian scream. It is not known whether Cahun was aware of the work of German artist, Hans Bellmer, who created his first doll (*Die Poupée*) in 1933 in response to the rise of Nazism and its cult of the "perfect body" popular at that time.[48] On the neck of Cahun's *Poupée* are the words "ASSEMBLEMENT MONSTRE (Monstrous Composition)." In 1930, Cahun wrote, "I only believe in the monsters I myself have created."[49]

Cahun and Moore left Paris for the British Isle of Jersey off the northern coast of France in 1937. Jersey was the place she had spent her childhood holidays and where she claimed to have loved herself for the first time. The two women lived there peaceably as "sisters" until 1940 when the Germans invaded, at which time they launched an active subversive resistance effort lasting four years. Although the Islanders were given the opportunity to leave the island during the final weeks of June 1940, Cahun and Moore chose to remain in order to directly resist the Nazis.[50] They then literally flooded the island with anti-Nazi propaganda to demoralize the occupying German army and encourage soldiers to desert.[51] Cahun and Moore created photomontages, wrote pacifist testimonies, and rewrote German marching songs.

In October 1940, Cahun failed to obey the Nazi call for Jews to register their identities. On July 25, 1944, the Nazis arrested Cahun and Moore at their home. The Gestapo had trouble believing that two middle-aged women were solely responsible for such a large-scale resistance movement. The "sisters" were tried and sentenced to six months imprisonment for possessing arms and a camera, six years for listening to the radio, and death for distributing propaganda aimed at undermining morale and inciting the German troops. With characteristic repartee, Cahun asked the judge which sentence they should serve first. She and Moore escaped execution but were imprisoned for nine and a half months, most of which was served in solitary confinement. Early on, the women made two planned suicide attempts and later they refused to appeal the judgment because they were willing to meet their death as Nazi resisters. Indeed, they even continued their resistance activities from within the confines of prison. The Nazis, who considered it pornographic, destroyed much of the women's artwork.[52] In 1945, a self-portrait shows an ever-defiant Cahun with a Nazi eagle insignia clenched between her teeth, the medal given to her by a German prisoner on the day of Liberation.[53]

Some of Cahun's art of the late 1930s and 1940s lacks the concentrated passion of her earlier work. She clearly had aged, was less concerned with issues of identity and more involved with political realities. Though her facial expressions remain intense, the older Cahun appears more resigned and sad in her self-portraits. Although they appear more prosaic than her earlier work, Cahun's face continues to stand out in its expressiveness, now burdened by experience, but still filled with mystery. Cahun's spirit was probably injured after her war ordeals and her passion for life overshadowed by a preoccupation with death. She is said to have been ill, both physically and mentally, and never to have fully recovered after her release from prison.[54]

By 1947, Cahun was plainly preoccupied with death. Many of her photographs were shot in a cemetery; some display a skull and others blot out her face. At times, she seems to mock death, for example in a portrait in which she poses next to a tombstone with a cigarette dangling from her mouth. She feigns a knowing expression and stands on a plot of ground on which the words "PRIVATE PROPERTY" are spelled out in large letters. Most certainly laughing at a private joke, Cahun played with death, with us, and with herself.

A series of eight self-portrait photographs from 1948 (*Le Chemin des Chats*) depicts a white-haired, barefoot, and blindfolded Cahun gripping a leash led by a cat on a narrow pavement in a cemetery. In 1953, the year before she died, she again approached the subject of death. Blindfolded and clutching a large bag, this time she follows the cat who leads her down a precariously dangerous and narrow chute, evidently to her death.

Although she made plans to return to Paris in the early 1950s, due to poor health Cahun remained in Jersey until her death in 1954. Moore moved after her companion's demise. She eventually found life unbearable and, in 1972, committed suicide.

The Art of Multiple Selves

Homosexuality is no longer regarded as a psychological disorder by mental health professionals. Desires of transexuals and transgendered individuals have begun to be acknowledged and queer theory conceived. Sex and gender are generally not considered clear-cut terms defining precise categories. Freud's theory of gender development is being reformulated by scholars like Irene Fast, who has shown that children's early experiences are undifferentiated with regard to gender.[55] In the 1920s and 1930s, Claude Cahun tackled subjects that we are only beginning to appreciate today. She was a pioneer in her highly original explorations of female identity in her art.

Cahun clearly eludes classification. Each theory seems too narrow to contain her multiple metamorphoses and too restrictive to comprehend the breadth and depth of her being. Breton's Surrealism, Butler's performativity, Rivière's masquerade, Lacan's mirror, and Freud's uncanny each enhances our understanding of Cahun and her art, but none do her justice.

It is tempting to understand Cahun's innovations solely in terms of postmodern conceptions regarding the fluidity and performativity of gender and identity. Although I have at times succumbed to this temptation, I have tried not to do so exclusively. While I believe that Cahun's art easily lends itself to interpretations based on theories that have been refined a little more than a decade ago, I think it is risky to apply such retrospective analysis to Cahun without considering the personal, social, and cultural climate in which *she* lived.

Cahun clearly enjoyed the transgressive pleasures entailed in gender-bending and cross-dressing. Nonetheless, she admittedly suffered from her use of mask and masquerade and was aware of the danger and potential violation of self entailed in her "games." She took on abundant identities, but her self remained firm and constant in its longing. I therefore believe it is crucial to not overly romanticize Cahun's strategic and aesthetic use of multiplicity, since at least one reason for her doing so derived from a deep sense of loss and confusion. The audacious assurance witnessed in many of her photographs is therefore best understood when combined with the insecure exclamations in her writing. Toward the end of *Aveux non Avenus,* Cahun reaches the following conclusion: "Make myself another vocabulary, brighten the silver of the mirror, blink an eye, swindle myself by means of a fluke muscle; cheat with my skeleton, correct my mistakes, divide myself in order to conquer, multiply myself in order to assert myself; briefly, to play with ourselves can change nothing."[56] Hers was also a ceaseless battle to manage powerful needs and anxiety through her art.

Cahun courageously brought to the surface previously hidden or feared aspects of the self, thereby empowering woman's ability for a more liberated self-definition, one that allowed for multiplicity and paradox. Her art foreshadowed much of what would later emerge in women's art. Feminist artists like Hannah Wilke, Carolee Schneemann, and Adrian Piper adopted her combination of the personal, sexual, and political. Cahun's use of the mirror, double, mask, and masquerade were also subsequently taken up by Frida Kahlo, Lorna Simpson, and Cindy Sherman in their work. The self-portrait in drag has become increasingly popular with male artists like Andy Warhol, Matthew Barney, Lyle Ashton, and Yasuma Morimora. That Cahun remains one of the only women (with the exception of Kahlo, Piper, and Sherman) whose art depicts her in drag again marks her enlightened and unique contribution to "herstory" in Western art. Her body of work represents one of the most advanced self-investigations of a woman artist up to her time and including our own.

Cahun's oeuvre remains remarkable for its inventiveness. Replete with theatrical gender bending and self-staging, the revolt against social and sexual conventions in Cahun's art possesses a powerful contemporary resonance. This fact, at first glance, makes it difficult to comprehend why so few people are familiar with her work today, especially since it seems to belong to our time as well.

Perhaps this omission is at least partly due to the artist's conscious and unconscious strategies of obfuscation. My suggestion that Cahun contributed to her own glaring absence from art history is not meant to excuse art historians who have taken years to unearth many talented women artists including Cahun. Rather, Cahun's "disappearing act" may be an uncanny replica of the way she experienced that of her mother. Therefore, in order to undo the obliteration of a truly fascinating woman and her significant art, it may be necessary to excavate not only Claude Cahun, the mature artist and master of deception; but also, Lucy Schwob, the young girl who, in search of her lost mother, lost herself and became lost to the world.

3
Charlotte Salomon: The Art of Trauma

Be thou with me. I go with joy to my dying and to my rest.
—Johann Sebastian Bach, *Bist Du Bei Mir*

"C'EST TOUTE MA VIE!" EXCLAIMED CHARLOTTE Salomon to Georges Moridis, a doctor and friend in the Resistance to whom she entrusted her thinly veiled autobiographical picture novel, *Leben? oder Theater?* (Life? or Theater?), before being ushered to her death. Indeed, the work she had frantically produced between 1940 and 1942, while exiled from Germany, *was* her life and her art. In addition to being a poignant coming-of-age story set among increasing Nazi oppression, it was the way she found to stay alive, to choose life over death, and to make an artistic bid for immortality.

Salomon (1917–43) experienced childhood trauma—seven suicides from her maternal line—that assumed a new form in the context of social tragedy—Nazi persecution.[1] Before she was murdered in Auschwitz in 1943, twenty-six years old and five months pregnant, she completed *Leben? oder Theater?*, a brave life-confirming artistic document that prevailed over the morbidity of its inspiration and content. Salomon crafted this amazing work of art because, in her words, "I have a feeling the whole world has to be put back together again" (774).[2] Rather than follow in the suicidal footsteps of the women in her family, she chose instead to transform her private trauma into a work of art, a work that has become a noble testimony to the power of spiritual preservation.

If we appreciate the full value of her statement to Dr. Moridis, then the bookends of this masterpiece are highly significant. Salomon chose to open her musical theater with the suicide of her aunt Charlotte, after whom she was named. Charlotte Grunwald (renamed Charlotte Knarre in the play) drowned herself at the age of eighteen in Lake Schlachter outside of Berlin in 1913. Salomon painted her aunt in an oval cocoon that resembles a womb, thus bridging death and birth, death and art. Despite the fact that her aunt's suicide took place four years prior to Salomon's birth, the artist considered this event an apt one to begin the story of *her* life. Born into a legacy of willful death, her blood tie to self-extinction was one against which she would struggle for the remainder of her life.

The work concludes in France's Cote d'Azur where she was sent to live in (temporary) safety with her maternal grandparents who had been living there since 1934. She and her grandparents were the guests of Ottilie Moore, to whom *Leben? oder Theater?* is dedicated. Moore was a wealthy American woman of German descent who housed many refugees in her villa, *L'Ermitage* (the Hermitage), in Villefranche during the war. While there, Salomon's grandmother, no longer able to bear life, made a suicide gesture by trying to hang herself. As if to speak both to her grandmother and herself, Salomon desperately drew attention to the sun, flowers, and mountains. She also sang Schiller's *Ode to Joy* from Beethoven's Ninth Symphony (702–4) as she attempted to rescue her grandmother through music. Finally, she implored her grandmother to make a choice: to write or to die. The grandmother jumped to her death from an opened window. Not long afterward, it became inevitable that Salomon confront the same choice: to take her life or undertake something "wildly eccentric." *She* chose the latter, the path of creativity. "I will create a story so as not to lose my mind," she proclaimed in her last communication to her parents before the Nazi invasion of Holland,

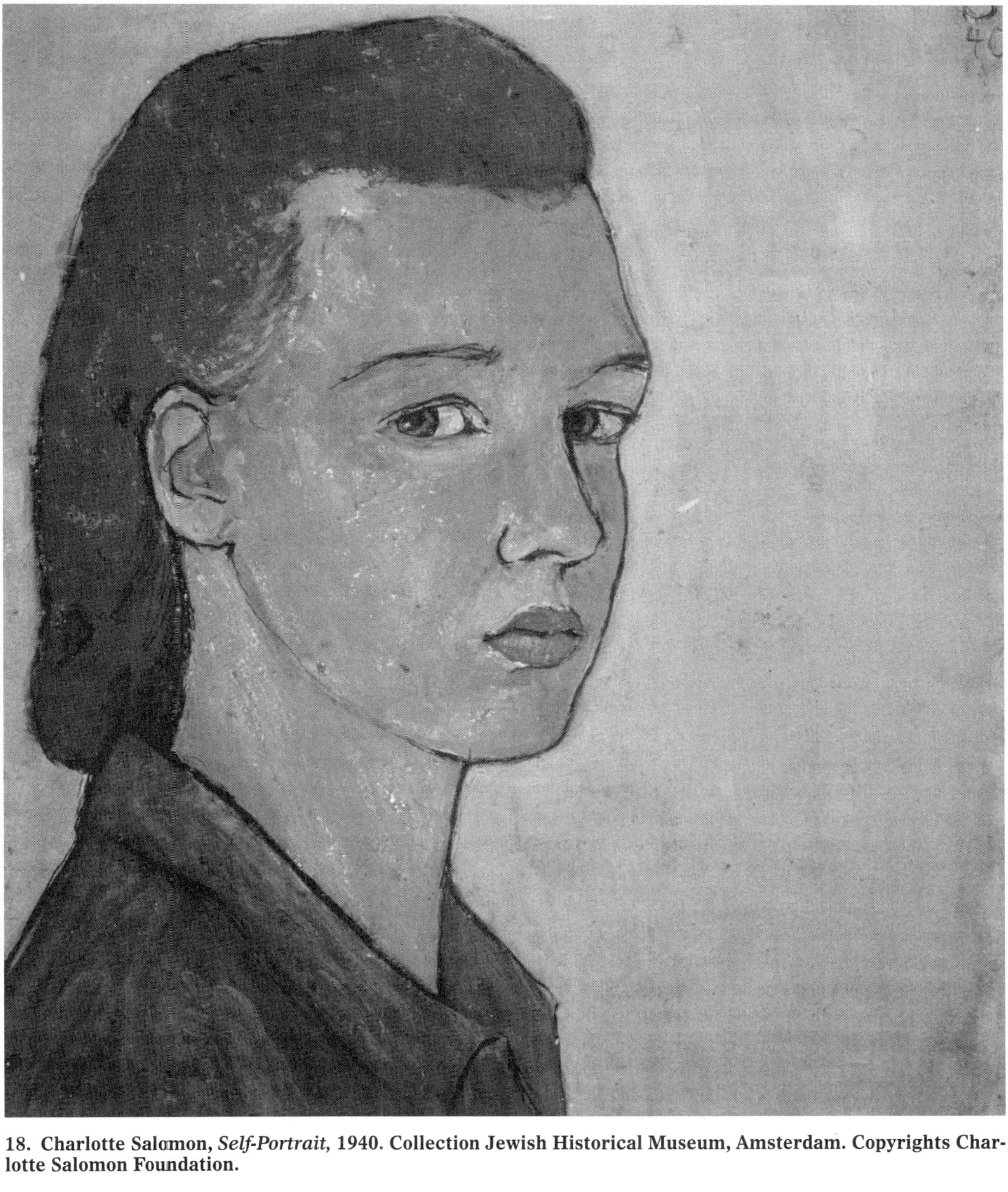

18. Charlotte Salomon, *Self-Portrait,* 1940. Collection Jewish Historical Museum, Amsterdam. Copyrights Charlotte Salomon Foundation.

where they had relocated.[3] Between her bookends of death, Salomon created a space for mourning—mourning the many losses she had had, mourning the future she would never have. Ultimately, Salomon's *Gesamtkunstwerk* can be considered a type of memorial, an artistic Kaddish, the Jewish prayer for the dead.

Leben

Since Charlotte Salomon's life was profoundly intertwined with her art, which weaves memory and fantasy, I will outline the facts of her brief life to allow the reader to keep them in mind while encountering her work. Born in Berlin on April 16, 1917, Salomon was the only child of Albert Salomon, a surgeon, and Fränze Grunwald, a nurse. Their family was cultured, middle class, and assimilated Jewish; they even celebrated Christmas. Her mother committed suicide when Salomon was eight years old; however, little Charlotte was told that she died of influenza. She was named after her mother's sister, Charlotte Grunwald, who had committed suicide thirteen years prior to her mother's suicide. The Grunwald sisters' grandmother, Salomon's great-grandmother, apparently tried to kill herself repeatedly for eight years. Up until the time of Fränze's death, her mother's family suffered seven suicides, all of which were kept hidden from Salomon. Her father's family was also filled with tragic deaths. Albert Salomon's mother passed away at his birth and his father died not long after.

In 1930, Albert Salomon married opera singer Paula Lindberg. The Nazis came to power in 1933 and, consequently, Albert's professorship was renounced and he was only permitted to practice medicine in a Jewish Hospital. Likewise, Paula was forbidden to perform in public, except with the newly formed *Kulturbund*, a cultural art organization created by and for Jews. In 1934, Salomon began studying at the Berlin Academy of Art but in 1938, her enrollment was annulled. Alfred Wolfsohn, a man who had been traumatized by his war experiences in World War I, was sent by *Kulturbund* to be Paula's voice coach in 1937.

Afraid for her safety, Salomon's parents sent her to the south of France where she joined her grandparents in 1938. Her parents then escaped to Amsterdam while Wolfsohn fled to England. Ironically, all but Salomon survived the war. In March 1940, after Salomon's grandmother committed suicide, her grandfather disclosed the family suicide legacy to her and began making sexual advances to her. In June of that same year, Salomon and her grandfather were interned in the French-run camp, Gurs, in the Pyrenees. Soon after their release in July, Salomon began work on *Leben? oder Theater?* In 1941, she left her grandfather in Nice and went to St.-Jean-Cap-Ferrat. She returned to Nice in 1942, probably after completing *Leben? oder Theater?* Her grandfather died in February 1943. Salomon married Alexander Nagler, an Austrian Jewish refugee, and became pregnant, not necessarily in that order. On September 8, the German troops occupied the French coast and Salomon and her husband were deported to Drancy, a transit camp near Paris. On October 10, Charlotte was transported to Auschwitz and is thought to have been murdered on arrival.

Leben? oder Theater?

Using only the three primary colors, Salomon produced 1325 gouaches, each measuring roughly 13 x 10 inches; 784 were numbered into a final version by the author. She divided her *Dreifarben Singespiel* (three-color opera) into three sections: a prelude, a main part, and an epilogue. The prelude describes her childhood in Berlin against the backdrop of Hitler's rise to power. It covers her mother's death, her powerful crush on her stepmother, Paula Lindberg (renamed Paulinka Bimbaum in the play) who entered her life when she was thirteen, and her acceptance to the Berlin Academy of Art. The main part centers around the figure of Alfred Wolfsohn (renamed Amadeus Daberlohn), voice therapist to her stepmother. Charlotte was as enamored of Wolfsohn as she had been of her stepmother. He became her mentor and lover and she recounts his lengthy pontifications on the subjects of love, death, and creativity. The epilogue takes place in France's Côte d'Azur where Salomon was exiled and where the family suicide secret was disclosed to her. Completely on her own for the first time, much of the epilogue is written in French rather than German, a move in which she consciously disassociated from her motherland and her maternal legacy.

The beginning of Salomon's work anticipates the ending and the ending brings us back to the beginning. The author and narrator, *CS*, introduces her readers to the various interwoven modes of representation—painting, music, text—by inviting them to imagine "A person sitting beside the sea. He [*sic*] is painting. A tune suddenly enters his mind. As he starts to hum it, he notices that the tune exactly matches what he is trying to commit to paper. A text forms in his head, and he starts to sing the tune, with his own words, over and over again in a loud voice until the painting seems complete . . ."(5). It is unclear why she chose to use a masculine pronoun to describe herself except that she later claimed to have inhabited each character, male, female, young and old. This choice may also reflect the strong identification she felt with her mentor, Daberlohn, whose words she later adopted as her own and whose perspective she eagerly assumed. The play ends with a self-portrait by the sea, an image that illustrates her opening words and demonstrates the work's circular rather than linear nature, a work that is simultaneously a world, complete in itself, spun from the artist's redemptive vision. Salomon informs us from the start that what we are about to witness will "penetrate" our souls.

Six pages make up a Playbill, probably written after she completed *Leben? oder Theater?* The playbill introduces the two settings—Berlin and France's Côte d'Azur—and the characters in her play; it also instructs us how to view and "hear" the work that follows. The names she gave her characters are both revealing and humorous. She called her alter ego, Charlotte Kann rather than Charlotte Salomon to emphasize her ability (*Kann* means *able*) to overcome her suicide legacy and to create something of value. Charlotte is not spoken of in first person, referred to instead as "she," never "I." This distinguishes the fictional self she created from CS, the initials that identify her as author, narrator, and interpreter of events. Her double identities are further distinguished from Charlotte Salomon, the historical subject. I will use the names Salomon herself employs when discussing her as artist (*CS*), character, (*Charlotte* Kann) or historical personage (Charlotte *Salomon*). Her multiple levels of consciousness additionally reflect Salomon's displacement and the in-between living to which she became accustomed.

Salomon's stepmother, mezzo-soprano Paula Lindberg, is given the playful and melodic name Paulinka Bimbam. Dr. Kurt Singer, a psychiatrist and opera director who created *Kulturbund*, a "cultural island" for Jews who were no longer permitted to participate in German arts, is renamed Dr. Singsong. At one point in the play, a character playfully pokes fun at the characters' names when he exclaims, "Singsong, Bimbam, Klingklang. What kind of dingdong am I?" (216). Alfred Wolfsohn, Charlotte's artistic mentor and first love, is renamed Amadeus (à la Mozart) Daberlohn, and grandiosely referred to as "The Prophet of Song." Her grandparents are named Knarre. Although more than twenty characters speak in soliloquies and dialogues in thousands of scenes from Salomon's external and internal life, two characters clearly assume utmost importance in her life and create a palpable family romance: Paulinka Bimbam and Amadeus Daberlohn. Charlotte's father, Albert Kann, is conspicuously absent in most of the work, a background figure in his daughter's drama, and portrayed as a workaholic who is preoccupied with his career as a physician and professor. In the only scene of its kind, she visits her father's office to say goodbye before departing for France and receives a farewell gift: a portrait of himself (668).

Because of its mixture of styles and its cross between art and theater, literature and music, Salomon's work is impossible to categorize. While it is narrative, it is not linear, and although it is autobiographical, it is partially fiction and fantasy. It is lyrical and has a folklike innocence and the figures are flattened and simplified; the shapes are presented in vivid, Fauve-like primary colors, suggesting a strong life force. Some recall the dream-like floating figures in Marc Chagall's paintings of his Russian Jewish childhood. Both Chagall and Salomon dispense with conventions of space and perspective; the art of both is whimsical, childlike, and vividly colored. Her work also recalls that of Edvard Munch and Vincent Van Gogh, two artists who struggled with family deaths and inner demons, including suicidal urges. Van Gogh, like Salomon,

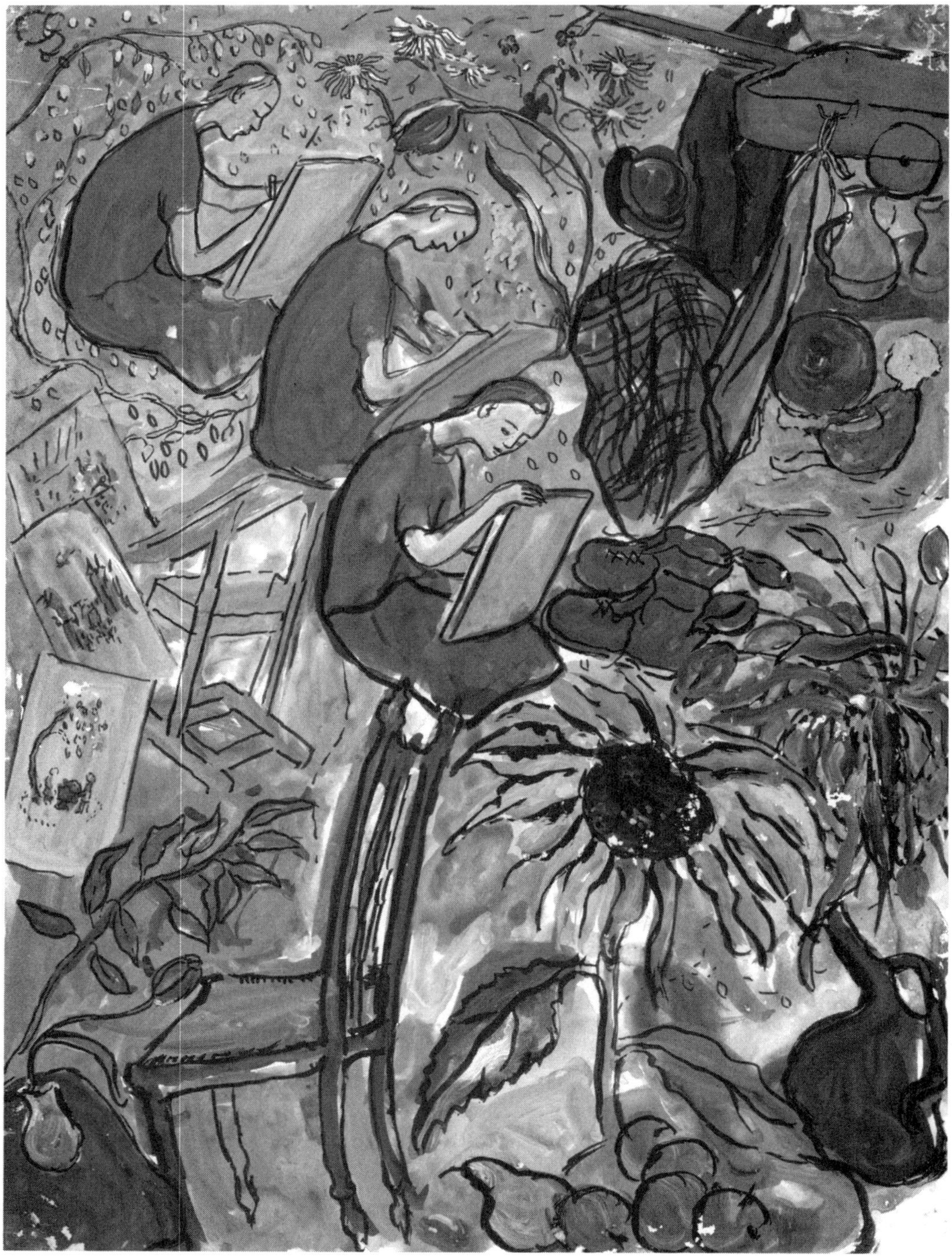

19. Charlotte Salomon, From *Life? or Theater?* 1940–42. Gouache, 13 × 10 inches. Collection Jewish Historical Museum, Amsterdam. Copyrights Charlotte Salomon Foundation.

was aware that time was running out and painted with a sense of urgency toward the end of his life. Salomon made a lovely self-portrait in homage to Van Gogh by surrounding herself with obvious symbols from his oeuvre: a sunflower, a wooden chair, a pair of boots (193) all of them swirling about her figure. Some of the facial and bodily distortions in her work look like portraits and figures of Russian-French Expressionist painter, Chaim Soutine, the tortured Jewish artist who died prematurely in 1943. Another artist who resembles Salomon's naïve, lyrical, vividly colored and nonconformist style is German-Jewish-American, Florine Stettheimer (1871–1925). Stettheimer's paintings, like Salomon's, represent a synthesis of drama, movement, setting, and implied music. Both artists were inspired by personal experiences and painted mostly portraits of friends and family; both provided witty social commentary. Finally, Nanette Salomon compares Salomon's art to Ludwig Bemelmans's popular *Madeline* books whose main character is an orphan girl. Salomon and Bemelmans, she notes, each produced work reflecting "steeped perspective, expressive color, and distorted proportions."[4] Despite these influences and similarities, Salomon's oeuvre stands out as unique and *Leben? oder Theater?* is truly one of a kind.

In Salomon's work, images alternately present close-ups, long shots, flashbacks and montages, winding from one person to another, from one angle to another, in a serpentine composition. Sometimes, the artist employed multiple angles to suggest the passage of time, placing the most recent events in the foreground and earlier incidents in receding planes. At other times, she applied an aerial perspective; in one painting she dispensed with ceilings in order to peer into the rooms of a house (19). In others, she set the images floating about the page with no discernible order. And, finally, she sometimes broke up scenes in a comic-book style. It is often difficult to know where one scene ends and the next begins. At times, her use of multiple selves in one frame is dizzying. Many pages depict one or two characters, yet it is not uncommon for a page to be inhabited by dozens of characters, or for the same scene to be portrayed a dozen times or more. Salomon thus attempted to achieve the effect of temporal unfolding common in cinema, partly because Wolfsohn believed cinema provided the most effective modern means to gain insight into oneself. Yet, hers was also a whirlwind of text, color, and image that must have mirrored the confused and terrified state of mind in which she found herself. It also conveys the artist's desperation to communicate, to bring forth her vision before it was too late. It is as if she rushed to finish her work, pouring it on the page in a tornadic mixture of image, text, and music as she fled death. Finally, Salomon's oeuvre possesses a Joycean quality, the repetition of scenes suggesting the movement of consciousness and the way events were burned into her awareness and her memory. Thus her work does not merely suggest the temporal unfoldment found in cinema but also the mythic enfoldment contained in human life and *experiential* time—made so by numinous events deeply significant to the person experiencing them. It shows how she needed to recollect and feel certain intense moments, especially the beautiful ones, as a way of building a potent inner life that could do combat with her family, its history, and the impending sense of doom that must have been the ambience of her time, an era of evil that reached mythic proportions. Pictures were not enough. There had to be description. There had to be music. She needed to turn her art into a theater of what was most inwardly real. She was trying to capture her life, trying to make her life mean something, and so she came at us with everything she had.

The clustering of images reflects the combination of memory and fantasy from which she drew the content of her stories. Some occurrences are pure fictional representations. (With myth this doesn't matter.) For instance, her mother's death took place when she was a child of eight, and it was not an event Salomon actually witnessed or even knew about. She was told her mother had died of influenza. In fact, she was enlightened of the family suicide trail only after her grandmother tried to hang herself in Nice. Her grandfather, apparently upset by his wife's attempted suicide and the encroaching war, callously confronted Salomon with the family birthright (four women and two men had committed suicide) and even prodded her to take her own life.

Salomon's grandmother killed herself the second time she attempted suicide. It is not difficult to understand why this event served as a pivotal catalyst for Salomon's creative endeavor. She wrote, in an unsent letter, "My life commenced when my grandmother wanted to take her life, when I found out that my mother had taken hers, as had her entire family—when I found out that I was the only survivor and when deep within me I felt the same inclination, the urge towards despair and towards dying."[5] After Salomon witnessed the attempted suicide of her grandmother, she was then told for the first time about the suicide of her mother. Both deaths resulted from the women jumping out of an open window. She depicted the two suicides similarly,

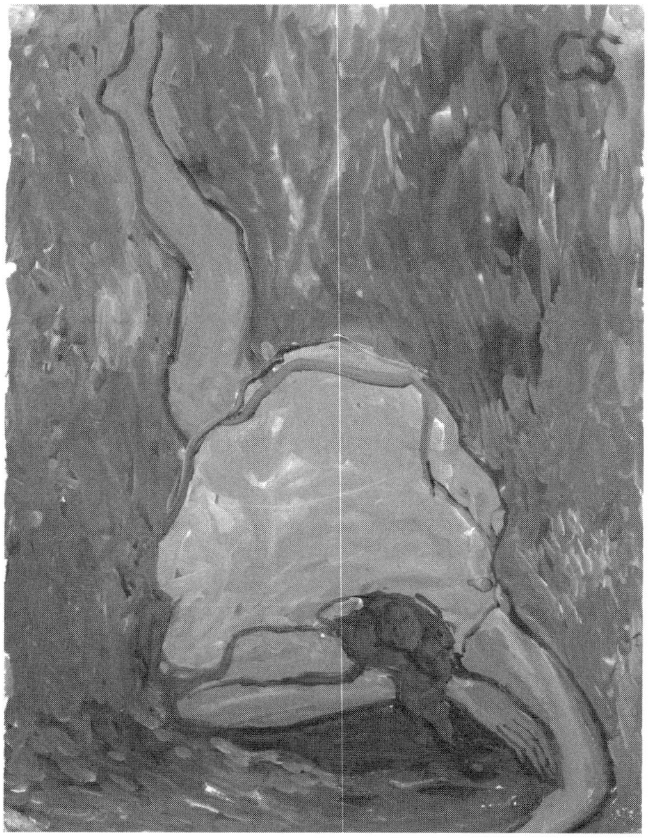

20. Charlotte Salomon, From *Life? or Theater?* 1940–42. Gouache, 13 × 10 inches. Collection Jewish Historical Museum, Amsterdam. Copyrights Charlotte Salomon Foundation.

one witnessed and one imagined, condensing the important women in her life and thus uniting adult pain with childhood longing. The bodies of both women lie on the ground in a pool of blood, a single, naked, raised leg the only sign remaining in defiance of the downward thrust (32, 748).

Text and Image: Love and Healing

Although Salomon's work is primarily visual, it is accompanied by text and is called a *Singespiel* (Operetta); scenes are escorted by suggestions for musical accompaniment culled from opera as well as popular sources. Both Paulinka and Daberlohn possessed strong ties to music, and CS observes that from the time Paulinka is introduced into Charlotte's life, her "feelings are expressed in songs" (58). Daberlohn, too, believed that "singing is more closely bound up with life than anything else" (251). Thus, music connected her to the important people in her life at a time when she was forced to be apart from them. In fact, Salomon hummed as she drew, thereby fashioning a type of "holding environment," a safe space, in which to create.[6]

In the first part of the work, Salomon added text onto tracing paper, which was superimposed onto the painted pages. It is possible that these overlays provided the author with the necessary distance from the tragic events she portrayed. CS is the narrator and director, more removed than involved, more observer than participant. Even her alter ego, Charlotte, is most often depicted from behind or in profile, and her identity as artist is displayed throughout with many pictures showing her hunched over a drawing pad. She is subject and object, image and voice, director and actor in her theatrical piece.

Salomon's overlays can also be understood as representing what Freud called "secondary revision," the ego's organizing, interpreting, and narrating function for the dream's somewhat puzzling visual imagery.[7] As with the dream, Salomon's seemingly disconnected fragments are allotted meaning and coherence in the textual narration and commentary provided in the overlays. It cannot be coincidental that she dispensed with the tracing paper and began to include text directly on the painted pages at the point at which she met the play's pivotal character, Amadeus Daberlohn. She had Daberlohn comically enter her tale to the tune of the toreador's song from *Carmen*. I believe that Salomon dispensed with the tracing paper when Daberlohn entered Charlotte's life because he came to represent the breaking down of barriers and the removal of defenses. Furthermore, since he was most probably her first sexual partner, the overlay could be likened to the female hymen, a virginal interposition between picture and text, penetrated by his presence. It is he who awakened her sexuality, and he who helped her break through her limitations, to become more innovative in her artistic project and in her life. Thus, Daberlohn represents the connection between image and speech, a connection that ultimately became Charlotte's song.

Daberlohn was a voice coach, called in to help Salomon's stepmother, singer Paulinka Bimbam. Charlotte idolized Paulinka and re-

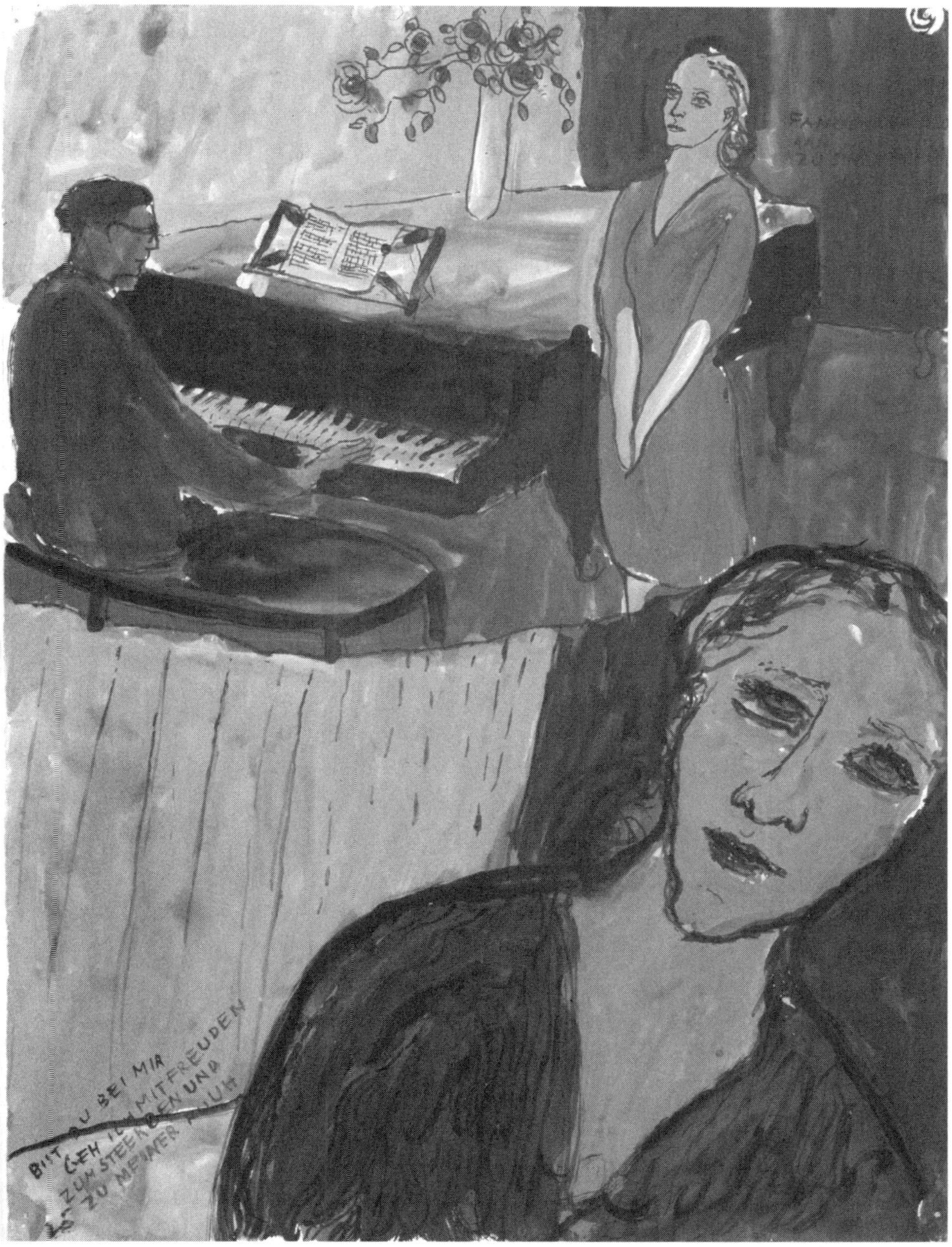

21. Charlotte Salomon, From *Life? or Theater?* 1940–42. Gouache, 13 × 10 inches. Collection Jewish Historical Museum, Amsterdam. Copyrights Charlotte Salomon Foundation.

ceived much love, warmth, and attention from this extremely positive figure, who replaced her own mother and who, coincidentally, had been an orphan herself.[8] Adolescent idealization swung back and forth between her stepmother and her Svengali-like mentor, Daberlohn, both recipients of serious crushes, creating palpable and shifting oedipal tension. One painting (fig. 20) pictorially illustrates Charlotte's own primal scene tableau: she is in the lower right corner facing the viewer while, in the background, Daberlohn and Paulinka crowd the piano and literally make beautiful music together (236).[9] Charlotte is inspired by her exclusion; she wants in and she dreads it at the same time.

Charlotte met with Daberlohn, often in secret, and absorbed many of his ideas, which are evident in the play. Daberlohn's theories, clearly influenced by psychoanalysis, are allotted a great deal of space. His axiom: "You must first go into yourself—into your childhood—to be able to get out of yourself" is quoted numerous times, echoing early psychoanalytic views which stress the importance of childhood in depth psychology. Page after page of text winds around Daberlohn's floating, disembodied head; at one point, his figure appears 191 times above each phrase of a rather lengthy pontification. Daberlohn believed that geniuses are made, not born, and that one becomes an artist only by getting in touch with one's inner self. He also preached that creativity is born of trauma and suffering. "The emotional life of the singer," he said, "must suffer a great upheaval to enable that singer to achieve exceptional results" (379). When reading these words, it is impossible not to think of the exceptional results achieved by Salomon in her artistic *tour de force.*

Secrets and Suicide

The secrecy surrounding the suicide of Charlotte's mother—and its abrupt disclosure at the moment of her grandmother's suicide—lie at the core of her art. The impetus to create her life's work begins at the moment she realized that her life, up until that point, had been constructed on a lie. *Leben? oder Theater?* is her attempt to reimagine her life in order to make it bearable. Angry at his wife's suicide, Charlotte's grandfather discloses the family suicide trail to her. The violent nature of this communication, coupled with his statement that she too should take her life, is only exacerbated by the sexual advances he makes toward her. He utterly traumatizes her, and she then realizes that she has been mired in a confusing morass of deception meant to protect the very familial relationships that have become toxic. Hidden alliances and splits regulate the closeness and distance in family relationships she can no longer trust. Out of this terrible pain she began her creation.

Salomon's strong need to imagine how the event of her mother's suicide took place made her depict the episode from both inner and outer perspectives. In one frame, we look directly into the mother's face, which is attached to profiles of her husband and daughter. Immediately afterward, we see her gazing dreamily out of the window. As the coloring becomes darker and more ominous, we observe her from behind. Finally, all that remains is a stark empty window frame. The next frame is a close-up of her dead face. Before the death, we witness a child who was very attached to her mother and who empathically watched as her mother became increasingly depressed and disinterested in life. Intimate conversations take place in a shared bed during which mother tells daughter how beautiful it is in heaven and that she would like to go there and become an angel (see Plate 1). She promises to write from heaven and, after her death, Charlotte repeatedly checks the mail for the letter that never arrives. As in her life, Salomon's endless repetitions in her art reflect her attempts to master a world that was quickly spinning out of her control.

The play has father and stepmother blaming the family suicides on Grandmother Knarre. More specifically, Paulinka blames Charlotte's maternal grandmother for having "stifled every natural impulse in her children by bringing them up to be stiff and formal . . . in such a way that . . . their only escape was through death" (94). In truth, suicide was rampant in Germany during these years. Germany ranked fourth in the Western world and Berlin came first in claiming hundreds of annual deaths by suicide, Salomon's mother only one among 5053 suicides in Berlin between the years 1925 and 1927. The suicide rates of women—especially Jewish women—surged during this period. Felstiner claims that, in light of these alarming figures, Fränze Salomon's suicide "was not anomalous, it was exemplary."[10] While this may be so, I find it difficult to convincingly argue that seven suicides, including those of men, in one family is reflective of an "exemplary" statistic. Buerkle argues that the Jewish female suicide rate in Germany was meant to efface these women's growing despair and that Salomon's work, aimed at bringing to light the truth surrounding these deaths, as well as her struggle with her own suicidal tendencies, served to refute such effacement, primarily through her use of repeated close-ups of female faces.[11]

Despite its widespread nature, the suicides in Salomon's family were evidently regarded as shameful and therefore kept secret. After being told her mother died from influenza, Salomon was not allowed to attend the funeral, so years later, when her grandfather revealed the family trail of suicides, Charlotte, stupefied, responded: "I knew nothing of all that" (713). Yet, the secrecy surrounding the suicide of her mother and other family members surely shaped Salomon's shy and withdrawn nature. Shameful secrets encourage isolation and thwart relationships because secrets limit opportunities to connect both within and outside the family.[12] The silence surrounding the secret and the verbal and nonverbal prohibition against asking questions shuts down dialogue, sending the message: "Don't ask. Don't tell. Keep it to yourself and keep to yourself." Salomon's biographer described her as a non-person, "not of this world," one who rarely spoke but became a keen observer and listener.[13] Salomon's aloof, even schizoid, character created distance between her and her experienced reality, a distance she later exploited when she created herself as a separate character. Salomon was forced to grow up fast. In one painting, Charlotte is shown seated on the rim of a bathtub following her mother's death. She stares at the toilet and muses, "So that's what they call life" (41), implying that life can be flushed away in an instant.[14]

Although Salomon had Albert and Paulinka describe Grandmother Knarre as the "murderess of her children," it is notable that Grandfather Knarre emerges blameless. Yet, she has us envision Charlotte alone with him after her grandmother's suicide; in his nightdress, he makes sexual advances to her: "I don't understand you," he says. "What's wrong with sharing a bed with me—when there's nothing else available? I'm in favor of what's natural" (764). Disgusted, she tries to keep her distance from him, but who knows if she succeeded. Stuck with him on a train completely crammed with people on their return from the Gurs camp, she confesses, "I'd rather have ten more nights like this than a single one alone with him" (763). Unable to avoid her grandfather, she seems to lose her sanity the more time they spent together. "Dear God, please don't let me go mad" (755), she exclaims in one painting which depicts her with her hands on her head in a blood-orange room that twirls around her body. In 1941–1942, Salomon eventually left her grandfather to board in *La Belle Aurore*, a hotel in St. Jean Cap Ferrat, where, "despite her utter weakness [she] . . . remained alone with her experiences and her paintbrushes" (776–77). It was there that she completed her masterpiece.

The sexual advances, sought by her grandfather after his wife's suicide, suggest another reason for the suicidal deaths of his children. It is quite possible that the grandfather abused his children, including Charlotte's mother, increasing their odds of suicide. Sexual assault is associated with an increased lifetime rate of attempted suicide, and the odds grow fourfold if the abuse occurs prior to age sixteen.[15] Charlotte perceived her grandfather as loathsome and evil and even went so far as to group him together with the Nazis: "For me, my grandfather was a symbol of the people I had to fight."[16]

Psychoanalysis and Orpheus

Wolfsohn exerted a profound influence on Salomon, taking on many roles for her, but it is his role as her therapist that proved instrumental in saving her life. Wolfsohn was no stranger to trauma. He suffered shell shock in World War I as a result of having been buried alive for several days beneath a pile of dead soldiers. After he heard dying soldiers cry out to him to rescue them and he did not respond because it would have cost him his life, he lost his own voice. The sound of the dying soldiers' voices had an unreal quality; they haunted him and led him to conduct voice experiments and, eventually, to develop a theory proposing that the voice and the soul are linked. His theory of song also incorporated the sounds of infants crying and those heard in religious prayers to God. Wolfsohn eventually became a voice therapist and dedicated himself to healing himself and others.

Wolfsohn noticed Salomon's strong defenses and her withdrawn nature. He stated: "Certain reasons induced me to undertake an attack on those fortifications"[17] Indeed, he was a man with an inflated self-perception, believing he had special prophetic powers and, like Christ, had risen from the dead. He enjoyed the attention of women, including Paulinka, whom he worshipped as a Madonna and whose voice he trained, his fiancée, Salomon, and many others.[18] He encouraged Salomon's amorous idolization of him and, at twenty-one years her senior, he served as an authority figure who took the place of her work-absorbed father. She was so impressed with his ideas that she painted 1387 portraits of his speaking face.[19]

Wolfsohn's familiarity with psychoanalytic theory and technique is evident from Daberlohn, his alter ego in Salomon's play. It seems he had a special affinity for Jungian analysis, known for its archetypal and mythological foundations, and for its androgynous theories of humankind. Daberlohn's favorite myth was that of Orpheus, the greatest musician and poet in Greek mythology; he even wrote a manuscript called *Orpheus or the Way of the Mask*. In the original myth, after his wife, Eurydice, died from a serpent bite, Orpheus became inconsolable and his songs were so mournfully beautiful that they caused the gods and nymphs to weep. Orpheus descended to the lower world and softened the hearts of Hades and Persephone with his music. The gods agreed to allow Eurydice to return to the world of the living with the condition that he should walk in front of her and not look back until he had reached the upper world. Orpheus broke his promise and Eurydice vanished from his sight, this time for good.

Because Daberlohn believed he had risen from death and that only music and love could heal his soul, his use of the Orpheus myth to depict his own story came naturally. The myth additionally paralleled the psychoanalytic process. Daberlohn repeatedly emphasized the necessity of descent back to childhood and to the darkest of human experiences. It is only when one can make this descent with love, he believed, that one can "create . . . [the] world anew out of the depths" (371). Many portrayals of Charlotte with Daberlohn are achieved in dark colors, signifying their secret meetings as well as the subterranean world of the unconscious. Years later, Salomon's stepmother would insist that her stepdaughter's love scenes with Daberlohn were fantasy.[20] Yet, she probably needed to believe that because she took her place in one corner of two very prominent oedipal triangles depicted in the work: Charlotte loves Paulinka and is jealous of anyone who approaches her stepmother, including her own father and Daberlohn; Charlotte loves Daberlohn who loves Paulinka. Positive and negative oedipal complexes have Charlotte wishing to possess both mother (Paulinka) and father (Daberlohn) in multiple scenes.[21]

Daberlohn urged Charlotte to work through her traumas and he believed in her talent. The main section of Salomon's play reads as a tribute to Daberlohn and documents her "analysis" with him. It is her memory of him and his teachings that inspires her while she is in exile and "preserve[s] her from suicide" (779).

Salomon's unusual artistic techniques resemble those employed in psychoanalytic treatment. The reconstruction and working through of trauma, and the repetitious and associative/nonlinear way of approaching one's life, are well-known aspects of the psychoanalytic method. When Charlotte's grandmother attempts suicide, Charlotte remembers Daberlohn and "starts her therapy" (607). This time, it is she who assumes the role of therapist, devoting herself completely to her grandmother's rescue. The young woman proposes creative therapy as an alternative to suicide: "Instead of taking your life in such a horrible way . . . why don't you make use of the same powers to describe your life?" (722–23). Similar to Kollwitz's grieving mothers, Grandma Knarre's body is bent over in the shape of a ball and painted in dark colors when she recalls her childrens' deaths (33, 103, 637, 643). Charlotte shows her grandmother a picture of several people, points to the figure of Daberlohn, and announces with confidence, "That man is going to save you" (721).

Charlotte becomes Daberlohn's protégé, his stand-in, and her face is multiplied as was his. She repeats the words he once said to her—"May you never forget that I believe in you" (717)—and assumes Daberlohn's role as therapist with her grandmother. She simultaneously identifies with her grandmother in her matching struggle against suicidal impulses. Attempting to shift the power relations by handing power to the weak and helpless, to those most in need of safety and support, Salomon's art became a warning system as well as a form of resistance against destructive forces.[22] Forty-two rescue scenes depict the two women, many of them showing Charlotte's body on top of her grandmother's, as if to hold her down to prevent her from committing the fateful act. The indistinct boundaries between the two women demonstrate that Salomon's efforts were aimed at keeping herself alive as well as her grandmother. She failed to save her grandmother, which left her facing her own life-or-death conflict. Salomon's fate differed from that of her grandmother, however, because she freely and passionately engaged in creative self-analysis.

Salomon's attempt to discover and communicate truth—truth about humankind and truth about her inner world—parallels the task facing psychoanalysis in its journey into the depths of the human spirit. Daberlohn's words echo throughout the play: "In order to go out of oneself one must first have gone into oneself" (374, 535, 569, 570). Using art to tame terror is a skill Salomon perfected, yet her creativity and humor are far more than defensive maneuvers because they invite us to appreciate the horror and absurdity in life all the while embracing the most important of human possibilities: the willingness to love in the face of uncertainty, loss, trauma, and death, the courage to say "yes" to life despite its innumerable miseries, and the determination to fight for meaning in the midst of chaos.

Art, like psychoanalysis, offers traumatized persons the ultimate creative experience: the possibility of creating a survivor who is strengthened rather than destroyed by trauma. As Salomon's audience, we become her witnesses to the reality that threatens to overwhelm her. Her art compels us to acknowledge, if only through unconscious identification, that we are all survivors of devastation from personal and cultural traumas and we all live with the imprint of death and the guilt which surrounds it.

The Art of Trauma

Despite the parallels between Salomon's creation and psychoanalysis, it is important to keep in mind that *Leben? oder Theater?* differs from psychoanalysis in that it is a work of art. The traumatic reaction to atrocious events involves the dissolution of connection to social structures and people as well as a disintegration of the illusions that are needed to make life tolerable. The art object attempts to restore these broken connections and to impose form onto the destruction if only by representing it within a new structure: the structure of art. By inviting dialogue with its spectators, the art object also acts to restore threatened social connections.[23]

Salomon's art was created at the intersection of personal, aesthetic, social, and political experience. It is art created in the service of survival; an aesthetic response to human emergency.[24] Multiple forces combined in her life and mind to propel her into the creative act as a way of saving her life.

After her beloved grandmother's suicide and fleeing her grandfather's sexual advances, Salomon experienced terrifying danger up close when she was sent to the Gurs camp in June 1940 where the threat of war, and even death, became a real possibility. She incorrectly wrote that war was declared in May 1940, when the Germans invaded France and her personal experience of war began, eight months after the war's official beginning. Her emotional reaction to all of these factors closed in on her and the window, by now a clear symbol for suicide, began to call to her. "I'm afraid it's starting with me too" (754), she cried at the same time as her paintings became sloppy and visibly unmanageable.

Salomon *knew* the essence of trauma. She strove to make sense of the trail of family suicides under conditions in which she found herself increasingly isolated and endangered as a Jew. Unsurprisingly, then, her work came to reflect the familiar discontinuity, disruption, and fragmentation associated with traumatic experiencing. A work of urgency, it suggests impending doom with images both intimate and claustrophobic.

Salomon's musical drama became her fight against her family and the Nazis who pursued them. It brings to mind the diary of Anne Frank, another young girl who chronicled her life in defiant refutation of death's menace. Yet, Salomon's visual diary is much more than an account of her daily adolescent life as she lived it; hers is a young woman's willful act of creation. Salomon's portrayal of young Charlotte in a train that transports her and her grandfather from the transit camp, Gurs, stands out from that of the other passengers; they weep while she sketches. She is an artist above all. Like Frank's, Salomon's work is impossible to view without placing it within the context of the war. Although we view *Leben?*

oder Theater? with our postwar insights and knowledge, it is important to recall the time she produced it (1940–42) and that much of the trauma she was dealing with was family related. In the end, *Leben? oder Theater?* is a story within a story; family losses are described against the backdrop of the millions of losses from the Holocaust. We view and read Salomon's play as she presents it, and we are constantly aware of her inevitable and abrupt finale.

Robert J. Lifton has controversially argued that we need human catastrophes like Hiroshima and Auschwitz in order "to deepen and free . . . imagination for the leaps it must make."[25] (I would argue that those horrors are not needed to deepen our imagination. Rather, they tell us of the evil of which we are capable.) Indeed, Salomon is not the first artist to respond directly to the personal and political tension and violence with which she was forced to live. Like Kollwitz, she did so by engaging, and having us engage, in an ongoing dialogue with death. Salomon bombards us with aesthetic repetitions, making us feel her incredible psychological burden as well as the ethical responsibility of containing it.

In addition to her heightened sense of inner and outer reality, Salomon had a strong need to repair the bleak and damaged world she saw before her.[26] After she cries "I have the feeling the world has to be put back together again" (774), she enlists a creative solution to restore and recreate a lost world. According to Melanie Klein's theory, creativity is born of the depressive position, during which one harbors a wish to repair the destroyed harmony with the mother. "True reparation," writes Segal, "must include an acknowledgement of aggression and its effect" because it poignantly articulates the reality of separateness and loss.[27]

Klein's theory reminds me of the response found in the Jewish mystical tradition of the Kabbalah to people who question why there is evil in the world or how a benevolent God can allow evil to exist. The Kabbalah teaches that because God made humans his partner, Creation remains unfinished. It is only through *Tikkun Olam*—acts of healing and repair—that Creation is completed and the world restored. Truly, human evil remains inexplicable, ghastly, and overwhelming. The individual must battle it within herself and from there the battle moves outward. Artists possess the singular ability to restore life from the most broken and damaged pieces. Salomon added color and humor to the tune of suicide and mass annihilation in her heroic tale.

Death and the Maiden

Salomon's epic, although heavily influenced by the political conditions under which she lived, allots surprisingly little space to the actual depiction of these events. She does, however, present us with the flavor of European prewar anti-Semitism. Interestingly, in nearly all cases, she does so with humor, perhaps to render these noxious experiences more aesthetic and palatable both for her readers and herself. For instance, during a visit to Italy with her grandparents, Pope Pius XI inquires, with arms open to those before him, "Tiens, tiens, tiens. What are those little Jews doing here?" (176). Later, an oddly amusing exchange takes place during her interview with a Mr. Schmidt at the Berlin Academy of Art:

Mr. Schmidt:	"I am Mr. Schmidt from the Academy, I do anything I am asked to do: Heil Hitler!"
Charlotte:	"Do you also accept Jews?"
Mr. Schmidt:	"Surely you aren't Jewish?"
Charlotte:	"Of course I am."
Mr. Schmidt:	"Oh well, we're not that particular." (184)

In fact, the Academy *was* that particular. Charlotte was accepted as the only full-blooded Jew because they apparently thought her nondescript qualities would deter her from seducing any Aryan males, leaving them safe from Jewish contamination. She participated in an art competition while a student there and, though her work was chosen for a prize, it was later denied her once the judges found out she was Jewish.

Another humorously depicted scene shows Dr. Singsong's visit with the Nazi Minister of Propaganda. He is greeted with, "I am the Ministah for Propagandah! I'm busy night and day, No time for rest or play—Come in, come in! Yes, this is a good project, he seems to be just the man. A pity he's a Jew—must see if I can't make him an Aryan." After Singsong's request to create a Jewish Kulturband is approved, the Minister politely shakes his hand

and invites him to call to which Singsong replies, " 'The honor would be mine.' (Under his breath—'You filthy swine.')" (162–64).

Finally, Salomon depicts with brutal clarity a scene of marching Nazis who meld into one mass, nondescript in personal features but conspicuous in the uniforms that create a large brown tapestry broken only by the red and black flags bearing the swastika. Salomon purposely painted the Nazi symbol in reverse at all times both to mock it and to diminish its power. The text accompanying this potent image is written tongue-in-cheek as it adopts the Nazis' prejudicial allegations against the Jews:

> The swastika—a symbol of bright hope—
> The day for freedom and for bread now dawns—
> Just at this time, many Jews—who with all their often undesirable
> Efficiency, are perhaps a pushy and insistent race, happened to be
> Occupying government and other senior positions. After the Nazi
> Takeover of power they were all dismissed without notice.
> Here you see how this affected a number of different souls that
> Were both human and Jewish! (152)

Salomon's reminder that Jews are humans who possess souls defied the Nazi attempt to dehumanize them.

Salomon illustrated, too, how her stepmother's celebrated singing career was brought to an abrupt end with the depiction of her final concert during which a crowd shouts her off the stage. Likewise, her father's university professorship was retracted. A scene shows him performing surgery with a large red X over it; now he is only allowed to work in a Jewish Hospital. Both parents were ousted from their professional milieus with the harsh commands, "*Aus—Raus* (Get out—out—get out)" (154, 156). Salomon also chronicled the Nazi attacks on the Jews that accelerated in 1938 and culminated in Kristallnacht, November 9, 1938. Her father was arrested and sent to Sachsenhausen, a labor camp. Nine thousand Jews passed through the camp ruled by Rudolf Höss. In one painting, a guard stands over the bowed shadow figure of her imprisoned father. The guard's words—"You have to work here, there'll be no loafing. You've done enough loafing in your lives" (644–45)—literally and figuratively weigh down on the father's hunched body. It is interesting that this is the first time Salomon employed a muddy palette. Paulinka, using her considerable charms, obtained false papers, granting Albert's release from the camp; he was nonetheless forced to walk fifteen miles home in his weakened state. The man who walked with him perished. Albert survived but was bedridden for four weeks (F83).

No image of Gurs, the French Transit camp in the Pyrenees where she and her grandfather were inmates during the summer of 1940, exists in her work, but it is known that art supplies were delivered to the camp by the Red Cross and that a large amount of art was produced there, possibly reconnecting Salomon to her art and to Wolfsohn. The transit camp served as a transition between life and death and between art and death.

In the midst of the beautiful south of France, beset by ominous forces, Charlotte's memories of her "fervid early love" revived. She recalled her drawing of *Death and the Maiden* which she had offered to Daberlohn along with *The Meadow with the Yellow Buttercups.* He contrasted the "despair" in the first work with the "hope and courage to face life" in the second (450). He told her that *Death and the Maiden* represented the two of them and (correctly) predicted, "One day people will be looking at us two" (590). While she was exiled in France, struggling with her own suicidal impulses, the memory of Daberlohn's words returned to save her: "And suddenly she knew two things, First, that Daberlohn's eyes seemed to say: 'Death and the Maiden, that's the two of us,' and second, that she still loved him as much as ever. And if he was Death, then everything was all right, then she did not have to kill herself like her ancestors, for according to his method one can be resurrected, in fact, in order to love life still more, one should once have died. So she was in fact the living model for his theories . . ." (780–781).

Toward the end of Salomon's oeuvre, text progressively crowds out image until it completely takes over. This is partly due to the fact that Salomon shifted her focus from actual memories to psychological complexities. For example, in one image of her grandfather after his wife's suicide, he makes sexual advances to Charlotte, and his body is covered with text as if to drown out his words and his power. It is clear that Salomon was feverishly trying to complete her work as she sensed that time was running out. At one point, she painted herself with brown-lettered words, "I can't take this life any more, I can't take these times any more" (636).

Irregularly sized letters and disembodied words become bolder and demand more room, often with barely a space between them. The last words in *Leben? oder Theater?* are: "And with dream-awakened eyes she saw all the beauty around her, saw the sea, felt the sun, and knew: she had to vanish for a while from the human plane in order to create her world anew out of the depths. And from that came Life or Theater?" (782–83). Her final image is one of herself seated at the beach in her bathing suit, paintbrush in hand (see Plate 2). She looks out to sea and contemplates her death, a death she willingly embraces but a death not caused by suicide. In large letters printed across her back are the words "LEBEN ODER THEATER." The question marks are gone revealing that in the end Salomon chose both life *and* theater. Salomon chose life, with its chaos and broken promises, its cruel surprises and assaults on meaning, its precious beauty that still peeks in on its seeming indifference. Salomon also chose to transform all of this, every bit of it, both bitter and sweet, into theater, into show and song and, most of all, into a meaningful and beautiful story forged from her own bleeding depths.

Salomon's boldness was expressed in the way she found to unravel and expose the many secrets with which she was compelled to live. Her courageous journey from secrecy to openness is evident in her behavior as well as her art. She actualized her plea, "Let us come out of the dark" (704), while in Nice after the Germans asked all foreign refugees to register themselves. Despite her Aryan looks, which would have made it easy for her to conceal her Jewish identity, Salomon, unlike Cahun, did what the Germans asked. She refused to lie about who she was; she refused to live with any more family secrets. On June 17, 1943, she married an Austrian Jewish refugee, Alexander Nagler and, when she became pregnant, once more inscribed her name, along with his, in a public registry.[28] Salomon's divulging behavior set her apart from her family, who had long harbored secrets and lived their lives in hiding. Although she paid with her life, she saved her identity.

In September 1943, Charlotte Salomon was taken from Nice, along with her husband, to Drancy, a camp a few miles from Paris where more than seventy thousand Jews passed through on their way to German camps. It is assumed that Salomon was murdered upon arrival in Auschwitz on October 10, 1943. Although her work did not succeed in saving her life, it seems to have given her life a purpose. It allowed her to visit her past, no matter how painful, in the context of a terrifying present and future. It brought to life her youthful passion and creative spirit. It connected her, in her isolated exiled state, to those most dear to her and breathed life back into the dead, in blatant refusal to accept their disappearance from her life. It helped her battle the death forces in her by facing the truth about her family and the world. It helped her to find herself. She wrote: "The war raged on and I sat by the sea and saw deep into the heart of humankind. I was my mother my grandmother indeed I was all the characters in the play. I learned to walk all paths and became myself."[29]

4
Frida Kahlo: Mirror and Mask

La Bailarinita! SHOUTED SOMEONE AFTER THE fateful bus accident that altered Frida Kahlo's life forever. Little ballerina. What an ironically lovely and fantastically feminine image for someone whose body was rendered naked because the violence of the crash had torn off every bit of her clothes, for someone whose body was sprinkled with gold dust unleashed from another passenger's grip, for someone who sustained a dislocated and crushed right foot, eleven fractures in her right leg, a dislocated left shoulder, an injured spine and pelvis, two broken ribs, a broken collar bone, and a broken pubic bone, and for someone who was pierced by a handrail that entered her abdomen and emerged from her vagina. *La Bailarinita!* The embellishment of pain and the interweaving of fact and fantasy, so poignantly captured by these two words, aptly describe the compelling and paradoxical qualities in Frida Kahlo, a woman who struggled desperately to transform her tragic reality by passionately and obstinately using her pain and wounds as sources of creative inspiration and survival.

Frida Kahlo (1907–54), known also simply as Frida, recently attained a degree of popularity and public fascination usually reserved for cult figures. For years after her death, she was primarily known in her native Mexico, and chiefly as the wife of internationally acclaimed muralist and painter, Diego Rivera. Over the last twenty years, Frida has begun to be hailed as a feminist icon and perhaps the most talented of all Latin American artists. One conclusion clearly emerges from discussions of Frida's celebrityhood: her star quality and larger-than-life status are due not only to her art but also to the whole of her life and personality.

Frida began painting at the age of eighteen following her near-fatal accident. Even prior to her accident, however, she struggled with polio since the age of six, a malady for which she missed a year of school and was taunted, teased, and called *pato de pago* (peg leg). The bus accident she suffered at eighteen added a host of extra problems. In the days following her accident, Frida felt that she had aged instantly and that she was robbed of her childish illusions: "I already know everything, without reading or writing. A little while ago, almost a few days ago, I was a little girl who walked through a world of colors . . . Everything was mysterious and concealed something; I took pleasure in deciphering, in learning, as in a game. If only you knew how terrible it is suddenly to know everything, as if a flash of lightning lit up the earth. Now I live on a dolorous planet, transparent like ice; but which conceals nothing, it's as if I had learned everything in seconds, all at once."[1] Throughout her life, Frida was hung upside down, naked, and obliged to wear plaster and steel casts and corsets to strengthen her spinal column, required to undergo over thirty operations, and was bedridden and incapacitated over long periods.

Frida said two things destroyed her: the accident and Diego. Indeed, her relationship with the man she viewed as larger-than-life consumed her. Frida twice married Diego, who was double her age and three times her size, and she was deeply distressed by his numerous infidelities. Just as she struggled with the many assaults to the integrity and vanity of her damaged body, so too she refused to give up on the tempestuous relationship with Diego which was the source of so much heartache and pain, but more than anything else, enduring loyalty and profound love.

Although at first glance Frida's artwork can be characterized as a bold self-disclosure revealing the anguish of her corporeal battles, there is much more concealed beneath the surface of her art. Ironically, though much of Frida's imagery deals directly with very personal feminine issues, it often does so with the purpose of creating a mythological identity. In this chapter, I unfold the mystique—both created and real—of the legendary Frida Kahlo.

Frida transformed a tragic reality into a theatrical production, and both her life and her art illustrate the various acts she staged. She dressed ornately with elaborate hairdos and jewels to assert her Mexican identity and to conceal her limp and the scarred parts of her body. She decorated her beautiful home with gay colors, Mexican folk art, and pre-Columbian artifacts as a way of identifying with her Spanish Indian mother and to distract from the fact that her husband was away having numerous affairs, including one with her sister. Frida created myths about herself by altering certain facts, such as her date of birth; she added three years to make it coincide with the 1910 Mexican Revolution and called herself the "daughter of the revolution." She immersed herself in communism in the hope of eliminating differences between herself and others and of finding new idols, including Marx, Stalin, and Mao, who might cure her afflictions. She was known for her scandalous affairs with both men and women, some of whom were quite famous (e.g., Trotsky, Noguchi); the purpose of these trysts was to redress the balance in her relationship with Diego and to reassure herself of her desirability, femininity, and physical integrity. Finally, and most importantly, she painted self-portraits to compensate for her maternal failure and to conceal and restore a wounded psyche. As a woman obsessed with her self-image, Frida compulsively sought mirroring. Painting herself again and again was the way she found to move beyond the constriction imposed upon her by her body and to communicate her experiences to others. In the process of validating her sense of self and confirming her very existence, she produced astonishing works of art, works that are magical, dream-like, and layered with psychological resonance, bespeaking a visionary dimension of human experience accessible to very few. From her suffering Frida gave birth to visions.

The Mirror

It is widely accepted that Frida's art—largely self-portraits that depict a resplendent mask-like face—allowed her to deal concretely with her pain (both physical and psychic) while feeding her narcissism, which had been injured along with her body.[2] She actually had an easel mounted onto her bed to allow her to paint while lying flat.

It is true that she seriously turned to painting only following her accident at the age of eighteen, yet Frida was coping with early childhood circumstances that predisposed her to a particular form of artistic expression with its strong emphasis on self-portraiture. Her mother, Mathilde Calderón, a devout Catholic Spanish-Indian, remained unavailable to Frida as an infant. Apparently a histrionic personality, Frida's mother suffered from pseudo-seizures that were curious replicas of her husband's authentic epileptic fits. One of Frida's childhood memories is of her mother drowning a litter of rats.[3] Trying to understand her mother's behavior, Frida speculated, "Maybe she was cruel because she was not in love with my father."[4] Unable to have her needs met by her mother, Frida turned to her father, Guillermo Kahlo, a Jew of German-Austro-Hungarian descent, for love and guidance. Her father was a sensitive, somber loner who, through his artistic work as a photographer and his physical handicap (epilepsy), served as a figure with whom she could identify. In her 1936 family portrait, she placed herself in line with her father as one way of demonstrating the strong bond she had with him. He, in turn, stated, "Frida is the most intelligent of my [six] daughters. . . . She is most like me."[5]

The infant Frida was not breastfed by her mother; instead, she was suckled by an Indian wet nurse and cared for by her older sisters. She explained, "My mother could not suckle me because eleven months after I was born my sister Christina was born. I was fed by a nana whose breasts they washed every time I was going to suck them."[6] In *My Nurse and I* (1937), Frida's early mirroring experience is represented as she is shown suckling the breast of a masked Aztec Indian goddess. Although her body is one of an infant, her face is that of an adult. This Rousseau-like painting, with its lack of proportion, reveals the blurred boundaries between childhood and adulthood. The nurse represents the Indian heritage that Kahlo found nourishing and from which she later adopted her persona. It is also significant to consider that she depicts

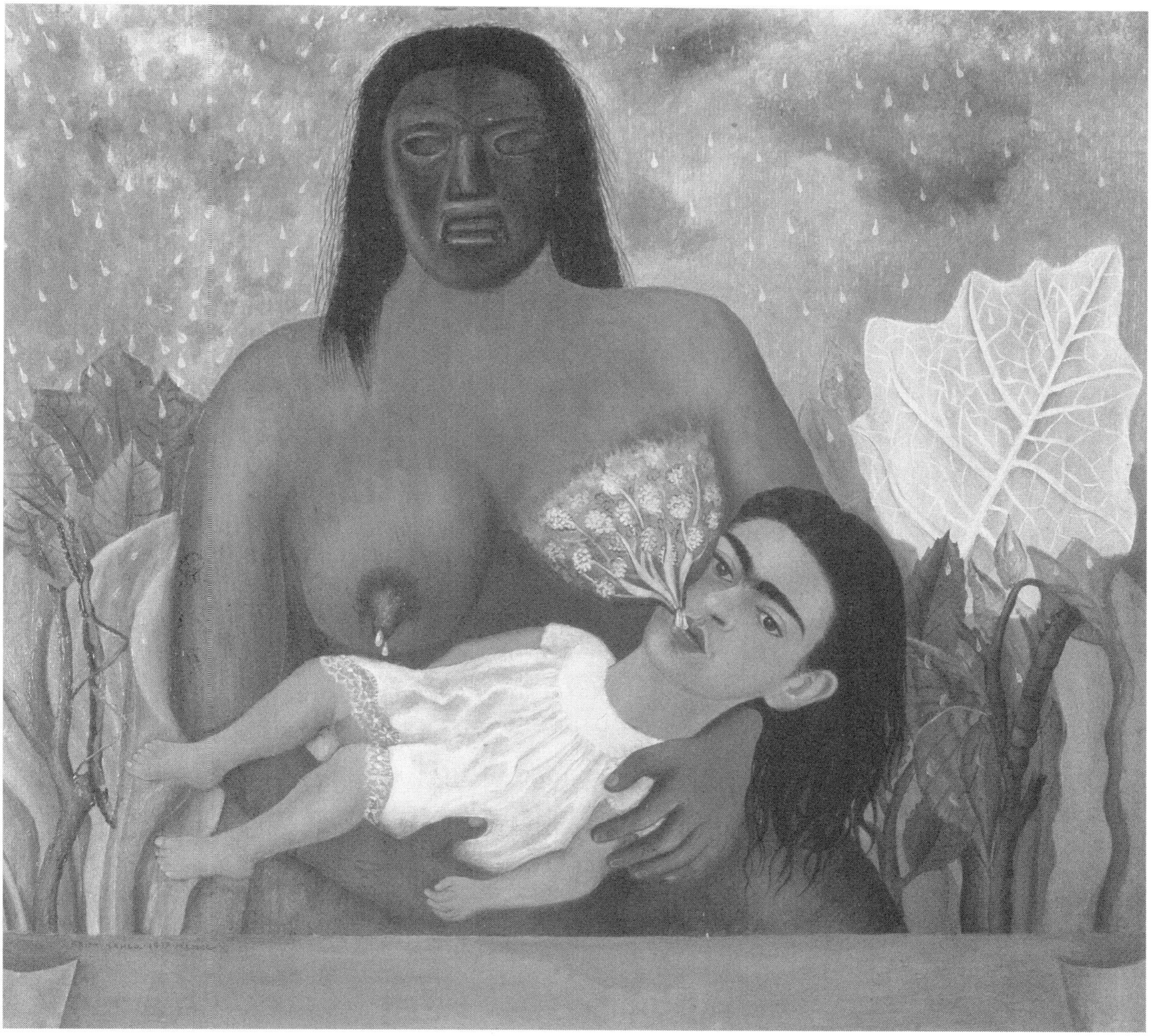

22. Frida Kahlo, *My Nurse and I* (Mi Nana y yo), 1937. Oil on metal, 11¾ × 13¾ inches. Fundacion Dolores Olmedo, Mexico City, D.F., Mexico. Photo credit: Schalkwijk/Art Resource, NY. © 2008 Banco de México Diego Rivera and Frida Kahlo Trust. Av. Cinco de Mayo No. 2, Col. Centro, Del. Cuauhtémoc, 06059, Mexico, D.F.

her own mirroring experience as one in which she was obliged to gaze into an impenetrable weeping mask of iron. Not only does the nurse look straight ahead instead of at the child she holds in her arms, but the infant Frida stares blankly as she turns away from the masked face and body of her "symbolic" mother. Frida not only lost her mother's attention at an early age, she also lost her nurse, who was fired when apprehended drinking alcohol.[7]

What astounds us in Frida's art, as well as that of the other women in this book, is the way she was able to transform a very personal pain into a unique, numinous image that possesses universal appeal and opportunity for identification. Though we have not all experienced troubled or disappointing relationships with our mothers, our primary nurturers, who among us received all that she longed for from that first, intensely important human attachment? Who among us does not continue to yearn for nurturance, warmth, protection, and mirroring from environments and people too frequently opaque and indifferent to our needs? It is not difficult, therefore, for us to be drawn into the early nurturing exchange between mother and child so poignantly rendered by Frida in *My Nurse and I.* The juxtaposion of the adult face with the child's body, the infant with the mask, the personal with the archetype, divides us along the rift it creates between the actual and the possible, between reality and the dream, between what is and what we hope for; a dimension of transcendence within the dimension of immanence is implied in this painting.

Frida's early mothering experiences, like those of Kollwitz and Cahun, were associated with unavailability, loss, and rejection. When the mirroring experience is unempathic, distorted, negative, absent—or, in Spitz's words, if there is a "derailment of the dialogue" between mother and infant—then the child's own existence becomes negated and suffers a disturbance in primitive self-feeling. According to Lacan, a failure in the mirror phase results in the infant's sense of body fragmentation, which he called *le corps morcelé* (the dissected body), as we saw in Cahun's photomontages.[8] Faulty mirroring may be explained by the mother's own self-involvement or depression, as was the case with Kollwitz's mother.

Although the Indian mother surrogate in *My Nurse and I* has plenty of milk, she also sheds tears of a "mater dolorosa" similar to the painting in Frida's portrayal of the scene of her own birth (*My Birth*). In both of these "mother" paintings, the mother's face is hidden, by a sheet or a steel mask, and replaced by depictions of a weeping martyred virgin or a tearful Aztec goddess. Frida's maternal images are too mythic and unreal to be representations of a nurturing mother whose face and expression are ready or eager to mirror her child and confirm its existence with pleasure. Nonetheless, these flawed mothers are incredible, beautiful, and shocking. By painting her mother in this manner, Frida transports us to a visionary world that in many ways speaks more accurately about the maternal universe than any precise formula could, a universe that makes no promises of comfort nor containment, where no individual rights exist, and even the next sixty seconds of life are not guaranteed. Thus, the infant Frida faces masks of mothers, masks that would eventually become the source of her own façade—an inaccessible mask alluding to profound pain on one hand, and Mexican femininity on the other. Diego insightfully wrote that his wife painted her maternal objects in this manner because she was "aware that in reality she had never seen their faces."[9] Interestingly, Frida was attracted to Diego partly because she loved "the sensitivity of his wonderful breasts" and his notable nurturing qualities.[10] In the early years of their relationship, she often signed her letters to him with the words, "your little girl, Fisita."[11]

Known for her unusual, even obsessional, relationship with mirrors and preoccupation with her appearance, Frida surrounded herself with mirrors of all sizes, placing them at varying angles from her bed (where she spent much of her time), installing an enormous one facing down at her from the underside of her canopy bed. She thus assured repeated encounters with her own reflection and the concrete assurance of her existence—a crucial need for Frida whose physical problems required that she repeatedly overcome new challenges.

To cope with her loneliness and feelings of abandonment, resulting from the prolonged bed rests imposed on her, Frida wrote numerous letters imploring her friends and lovers to visit her and, more importantly, not forget her. Haunted by the isolation foisted upon her by chronic pain and the sad solitude left in the wake of her lover's betrayals, the answers to her pleas were insufficient for her needs and so she transformed her canvas into a mirror in which she reflected a world of exquisite tensions, stark beauty, stoic strength, insidious will, and layered self-definitions. Incessantly drawing self-portraits, Frida seemed to be painfully striving to obtain what she did not receive from her mother's eyes: confirmation to help delineate a firm and cohesive sense of self while creating another world, one imagined to heal her physical and psychic wounds, yet radiant in its depictions of pain, longing, and transformation.

Clinicians have emphasized the importance of mirroring as a source of transference and cure in the psychoanalytic process. Freud compared the analyst to a mirror: "The doctor should be opaque to his patients, and, like a mirror, should show them nothing but what is shown to him."[12] Many others have followed in emphasizing the importance of mirroring in psychoanalysis. Winnicott viewed the major task of the analyst not as that of offering interpretations, but rather of serving as a mirror for reflecting back to the patient the patient's own self.[13] Kohut claimed that mirroring is an invaluable source of transference for the narcissistic patient. By acting as a confirming reflection of the patient's own grandiose infantile fantasies, the analyst validates the patient's self-esteem and gradually, by means of a selective process, restrains them within more reasonable limits.[14]

I believe that the same search for self which takes place in the mirroring reciprocity between mother and infant and between analyst

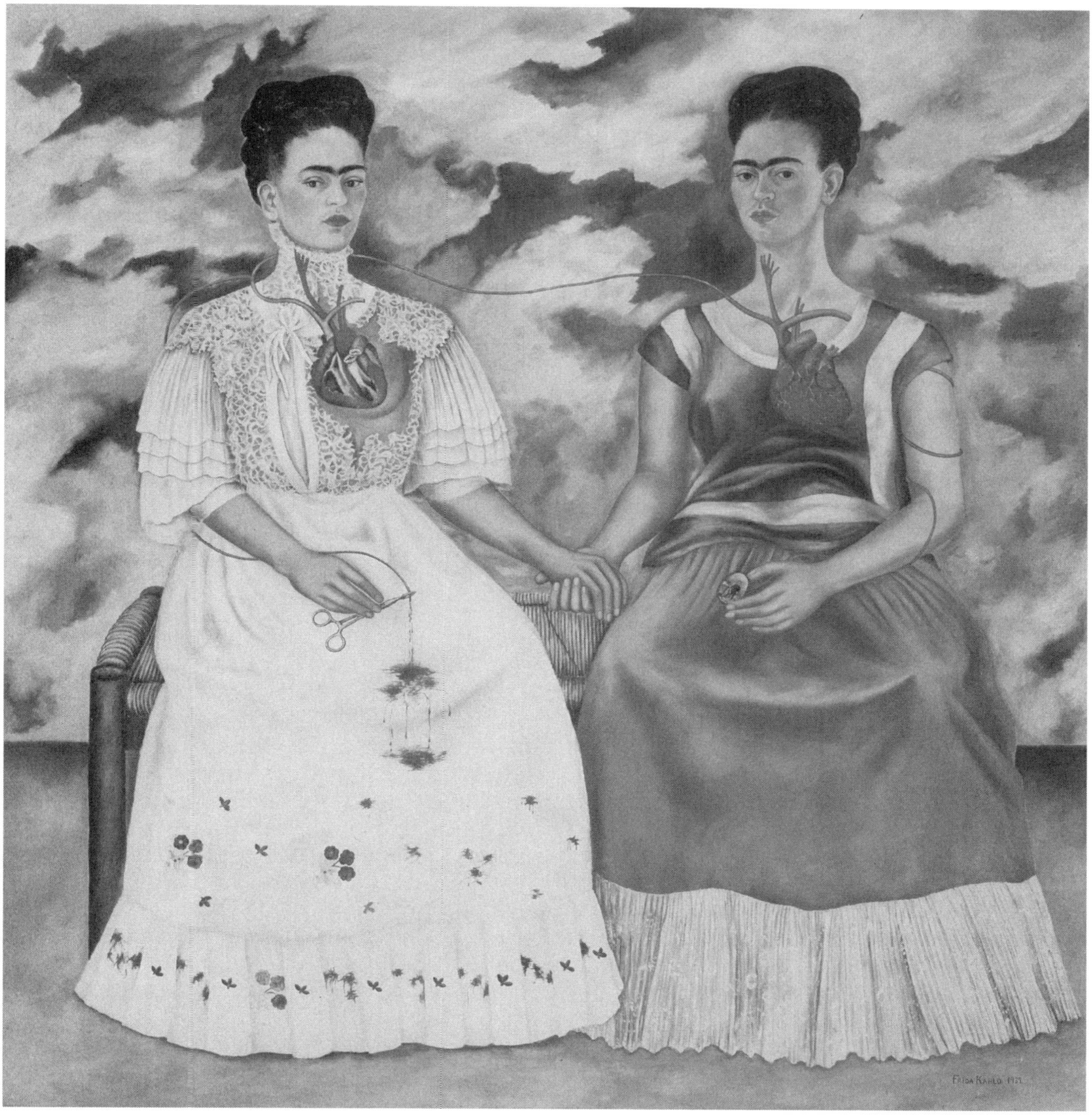

23. Frida Kahlo, *The Two Fridas*, 1939. Oil on canvas. Five feet 8½ inches × five feet 8½ inches. Museo Nacional de Arte Moderno, Instituto National de Bellas Artes, Mexico City, D.F., Mexico. Photo credit: Schalkwijk/Art Resource, NY. © 2008 Banco de México Diego Rivera and Frida Kahlo Trust. Av. Cinco de Mayo No. 2, Col. Centro, Del. Cuauhtémoc, 06059, Mexico, D.F.

and analysand can also be undertaken by the artist in the creation of her works.[15] The structure of art, by establishing preordained limits within which the artist must work, provides a more concrete dimension to the mirroring experience. For Frida, the self-portrait represented an apt, almost self-evident, means by which she was able to act as a mirror to herself, reflecting her need for self-definition while simultaneously attempting to achieve it. Through her art Frida succeeded in repeating the mother-infant dyad with its mutual gazing reciprocity. Creating her double in her self-portraits, she became her own mirror. At least in her art, Frida reached a state of forgiveness and reconciliation with her mother for she guaranteed not only that her image would live on to immortality, but that it would forever be mirrored. As spectators, we come face to face with Frida's painted figure and have taken over the artist's role of unceasingly mirroring her image. She thus created the perfect art, the perfect mother, and the perfect audience.

The way Frida *replaced* her mother by becoming the mirror she wished she had is best illustrated in *The Two Fridas* (1939), her largest painting. In it, the artist informs us about the way she survived: she kept herself together by appropriating the maternal function with which to nurture herself and by representing the ensuing self-containment of her world. Two Fridas seated on a bench hold hands and face the viewer before a dark sky filled with ominous storm clouds. One Frida has a broken heart and the other a heart that is whole. One Frida clasps a pair of surgical pincers in her hand to keep the other alive. Dispassionate and impersonal facial expressions produce an emotional remove from the poignant, near-death scene she is depicting. Frida thus reminds us that she is a perennial observer who looks at herself and then paints herself looking at herself, drawing the viewer into a dialogue with the observer and observed.

One Frida represents her Indian and the other her European heritage. One Frida holds a small portrait of Diego as a child near her genital, symbolizing the child—Diego's child —which she miscarried. The other holds the pincers near that same area, yet she cannot prevent the blood from spurting out onto the white bridal costume she wears. Blood stains, alluding to menstruation, castration, and her accident, combine with patterns of birds and flowers making it difficult to distinguish one from the other. For Frida, femininity forever united with pain and nature; loss, tragedy, and death speak in every human gesture.

Frida's double images further represent the mother who herself is divided between giving milk and giving poison, between nurturing the child and devouring the child—mother creator versus mother destroyer. Painted at a time when she divorced Diego, Frida additionally portrayed the divided feelings she harbored toward him. She herself stated that the painting depicted the Frida Diego loved and the Frida Diego no longer loved.[16] Perhaps she projected her own ambivalent emotions toward this man whom she both adored and despised. This remarkably complex painting with its multiple layers of meaning also reminds us that the structure of the self—this self that assumes itself to be singular, individual, and monolithic—is, in reality, mirrored, divided, plural, and distributed.

Beyond mirroring herself and creating a safe, self-enclosed world within which to meet her needs, Frida also acted against feelings of self-disintegration and fears of loss of self by reconstructing a novel self. In her diary, next to several small self-portrait drawings, Frida wrote, "The one who gave birth to herself"[17]

The Ancient Concealer

The self Frida birthed was in part a fabricated self, a false self aimed at concealing her vulnerability and terror. She signed many of her letters to Diego with the words "your ancient concealer" (*la gran ocultadora*). Unsurprisingly, then, Frida's self-image resembled a mask of strength; although it sometimes shed tears, it nearly always refused to display naked or uncontrolled emotion. What we see in its place is the noble struggle to contain a pain that cannot be loosed onto the world but instead must be rendered in dazzling and sometimes surreal scenes.

Masks have always played a significant role in the art and culture of Mexico.[18] Although Frida produced several paintings using masks (e.g., *Little Girl with Death Mask*), her most important mask was the one she wore herself. Indeed, most of her self-portraits depict her face wearing the same mask of expressionless determination. Frida once intimated at the origins of her mask when she commented, "No one in my house believes that I am really sick since I cannot even say so because my mother . . . gets sick, and they say it was because of me."[19] Unable to tolerate her daughter's infirmity, Frida's mother barely visited her for the entire year she was hospitalized following her accident. As a result, Frida became the heroic sufferer, and the one who protected her mother by pretending she was well and did not need her.

Anna Freud remarked on how children with bodily injury, often deprived of maternal care, learn to play the role of mother and child to their bodies.[20] Frida seems to have accomplished this by condensing her image with that of her mother in her art. In her paintings, Frida adopted the "mask" of her unresponsive mother. Having internalized her mother's unaffected face, she subsequently externalized it by projecting it onto her canvas as her own image. Frida therefore came face-to-face with the face she once internalized.

If the mother is the universal mirror and we are faced with mask upon mask over the mother's face in Frida's art, it is no surprise we find her wearing a mask-like face in her work and in her life. Yet these masks also mirror something about ourselves back to us. The mask in *My Nurse and I,* for example, is surrounded by the extraordinary beauty of the world. The mask shocks us into the realization that everything around us has so many hidden dimensions, layers beneath layers of structure and function. Frida's mask reveals the impersonal dimension of life; she brings us face to face with something absolutely true about our own reality: the sphinx shows us the stillness in the movement, the detachment hidden in involvement, the letting go within the holding on.

Frida's identification with her Spanish Indian mother was far-reaching. She preferred popular methods of representation, related to indigenous Mexican culture known as *Mexicanidad* to more academic European traditions. She also explicitly appropriated the traditional style of *retablo* or *ex-voto* painting in many of her works. Retablos are small paintings made on sheets of tin and nailed in church as thanks-offerings after a miraculous recovery from an accident or disaster. Frida also tried to imitate her mother, whom she depicted only in her white lace wedding dress (*My Grandparents, My Parents and I,* 1936). Like her mother, Frida painted herself (*Self-Portrait as Tehuana,* 1943) in an elaborate bridelike costume (see Plate 3). Yet, whereas her mother's dress suitably accommodates her body, Frida's gives the impression of being forced to fit like Cindarella's slipper on the foot of a wicked stepsister. In addition to the visual resemblance her outfitting herself in traditional feminine Mexican costume produced, the physical sensation of the clothing touching her skin perhaps symbolically created the bodily contact she so longed for with her mother.

That Frida's image was, in fact, an amalgamation of her mother's and her own is demonstrated in her groundbreaking painting, *My Birth* (1932), which in her own words depicts "how I imagine I was born (see Plate 7)."[21] Here we are shown in graphic detail the dark side of the mother-child relationship. The mother lies on a bed with a sheet covering her head and chest: a kind of dead mother. The position of the woman and the birth theme refer not only to pre-Columbian statues depicting a woman during the act of childbirth (*La Maternidad*) but, also, to Gustav Courbet's *L'Origine du Monde* [The Origin of the World], which shows a close-up of an anonymous woman's genitals (see Plate 8); the woman's upper body, like Frida's mother, is covered by a sheet. In Frida's painting, a picture of the Virgin of Sorrows, the grieving mother, pierced by swords, bleeding and crying, hangs above the bed to replace the mother's hidden head. The painting within this painting depicts the intense sorrow Frida felt, the agony behind the mask. The baby's head, emerging from between the mother's legs, is unmistakably Frida's because the joined eyebrows that became her trademark in her self-portraits are present. Covered with blood, the baby Frida looks dead as well. Yet, coming as it did after one of Frida's miscarriages, this painting also places her in the role of mother as it alludes to the recent death of *her* unborn child. Frida identified with the mother in the painting when she wrote, "My head is covered because coincidentally with the painting of the picture, my mother died."[22] Therefore, the condensation of her image with that of her mother is significant. Hating her mother for what she did not give her, Frida also identified with her as she too replaced her face with a mask of pain and gave birth to death.

Perhaps no other work of art shows such an ominous vision of birth and motherhood. There is no mercy in this painting. It is cruel and indifferent. The room around the bed is empty as is the retablo-like banner below—the sign that says nothing—reflecting the silence of life to our suffering and Frida's absence of prayer at that time. The sad mystic blue color she chose for the background is the same shade one sees on the ocean at twilight, a blue fading to black. Nature's cruel indifference to human fate screams at us from Frida's depiction of her birth—the arbitrariness of fate, her fate on that cursed bus, our fate, the fate of all humanity.

Despite the bleakness of its connotations, *My Birth* is, above all, momentous as an act of creativity. By painting this remarkable work, Frida shows how she gave birth to her art—the only arena in which she was able to express, rework, and master the conflicted relationship she had with her mother and her own body. Hers is a symbolic depiction of the act of creation, for creation is born of our need to cry out, our desire to matter and to make something out of the pain in our lives. Thus we wrestle with meaning and its opposite. We are eclipsed (like the mother in the painting) as we give birth to art, to something already fully formed, something mature, and of course something flawed (note the gashes in the baby's neck). So *My Birth* is more than simply about Frida making art; it is the process of making art itself. It is a painting about the beautiful madness of the artist who gives birth to creation.

Already, at the age of six, while homebound and physically restricted with polio for nine months, Frida discovered, perhaps for the first time, that she could turn to her creative imagination to compensate for a painful, restrictive reality. She created an imaginary playmate who, unlike herself, was agile and loved to dance.

> my imaginary friend
> always waited for me. . . .
> She laughed a lot.
> Soundlessly. She was agile
> And danced as if she
> Were weightless. I
> Followed her in every movement
> and while she
> Danced, I told her
> My secret problems. . . .
> LAS
> DOS
> FRI-
> DAS[23]

Continually creating her double in her self-portraits, Frida later struggled to prove that she could not only portray her pain, but in doing so, step outside of it and surmount it. Like her childhood imaginary companion, Frida's mask-like face in her self-portraits—her more mature alter ego with its unflinching, stoic gaze—declares that all is fine and under control. Of course, this is difficult to believe when one glances down at the ravaged body, bleeding, wounded, and cracked open (see, e.g., *Broken Column*). The origin of this split is especially interesting when one considers a statement she once made: "I have the eyes of my father and the body of my mother."[24] The maternal identification was for her that which had become associated with injury and attack. Consequently, the majority of her self-portraits leave out the hated body and focus exclusively on her strikingly handsome face.

Frida's portraits place great emphasis on the repercussions of her accident even though she only twice drew pencil sketches of it. Paradoxically, when she did show her body's wounds, the intact parts of her body were represented with flawless beauty. For example, *The Broken Column* (1944) depicts her body split in half with her spinal column replaced by a cracked and broken Greek column. Her naked body and face are punctured with nails. Notwithstanding the imagery of damage, Frida's face remains beautiful and her bare breasts are exquisitely shaped; her body is perfectly proportioned. Thus, while we expect to view a frail, weak body, we are confronted instead with one that is elegant and strong, even in its brokenness. Likewise, in *The Deer* (1946), despite the fact that her animal body is pierced by arrows and bleeding, à la St. Sebastian, it is a body capable of light, swift movement that seems to easily overcome the arrows and the broken twigs and trees at its feet along the forest path. Her tears refer to the awareness of the body proper while her stoic attitude and her noble carriage suggest her ability to step outside of her body, to exist beyond the pain and the constraints of her physical self.

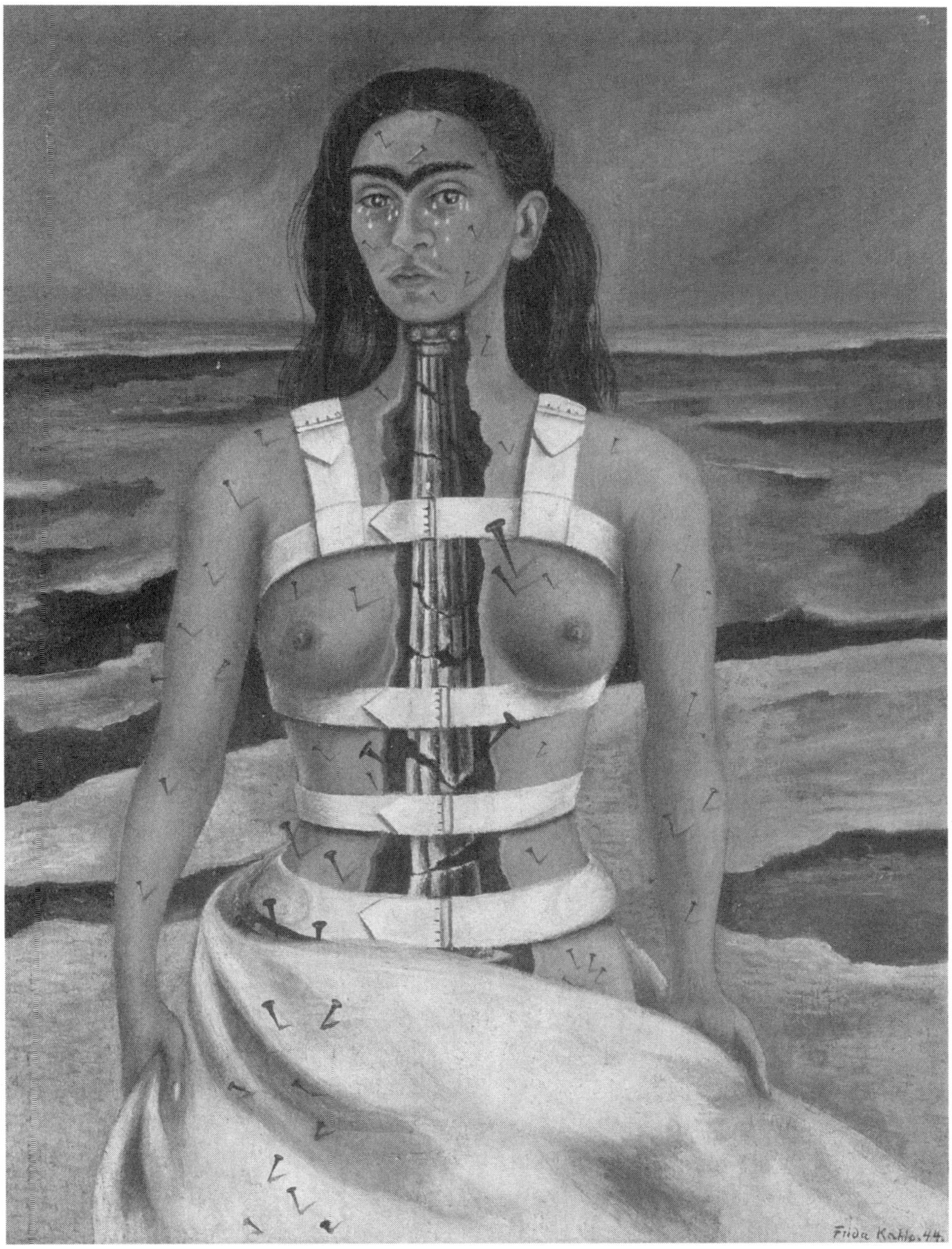

24. Frida Kahlo, *The Broken Column,* 1944. Oil on masonite, $15^{3}/_{4} \times 12^{1}/_{4}$ inches. Fundacion Dolores Olmedo, Mexico City, D.F., Mexico. Photo credit: Schalkwijk/Art Resource, NY. © 2008 Banco de México Diego Rivera and Frida Kahlo Trust. Av. Cinco de Mayo No. 2, Col. Centro, Del. Cuauhtémoc, 06059, Mexico, D.F.

While her paintings contain glaring emotional images, the atmosphere in many of them is, for the most part, flat and unemotional. Furthermore, her technique was a careful one that emphasized deliberate and steady strokes, perhaps reflecting the way her movements must have been—restrained and calculated, rather than graceful and spontaneous. The attention to detail contributes to some of the paintings' unemotional quality. Mental anguish is repeatedly transformed into physical pain; as her mental anguish increased, so did her glamorization of physical suffering. Ironically, Frida masked her weakness by exaggerating the painful. Yet, how do we explain the ease with which we respond with deep emotion to her art? Perhaps the suppression of anguish in her work incites an anguished response in us. Perhaps it is we who feel how much she is containing in her work the volcano of emotion brewing beneath the surface.

Although Frida's expression is rarely sorrowful, she allows the viewer to know that she is obsessing about her husband by placing his image on her forehead (e.g., *Diego on My Mind*). The stoic face she wears shows us the way pain—both physical and emotional—is a necessary part of the human condition. Yet, she also demonstrates that it is possible to transcend one's pain by drawing the self-torture out of it and meeting it with forgiveness and healing awareness. She thus turns into that force of nature that goes beyond the human condition; she becomes a goddess arche-

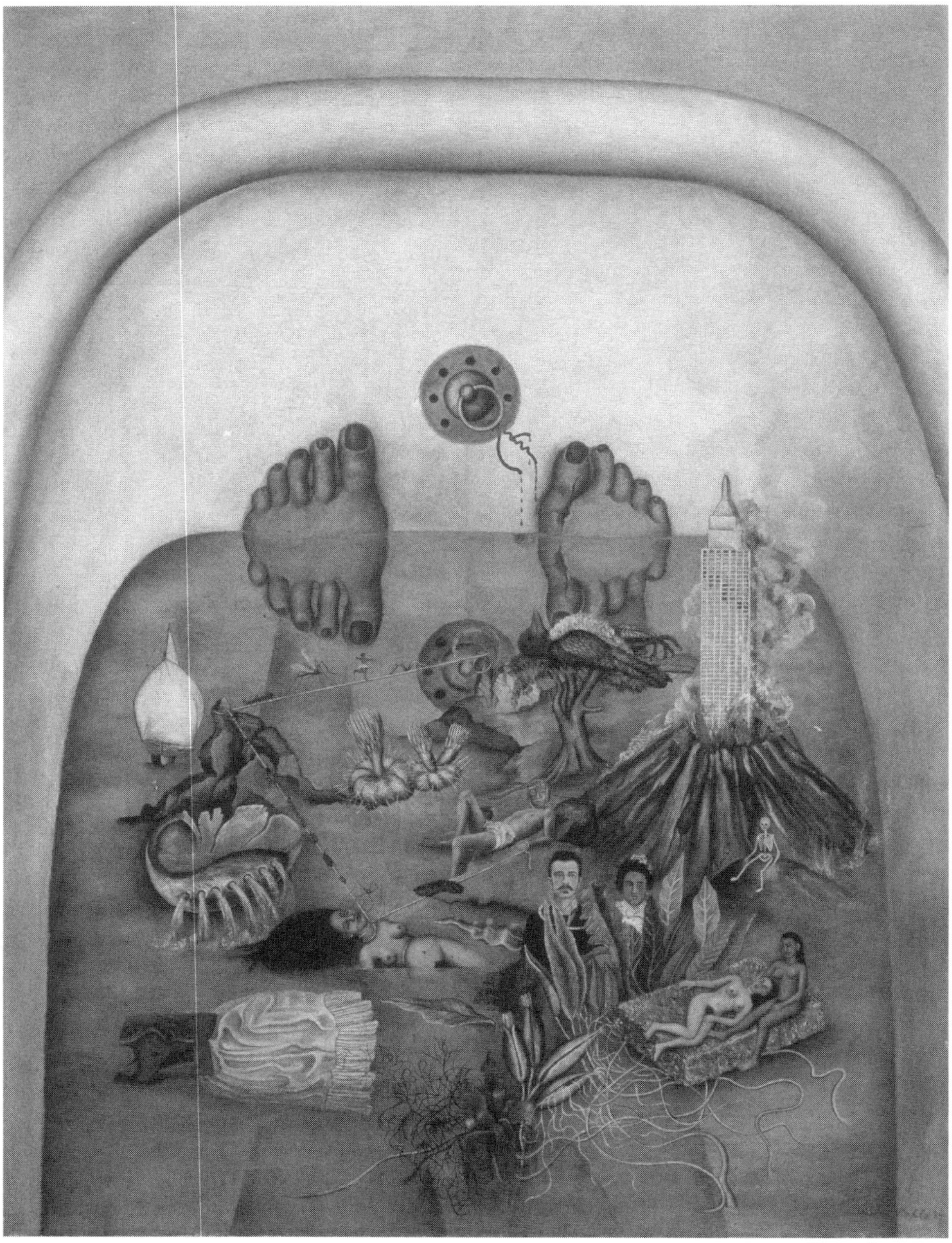

25. Frida Kahlo, *What the Water Gave Me* (Lo que el agua me dio), 1939. Oil on canvas, 69 × 88 cm. Photo credit: Schalkwijk/Art Resource, NY. © 2008 Banco de México Diego Rivera and Frida Kahlo Trust. Av. Cinco de Mayo No. 2, Col. Centro, Del. Cuauhtémoc, 06059, Mexico, D.F.

type—focused, indifferent, looking beyond the personal. She exists outside of her physical pain and outside of her lover's infidelities. Frida's work, in the final analysis, consists of the same "unemotional" self-portrait: a mask of strength and fortitude, a mirror of survival, and a flamboyant fête of pain and suffering. Even the bodies in her self-portraits merely display descriptive or symbolic damage. Only in *Tree of Hope* is her back cut open as it often was in reality.

Interestingly, her most emotionally revealing self-portrait omits her face. In what is arguably her most surrealist painting, *What the Water Gave Me* (1938), Frida drops her mask to disclose hidden parts of her self. The painting is drawn from her perspective as a bather in a tub looking down at her feet, which are doubled in the water's reflection. The right foot unashamedly displays its bloody wound. Below are blood-red hairy flowers suggestive of pubic hair and castration, menstruation, and damage to her vagina from the accident. Floating in the bluish water are Bosch- and Bruegel-like miniature forms that create a collage of images—a symbolic microcosm of her psyche—and denote her sense of bodily defect and castration. Aside from the damaged foot (castrated penis) and the bloodied female genitals, we also see a dead tree stump with a dead bird on it, a death ship sailing away (in a previous painting, *Remembrance*, she drew her foot as a boat), a volcano erupting with a smoky, phallic Empire State Building; a tiny skeleton on top of a mountain, and her parents covered by plants. Two women embrace while protectively covering their genitals; a boy lounges on the bank, the root of a tree wrapped around his head as he clutches a rope that extends to a naked, drowning woman who is strangled by the line. A ballerina (*La Baillarinita!*) and some insects balance on a tightrope. Frida's Tehuana dress floats away, signifying her relinquishing disguises. A string is held by a ghostlike figure, intimating that Frida's life and sexuality are kept alive by a thread (as in *The Two Fridas*) in an ominous sea of castration symbols. Even the stopper of the tub bleeds in symbolic reference to her bleeding, wounded vagina.

On one level, Frida *is* the damaged, castrated, and bleeding woman. Yet, on the other, she gives birth to these images which literally pour out from between her legs. Like the pregnant woman whose "water breaks" at the moment she is about to give birth, Frida emphasizes the organic connection of water to everything past and present. Note, too, the opened sea shell on the right—a miniature symbol of the painting as a whole—displaying water streaming through its many holes. In *What the Water Gave Me*, everything floats on the surface of an unfathomable depth, not the mere depth of a bathtub, but the depth of a mind looking in two directions at once—outside/inside, above/below, conscious/unconscious, here/beyond. Despite the fact that the tram's handrail impaled her vagina and resulted in her incapacity to bear children (she had three miscarriages), Frida's pro/creativity is her art making, an art filled with color and life even as it portrays pain and death. Many years later, Orlan would approach the subject of the castrated female body in her art, also showing bodily damage while simultaneously challenging popular assumptions of inferior female genitalia. Frida's depiction of the bleeding woman would also be taken up by Judy Chicago (*Red Flag*, 1971; *Menstruation Bathroom*, 1979) and Ana Mendieta (*Siluetas* and *Rape Pieces*).

Unlike the majority of her self-portraits, which tend to mask her feelings, Frida's diary, not intended for public viewing, offers a picture of the artist unmasked.[25] Her diary reveals what lay beneath the mask of the great concealer: pain, depression, loneliness, despair over her relationship with Diego, and terror of her illness. Littered with colorful drawings, we encounter a Frida who, as her health deteriorates and her husband cultivates relationships with other women, portrays her face as fragmented and her body as sprouting broken wings. Even the sun is broken. Eyes abound as she searches both inside and out for comfort and reassurance during a time she claims to have suffered the most in her life. Frida gained the determination to go on from her growing attachment to the Communist Party and its ideals which she treated like a religion whose gods are Marx, Lenin, Stalin, and Mao, and from her incredible love for Diego: "I love Diego more than myself."[26]

> Nobody will ever know how much
>   I love Diego. . . .
> I never want
> him to be sad

and if I had my health
I'd like to give it all to him
if I had my youth
He could have it all . . .[27]

Despite her all-encompassing love for Diego, she also grappled with the vast pain and anger she harbored for him. In *Ruina* (Ruin), a self-portrait drawing from 1947, her face is cracked like an ancient statue and held together by elaborate edifices resembling those attached to the sides of buildings during renovation. Its location: *Avenida Engano* (Deceit Avenue). Inscribed onto a stone (tombstone?) adjacent to her crumbling head are the words: "Ruin / House for birds / Nest for love? All for nothing." Even as she became increasingly suicidal, Frida continued to assert that what kept her from taking her life was the thought that Diego might need her.

Madonna of Sorrows

By embellishing her pain, Frida became a female martyr; she became a "mater dolorosa" in her own right. Attributing her creative impulse to the ruined possibility of motherhood, she once wrote: "My painting carries with it the message of pain. . . . Painting completed my life. I lost three children. . . . Paintings substituted for all this."[28] Forever embellishing what she most despised, Frida even decorated the plaster corsets she was obliged to wear. On one, superimposed on her abdominal region, she painted the image of a fetus with umbilical cord, thereby creating the desired illusion of pregnancy.

Frida's sense of having an inferior body seems also to have been tied, in her mind, to its being a female body. Encouraged to pursue "masculine" activities, like sports, to overcome her physical liabilities, Frida appears to have associated masculinity with strength and intactness and femininity with weakness, physical frailty, and defectiveness. The suffering she portrayed in her art was therefore also meant as a metaphor for all female suffering. For example, in *Self-Portrait with Cropped Hair* (1940), which she painted following her divorce from Diego, Frida acknowledged a powerful masculine side to her personality. Dressed in a man's suit, she symbolically castrated herself (scissors at crotch) by cutting off the feminine locks Diego loved. Frida painted many works that, like this one and *What the Water Gave Me*, depict symbolic castration. In *Henry Ford Hospital* (1932), painted after a miscarriage, she is shown lying naked in a pool of blood around her genital area. She holds six ribbons connecting her to a series of objects that symbolize her barrenness and maternal failure and that illustrate the way she viewed her body as a malfunctioning machine. She once confessed, "I am not sick; I am broken."[29] Indeed, *Broken Column* (see Fig. 24) is perhaps the most revealing of Frida's "castration" paintings. The title is suggestive and simple to interpret: her phallus, here a Greek column, is broken and crumbling, and causes her enormous pain. Interestingly, Frida initially painted herself nude but, later, decided to conceal her genitals with a sheet which she holds with affecting delicacy. The tears on her dispassionate face, the beautiful breast spilling from the truss, the spilt chest revealing the broken column, the nails symbolizing her constant pain, all combine to convey a state that is excruciatingly brutal, beautiful, erotic, and, ultimately, impossible. The triumph of the will and spirit over the broken body is reflected in the painting's beautiful sky canopied over the barren, cracked, sickly green-brown-black earth.

Indeed, it is questionable whether Frida really required all of the thirty-plus operations she had, most of them on her spine. These operations could have satisfied an unconscious need to be cut open, changed, corrected—castrated. Dr. Eloesser, her most trusted doctor, thought that most of Frida's operations were unnecessary.[30] Perhaps Frida's superfluous surgeries can best be understood as efforts to repeat the tragedy of castration, as well as the damage from her accident, in an attempt at mastery. As with her self-portraits, Frida felt compelled to repeat those events from her life most responsible for her pain. For instance, she produced several paintings combining her face with that of her husband, Diego (*Diego and Frida*, 1929–44, I and II) to concoct one asymmetrical and unsettling face. In addition to expressing her desire to merge with her husband, Frida also artistically fulfilled her wish to be half-male and half-female. In *The Deer*, we behold Frida's face attached to an animal body with male genitals, once more realizing her unconscious wish to have a male body, or a powerful, active one (translated as male in her mind). Finally, in what was meant as a humorous sketch drawn in 1932, Diego coyly displays a pair of women's breasts while Frida exhibits a sizable male organ.

Frida revealed the masculine side to her personality when she exclaimed, "In another period I dressed like a boy with shaved hair, pants, boots and a leather jacket. But when I went to see Diego [Rivera] I put on a Tehuana costume."[31] Although Frida loved to dress in male clothing most of her self-portraits show her in long, feminine, Mexican dresses typical of women from Tehuantepec in southern Mexico. Every day she dressed herself as if she were attending a festival, adorning her body with native jewelry and weaving colorful ribbons into perfect braided hairdos. Frida's elaborate Tehuana costume became such a significant part of her persona that, at times, she even painted it alone and devoid of a body; it had a life of its own (e.g., *My Dress Hangs There*). Despite the emphasis in her self-portraits on feminine dress and accoutrements, however, Frida coyly exhibited her "masculinity" by artistically focusing on her mustache and the hair connecting her eyebrows.

The intricate connection between clothing and self-image is traditionally feminine and one that Frida took to an extreme. The ornate dress she wore served to cover up the scars and physical deformities inflicted upon her from her dreadful accident. Children who suffer physical injury are known to create a secrecy surrounding the injury.[32] Even as a child, Frida wore three pairs of socks to hide her atrophied leg. As an adult, her flamboyant dress can at least partly be understood as a fabricated ideal of a feminine self that she cultivated and exhibitionistically flaunted to ward off disclosure of her flawed self. It was not only the mask she wore for her art, but the masquerade she lived.[33]

Toward the end of her life, Frida was no longer able to sustain her mask of affectless detachment. Her self-portraits increasingly began to uncover emotional as well as physical pain. Fear, depression, hopelessness, and suicidal longings became the themes in her final paintings. In 1943, she painted *Thinking of Death*, a self-portrait depicting a skull and crossbones in the middle of her forehead, to show us what was really on her mind. *Without Hope* (1945) is perhaps the only self-portrait that situates her in her sick bed, naked under a sheet, weeping and staring at us beseechingly. The easel she had attached to her bed is present but, rather than display a painting, it holds the vomit she spews from her insides, vomit that literally overflows with images of animal entrails, decay and death. A gem-encrusted skull bears her name. On the back of the canvas, she wrote: "Not the least hope remains in me. . . . Everything moves with what the belly encloses." Besides expressing her innermost pain and fear, Frida here shows us her blood and guts, the true source of her artistic inspiration.

Another painting from 1946 depicts two Fridas. One Frida sits facing us and wears a colorful red and yellow Mexican dress; she has red ribbons in her hair and holds a pink back brace in one hand and a banner with the title of the painting in the other. *Tree of Life, Stand Firm* is a patent communication meant to boost her spirit. This Frida has tears in her eyes but nonetheless appears strong and resolute. The second Frida lies behind the first; we see only her back which exposes a large, bleeding V-shaped incision. Her hair is undone and she is wrapped in a sheet, as in *My Birth*. She could be dead. Night and day divide the picture as do the moon and the sun. Once again, Frida here reveals what lies underneath her mask. The brace she holds is the same one she wears under her dress, as evidenced by its visible straps. She literally lets her hair down and shows us her lacerated body as she dared not before. Frida's two selves also represent the striking contrast between woman as object—here, a medical specimen—and woman as subject. Not willing to present herself solely in terms of illness, as the medical establishment often forces one to, Frida's Tehuana self sits proudly upright and stares directly at the viewer who is willing to face what illness means to a woman's body and self. Artists like Jo Spence, Matuschka, and Hannah Wilke would later follow Frida's lead in portraying their experiences with illness and the medicalization of their bodies.

Disguises and embellishments are shed as Frida faces us with her true emotions. It is this kind of pain which vivifies the world, revealing its secret treasures—nature's incredible beauty and incredible indifference. Nature's alterity, and ours too, is filled with wonderful presentations and wormy depths, the cloud and the maggot, and all the gorgeous visions sprung from the tension of these oppositions. The magnificent colors of her work, the florid excesses, the odd juxtapositions are stunningly rendered. Additional paintings in which she is wounded—*Broken Column* and *The Little Deer*—combine with several others showing her neck nearly choked by ribbons, hair strands, necklaces, and thorns. Such visual markings on the neck are known to indicate suicidal tendencies in the draftsman. Paradoxically, they also reveal Frida's desperately literal attempts to remain tied to her surroundings as she felt her grip on life coming undone.

In the year 1950 alone, Frida underwent seven operations on her spine. Following that year, she stopped producing self-portraits altogether and turned exclusively to still life painting. Weary from her deteriorating physical and emotional condition, Frida no longer desired its reflection. In place of her own image, she now filled her canvases with dazzling arrays of sensuous, colorful fruits. Yet, however much her fruits display nature's marvels and remind us of the organic unity of life, they are also anthropomorphized objects that clearly symbolize her emotional state of being at the time. For instance, many of the fruits have been sliced into pieces, as had her body, and some show deliberate resemblance to faces with tears streaming down improvised eyes. Some of the paintings are fragmented by clinging root tendrils, not unlike those that surround her face in *Self-Portrait as Tehuana* (see Plate 3). Quite a few of the opened fruits resemble female genitalia. Indeed, fruits are cultivated in gardens, represent fertility, and are, by definition, ripened ovaries. Thus, in painting her sliced flesh, fragmented body, divided self, weeping fruit, Frida painted her pain—female pain—a pain both personal and universal, yet a pain that never lost touch with life's beauty and mystery.

During her final years with Diego, Frida resigned herself to his adulterous ways. She refused to let him go, however, choosing instead to become financially independent of him; she tried to survive by selling her works and by teaching painting to a group of students who became known as *los Fridas*. Most importantly, the way she kept the relationship vital was to turn the tables and mother Diego; he became her child and she nurtured him: "He's my child every minute, my newborn, every minute of the day, my very own."[34] Interestingly, even Diego's famous fresco painted at about the same time, *Dream of a Sunday Afternoon in Alameda Park* (1947–48), portrays Frida as an adult who places a motherly hand on the shoulder of Diego, the child in britches.

Frida's ambitious painting, *The Love Embrace of the Universe, the Earth (Mexico), Diego, Me and Señor Xolotl* (1949), produced during Diego's affair with the beautiful actress, María Félix, is a remarkable work that illustrates the new relational balance between Frida and Diego as well as her final version of motherhood (see Plate 4). In the center of the painting is Frida, a wounded, weeping Madonna who holds a naked childlike Diego in a maternal embrace. He evinces a Buddha-like placid expression and possesses an enormous third eye in the middle of his forehead, pointing to the visionary powers she attributed to him. He also clutches an orange maguey plant that resembles a flame—the flame of his sex or that of his creativity. Frida, too, is embraced by a larger earth-mother, a pre-Columbian goddess who recalls her wet nurse in *My Nurse and I*. Her chest is cracked like Frida's and her breast leaks a drop of milk and/or a tear. Beyond her is the same face in the clouds, symbolizing the universal forces that embrace Mexico, Frida, Diego, and even her favorite dog, Señor Xolotl. Prickly cactus vegetation surrounds the figures, creating a natural protective hedge around them. Frida's neck is severed and bleeding, as it was in the painting *My Birth* and, through her dress, her heart/breast squirts blood/milk in the shape of a firework display.

Frida's *Pieta* is set in a pre-Columbian paradise and creates the chain of mothering embraces within embraces that extends to the cosmos itself and that she found necessary to survive. In this painting Frida identifies herself with the cosmic goddess, mother and devourer of her own children who unifies life and death in her embrace—ever creative and ever detached, an infinite originator of form, action, and possibility. This is a highly spiritual painting that implies a deep gnosis of cosmic unity, like the sudden knowing she arrived at after her accident.

During these years, Frida became addicted to alcohol and the painkillers she was administered; she made several suicide attempts. The only solace she found near the end of her life was in her nurse. It is interesting that at both the beginning and the end of her life, Frida found mothering in a nurse—first her Indian wet nurse who replaced her mother, and later the nurse who took care of both her physical and emotional needs and replaced Diego. Frida's nurse, who often cradled her in her arms and rocked her to sleep like an infant, recalled: "In my hands she was like a child. Many times I felt that she was my child because she behaved that way. She liked to fall asleep the way babies do. . . . So I always lay down beside her as a support for her back and she called me her 'little prop.'[35] Coming full circle, Frida expressed her unrequited longing for a mother's love and attention one last time.

In August 1953, gangrene spread in Frida's right leg necessitating its amputation. It was this amputation that, more than any other operation, appeared to have had the greatest impact on her. The amputation was the final coup, the final castration, the final offense to her vanity; it reactivated the feelings of pain and helplessness associated with her polio, the earliest assault to her body. One drawing in her diary depicts her as a one-legged doll on top of a pedestal. Unable to keep her balance, she topples under the heading: "*Yo soy la Desintegracíon . . .*" (I am disintegration).[36] Her attempts at compensation were futile as she became increasingly depressed and suicidal.

Making an Entrance, Making an Exit

After Frida underwent an unsuccessful bone transplant, Lola Alvarez Bravo, owner of the Galeria Arte Contemporaneo, sensed that the artist was approaching death. She wished to honor Frida while she still lived and arranged the first one-woman exhibition for Frida in her native land in the spring of 1953. On the opening night, Frida was in very poor health and her doctors advised her not to move. The town was buzzing with speculation and rumors as to whether she would be able to attend the opening night. Crowds of people waited impatiently to be let into the gallery in what became somewhat of a mob scene. At one point, ambulance sirens bellowed and Frida arrived on a stretcher. Her four-poster bed was set up in the middle of the gallery where she held court with the onlookers. Anticipating the performance and installation art that would become popular after the 1960s, Frida became as much, if not more, of an attraction than her paintings. She ensconced herself in the midst of her self-portraits, a fitting site for someone whose life and art were truly impossible to separate.

During her lifetime, Frida depicted the locale of her experience as existing somewhere between a dream state and reality, between the earth and the sky, between life and death. In 1940, she painted *The Dream*, in which she lies asleep on her side in a canopy bed that floats in a lavender, cloud-filled sky. A thorny vine spreads over her body, signifying her tie to nature at the same time that very nature threatens to carry her to the heavens. In a paradoxical image, a skeleton clasps a bouquet of lavender flowers while bound with explosives, reminding us of Breton's well-known description of Frida's art as "a ribbon around a bomb."[37] The skeleton is Frida's double, her mirror image and alter ego, as it lies in the exact same position as she on top of the canopy. A delicate explosiveness is expressed, externally in the skeleton, internally in her. In reality, Frida had a papier-mâché skeleton positioned on top of her canopy bed as a constant reminder of her mortality. Her death "dream," which threatens to burst at any moment and from which she can still awaken, reflects her powerful yet tenuous hold on life. She once commented, "They thought I was a Surrealist, but I wasn't. I never painted dreams. I painted my own reality."[38] Frida's reality embraced the death she caught sight of when glancing up at her reflection in the mirror on the underside of her canopy bed.

In *Roots* (1943), Frida lies on the ground as if on a bed, leaning on a pillow and facing us. The left side of her chest is carved open in the shape of a rectangle. Plants grow from this heart cavity and spread their leaves and tendrils onto the cracked, dry earth below. Although this painting depicts the nourishment she offers rather than receives, it contains an ominous quality, like that in *The Dream*, because the crack in the ground could widen to envelop and bury her body. Merging her body with vegetation was Frida's way of creating a lifeline that rooted her in organic unity and helped her feel connected to her surroundings. Such art, with its universal as well as personal symbolism, paved the way for later artists, like Ana Mendieta, who regularly merged their bodies with the earth. For Frida, paintings like this also announced her proximity to death. In her art, she frequently played with death symbols to render them less frightening and to help her prepare for the inevitable.

The last words in Frida's diary reveal her readiness to be released from a life crammed with agony and affliction: "I hope the leaving is joyful—and I hope never to return—FRIDA"[39] Her final drawing is of an angel with enormous green wings and big black boots. It recalls the words she wrote a year earlier under a drawing of an amputated pair of cracked feet: "Feet what do I need them for if I have wings to fly."[40] The drawing and the words are prophetic and seem to confirm that Frida took her own life (with drugs) on Tuesday, July 13, 1954.

In her final painting, Frida filled a canvas with ripe, cut-open watermelons. The pinkish-red interiors symbolize her bleeding flesh and recall all of the damage—physical and emotional, imagined and real—she endured throughout her lifetime. She carved the words "*VIVA LA VIDA*" into one of the melons, epitomizing her characteristic glorification of that which was most tragic in her life. At age forty-seven, Frida made her final toast to life as she welcomed death.

Before she died, Frida requested that her body be cremated, explaining that she had spent far too much of her life lying down and did not envision the prone position as restful, even in the grave. She probably wanted that reviled body to turn to ash. As with her accident and her final exhibition, Frida's cremation ceremony became a grand spectacle that united the life and death of this amazing woman. The cremation was well attended and included Diego, family, friends, members of the Mexican Communist Party, luminaries of the art world, and hundreds of guests, all of them willing to pay their homage in the rain. As the body began to move toward the oven, the mob grabbed Frida's hands and clung to them, refusing to let go of this woman who had come to symbolize Mexico, which was in a state of transition during the years she produced the majority of her art. Indeed, Frida's seemingly private self-portraits were also allegories of Mexico's public search for a utopian social body in its embattled post-Revolution state.[41] The horde threw itself on top of Frida's body and snatched the rings off her fingers.

Finally set free from the hysterical throng, Frida's body traveled toward the sweltering oven. As it crossed the threshold to the furnace, the intense heat forced the body to sit up as if of its own volition. At the same time, her hair burst into flames and encircled her face like a golden halo. She appeared to be smiling. With characteristic *alegría,* Frida—sunflower, angel, madonna, and martyr, *La Baillarinita*—forever defied the line between reality and performance and between life and death.[42]

5
Carolee Schneemann: Feminine Erotics

They're afraid I'll pull down my paints . . . you know . . . They suspect I get messages from my cunt and want to exhibit them.

—Carolee Schneemann

THIS CHAPTER DIFFERS FROM THE OTHER chapters in the book in that it is based on an interview I conducted with Carolee Schneemann on June 7, 2003, at a conference entitled, *Art Matters: Dialogues between Analysts and Artists.*[1] The conference took place at Mohank Mountain, New York, and was sponsored by the Regional Council of Psychoanalytic Societies. The interview was accompanied by slides of Ms. Schneemann's work. Since I gave her my questions in advance, some of her answers were prepared prior to the actual interview. I have inserted brief descriptions in brackets of several of the pieces she showed where I believed the reader could benefit from further clarification of the visual material.

Carolee Schneemann's (b. 1939) oeuvre has largely, but not exclusively, focused on feminine sexuality and erotics. It is best known for the instrumental role she played in launching nude female performance art in the 1960s and in advocating the validity of female sensual pleasure. Many consider her assertion of an unequivocal embodied female presence as helping pave the way for a number of artists, such as Marina Abramovic, Ana Mendieta, Karen Finley, Cindy Sherman, and Janine Antoni, who later became known for using their bodies in their work.

The purpose of my interview was to delve into some of the psychological dynamics present in Schneemann's creative process. Her openness, eloquence, and psychological sophistication offer a rare glimpse into the mind of an exciting artist who pioneered revolutionary changes in the art world at a specific time and place in American culture. It also reveals some intimate, personal layers of meaning and motivation that help enhance the appreciation of her oeuvre.

INTERVIEW

DK: *I'd like to begin by contextualizing your work and emphasizing that at the time you came onto the art scene in the mid-1960s, it was a scene dominated by male artists of a specific kind. Minimalism and pop art were at their peak. You clearly offered an alternative to the clean, cerebral surfaces these men were displaying. Your performances at the time took place in environments depicting an emotional landscape created by you, environments filled with raw sexuality and violence (or at least rage). Your work,* Meat Joy, *is especially salient here in its introduction of messiness into the artistic discourse. (Half-clad men and women frolicked about and smeared themselves with blood, chickens, and fish.) Messiness, of course, had been present in the abstract expressionist canvases of Jackson Pollock, but you brought that into a nonabstract, very physical and present world of performance. Suddenly the art world was filled with blood and guts, penises and vaginas. It is as if a Pandora's box had been opened and the id was liberated. How do you see yourself in the art historical context in which you came onto the scene? Were you, like Freud, someone who felt obliged to disturb the sleep of mankind by confronting, and having others confront, what they prefer to avoid?*

CS: Freud represented one of the megaliths that I needed to "penetrate" and disturb in

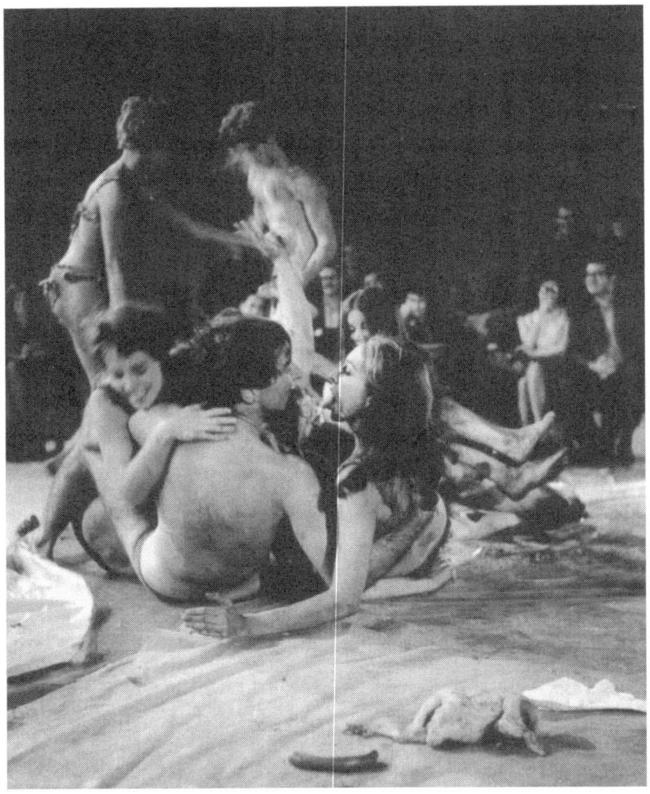

26. Carolee Schneemann, *Meat Joy,* 1964. Performance London: raw fish, chickens, sausages, wet paint, plastic, rope, paper scrap. Photo: Charles Rotenberg. Courtesy of the artist.

terms of the knowledge surrounding the belief systems of my college years that young women can be gifted but have no authority, and that we would have never been given a confirmation of our full potentiality. . . . Paintings from my first years of college were considered "impossible" but they introduce the complexity and visual rhythms, which will persist, as well as an insistence on momentum that characterizes all works. And I will ask you to follow these aspects both viscerally and structurally. During my first years in New York City, I find an abandoned fur cutters' loft on 29th Street and begin to build these large painting constructions—that have motorized parts. Within this intensified dimensionality, I activate a series of photographs, *Eye Body,* in 1963—an extended collage, which integrates fragments of photographs, mirrors, wood, painting, and motorized umbrellas. In 1963 the use of my nude body was a source of consternation. The *Eye Body* photographic sequence was considered narcissistic, exhibitionist. [*Eye Body,* one of Schneemann's first performance works, features the artist nude as she interacts erotically with various studio props and her own paintings and constructions. She covered herself with paint, grease, chalk, ropes, and plastic to explore the image values of her flesh as material.] The principle of embodiment, the extension of the self as a material—in a sense to obliterate the self and to turn the self into a collage—was not understood. My intention was contrary to most cultural interpretations at the time. This work evolved as a constant series of actions, of spontaneous physical engagements photographed by my inspiring friend, the Icelandic painter Érro.

A further layer of my process is the degree to which my works are generated by dreams (I have always wanted to have a chance to *enlarge* that aspect within a psychoanalytic context). The dreams are transferred to drawing just between waking and sleeping—a synthesia. If the need persists to continue drawings, they may lead to a dimensional work to be realized.

If you go back to your original question of what sustained my work I would claim a combination of joy as an artist, joy in my personal life, and an underlying outrage that this idealized historic art world would be so constrained, exclusionary of women artists, and subject to political machinations.

Central to my struggle as a young artist was surrounding cultural exclusion. The neutral pronoun did not enter common usage until the mid to late 1970s—due to the then determined concentrated efforts of feminist cultural analysis. In my college years I was outraged by the linguistic masculinization of all texts: "Man and His Images," "The Artist and His Materials," "Every student will remove *his* car from in front of the art building." I was automatically a girl gender criminal, because I didn't think that "He must empty his locker" really meant me. At the same time my creative essence was also denied its erotic core: there was no female genital sexuality . . . women's explicit sexuality belonged either to medical issues or to pornography. My lived experience was taboo, occluded.

DK: *Freud wrote that the ego is first and foremost a body ego, yet much of psychoanalysis (except for people like Didieu Anzieu) seems to have moved away from that body. You have said that you locate thought in your body and* *it is clear that you have tried in your art to correct for the displacement of physicality in many of our theories. The one psychoanalytic influence I found in your writing is Wilhelm Reich. Although Reich's emphasis on the body and its orgasms is a natural fit for you, could you please comment more specifically on how Reich influenced you and your work?*

CS: Reich's writings were a revelation from which my original partner (since college), James Tenney, and I would read to each other. Our shared intellectual and creative struggles were mutually inspiring. Jim's emotional support was crucial to my envisioning difficult work; I had no sense of whether or not my explored images could actually alter my culture or not. All that was quite unknown. In *Fuses* (1965–68), my self-shot [silent] erotic film [with companion, Tenny], the camera was situated in the way that women were portrayed in porno films. The camera, a wind-up 16mm Bolex, was tied up to the lamp, sometimes kicked off the bed . . . The editing took four years. Reading Reich inspired me to feel that I could examine images of heterosexual pleasure, the embodied sensuousness central to all my visual work. Our observant cat, Kitch, in her shameless regard offered permission to gather erotic interchange. *Fuses* was also a homage to Jim, (composer, pianist, conductor) whose music enriched our daily life and influenced the time structures of my films.

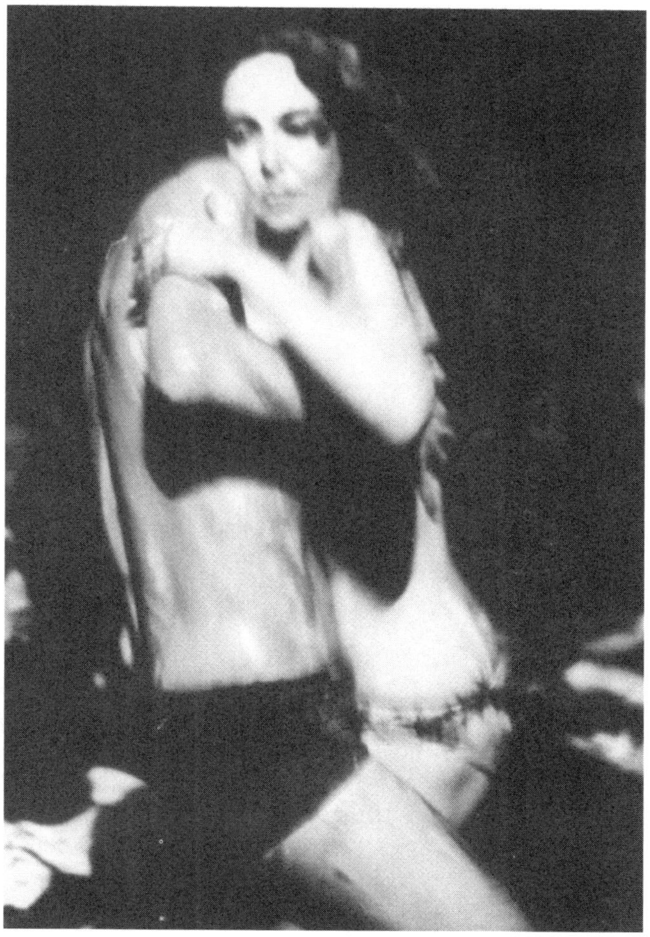

27. Carolee Schneemann, *Meat Joy,* 1964. Performance: raw fish, chickens, sausages, wet paint, plastic, rope, paper scrap. Photo: Harold Chapman. Courtesy of the artist.

DK: *My next question has a few parts. I would like to speak to you about pleasure because much of your work seems to celebrate pleasure, especially female sexual pleasure. Freud's purified pleasure ego or the French concept of jouissance, which has no direct translation because the English word, "enjoyment," does not carry the sexually orgasmic connotation that the French does, seems relevant here.*

Unlike American psychoanalysis, I think that the theories of French feminists, like Helene Cixous and Luce Irigaray, can be more easily applied to your work. Irigaray, for example, writes of women as the sex which is not one (ce sex qui n'en est pas un)—in other words, the sex that has been erased (in psychoanalysis and elsewhere), but also the sex whose zones of pleasure are not singular nor restricted to one part of the body as in the male, but plural, multiple. Your visibility as a woman with a body and a strong and positive degree of sexuality clearly makes the female sex one that cannot be ignored or erased, and your performances showing the pleasuring of that body in a variety of ways illustrate the multiplicity of its pleasure as well as its complexity and diffuseness.

You have said on several occasions that you have a body that is unconflicted about its pleasure. As psychoanalysts, we would be very interested to hear what you think contributed to that healthy (and rare) state in you and what forces (personal, political and aesthetic) you believe led you to share that sexuality and pleasure with the public.

CS: Early in life I recognized that there was certain ecstasy (akin to the sacred and holy—

orgasm) involved in creating images within a frame. I discovered this was a place I could go for a "higher" integration of where I was and what I could feel. Drawing and the erotic had this early bond—whenever the adult world would try to inhibit or discourage or confuse me, I would recognize that they were trying to separate these two realms. I was drawing before I knew how to talk—drawing was like breathing for me. All kids draw, but I drew action sequences resembling crude stills from a film. By college I had started keeping notebooks—not only of dream notes, but of dream drawings.

One issue was the permission *to* see. As the daughter of a rural doctor, I grew up seeing firsthand blood and guts, limbs that were injured—there was no editing—when there's an accident, body parts "you're not supposed to see" are sticking out! At a neighbor's farm, I worked in animal husbandry—if you're artificially inseminating a cow, you don't put a drape over it or close your eyes and hope that the syringe finds the right spot . . . And I wanted my father's knowledge of the female body!

As a painter you have to see. Isn't there something in a curved fruit as taboo as human genitals? You were never forbidden to look

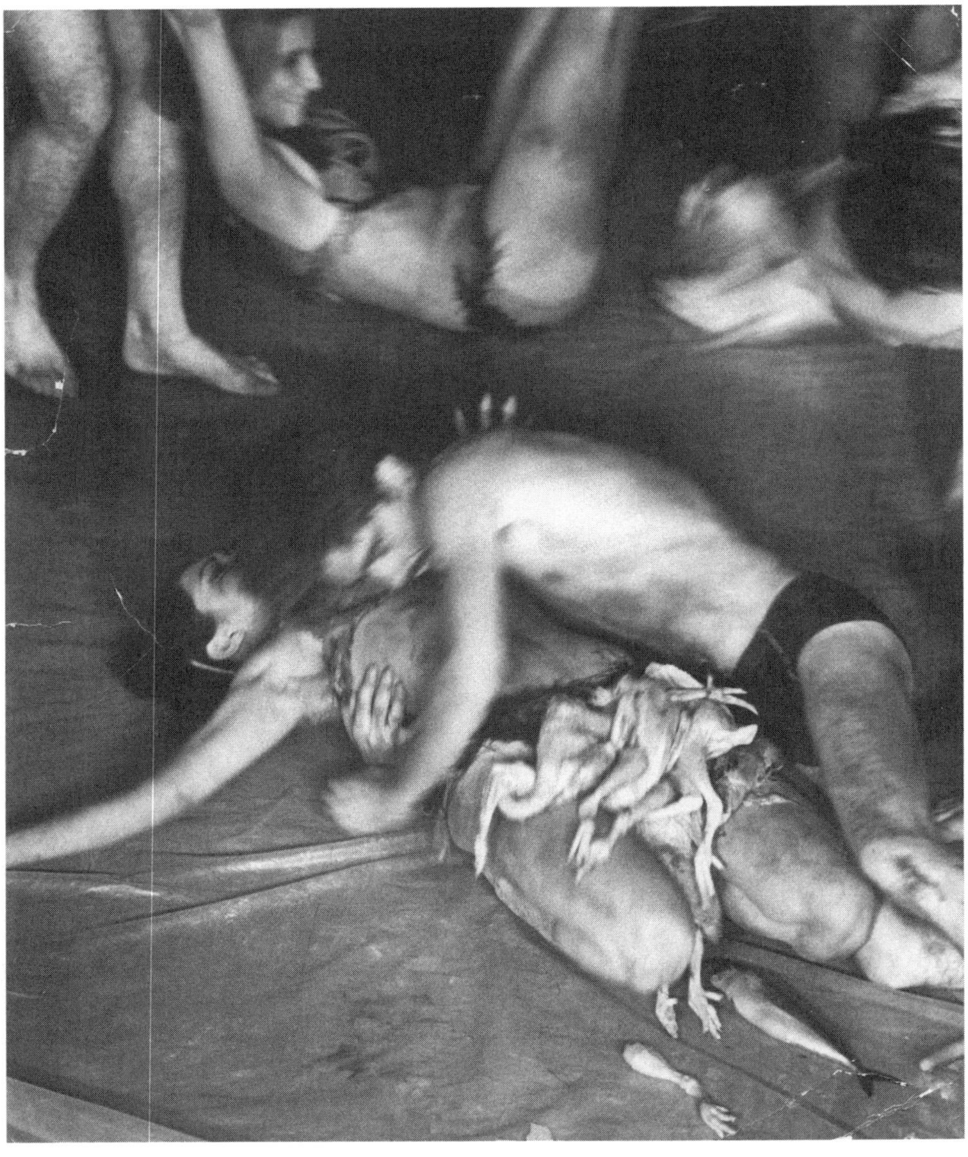

28. Carolee Schneemann, *Meat Joy,* 1964. Performance: raw fish, chickens, sausages, wet paint, plastic, rope, paper scrap. Photo: Al Giese. Courtesy of the artist.

into a concavity or convexity of anything that was animal or mineral or vegetable. Only human fractures were explicit and therefore taboo. So when I made the film [*Fuses*] of my longtime partner and me lovemaking, I wanted to see if the experience of what the film captured would have any correspondence to what I felt—the tactile intimacy. It was almost a Heisenbergian dilemma: will the camera distort everything? (There was no camera person present.)

For instance *Meat Joy* (1964) was an erotic rite that came through a series of very visceral dreams of expanding physical energy—off the canvas, out of the frame. *Meat Joy* developed from dream sensation images gathered in journals stretching back to 1960. By February 1964, more elaborate drawings and notes accumulated as scraps of paper, on the wall over my bed, in tablets. I'd been concentrating on the possibility of capturing interactions between physical/metabolic changes, dream content, and my sensory orientation upon waking: an attempt to view paths between the conscious and unconscious organization of image, pun, double-entendre, masking, and the release of random memory fragments (often well-defined sounds, instructions, light, textures, weather, places from the past, solutions to problems). I found the transition between dream and waking, envisioning and practical function, became so attenuated that it was often difficult to leave the loft for my job or errands. My body streamed with currents of imagery: the interior directives varied from furtive to persistent: either veiling or intensely illuminating ordinary events.

Meat Joy has the character of an erotic ritual —excessive, indulgent, a celebration of flesh as material: raw fish, chickens, sausages, wet paint, transparent plastic, rope, brushes, paper scrap. Its propulsion is toward the ecstatic—shifting and turning between tenderness, wildness, precision, abandon—qualities which could at any moment be sensual, comic, joyous, repellent. Physical equivalences are enacted as a psychic and imagistic stream in which the layered elements mesh and gain intensity by the energy complement of the audience (They were seated on the floor as close to the performance area as possible, encircling, resonating.) Our proximity heightened the sense of community, transgressing the polarity between performer and audience.

In precisely determined patterns, vertical, diagonal, and horizontal shafts of movement and lighting cut through the overall circular structures of *Meat Joy.* The popular songs occurring throughout most sequences are "circular" in their thematic and rhythmic three-minute disc-spun durations, and they introduce a literal, historic time—popular "ritual" sound centering the sensory flow. Tapes of Paris street sounds were superimposed: the cries and clamorings of Rue de Seine vendors selling fish, chickens, vegetables, and flowers beneath my hotel window where I first composed the actual performance score. These shouts dominate a layering of traffic noise, and displace the songs' recognizable continuity, interfering with their associative range.

DK: *This is where I believe your art was so innovative. Other women artists used their own naked bodies in their work to make statements about the female body, its genitalia, and the desire to be seen beyond their attractiveness or ability to procreate. Your work goes one step farther by emphasizing and depicting female pleasure as a compelling reality in the present rather than a means to an end. In* Fuses, *for instance, you filmed yourself with your lover having sex. Your aim in this film was to emphasize its contrast to pornography, which is characterized by a voyeuristic/phallic mode, by showing equality and mutuality in a sexual encounter between two subjects, an encounter in which the woman—you—both receive and give pleasure. There is a daring freedom and what at times resembles a "carnival" of female desire and sexuality in your oeuvre whose ideological aim, I believe, was at least partly to release women's sexuality from its repressive chains. You once said, "I made a gift of my body to other women: giving our bodies back to ourselves." By giving women back their bodies; so to speak, were you also trying to liberate their desire?*

CS: It was a conscious intention within great uncertainty as to the degree to which my overt imagery might effect cultural change. All that was unknown at the time. My creative risk taking is "privileged" by not having been abused, not having been overtly suppressed—but implicitly suppressed by a culture that was telling me my lived experience was insignificant, inappropriate—it should be *masculinized.* My resistance joined those of women moving against the roles predetermined by masculist culture.

DK: *As you know, I've written a lot about women's self representation in art. One finding I've found to be both fascinating and sad is that each of the women I have studied—these are women who use themselves and their bodies as primary subject matter in their art—has been labeled exhibitionistic and narcissistic. The more beautiful the woman and the more nudity is involved, the more these labels are directed at them and associated with them. What do you say to those who accuse you of using your nude body in your work as a sign of your narcissism and exhibitionism?*

CS: I was always shocked by that. Amazed and bewildered. In 1963 with *Eye Body,* I proposed the question: could the nude female artist represent both the image and image maker? My works created confusion between the erotic and the pornographic by not following predictive models—for instance the male cum shot, the very strict expectation of pornographic films. *Fuses* is collaged, layered and very particularly edited so that whenever there is a genital close-up of the male genital, that will dissolve into a shot of the female genital, and vice versa. The viewers' latent attitudes are constantly having to be re-shifted. When *Fuses* was featured at the Cannes Film Festival, some men in the front rows began slicing seats with razor blades, a rampage of disappointment that the film was not what they had hoped, predictably pornographic, that it was actually something else. It was quite bewildering to witness.

If I were short and fat, I couldn't have subverted the meanings I wished to since that type of body does not disrupt the ideal because it is not seen as part of it. So, part of this aesthetic contradiction has to do with the chance of having had an "ideal" body and using this as an instrument to question: can this ideal body enter the expectations of my culture and really disrupt these expectations by insisting that I occupy authority as both the image and the image maker? That this body will not be reabsorbed into the male expectations. But it was a question that I could not yet know the answer to.

DK: *I'd like to ask you about your creative process. You have said that your dreams have served as inspiration and actual direction for much of your work. Can you say something about the relationship between dreams and creativity? Do you think of your work as driven or guided by the unconscious? If so, how do you translate that raw material into more consciously directed production?*

CS: Another answer was no dream, no *work.* A dream leads to two strands; one is direct visualization of the drawings, notes, and scraps of information and then realization. So for instance a small troublesome drawing, *The Message,* was a simple image scrawled upon waking up, where I had had a dream of a figure extracting a scroll from her vagina. The dream message: "there is a message from within." Of course the image related to my research into archaic aspects of vulvic depiction, Paleolithic inscriptions, sculptures. Over time this little drawing kept coming back . . . and telling me: if you are going to follow the implications of that dream, then you are going to have to bring to life that dream. Which was certainly the last thing on earth that I wanted to do—but such is the power of the dream, if it is a compelling and convincing one. The dream is the work that I have to follow. Sometimes it is a very bald instruction. For a 1995 projection system *Mortal Coils* [an aesthetic and physical mourning installation/ritual that used the gallery as a vehicle and container for grief over fifteen of the artist's friends who had died within the two previous years, including Hannah Wilke and John Cage, whose faces were projected onto the gallery's walls], a dream solved a huge museum installation problem with a very strict voice declaring: "*6 rpm! 6 rpm!*" That was a mechanical dream instruction! It meant that the ropes that I had suspended had to be mechanized, to turn, to coil from 6rpm motors! [Fifteen ropes dangled from the ceiling and revolved slowly, their ends wiping away flour on the floor, in a gesture symbolic of the wearing away of memories and life.] Once that was constructed the entire projection system became powerful. What else about a dream?

DK: *The unconscious. . . .*

CS: It demands a lot of processing. Dreams are. . . . Mostly they are just processing what

I call the daily junk of everything. My job as an artist is to try to protect the threshold of the emerging unconscious, its helpfulness to my creative process. I can undertake research, meditations to encourage stronger psychic information, which in turn nourishes the potential dream directions.

DK: *It appears that you wish your audience to also move beyond simple observing of an artwork and, in some way, participate, feel, and respond viscerally to your work. How do you conceive of the role of the spectator in your work? What effect do you wish to have on your audience?*

CS: That's tricky. In one aspect I never think of the audience at all because it will confuse and deflect my need for uncertainty, for exploration. I need to think that "no one is there." And once the work has taken its form, I reverse my position and wonder how are they seeing this? What are they thinking? What will I find out from their response? How much resistance will I find, or how much integration into surrounding configurations?

DK: *How have you responded to the reactions that you have received over the years? There have been such a range of reactions.*

CS: My work is often censored in a network of reactionary demonization and an economic censorship. So that the work—its multiple manifest actual forms—is rarely financially supported, rarely entering the chain of collectors, museums. Images of the works belong to an intellectual art history—works are widely reproduced and written about and in that way become an influence. I am shocked when a work is censored. I always imagine that I haven't done a shocking work, but introduced formal properties or issues, which my own culture will see is a next obvious step and would be very pleased to absorb. That usually happens, if I am lucky, after a lag time of fifteen years.

DK: *You are most well known for what has been labeled "freewheeling body art." Yet, I see that your art, as much as it involves sexuality, is often fused with violence, rage, and the underside of humanity. I am not just referring to* Viet-Flakes, *your work on the Lebanon war or* Mortal Coils, *all of which clearly deal with violence and death. One could say that your art brings together Eros and Thanatos as postulated by Freud. Can you say something about these two elements in your work and how you see them as connected or disconnected?*

CS: Expressions such as "free wheeling," "messy," or "rage" have been used critically to reduce the structure, the formal properties of the work. My works—films, videos, installations—remain of concern, because they maintain a very coherent formal structure within which taboo imagery and issues evolve.

DK: *I didn't mean that as derogatory. The ripping apart and uncovering in your art reveal, I believe, a return to basic instincts—pleasurable and aggressive.*

CS: Certain resistant influences or materials may demand that I find a unique form, a filter. For instance, a video-sculpture responding to the destruction of Palestinian culture, *War Mop,* consists of a thirty-inch TV monitor on which is displayed a continuous video pan through destroyed Palestinian houses. The color is vibrant, bright, the rubble an incredible assault on the senses. Every six minutes a hovering mop on a series of plexiglass cams rises up and then slams down hitting the TV . . . it then again rises up, its cloth strands quivering . . . That political assault provoked research throughout the 1980s. After the recent attacks on the World Trade Center, I was led to photographic processes, enlarging details of falling bodies to configure photographic intimacy as a memorium.

DK: *You are always—as far as I can see—categorized as a feminist artist. Yet, it is interesting that at the height of feminism, while you were doing some of the performances you are most known for—*Meat Joy *and* Interior Scroll *—even some feminist critics had trouble with your work. Can you say something about your relationship to feminism over the years? Do you believe that it is so deeply ingrained in women to be ladylike—i.e., sit with their legs closed—that even ideological feminists have felt provoked by your works in which you display yourself in an active manner as a woman* *who owns her desires and refuses to be merely an object of desire?*

CS: It is complicated, coming in as a pre-feminist. In the sixties, I lacked a supportive community. Early feminist practice required the separatist configurations of the seventies. When women and men collaborated on social and aesthetic conflicts, the men wanted to tell us what our problems were and to solve them! An interesting time—the separatist years. Gender integration was rather fraught throughout the eighties and nineties; male artists struggled to maintain their areas of preeminence while relinquishing their assumption of historic dominance. It has been interesting to observe the male students having to share creative history, to accept creative equity while maintaining "manly" attributes. Now I am often in the position of a teacher having full respect and authority—while when I was a student no woman teacher ever occupied that place. I had no female teachers! My feminism implicitly developed from a sense of negative recognitions, even though I was at Bard College on a full scholarship, full tuition. When I wanted to study de Beauvoir, my philosophy professor, a gracious southerner said: "Honey, why do you want to study the mistress when you can study the master?" I was encouraged to write on Proust, Joyce, Mann. I wasn't allowed to write on Virginia Woolf. (This was the sixties!) I was told that she was a trivializer. Study Proust or Kafka! At the same time, the guy painters stole my paint brushes and they stole my Nicholaides book! ("We need this more then you do.") I was a feminist by life circumstance. Then the extraordinary transformations through the seventies in which research that I had started in a blind and uncertain way in the sixties burgeoned into feminist issues; the sciences, anthropology, philosophy, religion, etymology. The world was transformed, enlivened, deepened *and* inverted. And now we even have female and neutral pronouns! And "vaginal politics" . . .

DK: Can *you say something about the critics, even from within feminism?*

CS: I still experience miserable exclusion by feminist scholars. Until recently my films were almost exclusively written about and analyzed by male film historians. That is peculiar. I don't know what to make of it; I am in the middle of it still.

DK: *Interior Scroll, performed in 1975 and 1977, has become a classic reference piece for feminist performance art. It has always been referred to as a seminal work that celebrated female sexuality but, more importantly, one that brought the female inner space out for all to recognize and contend with. In it, you removed a thirty-six-inch long scroll from inside your vagina and read from it. On one level, it is clear that one purpose of the piece is to deny the all-importance of the phallus by demonstrating that female genitalia exist and can no longer be denied. Yet, some psychoanalysts might say that your creation of a growing phallic shape that extends from your genitals is a perfect example of penis envy and that you, in fact, have thereby transformed yourself into a phallic woman. What do you say to this?*

CS: Oh, I love it! Well you mentioned something earlier that needs translation so I will divert my answer for just a second to warn everyone about transcription, its Freudian slips, and how dangerous it is. I was having an interview with a Swedish historian and she talked about this work, *Interior Scroll.* She said, "I want to know how much it hurt," and I replied, "Oh no, it doesn't hurt." She asked, "Doesn't hurt? but how do you make it fit?" And I replied, "It is a very complex origami with three stages and you can work out the shape . . . you use a lot of cream, you can try different kinds, avocado, gardenia. . . . you know what ever makes the paper smooth." And she said, "Yes, yes but what about the *claws?*" Bewildered I asked, "Claws? What do you mean claws?" And she said, "Of the *Interior Squirrel!*" So talk about projection! Of course *Interior Scroll* followed an unconscious demand to confront Freud's displacement of a vital female genital and of course to challenge the dreaded Lacan and his insistent "lack." To make clear my concept of vulvic space.

So *Interior Scroll* is many things; it is an enormous metaphor. One of the interesting interpretations was made by a Wall Street Banker. He was very shaken by it and he said; "Now I understand my tickertape." So I am

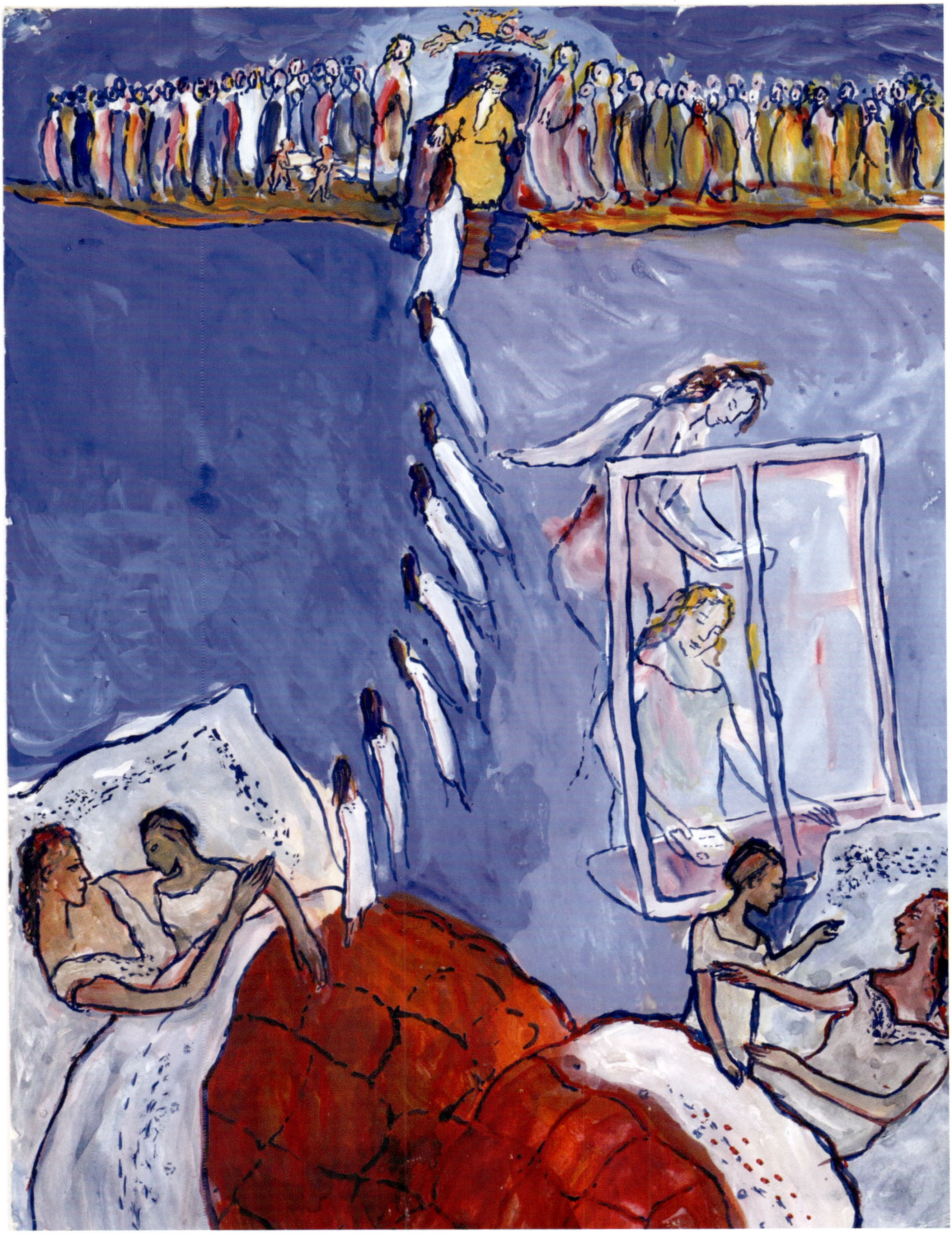

Pl. 1. Charlotte Salomon, from *Life? or Theater?* 1940–42. Gouache, 13 × 10 in. Collection Jewish Historical Museum, Amsterdam. Copyrights Charlotte Salomon Foundation.

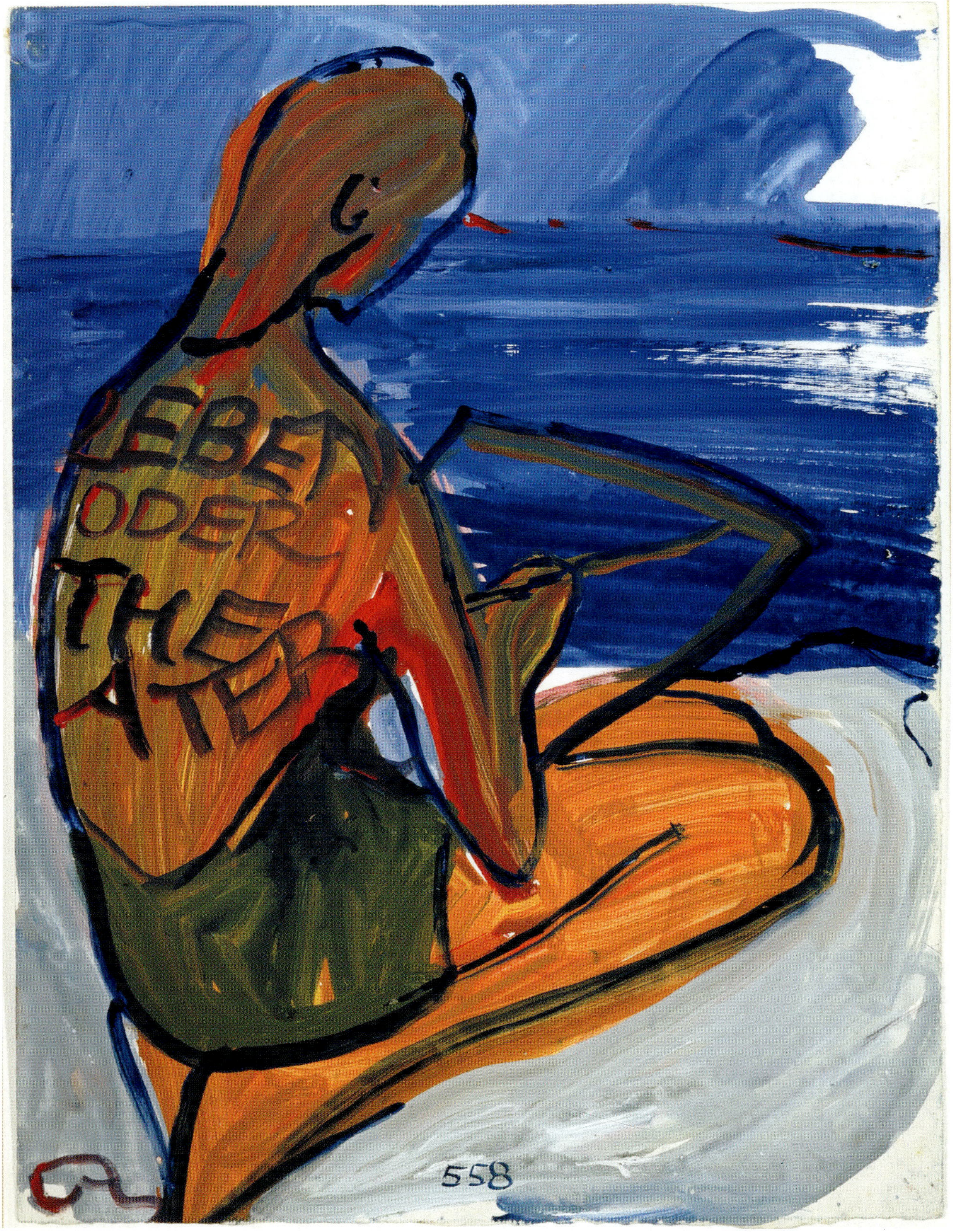

Pl. 2. Charlotte Salomon, from *Life? or Theater?* 1940–42. Gouache, 13 × 10 in. Collection Jewish Historical Museum, Amsterdam. Copyrights Charlotte Salomon Foundation.

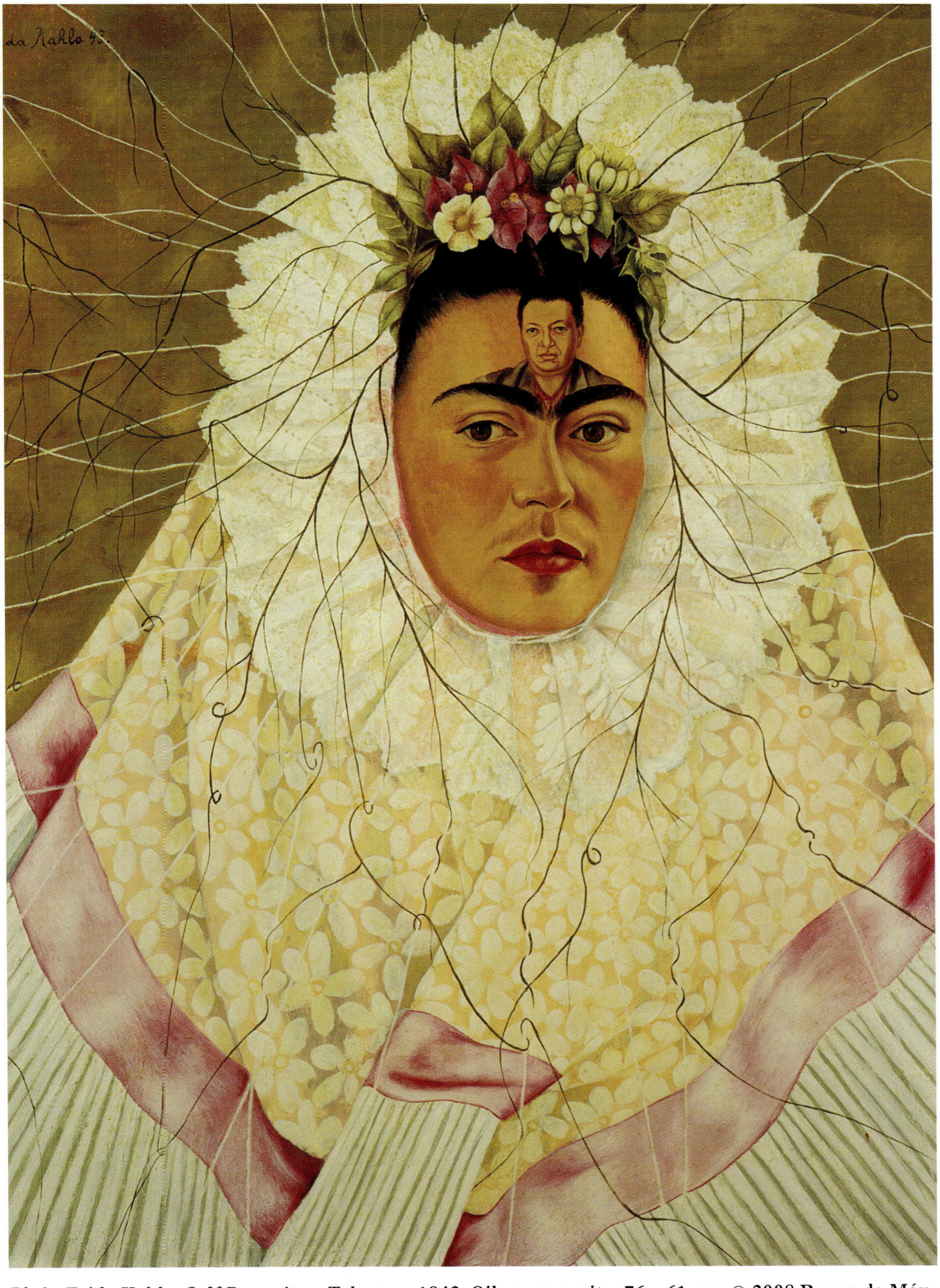

Pl. 3. Frida Kahlo, *Self-Portrait as Tehuana,* 1943. Oil on masonite, 76 × 61 cm. © 2008 Banco de México Diego Rivera and Frida Kahlo Trust, Av. Cinco de Mayo No. 2, Col. Centro, Del. Cuauhtémoc 06059, Mexico, D.F. Photo: Courtesy Rafael Doniz.

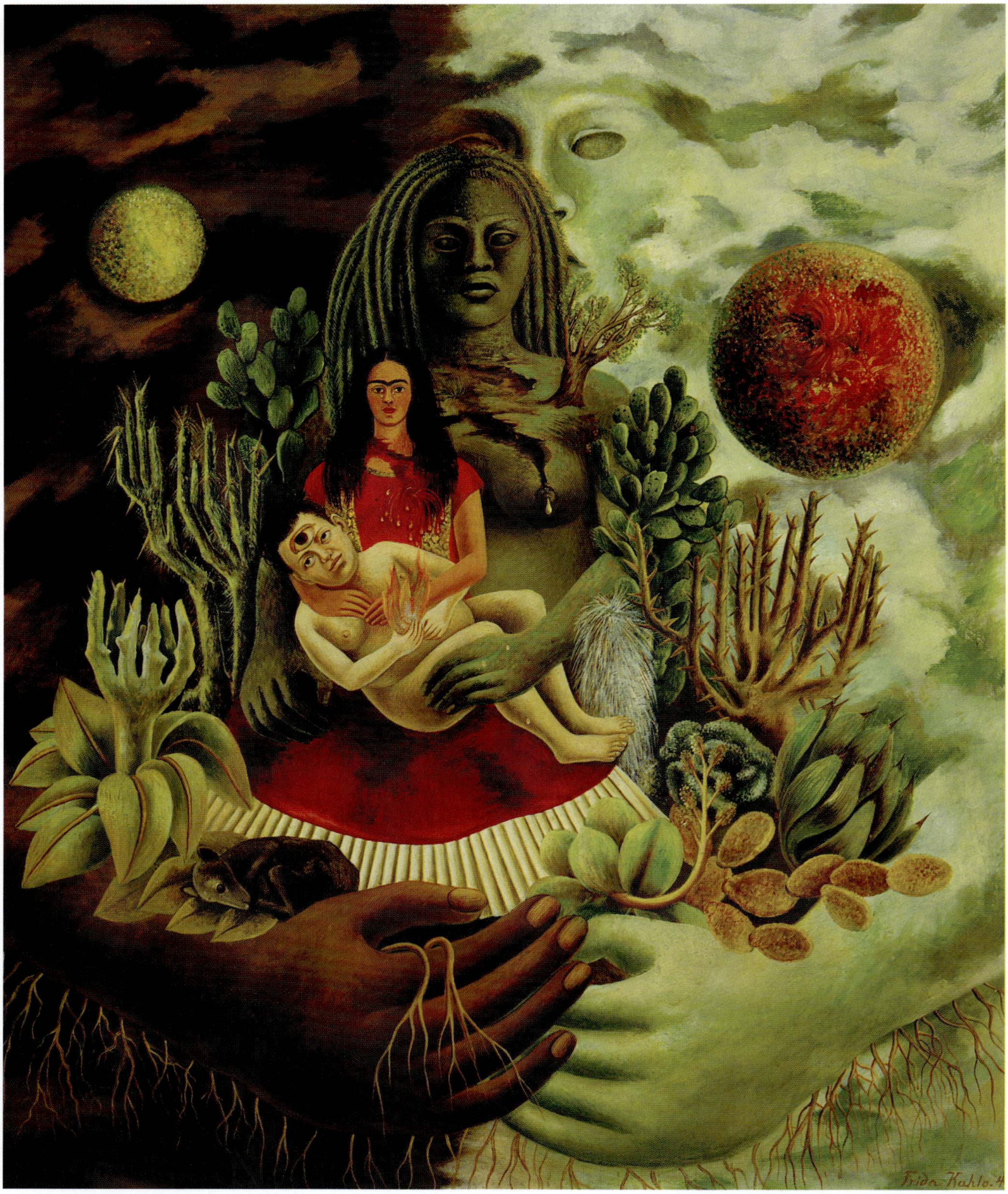

Pl. 4. Frida Kahlo, *The Love Embrace of the Universe, the Earth (Mexico), Diego, Me, and Señor Xolotl,* 1949. Oil on canvas, $27\frac{1}{2} \times 23\frac{7}{8}$ inches. © Banco de México Diego Rivera and Frida Kahlo Trust, Av. Cinco de Mayo No. 2, Col. Centro, Del. Cuauhtémoc 06059, Mexico, D.F. Photo: Courtesy Rafael Doniz.

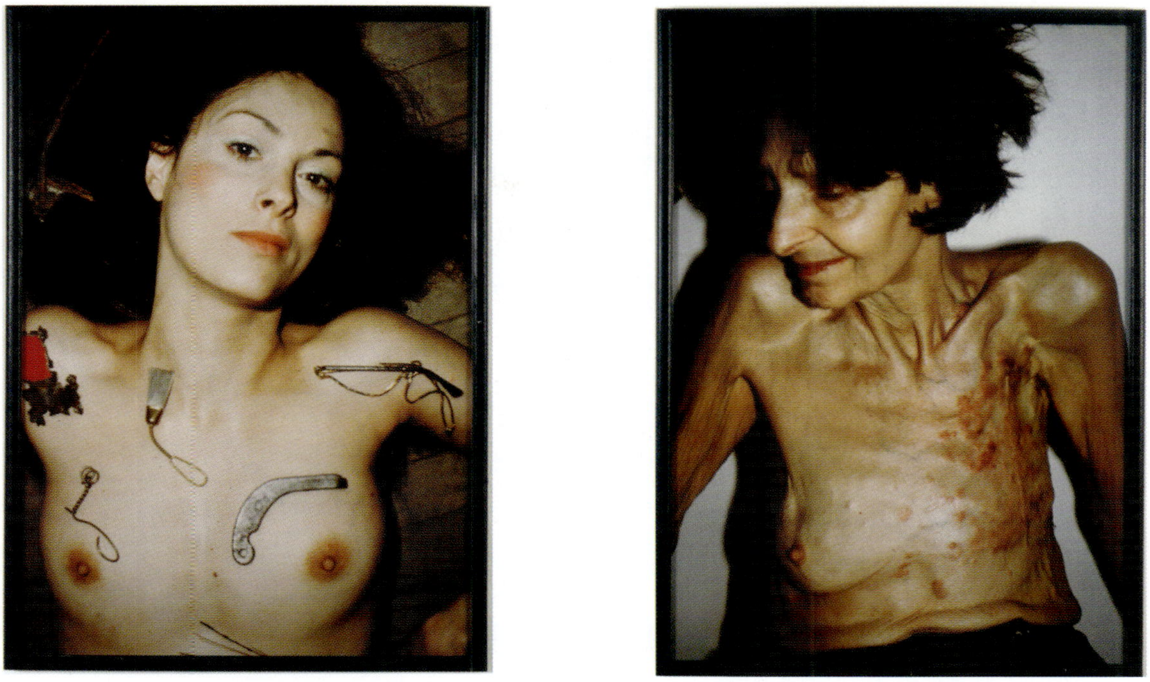

Pl. 5. Hannah Wilke, *So Help Me Hannah Series: Portrait of the Artist with her Mother, Selma Butter,* 1978–81. Cibrachrome diptych. 101,60 × 99,06 cm each. © Marsie, Emanuelle, Damon and Andrew Scharlatt/Licensed by VAGA, New York, NY. Photo: Courtesy Ronald Feldman Fine Arts, New York.

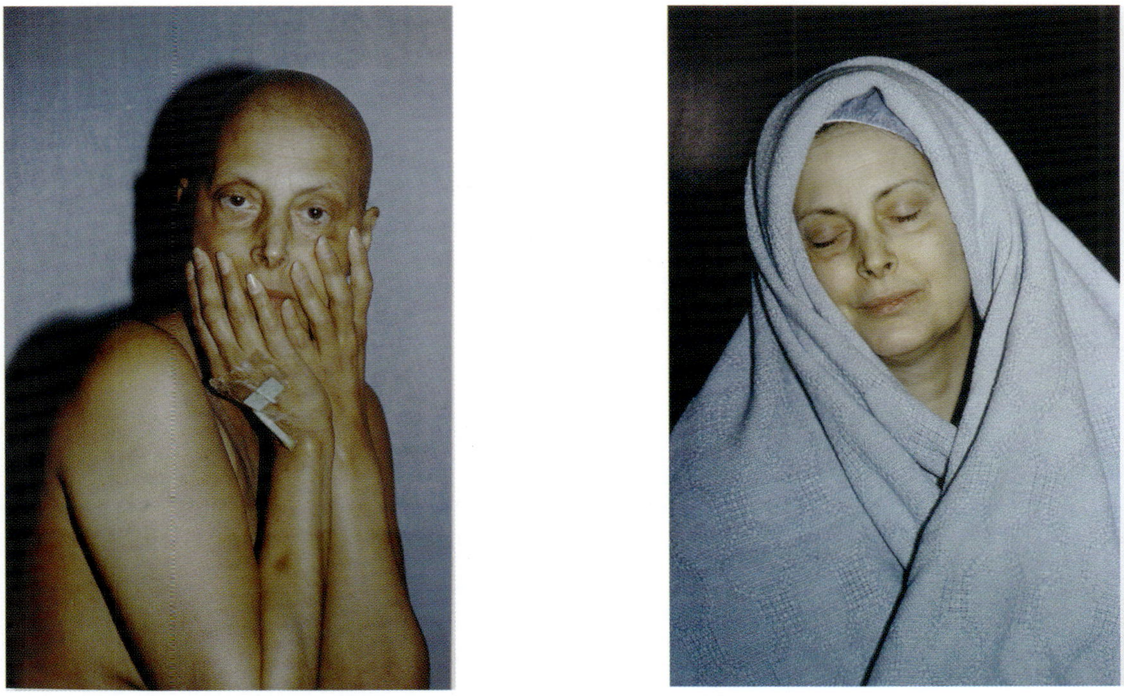

Pl. 6. Hannah Wilke, Performalist Self-Portrait with Donald Goddard. From *Intra-Venus Series # 4.* July 26, 1992/ February 19, 1992. Chromagenic supergloss prints. Two panels: $71\frac{1}{2} \times 47\frac{1}{2}$ inches each. Courtesy Donald and Helen Goddard and Ronald Feldman Fine Arts, New York.

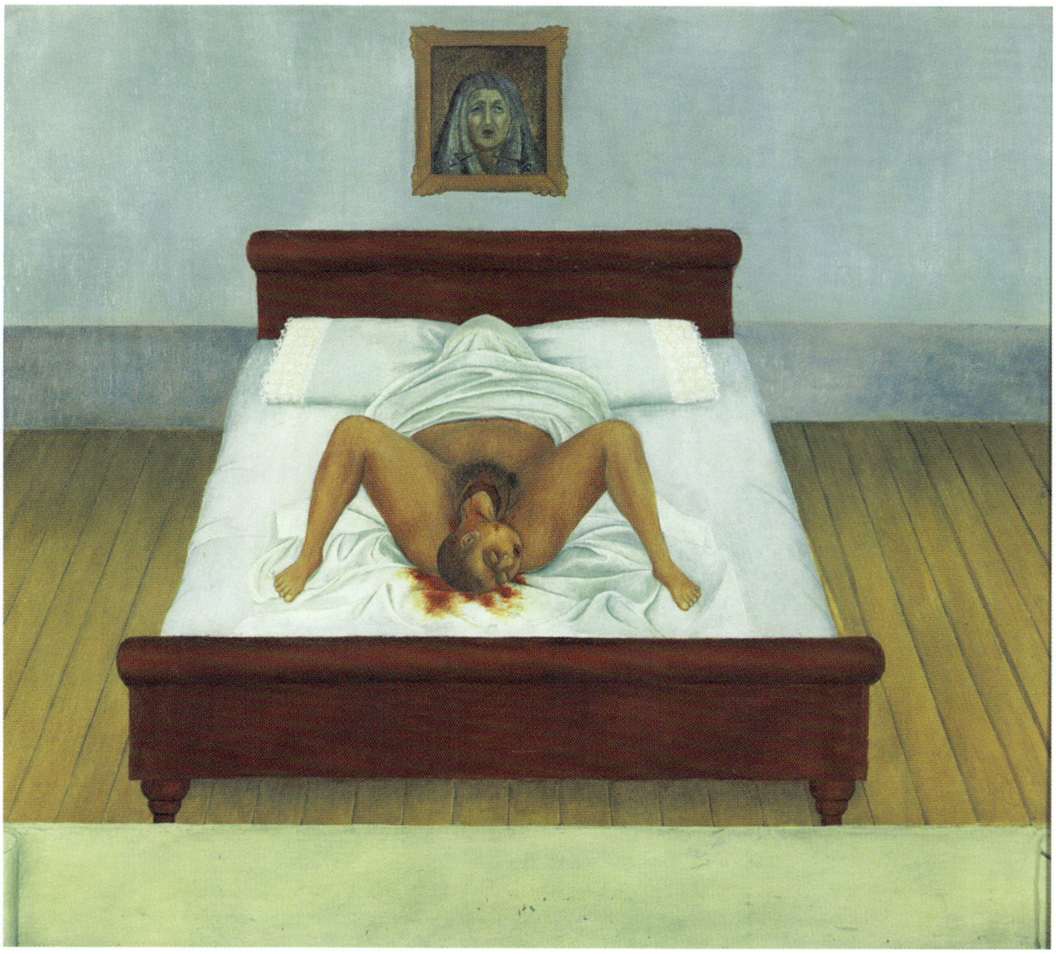

Pl. 7. Frida Kahlo (1910–54). *My Birth,* 1932 (oil on copper). © Private Collection/Photo: Jorge Contreras Chacel. The Bridgeman Art Library. © Banco de México Diego Rivera and Frida Kahlo Trust, Av. Cinco de Mayo No. 2, Col. Centro, Del. Cuauhtémoc 06059, Mexico, D.F. Photo: Courtesy Bridgeman Art Library International.

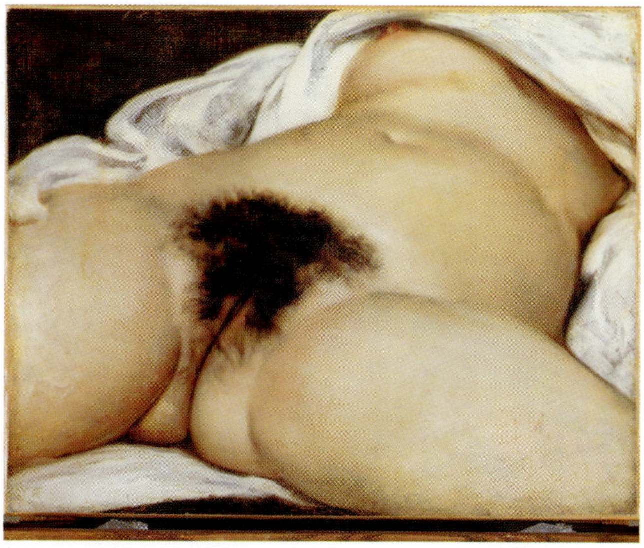

Pl. 8. Gustav Courbet, *L'Origine du Monde* [Origin of the World], 1866. Oil on canvas. Photo: Hervé Lewandowski. 55 × 46 cm. Musée d'Orsay, Paris, France. Réunion des Musées Nationaux/Art Resource, NY.

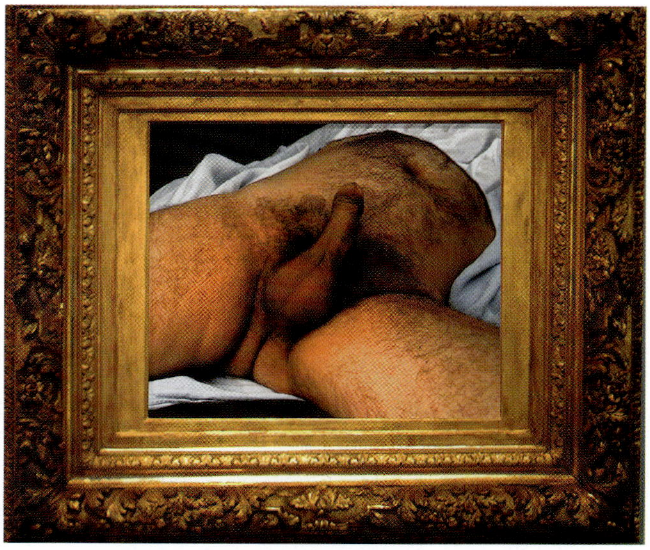

Pl. 9. Orlan, *L'Origine de la Guerre* [Origin of War], 1989. 55 × 46 cm. Cibrachrome stuck on a piece of aluminum. © 2009 Artists Rights Society (ARS), New York/ASAGP, Paris. Photo: Courtesy of the artist.

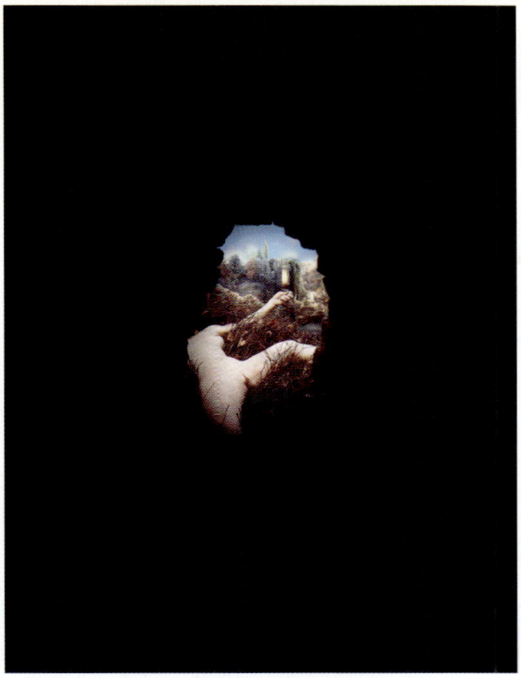

Pl. 10. Marcel Duchamp, *Etants Donnés: 1 La chute d'eau, 2 le gaz d'eclairage [Given: 1 The Waterfall, 2 The Illuminating Gas),* 1946–66. Mixed media assemblage: wooden door, bricks, velvet, wood, leather stretched over an armature of metal, twigs, aluminum, iron, glass, Plexiglas, linoleum, cotton, electric lights, gas lamp (Bec Auer type), motor, etc., 7 feet 11½ inches × 70 inches. Philadelphia Museum of Art: Gift of the Cassandra Foundation, 1969.

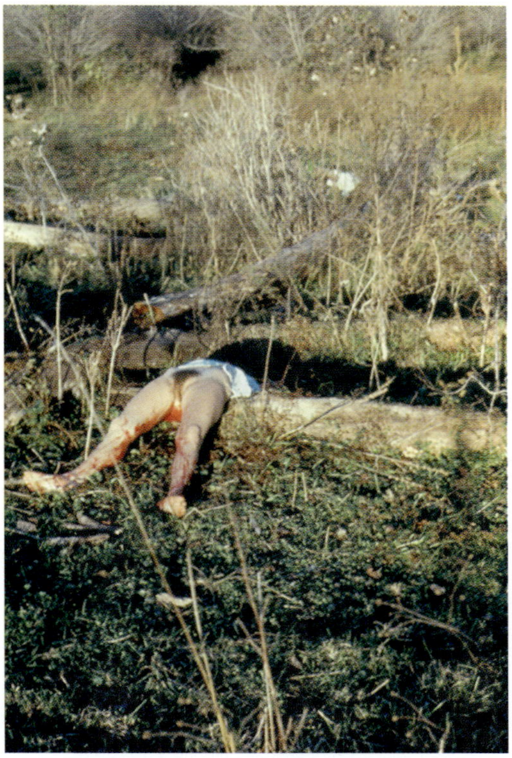

Pl. 11. Ana Mendieta, *Untitled* (Rape Performance), 1973. Estate print: 1993. Color photograph. 10 × 8 in (25.4 × 20.3 cm). © The Estate of Ana Mendieta Collection. Courtesy Galerie Lelong, New York.

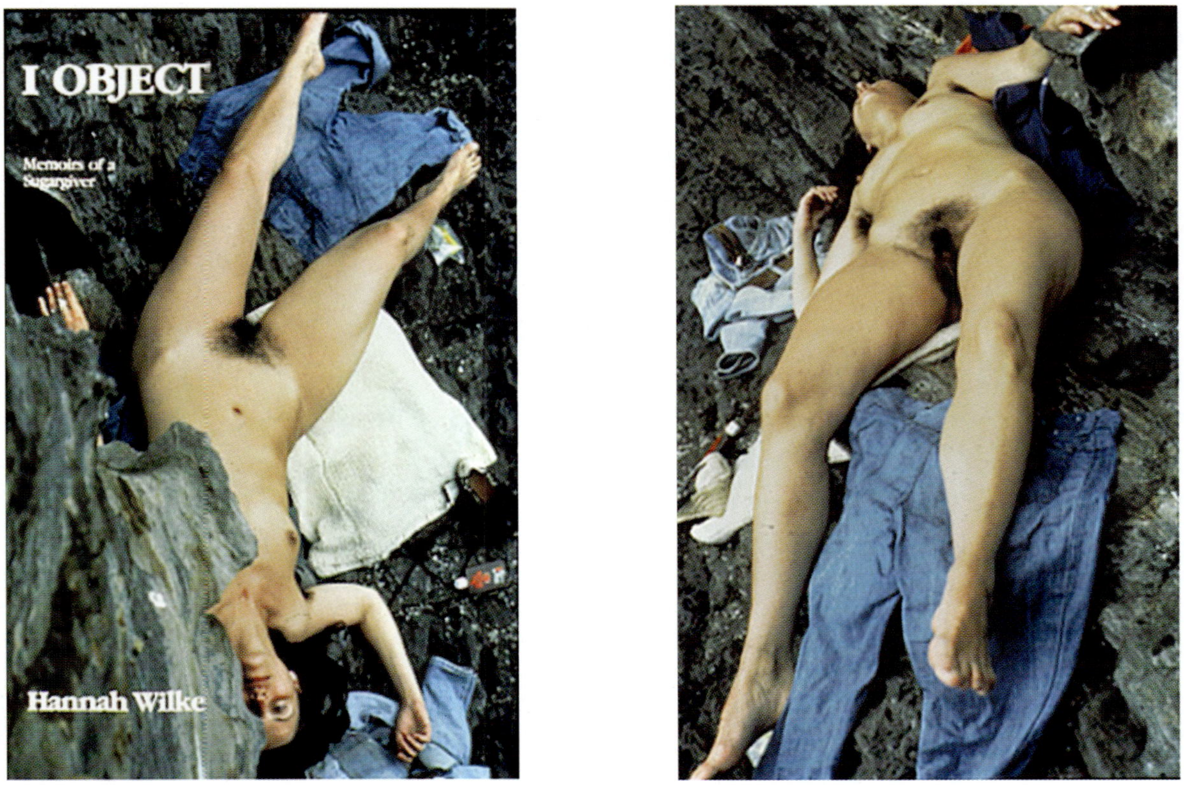

Pl. 12. Hannah Wilke, *I Object: Memoirs of a Sugargiver,* 1977–78. Performalist self-portraits with Richard Hamilton. Cibrachrome diptych. 60,96 × 40,64 cm each. © Marsie, Emanuelle, Damon and Andrew Scharlatt/Licensed by VAGA, New York, NY. Photo: Courtesy Ronald Feldman Fine Arts, New York.

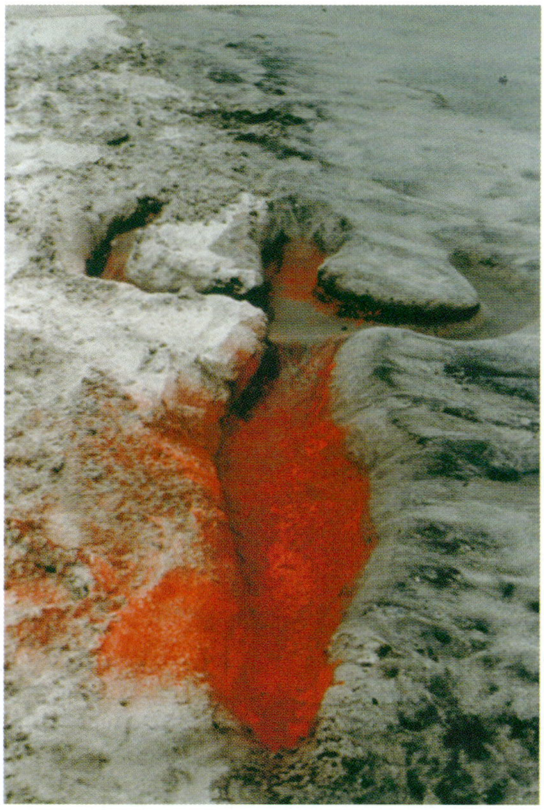

Pl. 13. Ana Mendieta, *Silueta* Works in Mexico, 1976. Estate print: 1991. Color photograph. 16 × 20 in (40.6 × 50.8 cm). © The Estate of Ana Mendieta Collection. Courtesy Galerie Lelong, New York.

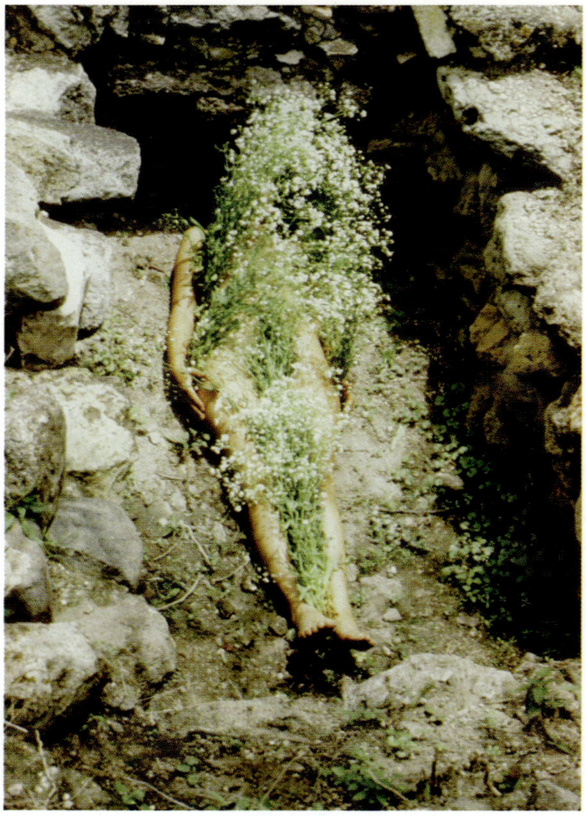

Pl. 14. Ana Mendieta, *Imagen de Yagul*, 1973. Lifetime color photograph. 20 × 13¼ (50.8 × 33.7 cm). © The Estate of Ana Mendieta Collection. Courtesy Galerie Lelong, New York.

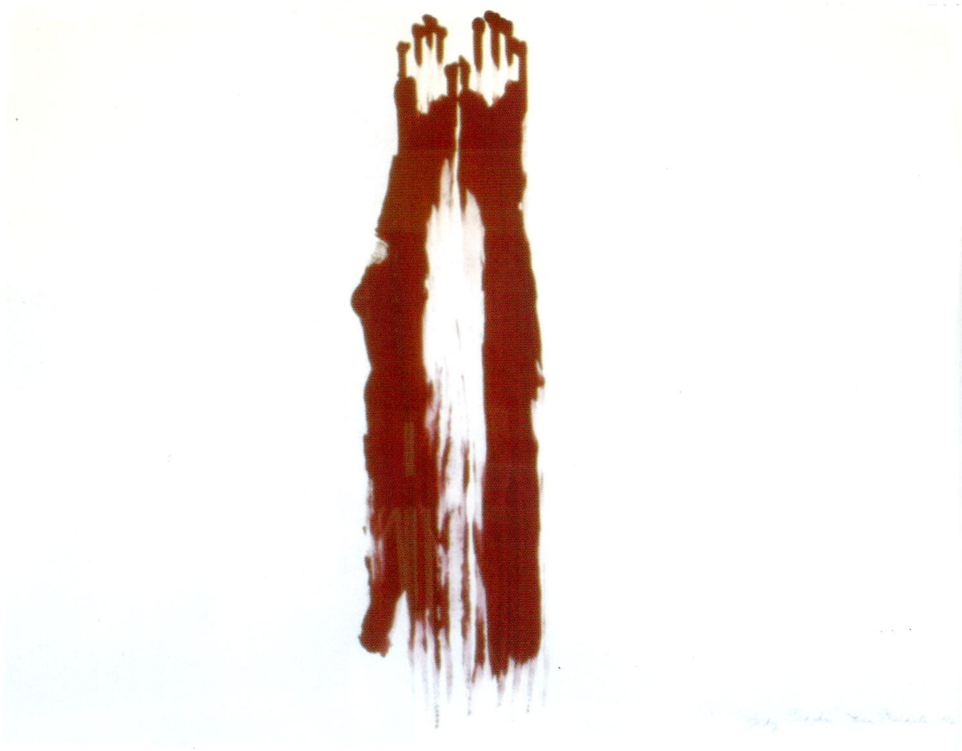

Pl. 15. Ana Mendieta, *Rastros Corporales* [Body Tracks], 1982 (detail). Blood on tempura paint and paper. Three works, each 38 × 50 in (96.5 × 127 cm). © The Estate of Ana Mendieta Collection. Courtesy Galerie Lelong, New York.

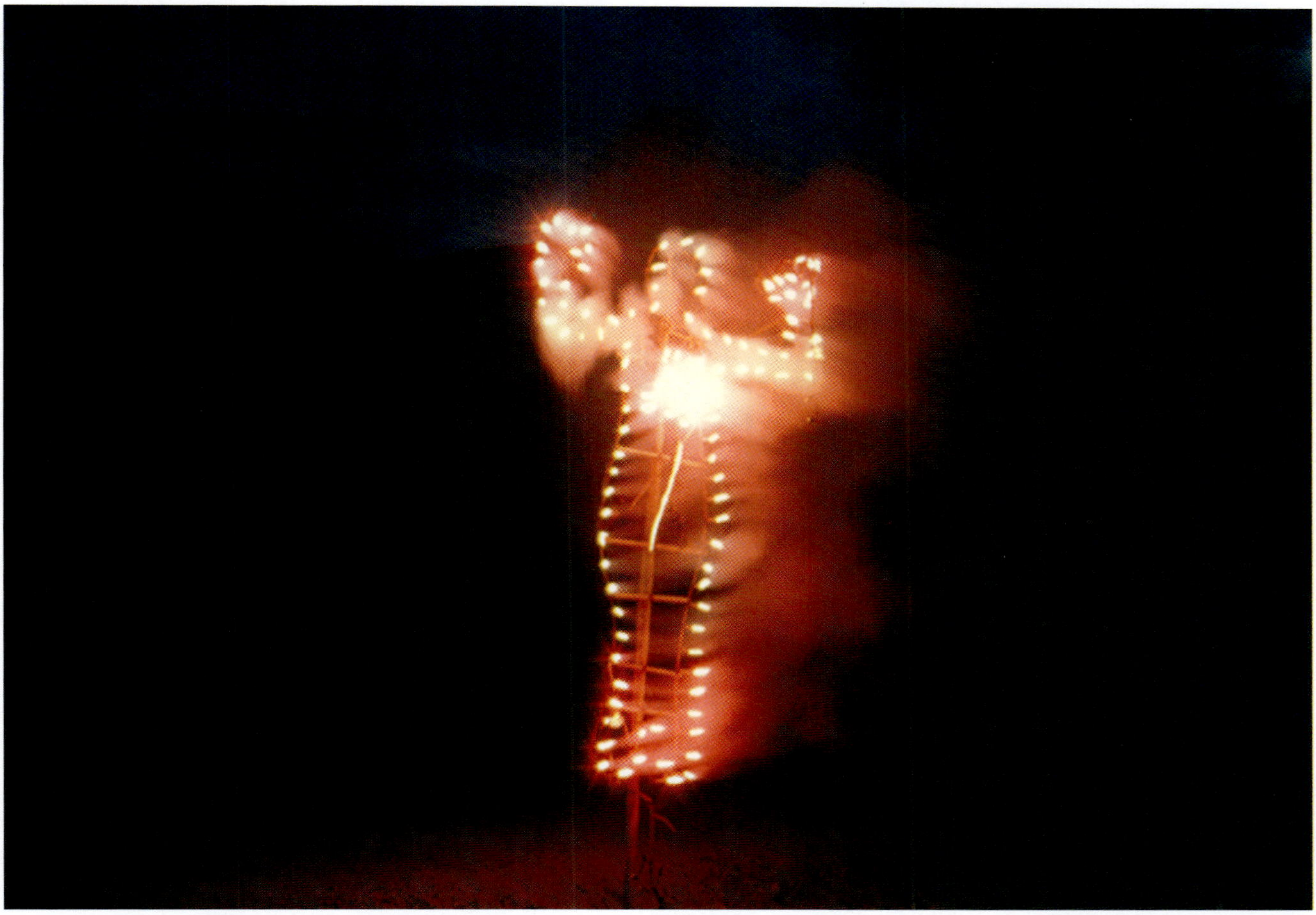

Pl. 16. Ana Mendieta, *Ánima, Silueta de Cohetes* [Soul, Silhouette of Fireworks], 1976. © The Estate of Ana Mendieta Collection. Courtesy Galerie Lelong, New York.

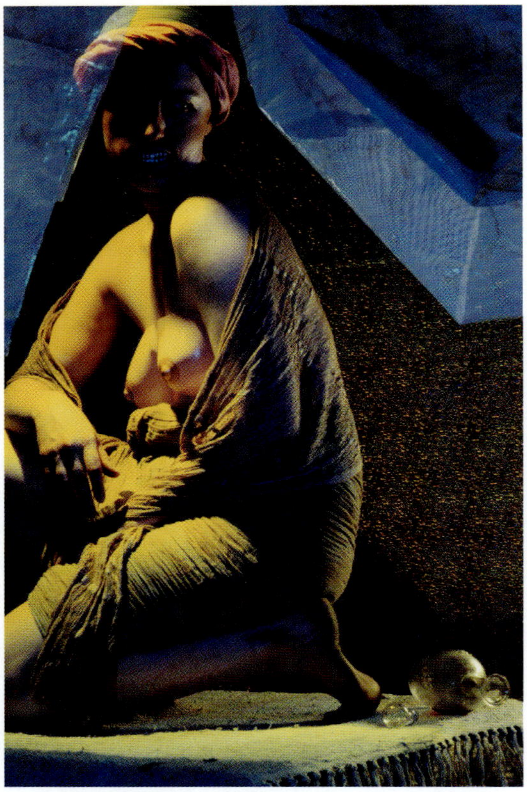

Pl. 17. Cindy Sherman, *Untitled #146,* 1985. $72^{1}/_{2} \times 49^{3}/_{8}$ in. Courtesy of the artist and Metro Pictures.

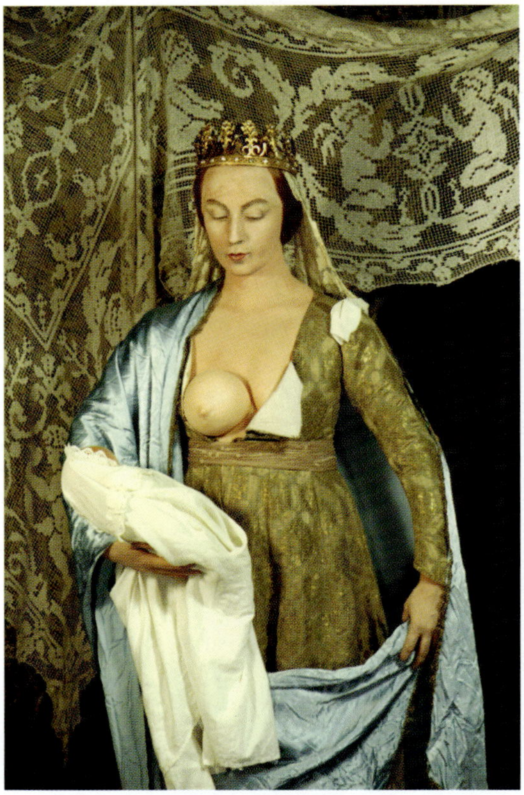

Pl. 18. Cindy Sherman, *Untitled # 216,* 1989. 87×56 in. Courtesy of the artist and Metro Pictures.

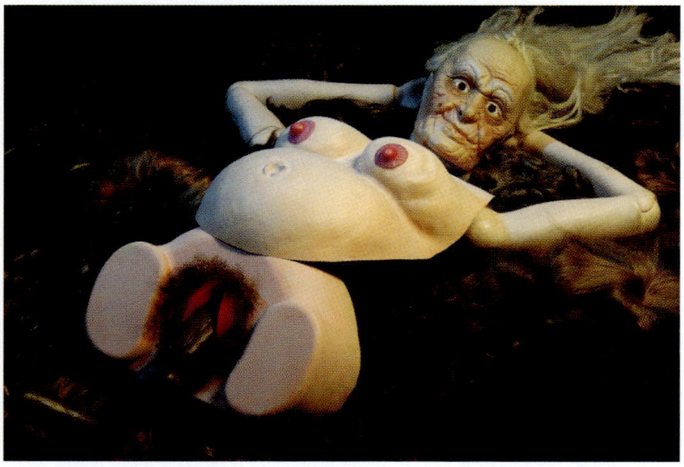

Pl. 19. Cindy Sherman, *Untitled # 250,* 1992. 50×75 in. Courtesy of the artist and Metro Pictures.

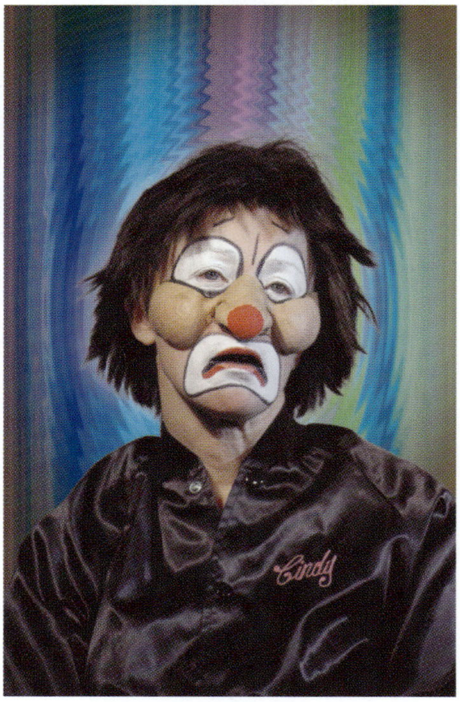

Pl. 20. Cindy Sherman, *Untitled # 413,* 2003–4. $46 \times 31^{1}/_{8}$ in. Courtesy of the artist and Metro Pictures.

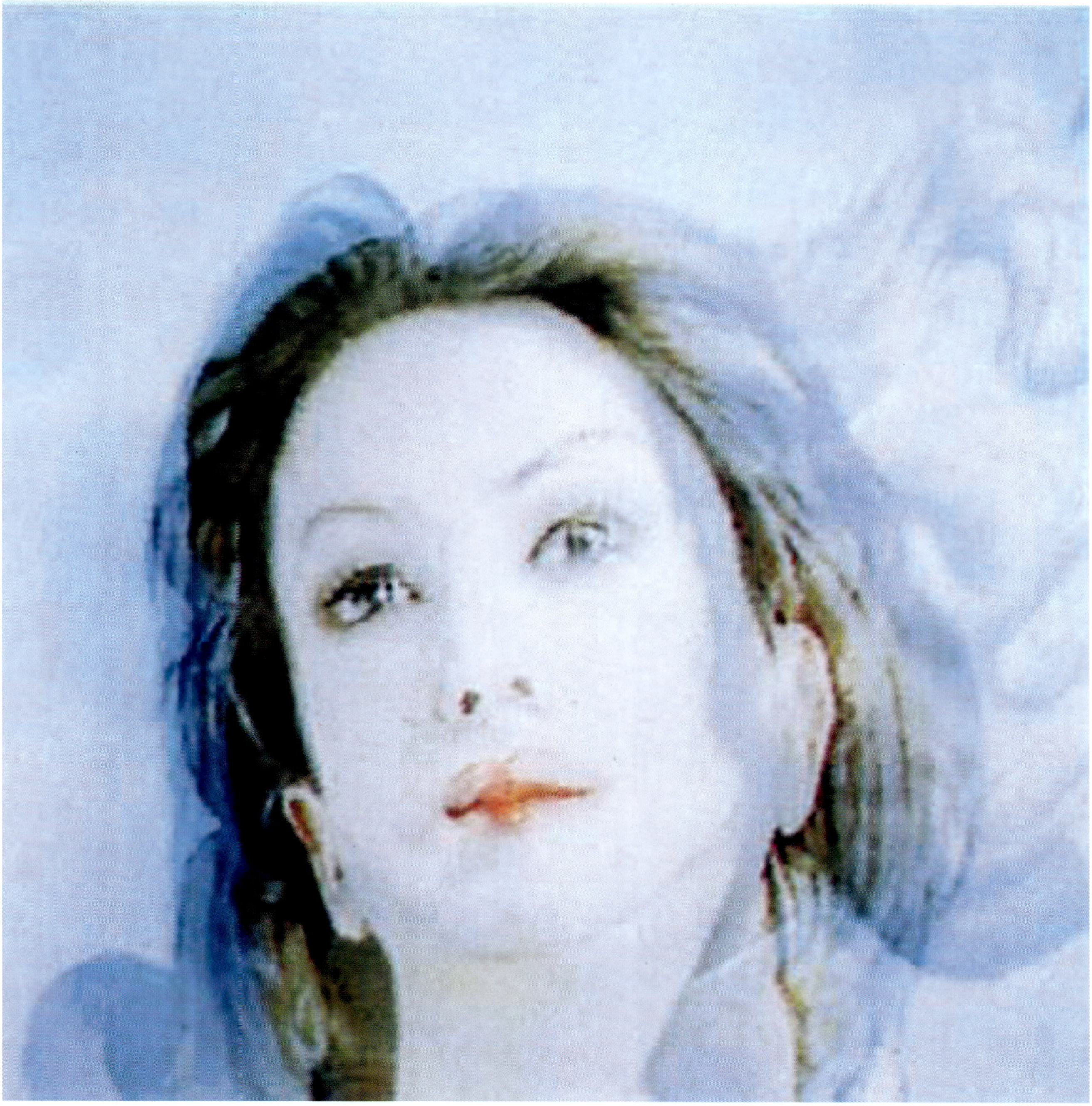

Pl. 21. Orlan, *Entre-Deux, No. 7,* 1994. 120 × 160 cm. Color photograph in light box. Photo: Courtesy of the artist.

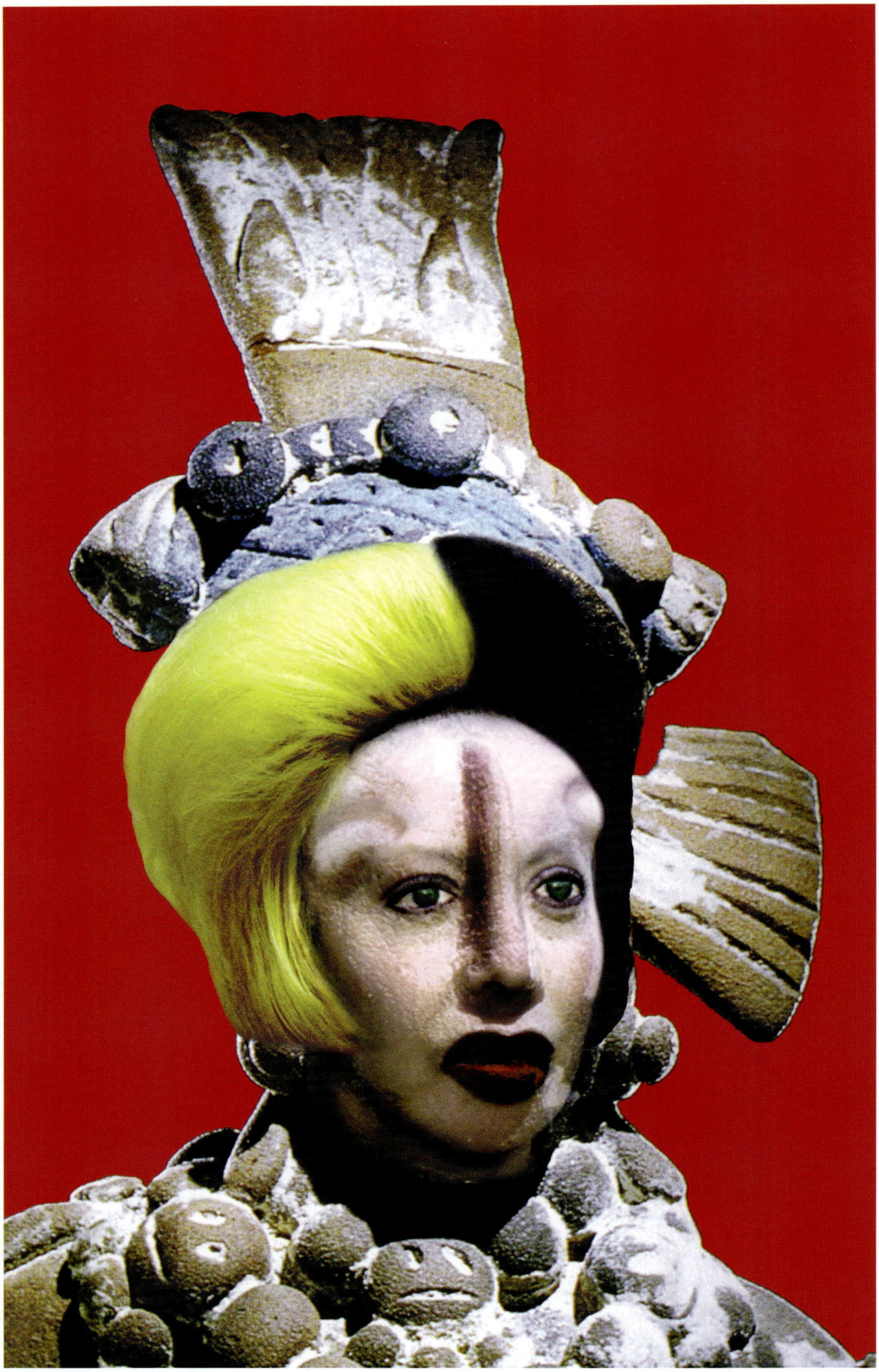

Pl. 22. Orlan, *Refiguration/Self-Hybridization, no. 27,* 1998. 2 formats, 100 × 150 cm. Cibrachrome stuck on a piece of aluminum. Technical assistance to digital image editing by Pierre Zovilé. © 2009 Artists Rights Society (ARS), New York/ASAGP, Paris. Photo: Courtesy Stefan Stux Gallery.

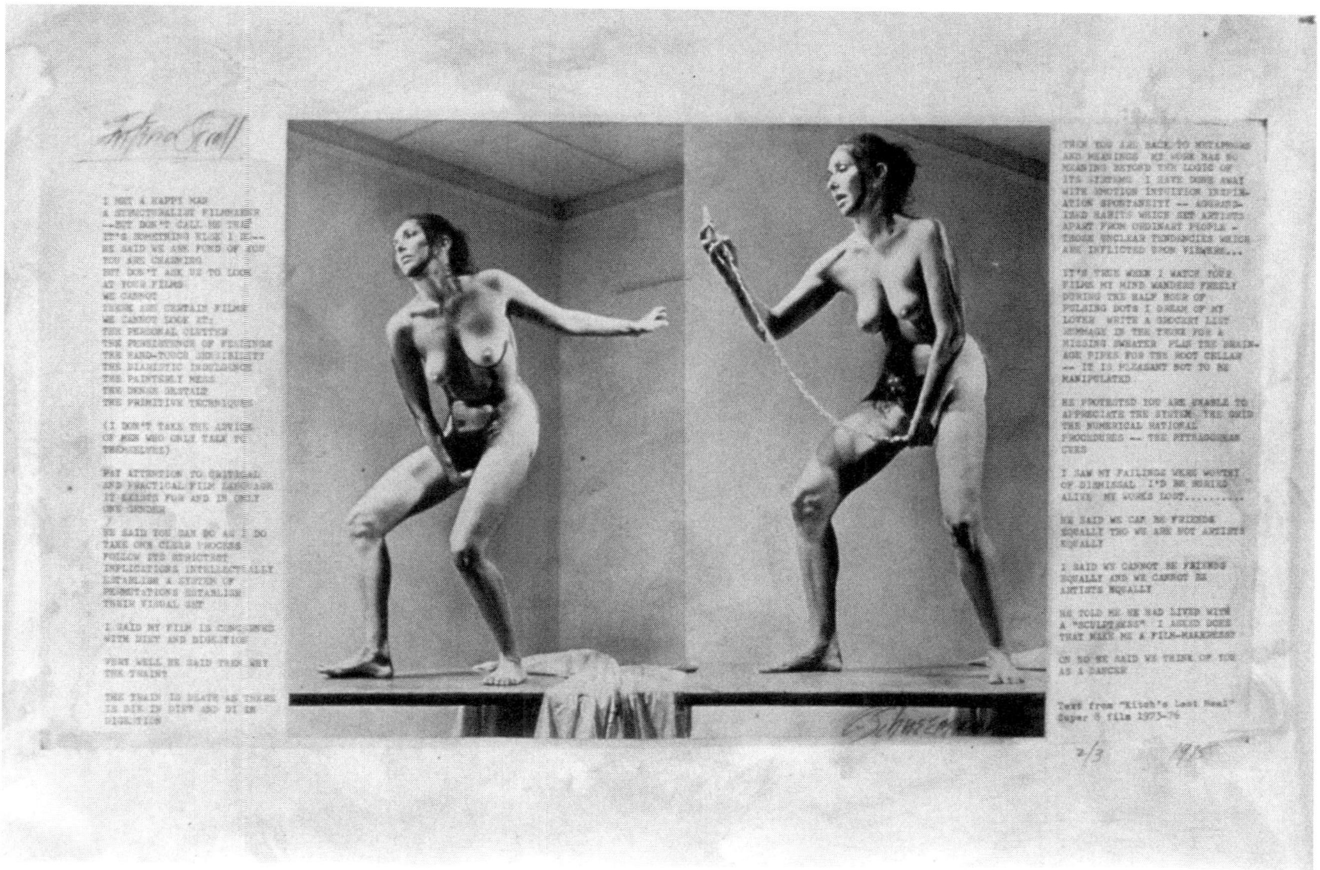

29. Carolee Schneemann, *Interior Scroll*, 1975. Performative action. Photo: Anthony McCall. Courtesy of the artist.

thinking of the vagina as a mold, as the positive shape. It is the muscle, the form in which the phallus takes its energy power, and identity. It is the clasp; it is the grasp. It is the interiority of a tremendous source of vitality and activity, the G-spot, the vaginal orgasm, the birth canal. But going inside is an enlivening vitalization of suppressed knowledge.

DK: *Texts that are scrolled remind me of religious texts like the Torah. Did you have in mind holy writings when you performed* Interior Scroll *and were you attempting to convey the holiness of the female sex (Sexuality is near to Godliness)—something akin to what is found in the Song of Songs?*

CS: No, I wasn't thinking about that, but I like it as an added level of meaning to the work. Actually, the text is ironic because it implicates semiotic theory. The scroll text functions as an aggression against conceptual presumption. It is a highly coded text attacking semiotic constraints on gender, the erotic merge of body and thought: and "vulvic space" as generated both physically and thoughtfully. "I met a happy man," . . . "a filmmaker," he said. "We are fond of you but we can not look at your films."

Text is very important in many of my works. My recent work, *Vulva's Morphia* [1992–97], consists of a photographic grid with rows of text. This work came from a dream I had in which there was a pile of research strewn over the floor of my studio. A voice remanded me: "You will never be an artist again unless you sort out these piles on the floor." The voice added, "Why don't you let Vulva do the talking?" I woke up and ran upstairs and began sorting the piles of research I had accumulated on witchcraft, clitorectomies, Lacan, Freud, Masters and Johnson, asking Vulva for a statement on each. I finally accumulated the statements which compressed a large morass of material. It was then that I added visual images to accompany the texts. So, you can see how the dream, the written word, and visuals

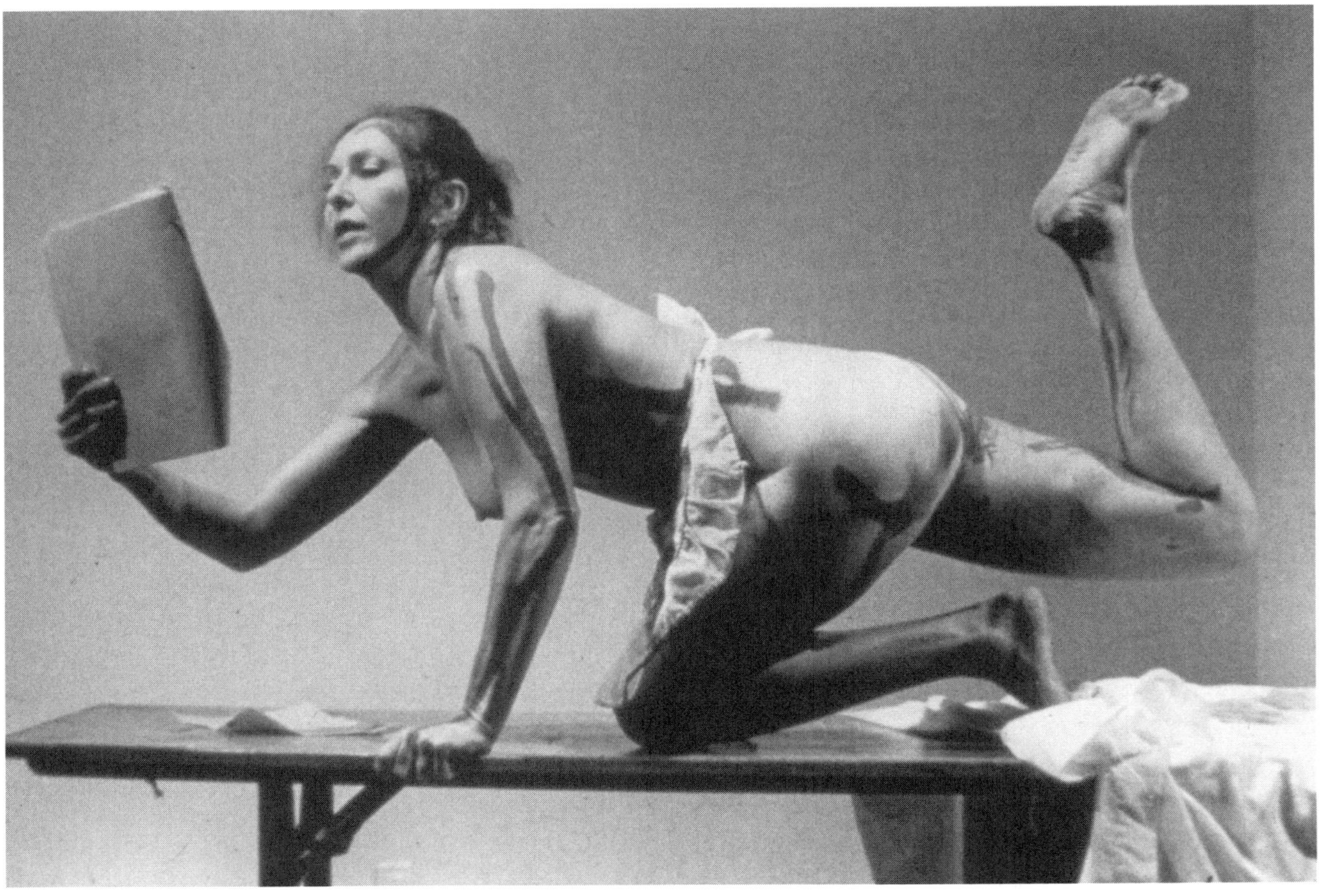

30. Carolee Schneemann, *Interior Scroll*, 1975. Photo collage with text: beet juice, urine and coffee photographic print; 72w × 48h inches. Photo: Anthony McCall. Courtesy of the artist.

work together for me. [Samples of Vulva's words are: "Vulva goes to school and discovers she doesn't exist. . . . Vulva studies Freud and realizes she will have to transfer her clitoral orgasm to the vagina. . . . Vulva decodes feminist constructivist semiotics and realizes she has no authentic feelings at all; even her erotic sensations are constructed by patriarchal projections, impositions, and conditioning . . ."]

DK: *Your artistic concern with the inside of the female body makes one (if one is a psychoanalyst) think of the mother, pregnancy, and what the mother possesses/contains inside her body. What do you think of the interpretation of your art as an externalization not merely of female genitalia—as you did in* Interior Scroll *—but an externalization of fantasies about the insides of the mother's body?*

CS: I think it is sad that for so many women, there is no way to attain our freedom unless we disown our mothers. I had a dream in which my mother was bringing me and my siblings lychee nuts, nuts covered in a brown shell with a milky white, almost fleshy, inside. My mother brought me a gift but I realized it was tainted because it represented her as both a leech and a nut!

These are drawings from a work that would overwhelm my concerns for eight or nine years; the initiatory drawings from a menstrual dream that I came to call *Fresh Blood—A Dream Morphology* [1981–87]. In the dream, my lover gives me a bouquet of dried leaves that have little dolls' heads in them. With the second part of the dream I am in a taxi in London and I accidentally pierce a man in his thigh with my red umbrella producing a spurt of blood from his thigh. I am very worried about this and I tell the taxi driver that we should go to a doctor. The driver says, "I am a doctor, but I will take you to the famous Viennese Veterinarian on the Mezzanine." I

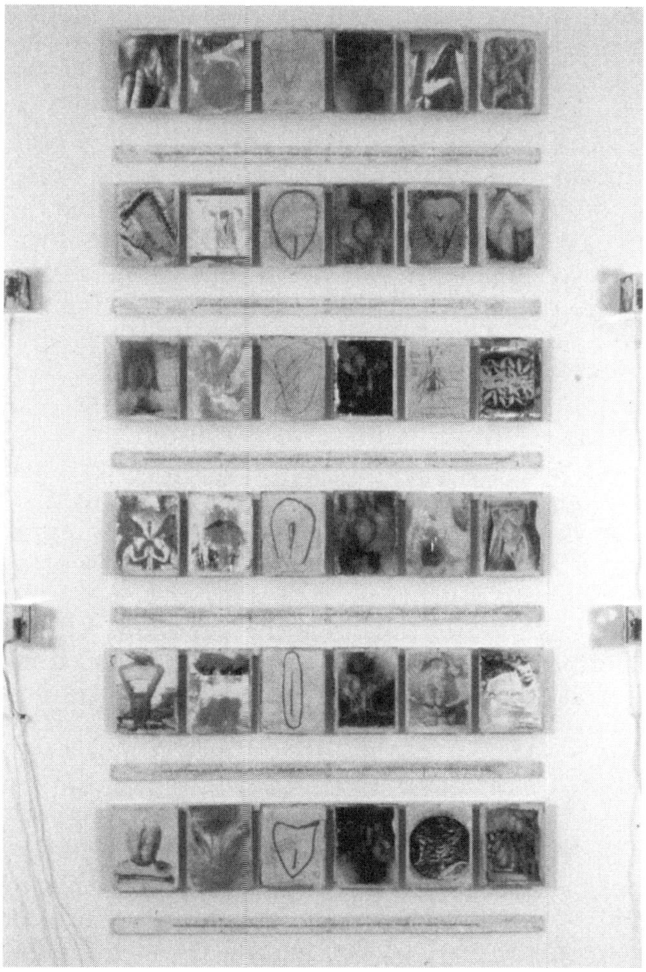

31. Carolee Schneemann, *Vulva's Morphia*, 1995. Photo-grid wall installation with 4 fans. Total 8 × 5 feet; each image 11 × 8.5 inches; text strips 2 × 58 inches. Courtesy of the artist.

wake up carefully considering these images—all very delicious—and I am menstruating. I am red, wet, and my dream mind has connected a red umbrella and a bouquet. What do they have in common? I start to draw. What they have in common is the vector like a vaginal "V," or the "V" for victory, or the bouquet and the umbrella as "V" shapes. I become very preoccupied with the implied language of the dream, these dried leaves. What leaves? Little babies' heads . . . menstruation leaves . . . the babies . . . go into dried leaves, leaves my body. So it is a dream of very funny and intensive interiorities and it is also delightfully playful—the umbrella is both vulvic, unfurled and rolled up, pointed and phallic. What I begin to do out of the dream is build a vocabulary of vector forms from nature, from science, from archaic religions. I photograph them and then I project them as slides. It becomes a kind of an enacted lecture . . . putting my body in the center of all of the projections . . . then composing my body responding with echoed "V" actions to the rhythmic projection of images all containing vector shapes. I keep a hold of a red umbrella. When the umbrella is opened out it becomes female and when closed, it becomes phallic and when it is turned upside down it becomes a question mark! As I worked on this piece I had subsequent dreams where I was told that I had to have an alter ego—a nurse carrying blood-stained white underpants on a fishing pole, a judge, and a grandmother—and that my alter ego had to be a Native American or black woman. Various performances were videotaped and then I edited these documents into another art form. A large circular plexi-glass sculpture incorporated the vocabulary of the printed vector shapes and includes moving video images of *Fresh Blood* on two monitors set into the sculpture, *Venus Vectors*. An eight-year process from those two originating drawings.

DK: *In a very moving essay you wrote in 1994, "Anti-Dementer: The More I Give The More You Steal," you equate a lump in your mother's breast with the imagined sensation of an alien lump you would feel if pregnant. What do you think of the idea that the alien lump in your mother not only refers to her cancer but, also, to the alien (unwanted) presences of your two younger siblings with whom you had to contend? This, of course, can apply to the possibility that you picked up your mother's ambivalence regarding her babies (including you) and viewed them as intrusions. Could it be, then, that one purpose of your art has been to emphasize sex for pleasure rather than sex for procreation because the latter is a reminder of a more painful situation related to unwanted babies?*

CS: I had a significant dream in which I was wearing a dress I had actually sewn out of a lace tablecloth. In the dream, I was wearing the fragile dress and realized suddenly that a mouse was caught under the dress and it was clawing at my back. To get the clawing off my back, I would have to tear the dress or kill the animal. I realized that the claws were my mother's hands with the pins she poked me with when sewing garments for me.

DK: *That's so interesting, both because of the animal under the dress—as in pregnancy—and your dilemma of which aggressive action to take to deal with it.*

CS: I couldn't be an artist if I had babies . . . it is real simple, there is no way that I could do it. As a twelve-year-old, I raised my brother and sister when my mother was ill. It was all-consuming. Children take up time, they require constant attention; and they mess up your pencils! You can't tell them you have to record a dream. A baby is crying; you need to nurse it. You have to get it diapers and food. I have fought like a devil to avoid being a mother because that is all that was expected of me. I will tell you a funny story. A friend who is a healer of a certain nutritional method, we were driving in his car and he said, "I am really horrified by abortion since I have had my daughter; it has gotten to the point where I think that they are absolutely intolerable. I don't think that they are okay at all." And I said, "If I hadn't had abortions, I couldn't have done all this art." He exclaimed, "Yes! But you might have had an artist!"

DK: *That's intense. I'd like you to talk a bit about performance. You once said: "There's something female about performance itself, I think because of how it's ephemeral and close to the unconscious—involving display, use of the self." Do you still believe that performance is more naturally feminine? This belief sounds rather unfeminist and recalls John Berger's distinction between men who act and women who appear.*

CS: I think that it is part of the unconscious that women's bodies are a source of pleasure, arousal, stimulation, titillation, and use. The Western obsession with the female nude as a source of arousal and pleasure has remained talismanic for male sexuality, ranging from the esteemed, the subversive aesthetic to pornographic. Traditions of erotic sensuous entertainment feature dancers, actresses, models. It is part of a social revolution to shift the fixity of those layers around perceiving the female body. For a woman to stand up and do a monologue about her life and her body enters the range of what is called performance art on preexisting traditions, even as she confronts, disrupts those conventions. Whereas for a man to stand up and do a confessional, expressive, vulnerable monologue about his life and art, we usually think: Oh, he is gay. Because masculinity still defines itself as avoiding vulnerability, keeping masculinity hard, impenetrable, and not exposing the self but using that self or its heroic anthologies to sustain hierarchical authority. That guy is the *director* or the *producer* or the actor assuming a "role." He is not out there on his toes, stripping his clothes. And there are deeper traditions around it too, if you think of Karen Finley. The wailing, the screaming of an Irish Shaman who goes naked in front of her whole culture in order to express grief and rage while the men are out there killing themselves. Heroics, erotics remain gendered even in the ways they are subverted.

DK: *So that is the position that you were taking in your work?*

CS: My live-action works, performative, kinetic, ritual, came out of painting, came out of the visual realm. . . . to be able to use film, movement, live-action, language as a material was highly enriching. Now "performance" belongs to MTV, Warholian narratives, glamour, seduction, confession, self-display—everything that my group was against.

DK: *Is there a difference between Carolee Schneemann the performer and Carolee Schneemann the person?*

CS: Performance can be an entrancement; if it is really working it is just an absolute otherness. It is ritualized, transcendent—a full physicalization meshed as imagery. It is also very physically demanding. (You meet each other in the street and you see that your friend is all crumpled over and you say, "You don't look so well, what is wrong with you?" and she says, "Well I am kind of fine but I am working on this performance." I say "Ok, I know where you are." You are generating and we can not even *speak* to each other.) This invisible process is going on and you can barely get up the stairs. You really think that you are not going to make it and then you enter the lights and a delicious possession, a certitude comes through—you don't know where it is coming from—you are its willing slave, it feeds on you as images, actions, the musicality unfolds, you have become the forms you envisioned, drew, scored, rehearsed, edited and layer in time. I never know what happened. What did I do? Well I know that I drank half a bottle of vodka, but were the cues on time, the slides with the light changes, images overwhelming? And when it is not wonderful, it is a nightmare because you are in this transformed state aware that the projector is chewing up sprockets, or the sound cue is fucked up, or you are not subsumed by the momentum of the dream . . . an exile observed by rows of shining eyes.

But I have pioneered the means to—in effect—paint within time, with words, with video, film—with the body an extended structure as space.

I will no longer create in the performative realm. It is essential to remove my body so that the body of work can be considered. For now I want the solitary concentrations of a visual artist. The privacy and focus on materials with which my work as a painter began. No audience. No fixed time frame.

It is important to note that Ms. Schneemann is a very vital woman who continues to be extremely productive and visible in the art world.

6
Hannah Wilke: The Naked Truth

Exposing the truth is like nudity.
—Hannah Wilke

THE LIFE AND WORK OF HANNAH WILKE (1940–93) are reminiscent of Hans Christian Andersen's fairy tale, *The Emperor's New Clothes.* Although those familiar with her work might think of her as the Emperor, strutting her stuff for all to behold, I see her as the boy who points to the Emperor, calling his bluff. He is the only person in the story with the courage to disclose the secret everybody knows but dares not speak.

Wilke played an endless game of *Show and Tell,* exposing and revealing what she believed to be the truth. A clever artist, she knew her audience would find unadorned truth unappealing and so she turned herself into a "Sugargiver," one who offers sweets—in the form of *Pink Champagne,* chocolate body casts (*Venus Pareve*), and chewing gum (*S.O.S.*). Wilke offered the sweetness of her naked body, as well as the quick wit of her mind, to captivate her audience. But once she had us where she wanted us, she delivered the punch.

Like the boy in *The Emperor's New Clothes,* Wilke pointed her finger at what others chose to ignore, or at the very least left unspoken. She revealed tough truths about female sexuality and the relations between the sexes; interdependency and daughterhood; aging and illness; and the deep need to be seen beyond the body. She remained true to her mission until the end of her life.

VAGINA AS ART: UNITING EROS AND AESTHETICS

In the 1960s, Wilke broke new ground when she created artistic representations of the female genitals, first in ceramics, then in latex, laundry lint, chewing gum, and kneaded erasers. Like Schneemann's *Interior Scroll* performance, Wilke brought her female "inner space" to the surface for all to behold by pressing her vaginal forms onto her naked body. These forms have been compared to fortune cookies and pastry shells, but the fact is that they are first and foremost female genital shapes. Wilke's vaginal forms also became the hallmark of feminist art, one of whose primary aims was the portrayal of woman's body in positive terms.[1] The aim of "cunt positive art," as it was sometimes referred to, was to display the beauty of female genitalia. By pasting her vaginal forms onto her entire body, Wilke suggested a vaginal embodiment, a sensuality that permeates the female body rather than one that is solely concentrated in the vagina, providing an added meaning to Irigaray's phrase, "the sex which is not one."

In the 1960s and '70s, feminists rejected traditional Freudian assumptions about female development, refusing to accept inferior genital status. Wilke went so far as to reverse the position of envy: "There is no reason for envy, but it's fashionable. The fact is women are biologically superior. I can have a baby, you can't. Penis envy really equals venus envy."[2] Wilke made a photograph titled *Venus Envy* (1980) in which the head of friend and lover, artist Richard Hamilton, emerges from between Wilke's legs, creating the impression of birth. Here, a woman artist gives birth to a male, thereby reversing the Pygmalian theme.

In the seventies, Wilke worked with latex, a flexible material that invokes the impression of translucent flesh, moisture, and movement. She poured the liquid into strips or circles, folded and clipped them together with snaps, and hung the whole with pushpins. These latex sculptures, with their soft, glistening, light beige and pink skin tones, remarkably produce the effect of giant labia. Along with Schneemann, Wilke championed the legitimacy of sensual pleasure for women. The titles she chose for these pieces were meant to be purposely suggestive of female genitalia and erotic delight: *Venus Cushion*, *Centerfold*, *Pink Champagne*, and *Agreeable Object*. Frueh (1975) describes *Pink Champagne* as "a heroic figure of 'cunt-positiveness,' masturbation, and multiple orgasms." She goes on to say that "Pink Champagne is a pleasure to look at and to taste and drink, and Wilke's *Pink Champagne* is a visual treat and a multiplicity of lips, which are beautiful forms that speak of morphological sameness and difference, of plural pleasures, not only in orgasmic capacity but also in regard to the many areas of sensitivity in women's external and internal anatomy."[3]

But more than this, the richly detailed labial forms of these works imitate and yet greatly exceed the actual physiological detail of the labia majora and minora. They offer the female genitalia a mythical expanse: the female body is the site of envelopment, conception, gestation and procreation; her vagina is the doorway to the world and through that doorway each of us enters, a person *and* a world. Her labia suggest the enveloped beauty of this ability and this gift, and so her experience is *vaginally informed*. This truth is captured exquisitely in Wilke's pieces. It is small wonder that she pasted vaginal forms all over her body, as if to express a kind of vaginal omnipresence, a world-womb pulsating with creative potential.

As the eye travels over *Agreeable Object* and *Venus Cushion*, it is drawn into pink folds, spaces, and overlaps, centering about two-thirds down on the vertical axis dividing the pieces into two nearly symmetrical halves. These works have a center of gravity and it is there the eye settles, before being restlessly drawn out again by tiny tongues, pink spots of soft fire and the mystery hidden behind the flower petal layers. The forms envelop the gaze, drawing it in but also pushing back against it, since the movement suggested in the multiplicity of petals and folds, of fiery lips, causes the eye to move and be discouraged from settling on any particular aspect of the work. The sculpture is pinned to the wall, suggesting the biological, historical, and existential bondage that is part of the feminine experience. The overall shape resembles a tear and also a large flame and the insides show tiny breaks and lacerations (tears) through-

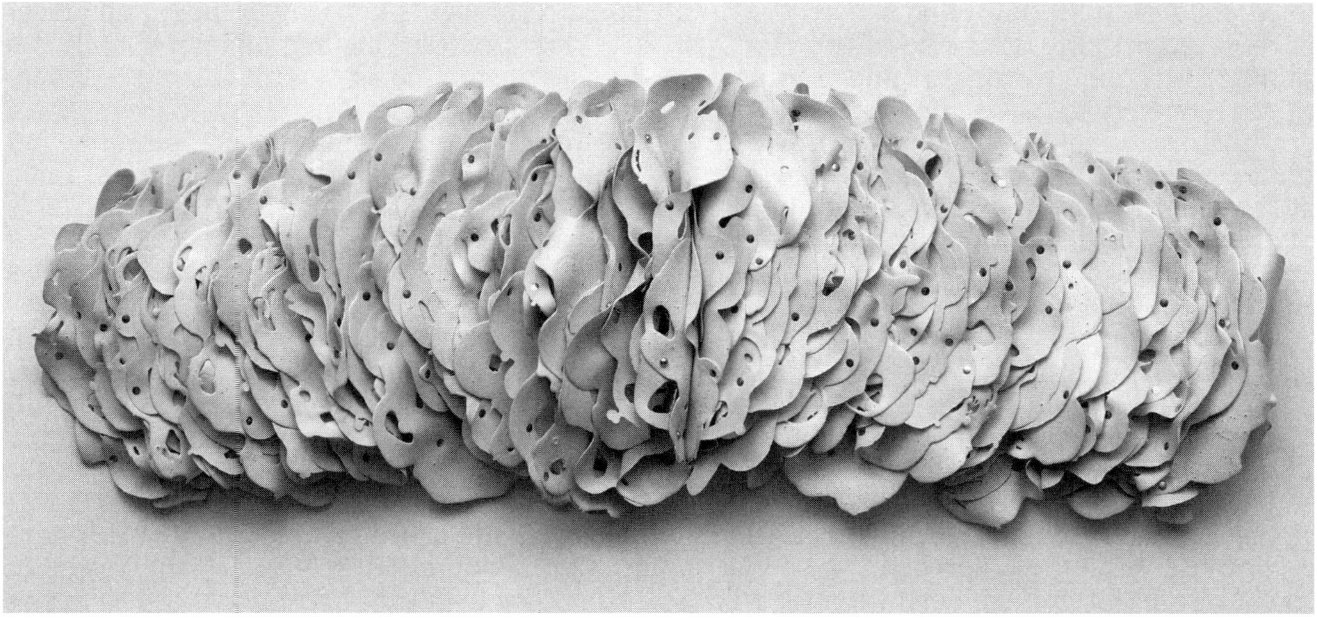

32. Hannah Wilke, *Pink Champagne*, 1975. Latex rubber with acrylic paint and metal snaps. 137,16 × 45,72 x17,78 cm. © Marsie, Emmanuelle, Damon and Andrew Scharlatt/Licensed by VAGA, New York, NY. Photo: Courtesy Ronald Feldman Fine Arts, New York.

out, revealing the delicate fragility that constitutes femininity. Many dimensions of female experience are symbolized in works like *Venus Cushion:* the complexity of a woman's body and feelings, the multiple dimensions of her erotic pleasure, the mystery of giving birth, her physical connection to life and death, and the strength, vulnerability, and centrality of the female.

Unlike her latex pieces, Wilke's early clay sculptures were not only vaginal in appearance, but also phallic, androgynous, and even excremental.[4] She clearly sought forms to represent the immediacy of the body and its carnality. Wilke wrote that creating "a specifically female iconography for both sexes in the early 60's was in direct conflict with a society that prohibited its citizens from and sometimes arrested them for using the words *fuck, cock,* and *prick.* In the United States the state of nudity is still a problem. My concern is with the word translated into form, with creating a positive image to wipe out the prejudices, aggression, and fear associated with the negative connotations of pussy, cunt, box."[5] She also understood that people felt profound fear in accepting and celebrating their sexuality: "Asking people to take pleasure in their own bodies puts them in fear more than anything else."[6] Wilke conceived of her art as uniting the erotic and the aesthetic and hoped her work could help overcome such fear. Indeed, she repeatedly called on men and women to cease repressing their sexuality.[7] Her own pulling, twisting, wrapping, and folding actions required to make her sculptures recall gestures involved in acts of self-pleasure. Wilke's continued insistence on the rights of the female body and its sexuality in a sexphobic and misogynist culture is what characterizes her work, most of which finds her in a state of nudity.

Wilke's Nude

The transgressive aspect of Wilke's nudity is key to the way her art became a political act, charged by the public spectacle of a woman dictating how to view her body. In doing so she and other feminist performance artists certainly had antecedents to work with and interrogate: Marcel Duchamp's oeuvre, which included his game of chess with a nude woman and *Etant Donnés,* Yves Klein's women who served as live paintbrushes, and of course Meret Oppenheim's 1959 *Spring Feast,* a live tableau of a female nude reclining on a table surrounded by male "diners." Wilke's work declares that the body is the chief point of contention in any debate concerning representation and gender in art. Whereas this attitude was revolutionary in her time, today one regularly encounters art focusing on sexuality and the self in both male (e.g., Matthew Barney) and female (e.g., Karen Finley, Janine Antoni) artists.

Some critics, including feminists, believed Wilke's flaunting of her body to differ little from male-generated art or pornography. Her art, at least that consisting of photographs or live performances of her "body beautiful" in "pinup" or *Playboy* style poses, has frequently been labeled narcissistic and exhibitionistic. To Wilke's dismay, even noted feminist art critic, Lucy Lippard, was among those who took issue with her naked performances.[8]

Whereas she admitted that she produced her art to love herself and that she posed even in her sleep,[9] Wilke's narcissism and exhibitionism are complex matters. Many of her critics failed to understand the distinction between the artist's autobiographical involvement and her social commentary, both of which are present in her art. At least on one level, Wilke's portrayal of herself as a sexual object represents her way of taking on an active and creative role in a tableau usually depicting the female as passive and without a vital psychic interior—as a "fuck toy." Thus, she reverses the situation of the pinup by becoming the pinup who pins the lustful male gaze.

A self-portrait photograph (1978–84) that offers direct critique of the female nude shows Wilke seated on the floor in a corner, legs spread wide open. She surrounded herself with guns and Mickey Mouse dolls, indicating the frightening and amusing nature of our cultural icons. She portrayed herself as literally cornered by the male gaze, adopting the words of Ad Reinhardt to question: "What does this represent? What do you represent?" Her gaze is blank and nonseductive, even frozen in sadness, a look that contradicts the viewer's natural temptation to eroticize such an image. Thus, Wilke objectified her naked body, as male artists had done with women for cen-

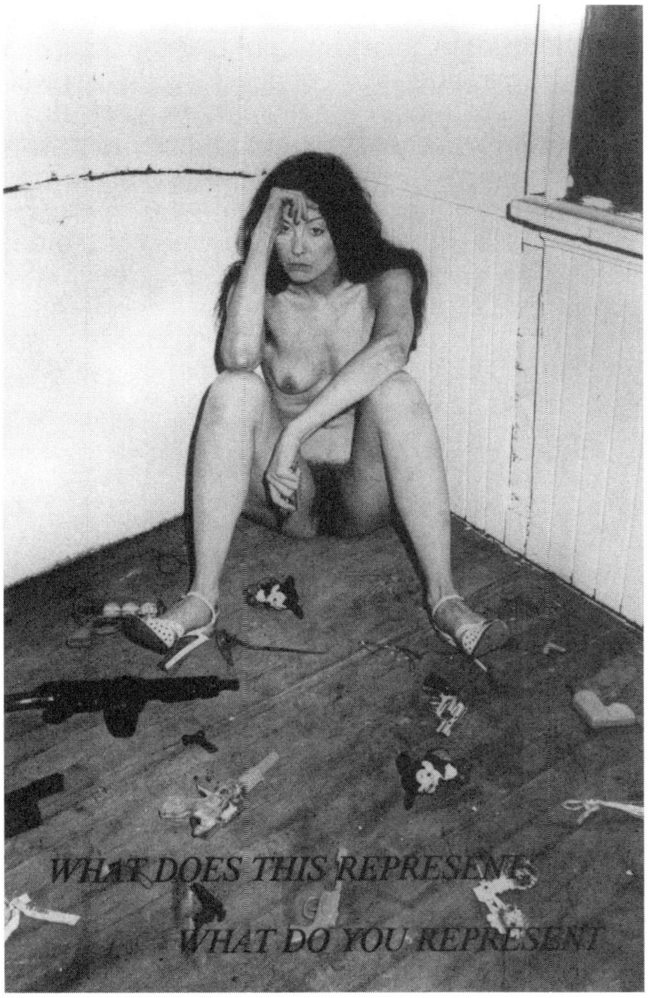

33. Hannah Wilke, *What Does This Represent? What Do You Represent? (Ad Reinhart),* 1978. From *So Help Me Hannah* Series. Courtesy Donald and Helen Goddard and Ronald Feldman Fine Arts, New York.

turies; yet, she did so in a way that made her sexuality ambiguous and confrontational; she appropriated male intellectual text as well as ownership of the gaze, and challenged the viewers to question themselves. Wilke's use of nudity in her art, unlike pornography or even male painted nudes of women, is therefore undoubtedly a two-directional process. Although she enjoyed being able to give pleasure, her nude is not submissive; she speaks, questions, and demands control over her erotic and intellectual life. The spectator's gaze is also brought into the art experience and becomes an integral part of it. Men are offered a reflection of their erotic objectification of the female subject while women are invited to identify with that objectification and its reversal.

Though feminists made famous the axiom that the personal is political, Wilke attempted to show how the relationship between the personal and the political is a mutually influencing one. For example, the guns in her piece, which derive from her original *So Help Me Hannah* (1978 and 1985) installation at P.S. 1 (1978), refer not only to male symbols of personal and political aggression, but specifically to ex-boyfriend, artist Claes Oldenburg's famous ray guns. Wilke's eight-year relationship with Oldenburg ended badly, and she never completely recovered. One way she found to express her pain, take revenge, and even keep the relationship with Oldenburg alive was to address him directly ("What do you represent?") through her art. Oldenberg admittedly influenced Wilke to become a serious artist in her own right.[10] She was inspired by his witty and provocative soft sculptures (his *Upside Down City* is a grouping of soft, hanging phallic forms in contradistinction to Wilke's vaginal forms) as well as his use of the multiple form. Whereas Oldenburg endlessly reproduced angular ray guns in the sixties and Mickey Mouse heads in the seventies, Wilke multiplied her curvilinear vaginal forms ad infinitum.

Although Wilke acknowledged Oldenburg's influence directly (in interviews) and indirectly (symbols, guns, and text aimed at him), much of her feminist stance seemed to draw strength from his betrayal. *So Help Me Hannah,* whose original subtitle for the P.S. 1 installation was *Snatch-shots with Ray Guns,* clearly refers to Oldenburg's ray gun collection which she helped him acquire. Among other things, her piece is meant to be a bold statement expressing women's rights to receive credit for their collaboration and participation in works of art.[11] In addition to dramatic black-and-white photographs of herself taken by her companion Donald Goddard, in which she appears to be running from danger, Wilke presented one hundred quotations from men and a handful of women, many of which refer to exploitation in relationships. In the final analysis, *So Help Me Hannah* is a plea to men who have hurt her, critics who have erased her, and all who have used or, worse, forgotten her. In this and other works, Wilke's needs cry out far louder than does her nudity. And her nudity is, in truth, a declaration of her vulnerability, the vulnerability of a woman whose emotions are not far from the skin.

In the five performances Wilke gave of *So Help Me Hannah* (1979–85), she actualized the wish for complete autonomy: to be sole director, actor, and creator. She also gradually transcended Oldenberg's influence in the piece, allowing it to address broader social and cultural issues. In the end, a live performance replaced the photographs, and she spoke the men's words that were previously on the wall. By showing the two cameramen who film her naked body on the move, Wilke not only incorporated the male gaze into her work; she exposed the collaboration necessary for the production of her art. Her insistence on authorship is revealed in her description of the role of her cameramen: "The cameraman participates as dancer, voyeur, lover, and artist, but under the direction of the woman, who retains the authority of artist, the creator of this performance."[12] Thus, Wilke's focus was never meant to be on her striking body alone but, rather, on the interpersonal relations between man and woman, artist and photographer, artist and audience, and between the artist and herself. She transformed the menacing gun from *Snatch-shots* into a sensual object that she no longer used in self-defense but, rather, as an object to caress and become intimate with. In her art, Wilke repeatedly turned her "enemy" into her lover.

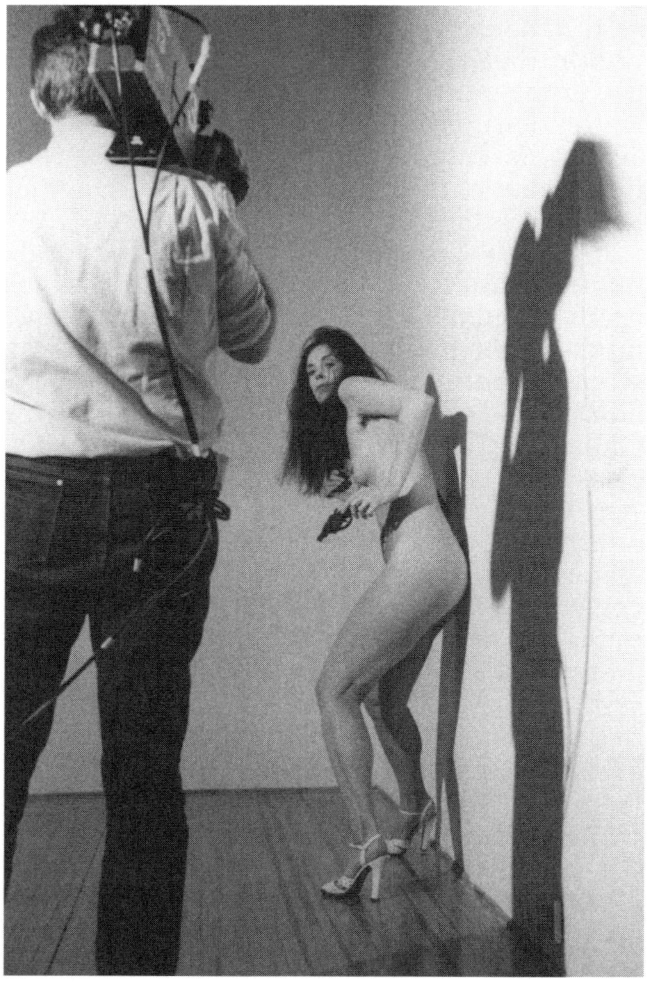

34. Hannah Wilke, *So Help Me Hannah*, 1979–85. Forest City. Courtesy Donald and Helen Goddard and Ronald Feldman Fine Arts, New York.

Relational Art

For Wilke, life's meaning was always found in relationships. A passage from a letter to Oldenburg describes the significance relationships had for her art: ". . . these works of art were created with affection for our past relationship of many years, as part of a larger effort to understand human relationships and social contracts. This is true of all my work over the past thirty years, whether it involved my mother, Stanley Landsman, Richard Hamilton, Don Goddard and his children, you, or anyone else."[13] Indeed, although she usually appeared alone in her art, the people in her life were never far away. In *Double Portraits: Name Brand* (1965–83), Wilke combined text and image; names of men she quoted in *So Help Me Hannah* are juxtaposed with scenes from her life. She expanded the series and changed the title to *Advertisements for Living*. Playing with the deceptive nature of words and their potential for false advertising, she contrasted famous names that trigger instant expectations with quotidian scenes of interactions between her and others. Like the child who points out the emperor's nudity, she is saying that what we want from relationships—to be seen as we imagine ourselves to be, somehow whole, to have permanence and real security, to be saved from death—is not possible. Yet we must want the impossible in order to live. The nude emperor represents the sad truth that we can never have what we want and his false/imagined clothes are our illusion that we can.

Wilke also brought the centrality of relationships to the forefront of her work in *Intercourse with . . .*, a 1977 video performance piece in which she played tape-recorded messages left on her answering machine over a period of two years, marking the relationships that were important to her. In this piece, she wore a black mink coat and a sweater which she gradually removed to reveal her bare chest inscribed with the names and initials of friends and lovers. She then peeled off the letters of the names, one by one, and contemplated the messages she missed (she was not at home) and the people who marked her in one way or another. Like the vaginal forms pasted on her body, names of significant others mark her body and soul, leaving their imprint. As a result of encounters she has had with people in her life, she is scarred as well as motivated to free herself from their influence. Until the end of her life, Wilke struggled with issues of autonomy, dependence, and victimization in her relationships. Even on her sickbed, she continued to write Oldenburg to try to settle their differences. In one poignant letter, she entreats him to "please help me not to feel so victimized . . ."[14]

Scarification/Starification

Wilke's sense of victimization is perplexing when considered alongside the glamour attending her celebrity in the art world. Yet these two facets were intimately related for her. *Hannah Wilke Super-T-Art* (1974) recreated, in twenty black-and-white photographs, her performance as part of Jean Depuy's "Soup and Tart" evening at the Kitchen in New York. These "performalist" self-portraits present her as a star, à la Jesus Christ Super Star. The first of these photographs recalls a pure and virginal Mary Magdalene, draped in a long cloak with arms held close to her body. By way of shifts in pose and garment, Wilke transforms herself into a Christlike figure, crossing both gender and human limitation. The robe becomes a loincloth and her movements, once constricted, turn expansive. Her arms project upward and outward and, liberated from constraints, she dances. Wilke reveals her self-sufficiency and neediness all at once: because the loincloth also resembles a diaper, she recalls both Jesus and a child. The final pose is that of a crucifixion. She is a star but, like many stars, she is also a martyr.

Therefore, in addition to celebrating her sexuality and its visibility, Wilke's vaginal gumfolds can be seen to represent the "invisible" scars she wore despite her perceptible beauty. Although many agree that a beautiful woman is "marked" by the male gaze and envied by the female, one is not in the habit of considering the suffering plight of an attractive woman. Her scars, invisible to the eye, are not appreciated and she hardly elicits empathy or sympathy. Wilke was acutely aware of the oppression of beautiful women and one purpose of her art was to challenge stereotypical responses to beauty. She said, "It was risky for me to act beautiful, but the scars representing the ugliness of society sometimes went unnoticed . . . people are first visually prejudiced and that's why I made myself very visual."[15] Wilke deliberately transformed herself into a star ("starification"), a beautiful, naked pinup girl who, at the same time, cries out for help and wears her feminine, vaginal scars ("scarification") on the outside for all to see. She said, "My work is about scars, being wounded."[16] Scarification, for Wilke, also alluded to clitorectomies performed on young women around the world and to African women's cicatrization wounds endured without anesthesia on faces and bodies for beautifying purposes. Present-day cosmetic surgery represents Western women's rituals of torture for beauty's sake. We will see how Orlan takes up the issue of beauty and scarification in her postmodern art.

Ahead of her time, Wilke directed our attention to how we objectify the other, in this case "beautiful people" and celebrities, foreshadowing the work of Piper and Orlan. Today, it is widely understood that the perverse fascination with stars, like that with Princess Diana, Paris Hilton, and Britney Spears, involves powerful aggressive drives intended to objectify and violate. In the 1970s, Wilke's focus on this matter was revolutionary. Her claim that "Saying 'beauty' is the same as saying 'Jew' and 'nigger' " was largely ignored; yet, through her chewing gum vaginal forms and many other works, she made a powerful statement about the ways women, especially attractive women, are victimized and treated as objects. "I chose gum because it's the perfect metaphor for the American woman—chew her up, get what you want out of her, throw her out and pop in a new piece,"[17] she explained when asked about the meaning of her 1975 *S.O.S. Starification Object Series.* With characteristic biting wit, she created a game from her *S.O.S.* series subtitled "An Adult Game of Mastication," in which chewing gum packs, vulvar sculptures made from chewing gum, and baseball card format photographs of Wilke fill a box for the pleasure and exchange of the players. Later artists, like Maedbhina McCombe, also used sweets to highlight the female association with eating, sex, and pleasure (e.g., *Clitoris Allsorts,* 1990, and her self-portrait series, *Appetites*). For Wilke, starification was equivalent to scarification and she often used the words interchangeably.

S.O.S, includes professional photographs of Wilke in classic seductive poses as those frequently encountered in fashion and *Playboy* magazines. By mimicking representations of women in popular culture, she simultaneously attempted to control and mock them. The middle word in her title, *Object,* indicates Wilke's awareness of her status as object. In her art, she exploits that status rather than allow herself to be used by it. She turns her

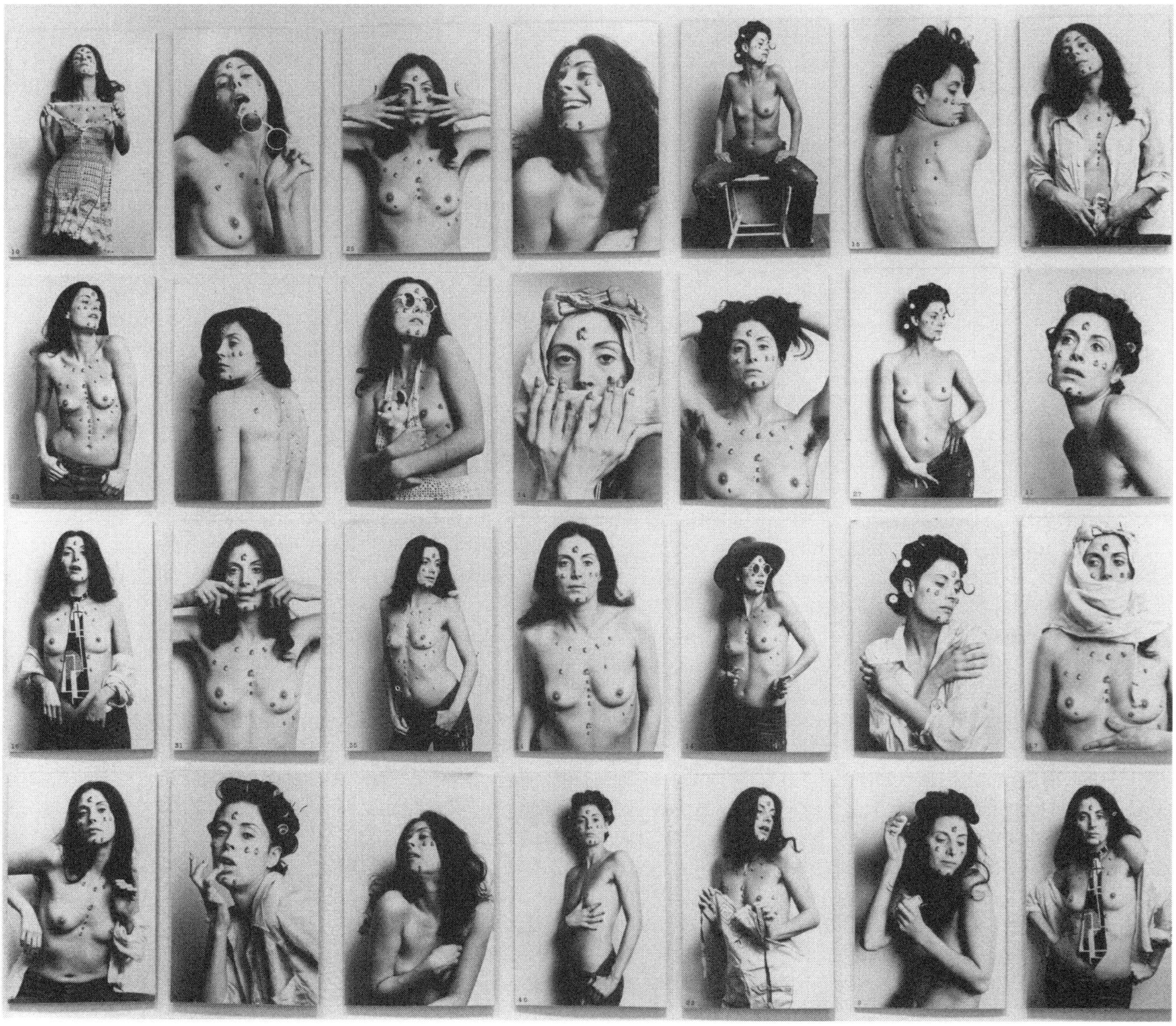

35. Hannah Wilke, *S.O.S. Starification Object Series,* 1975. Twenty-eight photographs from *Mastication Box,* $6^3/_4 \times 4^1/_4$ inches each. © Marsie, Emmanuelle, Damon and Andrew Scharlatt/Licensed by VAGA, New York, NY. Photo: Courtesy Ronald Feldman Fine Arts, New York.

anger into biting, dark humor that renders her work provocative and challenging. At the same time, the title itself (S.O.S.) is literally a coded cry for help, for rescue from the desperation of feeling exploited. Still, there is much fun and play in photographs of her with curlers in her hair, a Mickey Mouse apron, or a Muslim headdress. Wilke clearly enjoyed her beauty and took pleasure in sharing it with others. Yet, she critiqued the fashion industry, dominated largely by male ideals, as well as feminists who felt the need to deny beauty in order to be taken seriously. Wilke desired the best of both worlds: she was smart and pretty and she wanted others to acknowledge her as both. More than anything she wanted to be treated as a whole woman, as a life deserving respect, acknowledgement and support.

Dialogues

An excellent example of Wilke's playfulness with her status as object is her fake book jacket, *I Object: Memoirs of a Sugargiver* (1977) (see Plate 12). Both sides of the book jacket display a naked Wilke self-portrait reclining on a rock with legs apart. Her pose recalls that of the headless naked female lying on a bed of twigs in the foreground of Duchamp's *Etant Donnés* (1946–66), viewed through a small peephole (see Plate 10). It is known that Wilke found *Etant Donnés* "repulsive"; she spoke of its "distorted vagina . . . and voyeuristic vulgarity."[18] That one of her photographs is presented upside down most probably represents her revolt against the meaning of Duchamp's objectified girl. Wilke's use of language, especially puns and *double entendres* is evident from the title of this and other works. Thus, if the word "object" is read as a verb, her protest at being viewed as an object is stressed. If one reads "object" as a noun, however, Wilke's acknowledged participation as sex object and focus for a voyeuristic gaze comes to the fore.[19] Her subtitle, *Memoirs of a Sugargiver,* refers back to pieces like her chewing gum sculptures, *Venus Pareve,* and *Pink Champagne;* she offers the sweetness of her body, but not without commentary and a demand for self-reflection. It also contrasts with an anagrammatic play on Duchamp's name as salt seller (*marchand du sel*).[20] In a text (also called *I Object*) which she wrote for an exhibition at the Ludwig Museum in Cologne commemorating the centennial of Duchamp's birth, Wilke asked contemptuously: "Did he [Duchamp] actually touch the Venus Mound himself, or did he use woman, in need of helping the male artist, as muse, mentor or mold maker—the ultimate act of getting even by giving birth to a dead impenetrable object—Art."[21] Clearly, *I Object* was meant to present Wilke's live, sexual female body as a counterpoint for Duchamp's dry, cerebral allusions to sex and the body.

In her art, therefore, Wilke constructed an arena for staging dialogues with Duchamp, as well as other important men and women in her life. Like Duchamp, she shared an interest in sex, irony, and language. In addition, she elevated her status as artist by aligning herself with this great male artist, forcing both comparison and contrast. In *C'est La Vie Rose* (1976), for instance, she created a performance piece that inverted Duchamp's symbolism from *Large Glass* (1915–23) in which he, a male artist, played chess with a naked woman. Wilke posed nude in front of a photograph of Duchamp's *Large Glass* while she played chess with a male opponent.

For the exhibition honoring Duchamp at the Ludwig Museum, she added a text to the book jacket that included letters from her lovers, Claus Oldenburg, Richard Hamilton, and Donald Goddard, all three of whom had been seeing her when the original photos were taken in 1976. The letters had been written from faraway places and noted longing and absence. As in *Intercourse With . . . ,* Wilke has us ponder the repercussions of separation, the lingering presence of absent people. For her, the fact that someone was absent seemed merely to intensify his/her effect on her. Rather than depict herself in a position of need, it is the men who describe their longing for her.

Wilke's attachment to older, famous men reveals the earlier attachment she probably had to her father, whom she idolized. Indeed, she called herself "my father's daughter."[22] Her preoccupation with issues of separation and abandonment similarly refer to her father's premature death that left her, at age twenty, permanently grieving. Memory and desire combine and result in Wilke's ever present need for kindness. She inserted an anagram, essentially equating her name with the attribute of frailty, from an earlier work:

Handle with care
h**A**ndle with care
ha**N**dle with care
ha**N**dle with care
h**A**ndle with care
Handle with care

In one photograph, she lies in a fetal position with a brace around her neck. Yet, she also ended the 1987 text with lyrics from a song she wrote, *Stand Up* (1982), in which she directed herself to be strong and stand up ("stand up, or you might disappear"). In *His Farced Epistol* (1978–84) a photograph from the *So Help Me Hannah* series, she stood naked over a toilet while clutching a gun in her hand. Like a man, she seemed to be saying with a big smile on her face, "I can pee standing up!"

Wilke's dual expression of need (*SOS; So Help Me Hannah; Handle With Care; Give: Hannah Wilke Can*) on one hand, and the desire for autonomy (*Stand Up*) on the other, characterizes Wilke's work and reflects the major conflict with which she dealt: separation-individuation. Separation-individuation is a term that refers to the infant's early separation process from a symbiotic tie with its primary caretaker, the mother. Mahler, Pine, and Bergman described the phases the child passes through to achieve the very difficult developmental task of separation.[23] Whereas Wilke was very much aware of her neediness and dependency; she also tried hard to be independent, the author of her life—a star of her own making.[24]

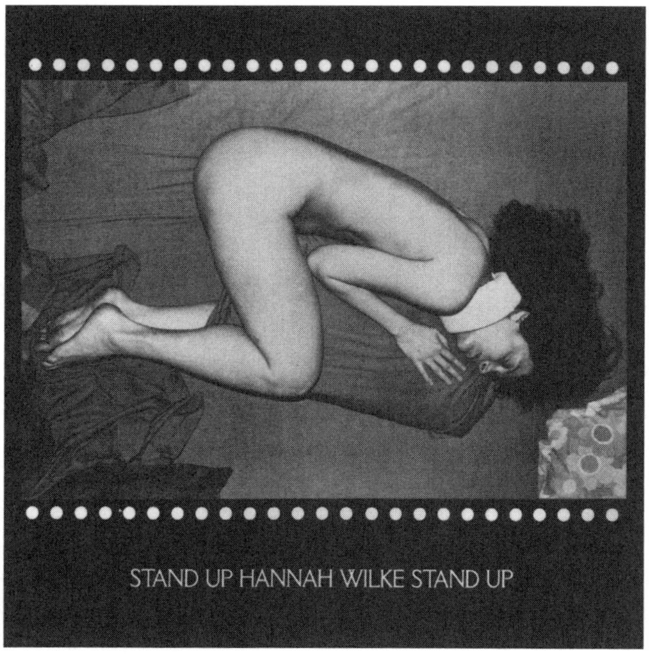

36. Hannah Wilke, *STAND UP*, 1982. Photograph and photo-phono-loop with song by the artist. Courtesy Donald and Helen Goddard and Ronald Feldman Fine Arts, New York.

Performance

From the early 1970s on, an important and consistent part of Wilke's art was her performance pieces—labeled "performalist" by her in 1979—in which she was the sole star. In the live "*So Help Me Hannah*" video works, which she performed from 1979 to 1985, she displayed her nudity wearing only high heels. On a pedestal, she likened herself to a sculpture, as she had done in a 1978 performance at the Susan Caldwell Gallery in New York called *Hannah Wilke Can: A Living Sculpture Needs to Make a Living.* She brandished a gun, a phallic prop that served as a reminder of male violence as well as a personal message to ex-boyfriend, Claes Oldenburg. In reality, Wilke brought a lawsuit against Oldenberg, part of which dealt with her demand to be properly credited for her involvement in his art, most specifically his ray gun collection.

As two cameramen follow her, she moves slowly to a soundtrack on which she quotes the words of famous men—artists, philosophers, and critics—forcing a brilliant recontextualization of men's words when spoken by a beautiful, naked feminist artist.[25] For example, she recites Marx's words, "Could commodities themselves speak, they would say: Our use value may be a thing that interests men. It is no part of us as objects. What, however, does belong to us as objects, is our value. Our natural intercourse as commodities proves it. In the eyes of each other we are nothing but exchange values."[26]

Hannah Wilke Can (1974–78), a donation can with the half-naked "Christ" photo from *Hannah Wilke Super-T-Art* and a slot/slit for those willing to support her "charity," plays with sex and humor but is about much more.

Wilke admitted that "because it's a naked woman on the can, a lot of people might just say 'Naked!' but it is about being scarred, still; it is still about religion, it is still about being the martyr. . . ."[27] Indeed, the *Can* is about Wilke's neediness as well as her self-sufficiency. She seemed to be saying that she needs others to survive; but if she can get her needs met, she will be able to support herself. Wilke considered herself a child and a martyr, a female Christ, a suffering Venus. In fact, many of the titles of her works refer to her role as Venus—*Venus Envy, Venus Basin, Venus Cushion,* and *Venus Pareve.*[28]

Venus was a Jew

Wilke was a Jewish Venus. From a 1982 self-portrait clay model she made a rubber mold and several casts in edible chocolate. *Venus Pareve* combines the Roman goddess of love with the Hebrew word for food that is neutral (can be eaten with either milk or meat products) according to Jewish orthodox dietary laws. Wilke challenged the assumption that Venus originated from the classical Western tradition and, by flaunting her sexuality, attacked the stereotype that Jews are merely "people of the book."[29]

Her Jewish consciousness, therefore, underscores another scar. In fact, she claimed that her feminist awareness originated in World War II: "To also remember that as a Jew, during the war, I would have been branded and buried had I not been born in America."[30] By imprinting her body with stick-on sculptures and marking herself like the concentration camp inmates with their numbered tattoos, she identified with Jews who had been victims of Nazis. Wilke believed that, like Jews in the Holocaust, women had been denied personal identity, definition, and belonging. She even connected her nakedness with her Jewishness: "When they walked into the ovens, they were nude . . . In the history of art, women are nude."[31] To view Wilke's nudity solely as an expression of her narcissism misses the ways she purposely accentuated her vulnerability by putting herself in a naked state and identifying with children and people who are scarred, disadvantaged, or unwillingly exposed and objectified.

Narcissism and Exhibitionism

Wilke's narcissism is nearly always mentioned by her critics despite the fact that they are sharply divided on the topic. Wilke herself exclaimed (or disclaimed) "it doesn't have to do with narcissism."[32] There is no doubt that the artist dealt with narcissistic issues; she recalled always feeling like "the victim of my own beauty" and "made to feel like shit [by her mother] for looking at myself in the mirror."[33] In defiance, Wilke turned her art into a mirror that allowed for consistent play with the fuzzy lines dividing narcissism, exhibitionism, and healthy self-esteem. One of her aims was to help free women from their enslavement to standards of beauty and to encourage and build their confidence in matters of appearance and sexuality. By creating innovative and provocative frameworks for displaying female beauty, frameworks which interrogated the standards and values of both genders, she simultaneously invited viewers to recognize the oppression implicit in those standards and opened the way to freedom from their constraints. *I Object* is an example of this cunning double play alive in her work; Wilke, the sexual object, has a voice, a mind, and a self and uses them all to escape the incarceration of sexual reduction. Her art does not allow her to be grasped solely as a sexual object and yet brings such grasping fully into view. Hers is therefore a "narcissism" in the service of social transformation.

Compensatory structures underlie Wilke's claim that she was an ugly duckling growing up. Yet, childhood photographs show her to be far from an ugly duckling; she, in fact, exhibited a strong self-presence and posed self-consciously for the camera, both qualities she later enlisted in her art.[34] Wilke's exhibitionism began early and, in 1977, she placed a nude photograph of herself as a teenage girl in high heels wrapped in her mother's mink stole next to an art magazine cover shot (for *Appearances*) of herself as an adult. She has said that making art was a way of loving herself. What she didn't say was that making art was a way to wrap herself, once again, in her mother's warmth.

Wilke's need for attention, as well as her competitiveness, brashness, and humor were frequently apparent in her behavior at exhibition openings of other artists. In 1975, she appeared topless at a Lynda Benglis opening at the Paula Cooper Gallery in New York, saying that Benglis's classical motifs needed a goddess. *Village Voice* photographer Fred McDarrah documented the occasion on film and Wilke later called it an "invasive performance." Similarly, she attended an event honoring German artist Josef Beuys, and shouted above the crowd, "Hey Joe, What About My Show?!"[35] Wilke competed with other women artists who enjoyed wider critical acclaim. She attacked Judy Chicago and Cindy Sherman for using ideas she claimed to have originated. She disliked Chicago's *Dinner Party* because "Sexuality has to do with procreation and recreation—not accomplishments . . . women don't sing with their cunts."[36] She also accused Sherman of belonging to a class of women who are "hostile to women who are traditionally beautiful and use their minds as well as their bodies."[37] While some of her criticism may be justified, it is clear, from both her actions and tone, that she was envious of the attention other artists received. This was especially the case when she felt such attention was her due. Not content to sit silently on the sidelines while others basked in glory, Wilke used her art and humor to transform what was, in fact, the source of profound pain. Her behaviors and statements are provocative and, at times, seem childish. The child within her grabbed at what she desired and became angry when she did not receive it. The origins of some of these feelings can be found in Wilke's own childhood. Growing up, she not only felt herself to be unattractive; she also believed her mother loved her older sister more than herself.[38]

Wilke's feeling of being unappreciated also surfaced in relation to feminism. Although she clearly identified with the movement, she felt she wasn't given her proper place in its inception: "I started feminism."[39] She was infuriated that Judy Chicago, with her famed *Dinner Party,* received public acclaim and recognition for the novelty of its vaginal imagery. Wilke frequently tried to set the record straight to whoever would listen. The truth is that she had been making vaginal art since 1959, much earlier than Chicago became recognized for it, and that this work had been known in Los Angeles, where Wilke had spent several months with Oldenburg in 1970. If Chicago was considered the matriarch of feminist art, then Lucy Lippard, a close friend of Chicago's in the 1970s and '80s, was the matriarch of feminist art criticism. Wilke could not rise above the fact that Lippard wrote in 1976 that "Wilke, a glamour girl in her own right . . . sees her art as 'seductive,' . . . her confusion of her roles as beautiful woman and artist, as flirt and feminist, has resulted at times in politically ambiguous manifestations that have exposed her to criticism on a personal as well as on an artistic level."[40] Wilke wrote numerous letters to Lippard, albeit probably never sent, to express her anger at being misunderstood. She seems to have been most pained by Lippard's excision of Wilke in a reprint of an article written in 1966. A staunch feminist, Wilke was nonetheless somewhat of an outsider to the feminist movement and she typically took her revenge in her art. In 1977, she responded to the prejudice she experienced against her by creating a poster with a photo from her "S.O.S." series. With hands on hips, wearing an opened shirt and bold geometric tie, her torso plastered with vulval forms, she casts a defiant stare. The text cautions: *Marxism and Art: Beware of Fascist Feminism.*

Wilke's narcissism represents far more than a vain woman searching for her beautiful reflection in others' eyes. It is as if she was saying, "If I am not seen, I cannot exist, much less be loved or love myself. To be loved, I cannot be simply an object. My inner wounds must be seen as well as my outer beauty."

Mother

The men in Wilke's life parented her and she did not hesitate to use them as props, facilitators, and mirrors. They became the subject matter of her work (she quoted from their letters and telephone conversations) and the eye through which we see her (because they photographed her). The display of her independence notwithstanding, she never stopped needing others. In 1974, she created *Needed-Erase-Her,* a series probably referring to Oldenburg's rejection of her, in which she placed kneaded erasers in vulvar forms on boards.

Thus, in many ways, Wilke remained a child, though she was aware of her neediness and not ashamed to seek support and nurturance. She commented on the support she sought when discussing a series of large, painted ceramic vaginal sculptures placed on masonite base (*Of Relativity* series, 1980–84): "These vaginal sculptures represent myself and my mother and the base represents the support I received from my mother."[41]

As with Kollwitz, motherhood became an important theme in Wilke's art. After her mother took ill with cancer and a stroke, Wilke devoted most of her time and energy to solidify the bond she had with her. She took thousands of photographs of her mother, magically hoping that they would keep her alive after the recurrence of her breast cancer. In a memorial exhibition two years after her mother's death in 1982, Wilke showed a large photograph of herself next to one of her mother, both of them bare-chested (see Plate 5). The daughter wears makeup and stares into the camera as she displays her familiar beauty. Her mother, Selma Butter, is beside her, gaze averted, chest hollow and reddened, marked by a long mastectomy scar. Wilke bridges the gap in this series between the fantasy woman and the woman whose scars are visible; the young woman and the old; the healthy woman and the sick. This photograph evokes a primal visceral reaction in the viewer who is compelled to reluctantly gaze at two bodies in cruel juxtaposition, mother and daughter, one scarred by disease, the other beautiful and still in her prime, life and death side-by-side, tied together by time and blood. Her own chest displays small ray gun stick-ons, recalling the scars she collected from her ex-lover Oldenburg, scars that are emotional, constantly recalling the pain of her lost love; her mother's are the external, physical scars of disease. For Wilke, starification was intimately linked with scarification, as womb was linked with wound. Anyone accusing Wilke of vain narcissism simply has to spend a few moments with this work to see how glib and superficial the charge.

Wilke's double portrait with her mother influenced artists like Melanie Manchot who also photographed herself and her mother naked in *Double Portrait—Mum and I* (1997). These double photographs of mother and daughter begin to emphasize the significance of the mother for the daughter's identity; they additionally stress the emotional closeness between the two women.

Wilke's art shows us that separation between mother and daughter is never fully achieved, and that it may not even be a worthwhile goal. When speaking of this work, she said, "I made a memorial exhibition for my mother, with life-size photographs of her and womb-like sculptures . . . to comfort me, to be with her again, to watch her wave, to see her eat. To wear her wounds, to heal my own . . . circles becoming three-dimensional wombs representing the oneness of our relationship . . ."[42] Wilke's art implies the desire to reunite with her mother in order to correct an early derailment in the exchange between them. Mother and daughter, beauty and scars, join together in Wilke's art and life.[43]

Upon reflecting on her works from her 1984 *Support Foundation Comfort* exhibition, Wilke herself noted the centrality of her mother's place in her entire oeuvre: "The main thread that wove itself through my art was my mother's life and death. Most of my work had something about mother in it. She has always been the real constant figure in my life. It was always, *mother*, it wasn't *cunt*. I was never thought of as Earth Mother. I was always thought of as 'Sex Goddess.' I think they are the same thing."[44] Certainly Wilke's explanation offers an expanded appreciation of her work, perhaps most significantly of her vaginal forms. They are not merely representations of female sexuality; they are symbols of motherhood, maternity, female power, the source of all life. Thus, Wilke was never guided by the pleasure principle alone. Her sculptures usually litter the ground and recall tombs, perhaps those of concentration camp victims, the death of her parents, and even the end of her opportunity to procreate. In her diaries and unsent letters to Oldenburg, Wilke laments the fact that he refused to marry her and father her children. It is perhaps for this reason too that she felt compelled to multiply her images, a gesture indicating fertility and abundance, representing a need to compensate for ways in which she felt barren and near death. In her *Generation Process* series (1980–82), Wilke lined up multiples that reproduce themselves, suggesting both sexual reproduction as well as the cell division that takes place with the spread of cancer.

Illness and Death

At critical times in her life, Wilke's focal point turned to her face. In 1974, after being notified that her ex-brother-in-law had died, she made a thirty-minute video titled *Gestures* during which she manipulates her face. She pulls at her skin, caresses her mouth and tongue, and makes faces in the mirror/camera as if to prove again and again that she is alive. Her dead stare contrasts with the slow and sometimes sensual gesturing and gesticulating. Although it is true, as Amelia Jones claims, that Wilke's face is a stand-in for her body, with mouth suggesting the vaginal orifice, I believe it is more probable that Wilke turned to her face, her most intimate part and representation of self, at times in her life when she faced illness and death most directly.[45] Thus, the manipulation of her face became Wilke's metaphor for the innumerable expressions of life, the many vicissitudes of joy and pain, shock and complacency, laughter and tears. She held up her face as a mirror to the world and engaged its marvelous plasticity and nuanced language of intent, reflection, desire, hope, and anguish. Confronting the most poignant of human truths, Wilke's "gestures" alert us that nothing is really solid, that the face is always on the move, that she can pull and push her face, stretch it and compress it, put it through every possible expression, to assert life while attempting to assuage grief.

In November 1986, Wilke again focused on her face. She began painting watercolor self-portraits in somber colors, at first somewhat realistic, then more abstractly. Unlike her numerous sexual images, these portraits, despite their increasingly lively colors, intimate death in their skeletal appearance. As with Salomon, who used primary colors as she approached death, Wilke, too, employed red, blue, and yellow in her large face self-portraits as she tried to hold onto life. Wilke did not yet know that she was suffering from cancer, but she was aware that something was wrong. Six months later, she was diagnosed with lymphoma. Her meditations on her face became a ritual that she continued until her death. Filling her sketchbooks and covering watercolor sheets, up to seventy-two by forty-eight inches in size, she provided herself with imposing, constant reassurance that she was still alive, still a self. In an interview, she said, "Right now, I am more concerned with my head than my vagina because I have an illness . . . With my big face drawings, I'm trying to save myself."[46] In a video she elucidated, "It's not my body I want to save, it's my mind."[47] Wilke guilefully titled a 1989 exhibition of these works *About Face.*

As was her habit, Wilke turned to art in order to cope with the slings of fate. In this respect, she resembles Frida Kahlo, who was also known for an oeuvre filled with self-portraiture, her liaisons with famous men, and her documentation of her physical handicaps in art. Wilke, too, survived what she called "tortures"—attacks on her emotional and physical integrity. Interestingly, both artists insisted that their illness not detract from their sexuality. "Nothing's bothering me anymore" claimed Wilke, "I'll make it into art."[48] Like Kahlo, Wilke equated the physical pain she suffered with the emotional pain all women endure by virtue of being women: "I've really been bombarded. I'm going to show how tough I am. I'm the toughest woman artist in the world. Nobody's been through this torture. Except mentally most of us women have, I must admit."[49]

The art Wilke created during her hospital stays was smaller in scale than her previous images. She began to incorporate syringes, medication bottles, bloodied bandages, and hair lost due to her treatments. She cleverly called the bloodied tissues "Marcels," referring to Duchamp; her "hair" pieces were named *Brushstrokes,* providing a pun on their sexual and aesthetic meanings.

Wilke succumbed to lymphoma in her mid-forties, only ten years following the death of her mother. She suffered for ten years before dying, years devoted to staying alive and transforming her physical and emotional battles into art. In retrospect, this makes her *So Help Me Hannah* and *Intra-Venus* series eerily resemble "before and after" pictures. She playfully referred to her transformation in appearance as that from "beauty to beast" and to her self-portrait watercolors prior to cancer as B.C. (*Before Cancer*).[50] In one of the most poignant images from her final series,

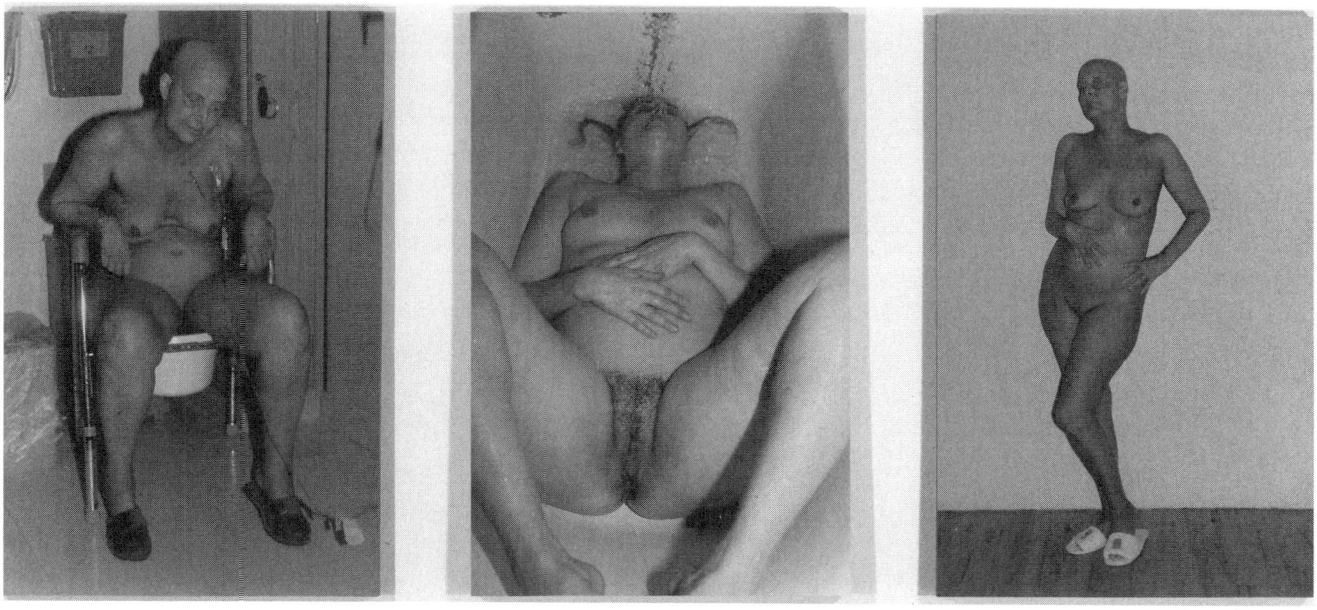

37. Hannah Wilke, Performalist Self-Portrait with Donald Goddard. From *Intra-Venus # 3,* August 17, 1992, February 15, 1992, August 9, 1992. Chromagenic supergloss prints. 3 panels: 71.5 × 47.5 inches each. Courtesy Donald and Helen Goddard and Ronald Feldman Fine Arts, New York.

cunningly titled *Intra-Venus,*[51] she is bald, the result of chemotherapy, and sits naked on a toilet hunched over wearing a beatific smile as she awaits death. Hospital slippers replace the high heels worn in her previous works and tubes are attached to the chest that once exhibited tiny vaginal forms. The directness of her gaze now aims to the ground as it begins to convey her detachment from this world. In another, ever-daring, photograph taken from a bird's-eye view, we observe the naked artist with her legs spread apart as she lies in the bath; a shot, with its close up of her vulva, that would ordinarily be considered pornographic. But this picture is far from pornographic since Wilke's pose likens her to an infant girl; her arms are folded over her belly and her hair is laid out on either side like pigtails. This disquieting work, with its focal point on Wilke's exposed vagina, is an uncanny remake of the earlier *What does this represent? What do you represent?* It is perhaps no coincidence that many of the *Intra-Venus* works depict Wilke in a fetal position. Her regressive aspirations to return to the comfort of the womb are poignantly straightforward.[52]

Several of the works are diptychs which use one daring image as counterpoint for an even bolder one.[53] In an example, one side shows her with bandages and tubes and a plastic shower cap on her head while, in the other, she holds a pot of flowers on her head and displays her bloated body in a coy, feminine pose reminiscent of an Ingres model. Although these achingly beautiful pictures expose the ravages of disease and the prospect of impending death, they do so with no sentimentality or self-pity.

It is in this last series that the depth of Wilke's lifelong commitment to truth makes itself most known and her unique form of radical narcissism is so potently put at its service. Here we see Venus completely naked and exposed, both in body and soul. She is bloated with illness, bruised with needles, swaddled in bandages, laid low by oncoming death, weary and broken, but still able to mug a smile, or strike a classical pose. She does not emerge from a shell but, rather, frumpy hospital slippers, or repose in beatitude, a meditative Madonna, her face and head encircled by a blue blanket (see Plate 6). Fully exposed is the existential nudity that lies beneath all of our skin, however beautifully shaped, the skeletal truth of our fragile mortality shining through the transparent clothing of culture and history. Through these images of Hannah Wilke dying and fading from life, we are forced to acknowledge the vertiginous paradox at the heart of desire: wanting perma-

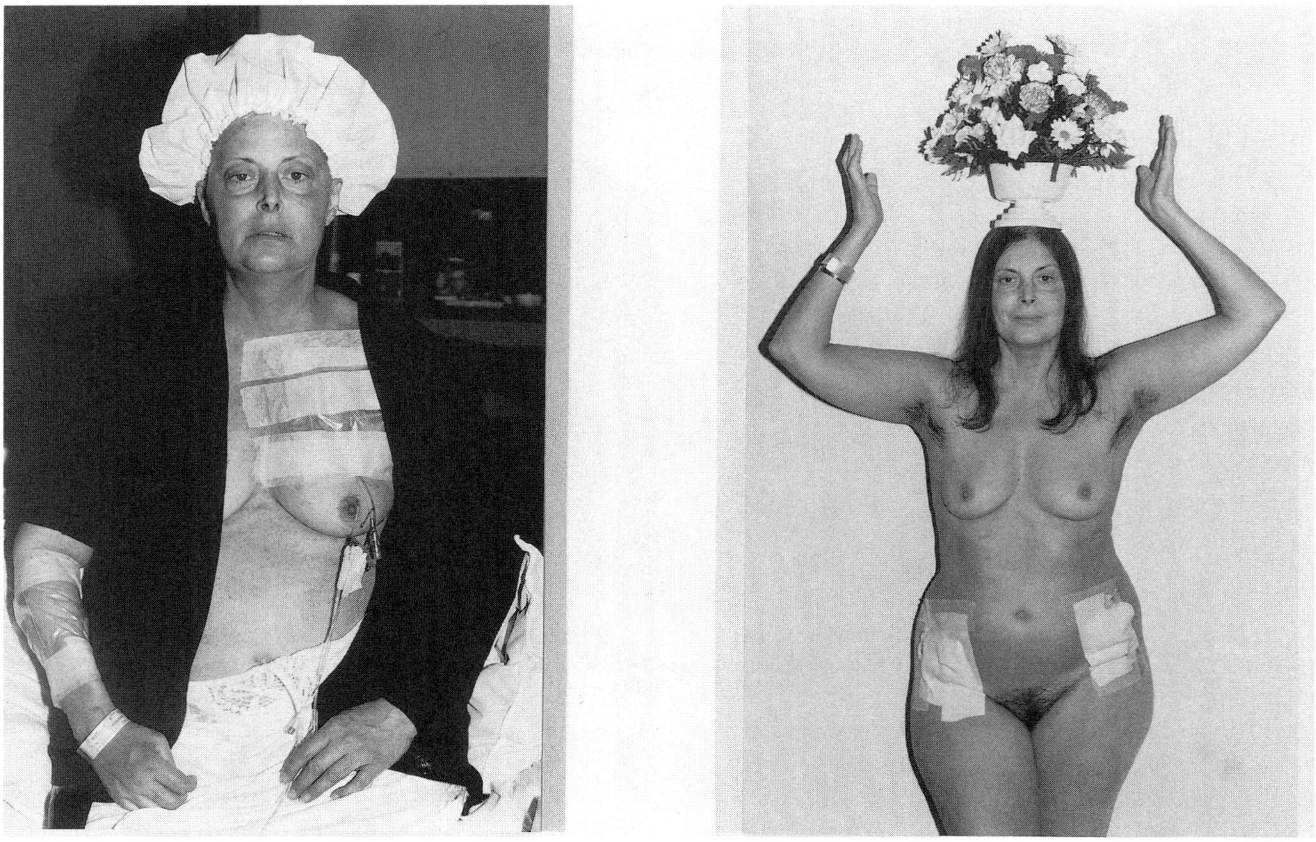

38. Hannah Wilke, Performalist Self-Portrait with Donald Goddard. From *Intra-Venus # 1,* January 30, 1992/June 15, 1992. Chromagenic supergloss prints. 2 panels: 71½ × 47½ inches each. Courtesy Donald and Helen Goddard and Ronald Feldman Fine Arts, New York.

nence and denying its impossibility with a pleasing and static image or idea. Here, in this breathtaking collection, the viewer is forced to confront every bias, including that of Wilke's relationship to her own beauty, as well as those about female representation and the illusionary nature of representation itself. *Intra-Venus* is both a highly spiritual and deeply philosophical work.

Wilke died at the age of fifty-three. Her final works were shown posthumously to rave reviews.

The Naked Truth

It is ironic that many critics did not take Wilke seriously until she portrayed the ravages of her own illness in her series of nude photographs taken of herself during the final year of her life. In the end, perhaps no longer envious of her remarkable beauty, some critics finally acknowledged that she could not have been truly narcissistic if she was willing to expose the devastating effects of chemotherapy and bone marrow treatments on her wasted body. Carol Diehl wrote, "*Intra-Venus* cancels out the narcissism of [Wilke's] earlier work."[54] Paradoxically, Wilke's cancer allowed such critics to finally see the scars she had been exposing all along. In fact, the purpose of her art—to make the invisible visible—never really changed; the only thing that changed was the ability of her viewers to respond to what she had been showing them from the start. Her use of poses taken from her early work not only speaks to the fact that she was her own point of reference but, also, demonstrates the continuity of purpose throughout her oeuvre.[55]

That the *Intra-Venus* photographs were taken in collaboration with her partner of many years is significant. Goddard described the photographic process as "the relationship" and claimed that he disliked the pictures he took of Wilke when she was asleep or unconscious because they lacked her active involvement.[56] He explained how they had never discussed taking the photographs that documented Wilke's illness and medical treatment: "There was no question we would do this, no discussion. It was natural to photograph Hannah dying. It was dramatic. There were so many visual opportunities."[57]

Goddard was the man who helped Wilke nurse her mother during her illness and the man who remained devoted to her until the end. Wilke could laugh and play in the face of adversity largely due to her relationship with this loving man. She proudly exhibited her wounds—now real physical scars—because they were seen not through the eyes of a male chauvinist but, rather, through the lens of a man who loved her, a man who saw her beauty and *joie de vivre* in all situations, a man who was as invested in keeping her alive as she was. Goddard became Wilke's comfort and support at the end of her life. Just as she had made peace with her mother at the end of her mother's life (she apologized to Wilke before she died for having loved her sister more) so too she made peace with the men in her life, men she previously experienced as having used, betrayed, or abandoned her.

Until her last breath, Wilke continued to force her audience to face what they dared not see and to name what they could not speak. And, until the end, she compelled us to confront our limitations, as men and women, as mortal beings who cannot know or control our fate. In one acrostic she invented, the name Hannah means *Handle With Care.* If we learn to look beyond appearances, to make the invisible visible, then we too need not wait until old age or illness strikes in order to notice the physical frailty and emotional vulnerability, the scars worn by every human being, each of whom deserves to be handled with care.[58]

It is unfortunate that so many who followed Wilke's art over the years were able to see her only in the role of the Emperor, a nude exhibitionist who treated the female body as a fantasy sight for male desire. Others, myself included, remain forever touched by Wilke's art. For us, she was not only the Emperor; she was the child. For us, Wilke was the voice of truth.

7
Ana Mendieta: Goddess in Exile

Exile is . . . the unhealable rift forced between a human being and a native place, between the self and its true home: its essential sadness can never be surmounted.

—Edward Said

Pain of Cuba
Body I am
My orphanhood I live.

In Cuba when you die
The earth that covers us
Speaks.

But here, covered by the earth whose prisoner I am
I feel death palpitating underneath.

And so,
As my whole being is filled with want of Cuba
I go on to make my mark upon the earth,
To go on is victory.

—Ana Mendieta

Ana Mendieta fashioned sand and water into dimensions matching her silhouette, creating an earth-body work in 1977 as part of her *Fetish* series. Executed at Old Man's Creek in Iowa City, she dug a shallow moat surrounding the figure and pierced it with sticks projected vertically from the body's center. Years later, Mendieta tied the making of this piece to the fact that her mother had undergone an operation for cancer at that time. Subconsciously using art in an attempt to restore her mother's physical health,[1] as did Wilke, she fused her own image with that of her mother, and then melded that shared body with Mother Earth. Mendieta created a ritual which she repeated time and time again: creation, destruction, death, and regeneration.

Torn from her mother and her motherland at an early age, Mendieta (1948–85) used her art to come to terms with maternal loss. The attempt to master the painful fissure of separation and loss was the raison d'être of her art. In her best-known, self-titled "earth-body works," Mendieta created sculptural pieces that blend into the natural landscape. Though her art deals with matters of loss and death, it exhibits a transformative power derived from the artistic gesture that breathes life into natural materials.

Making art became a spiritual act for Mendieta. She saw herself as a dynamic conduit, the willing shaman who left a talisman to work its magic with the elements. In creating her earth-body sculptures, she performed self-imposed rituals, usually working alone, preparing the land and claiming her territory, rendering it sacred, before creating fetish objects that in her mind possessed magical and spiritual powers. She appropriated the "healing imagery" from Santeria, a New World form of Yoruban religion created by Nigerian slaves who came to Cuba in the sixteenth century, and drew on ceremonies and symbols that affirmed social bonds, connected her to the past, and ultimately sought to overcome the limitations of time, place, and separation.

The ephemeral quality of Mendieta's earthworks reflects her subject matter: the disso-

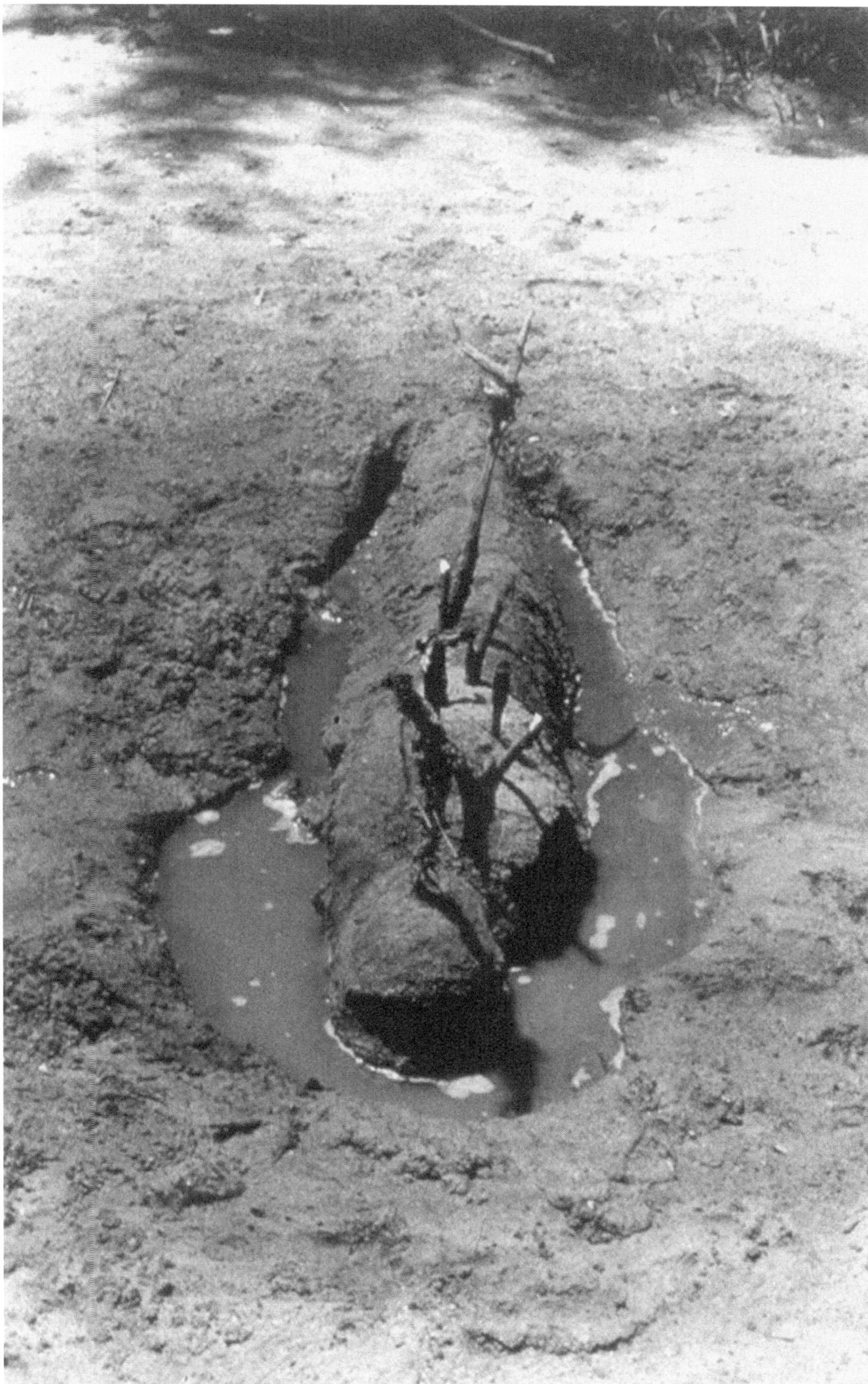

39. Ana Mendieta, *Untitled* (Fetish Series), 1977. Lifetime color photograph. 20 × 13¼ in (50.8 × 33.7 cm). © The Estate of Ana Mendieta Collection. Courtesy Galerie Lelong, New York.

lution and fragility of our ties to people and places. An artist in exile, Mendieta claimed space after space only to create a powerfully felt absence within them. She reproduced her concrete form by shaping her silhouette into the earth; yet that very form, so fragile and delicate, susceptible to weather changes and the forces of nature, gradually vanished, leaving only a trace of what once was. Mendieta's physical body became, in the end, a numinous presence. Although her art, like a child's sandcastle, was not protected against change and dissolution; its restoration was ironically guaranteed through its gracious return to and merger with the surround that furnished its existence.

The "disappearance" of Mendieta's earth-body sculptures begs the question of what the actual artwork is and where it belongs. Indeed, many of her pieces were never seen by anyone but herself. All that remains of them are 35 mm slides, Super-8 films, and color and black-and-white photographs, images of a fleeting art, simulacrums expressing the foreboding tension between time and timelessness and the profound anxiety attending the encounter with the transitory nature of all things. Mendieta repeated her own private trauma in these performative dramas and, at the same time, introduced a powerfully evocative aesthetic language for the universal problem of exile, dislocation, identity, and transcendence.

Beginnings

Ana Mendieta was born into a well-to-do, politically connected Havana family in 1948, a family dominated by her maternal grandmother, Elvira, the daughter of General Carlos Maria de Rojas, a leader in Cuba's war of independence (1895–98). Her granduncle, Carlos Mendieta, had been president of the nation in the 1930s.[2]

Following a difficult pregnancy, the last three months requiring complete bed rest, Mendieta's mother, Raquelin, gave birth to Ana, her second daughter, a sickly child who suffered from anemia and chronic bronchitis. She received three transfusions of her father's blood during her first year of life.[3] Consequently, she was overprotected and indulged, developing a particularly close attachment to her mother. Though young Ana received a great deal of attention, warmth, and nurturance from a large extended family and from a variety of maternal figures, including her mother, grandmother, nannies, and older sister Raquel, she also suffered numerous painful separations from all of them.

Mendieta's mother, a professor of chemistry and physics worked full-time and left much of the daily caretaking responsibilities to nannies who came and went, including Mendieta's favorite, a Chinese-African nanny who left for the United States when Ana was eight. The two Mendieta sisters, along with their two female cousins, spent every summer and holiday at their beloved grandmother's house in Cárdenas, and Ana always cried when it was time to leave.

Mendieta's father, Ignacio, a lawyer by profession, possessed the soul of a radical. During World War II, while working as an attorney for the Police Department, he identified members of the Communist Party for the CIA. The only way to later redeem himself and obtain employment was to join the Communist Party. He refused. Unemployed and blacklisted, he engaged in Cuba's counterrevolutionary struggle.

After the United States had severed ties with Cuba, political events frightened many Cuban families. Catholic schools were closed and members of the religious community advised to leave the country. Families feared governmental influence would weaken their ties with one another. Recalling Cahun and Moore's anti-Nazi campaign, during Castro's period of prenationalization, Mendieta and her older sister, Raquel, took it upon themselves to distribute antigovernment flyers. When their father discovered their dangerous activities, he feared for their safety and felt it necessary to impose drastic measures. Along with many other families, Mendieta's parents decided to send her at age twelve and Raquel at age fifteen to the United States in 1961 through Operation Peter Pan, a program created by the Catholic Church to encourage emigration and preservation of the children's Catholic upbringing. Although Mendieta's parents believed the separation would last only one year, it extended far longer. Mendieta's mother and younger brother, Ignacio, joined the girls after five years. Her father was arrested in 1965 for his CIA spying, and not permitted to leave Cuba until 1979, eighteen years later.[4]

Cast out of their homeland, Ana and Raquel lived for several months in a camp in Miami before being sent to an orphanage in Dubuque, Iowa. Although initially thrilled by what she perceived as an exciting adventure, Ana cried incessantly when she realized the grave reality of her situation. The orphanage housed many adolescent delinquent girls, and the nuns often separated and mistreated the Mendieta sisters.[5] From the orphanage, the sisters shuttled among a number of foster homes, and soon Mendieta began to regard herself as an orphan.[6] When her sister left for college, Mendieta again endured an agonizing separation, now from the person who had become the sole constant companion in her life *and* her primary mother figure. Mendieta's pain was exacerbated by the fact that her high school classmates teased her with racial epithets.[7] At this point, she stopped eating and became so depressed that her foster family sought psychiatric help for her. The tearing apart of her family began to tear her apart. Later in life, she understood the need to make art that was very physical to express the concrete as well as the symbolic aspects of her trauma.

In her adulthood, Mendieta followed in the footsteps of Frida Kahlo, fellow Latina artist whom she greatly admired, by making art her vocation and by transforming Mexico into her surrogate mother/land.[8] Like Kahlo, Mendieta became involved with an older married mentor, Hans Breder an art teacher at the University of Iowa, where she studied. Years later, living in New York City, she married the older, physically imposing (Mendieta stood at a mere four feet eleven), well-known minimalist sculptor, Carl Andre. Mendieta's oedipal search for a father replacement in these men, each of whom was thirteen years her senior, appears obvious.

In the 1980s, Mendieta's career was on the rise. She was exhibiting in the United States and in Rome, a city she lived in and felt more at home in than New York. Her confidence grew and her future seemed promising on all fronts except for her stormy marriage, their clashes fueled by alcohol and Andre's infidelities. At age thirty-eight, Mendieta became the victim of an infamous and unresolved death resulting from a fall from the thirty-fourth floor balcony in the apartment she shared with her husband. Andre was tried and acquitted of her murder.

Mother Earth

Mendieta's oeuvre is multifaceted, consisting of body art, performance pieces, and well-known earth works built-up with twigs, grass, mud, sand, stone, clay, snow, and ice on riverbanks, beaches, archeological sights, trees, and limestone caves. Most of her art uses her body or its silhouette to express an exquisite relationship with the elements and her longing for merger and re/union. She also made delicate petroglyphlike drawings and carvings on fig leaves and paper. "Art must have begun as nature itself," she wrote, "in a dialectical relationship between humans and the natural world from which we cannot be separated."[9] Mendieta saw deeply and correctly that humanity emerged from nature, and the two exist in reciprocal connection, whose underpinning is communion. Experientially, one cannot exist without the other. In so many ways, her art suggests this ontological viewpoint, which she felt emotionally and physically, in her being and in her body.

The many natural elements embodied in Mendieta's art are laden with both cultural and psychological meaning. Her oeuvre is linked with that of a group of artists who emerged in the late 1960s and 1970s. These "land artists" wished to challenge the museum and gallery spaces by creating art in outdoor sites. They made a strong statement against the commercial exploitation of art objects by using natural materials, like dirt and mud rather than paint, wood, or marble, to reconnect the art world with the real world. Mendieta described the shift in her artmaking: "The turning point in my art was in 1972 when I realized that my paintings were not real enough for what I wanted the image to convey—and by real I mean I wanted my images to have power, to be magic. I decided that for the images to have magic qualities, I had to work directly with nature. I had to go to the source of life, to mother earth."[10] The nature-culture dialectic is most noticeably experienced in the ephemeral quality of the land works because they are typically and freely given over to the forces of entropy and decay.

As part of a larger trend of environmental activism, back to the land movement, and eco-spirit groups, land artists not only dematerialized what they believed to be narrowly defined, commodified art objects; they also rematerialized landscape.

In contrast with the large-scale, mostly abstract, monumental, and often invasive, works executed by Michael Heizer, Robert Smithson, and Walter De Maria, Mendieta expressed more personal pieces and nearly always left the natural elements undamaged. She said: "I have thrown myself into the very elements that produced me, using the earth as my canvas and my soul as my tools"[11] Artist Nancy Spero distinguished Mendieta's approach to the earth with that of male land artists: "Ana did not rampage the earth to control or dominate or to create grandiose monuments of power or authority. She sought intimate recessed spaces, protective habitats signaling a temporary respite of comfort and meditation."[12] Restricted to the shape of her diminutive body, Mendieta's pieces were also much more modest in scale.

Even though most of her figures reveal few, if any, distinguishing feminine features, Mendieta's oeuvre is undeniably concerned with the female form and its cultural history. In fact, some of her earthworks are carved *into* the ground rather than superimposed on top of it. With their dark, oval crevices, these works suggest a mysterious inner space; they therefore also create vaginal forms not unlike those in Wilke's oeuvre. Unsurprisingly, then, in addition to the land art movement, the feminist movement had a profound effect on Mendieta's self-portrayals and performances. Influenced by fellow artist, Mary Beth Edelson, Mendieta joined the feminist art movement, Reclamation of the Goddess, whose primary aim was to find and use historical images of powerful female forms.[13] Yet, prior to this Mendieta knew that the mythical projection of the feminine onto nature served as a chief metaphor for the source and sustenance of life. Indeed, the earth is often associated with the womb and birth—the word nature, coming as it does from the Latin word *natura* which means birth or character; yet the earth also connotes an intimate tie to death as it is the most frequently used burial site. Biblical words from Genesis (3:19) proclaim: "In the sweat of the face shalt thou eat bread, till though return unto the ground; for out of it wast thou taken: for dust thou art, and unto dust shalt thou return." Life and death unite in Mendieta's earthworks as they bring together the most powerful forces with which we contend.

Mendieta's strong need to merge with the earth and to repeat its natural cycles by creating "living" artworks is illustrated in a highly evocative and powerful earth-body performance she executed in 1974 and documented on a film lasting three minutes and fifteen seconds. At the beginning of *Burial Pyramid*, Mendieta's hardly discernible body is buried beneath a pile of large stones at a temple structure in Yagul, Mexico. We watch as she takes deeper and deeper breaths that cause her torso to swell and the stones to rise and fall, eventually dropping from her body. Mendieta slowly emerges as if excavated from among the archeological ruins. Her naked body then begins to undulate, simultaneously miming the act of birth and the act of sex. Both acts revive her from a death-like state and reconnect her to life forces. Literally breathing life into what appeared to be dead and buried matter, Mendieta leaves us awed by the power of her interaction with the universal forces of nature and her ability to endow them with human form. Reminiscent of Freud's famous archeological metaphor for psychoanalysis, Mendieta exemplifies his statement that "stones talk."[14]

In her ongoing reverential and intimate dialogue with nature, Mendieta expressed a sacred perspective: that the earth is vibrant, creative, and everlasting, a modifiable source of life to which we owe our existence and without which we cannot take a single step. And, like the early psychoanalytic assertion of a sex and death drive to explain human behavior, Mendieta exclaimed: "All of my work is about two things . . . it's about Eros and life/death."[15] In a performance piece from 1975, *On Giving Life*, she placed her naked body on top of an adult human skeleton that lay on the grass and kissed its mouth. The image is shocking and provocative; she engages in what resembles mouth-to-mouth resuscitation and nakedly embraces death, daring to breathe life into dead bones and to show the natural yet discomforting intimacy between sex and death.

Since the prehistoric epoch, women have been identified with the earth and the earth

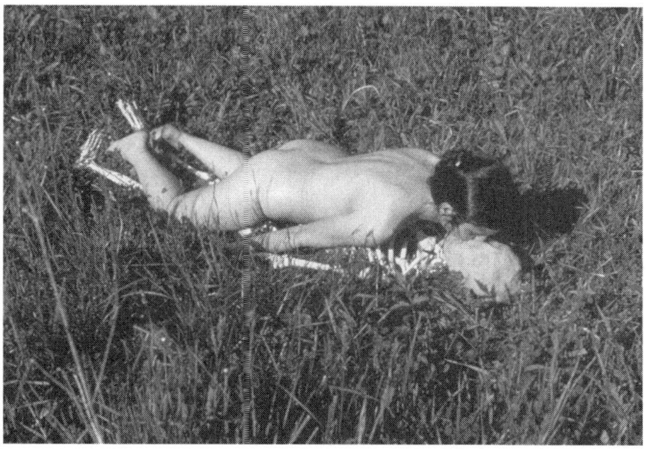

40. Ana Mendieta, *On Giving Life,* 1975. Lifetime color photograph. 8 × 10 in. (20.3 × 25.4 cm). © The Estate of Ana Mendieta Collection. Courtesy Galerie Lelong, New York.

has been regarded as symbolizing the womb, hence the terms Mother Earth and Mother Nature. For Mendieta, the earth became a surrogate mother with which she played out her issues of separation, loss, and creation. She treated the earth as if it were her mother's body and used it to simultaneously repeat and repair her trauma of exile. Mendieta accomplished this through a continued exploration of the concepts of figure and ground. She literally grounded herself in each new site, thereby becoming not only a figure within the ground, but also, a grounded figure. Mendieta's need to remain grounded was so intense that she suffered from a crippling fear of heights throughout her life. She blurred the boundaries between self and object by joining figure and ground, thereby representing the longed-for symbiotic reunion of mother/ground and child/figure.

Freud's concept of repetition compulsion as a defensive attempt to master trauma helps us comprehend the reasons Mendieta returned to her silhouette hundreds of times in a relatively brief period.[16] To make his point, Freud described the *fort-da* game of a child: after the disappearance of his mother, the boy repeatedly hides and then rediscovers a string as he replays the actual loss and its correction through his own creative efforts. Freud understood children's play and artists' works as existing in the service of such mastery. Psychologically, Mendieta's art expressed both a reaction and response to the forced exile she experienced as a youth. She was traumatized by the loss of a protective mother, someone who could contain her sense of disorganization and dissolution. Metaphorically repeating her merger and extraction from her mother's womb in her art, she attempted to master these feelings. With its dissolution of boundaries, Mendieta's art stresses the importance of loss and the attendant hunger to reunite with the lost object, as well as the need to preserve and remember the past not merely through recollection but, perhaps more poignantly, through repetitive action.

The impermanence of most of the materials Mendieta used—soil, sand, fiber—and also their volatility—gunpowder and fire—demonstrates the sudden, powerful, and ever-present forces of nature and the fragility of form as it is ever altered by wind, rain and time. Perhaps most importantly, the materials reflect the transient nature of the primary subject of her work: the ephemeral bonding with the mother and its vulnerability to unexpected and even explosive change. Mendieta was clearly aware of the psychological sources of her artwork when she wrote the following:

> I have been carrying on a dialogue between the landscape and the female body (based on my own silhouette). I believe this has been a direct result of my having been torn from my homeland (Cuba) during my adolescence. I am overwhelmed by the feeling of having been cast from the womb (nature). My art is the way I re-establish the bonds that unite me to the universe. It is a return to the maternal source. Through my earth/body sculptures I become one with the earth. . . . I become an extension of nature and nature becomes an extension of my body. This obsessive act of reasserting my ties with the earth is really the reactivation of primeval beliefs . . . [in] an omnipresent female force, the after-image of being encompassed within the womb, is a manifestation of my thirst for being.[17]

The artist's awareness encompasses the ultimate realization that her work dealt with the undifferentiated state between mother and self. In fact, the need to repeatedly return to the "obsessive" theme of separation and reunion grew into the main focus of her art. Aside from what she consciously acknowledged, this awareness emerges clearly from her work. Her longing to recreate the *oceanic feeling,* which Freud described as "an indissoluble bond, of being one with the external world as a whole" deriving from the mother-infant merger, is granted concrete expression in one of her early performance works in which she floats naked in the ocean (see Plate 13).[18] Mendieta deliberately executed this piece, and several others, in Florida's southernmost points to be as physically near to her homeland as possible. Striving to reconcile the unbridgeable distance between the United States and Cuba, and between her mother and herself, the artist laid her body in the sand facing in the direction of Cuba and allowed the tide to wash it up. Mendieta's "aesthetics of disappearance" movingly recreate the tragedy of exile.[19] They also represent her way of mourning her losses.

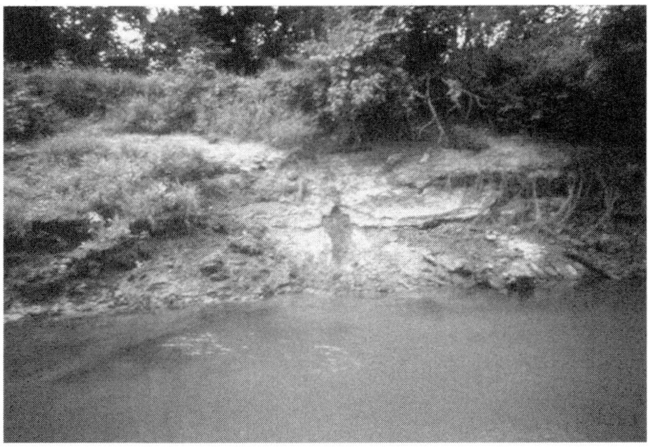

41. Ana Mendieta, *Untitled* (Silueta Works in Iowa), c. 1976–78. Estate print, 1991. Color photograph. 20 × 16 in (50.8 × 40.6 cm). © The Estate of Ana Mendieta Collection. Courtesy Galerie Lelong, New York.

In contrast with classical psychoanalysis, which views the mother-child relationship as solely influenced by the mother, recent research on the mother-infant dyad emphasizes the reciprocal influence that mothers and infants have on each other.[20] Mendieta, too, was aware of the mutuality of the mother-infant bond, the reciprocities and resonances that mirror, echo, reverberate, and transform both parties. Although she chose the sites of her earth body sculptures and the materials she used to make them, she could not control what happened to them. Nature was left to take its course and acted on her as much, if not more, than she acted on it.

Silueta

Mendieta's *Silueta Series*, produced in the 1970s, best illustrates the artist's dialogue with her lost mother by way of her art. These "earth-body" sculptures are distinguished by the lingering shape of Mendieta's body which had been literally hewed into landscapes, traced in sand, etched in dirt, carved in rock, and at times, covered with blood. Freud wrote of how the "shadow of the [lost] object" falls on the ego of the person in mourning and leaves a trace of its existence.[21] Mendieta's title *Silueta*, or silhouette, can be understood as referring to this shadow, or in her own words, the "after-image" of her mother whose imprint had invariably remained in her life and art. Incorporating the lost object through a process of identification, she tried to reestablish her place in the world.

In her first *Silueta* executed in 1973 in an ancient Zapotec stone grave at Yaagul in the Valley of Oaxaca, Mendieta called attention to the convergence of life and death forces (see Plate 14). She converted the rock-hard burial site into a womb-like cavity in which she laid her soft, live body covered with fresh, white blossoming flowers. This work nicely demonstrates the manner in which she made art by using her body to bring back to life what, for her, had seemed to die. After all, exile is a kind of death from which one must strive to emerge again as a new being. Furthermore, exile is itself a kind of womb, a container of isolation, a merger from which one must leave to embrace life and find a future. As she did when she mimicked making love with a skeleton, Mendieta here faced death and her fear of it; she also welcomed death as the end of pain, and connected it to life by exposing one undisputable truth: to be born is to be dead at some future time.

Mendieta's exile separated her not only from her mother but, also, from her father, whom she was prevented from seeing for eighteen long years. Ignacio was a frustrated artist who had created wood carvings in a studio attached to the family home.[22] Mendieta identified with her father by becoming an artist herself, a choice that allowed for a release of emotional expression, a mastery of trauma, and a means by which she kept him close to her. The first man she found to replace her father was Hans Breder, her art teacher at the

University of Iowa, married and thirteen years her senior. Mendieta and Breder had a ten-year relationship that proved romantically and professionally fertile. A self-imposed exile from Germany, Breder most probably possessed an implicit understanding of Mendieta's displacement issues. Breder's influence on the evolution of Mendieta's artistic idiom is unmistakable. He exposed her to a wide variety of performance artists, artists who employed their bodies in their work, while actively encouraging her to use her body in artmaking.[23] Breder watched approvingly as Mendieta joined her body with Mother Earth, and he filmed her during the creation of most of her siluetas.[24] Mendieta's works, like Wilke's, incorporated the male gaze in them. Yet, the male gaze in Mendieta's earth sculptures was one of awe and reverence rather than chauvinistic appropriation.

Mendieta sought out various sites in Iowa and Mexico for her Silueta works and visited Mexico with Breder every summer in the 1970s. In Mexico, she discovered a culture possessing similarities with her own. She liked that the Mexican people were short and dark, like her; and she appreciated their commemoration of death in their annual Day of the Dead celebrations. She adopted several elements from Mexican iconography, like the posture she frequently assumed with upraised arms.[25] Most importantly, she used the land to explore the relation to her lost tribe. In essence, Mendieta, the self-proclaimed "orphan," created a family romance with Mexico as her new mother/land. "There is above all the search for origins,"[26] she wrote in 1983. She also said, "Plugging into Mexico was like going back to the source, being able to get some magic just by being there."[27] Mendieta made certain to visit Kahlo's home in Coyoacan whenever she was in Mexico.[28] Due to her own personal tragedies, Kahlo was preoccupied with forces of life and death and had made several paintings of herself and others literally rooted in the soil. She served as a natural and logical artistic ancestor for Mendieta.

Mendieta chose to work in Mexico's archeological sites due to her deep fascination with ancient civilizations and indigenous societies. Since Freud's time, archeology has been employed as an apt metaphor for psychoanalytic excavations into buried (repressed/unconscious) memories of one's individual and collective past. Mendieta, too, perceived her goal as that of mining societies that had been lost and forgotten, misunderstood and hidden, to keep their memories and customs alive and to prevent their total obliteration. Clearly, her attempts to revive these lost civilizations acted as a way of symbolically reconnecting to the land, people, and life that she had lost. Mendieta seemed never to tire of resuscitating the dead.

Blood

During Mendieta's student years at the University of Iowa, she incorporated blood into many of her performance pieces. In her first such work, she created a voodoo-like ritual by grabbing a recently beheaded chicken whose blood gushed all over her face and body. Committing a scene of violation as well as one of sacrifice, Mendieta identified the animal's decapitated body with her own naked female body. After performing this piece, she remarked that she "immediately started using blood, I guess because I think it's a very powerful magic thing. I don't see it as a negative force."[29]

Certainly, blood is the substance we cannot fail to notice, the red liquid, the bright stain that shocks the eye with its reminder of the vulnerable, dark inside, the wound, the injury, the "monthly curse," the pain of the blade and the cutting edge, the bleeding that must stop less cold, shock, and death result. Blood, so much "thicker than water," transports life in the form of food and oxygen through the arterial pathways, nourishing every cell of our body. To see someone pouring blood is to be shocked with the stunning visual reminder of one's own animal mortality. No wonder blood furnishes so much symbolic meaning as sacrifice, suffering, rebirth, unbreakable bond, omen and oath, life and death. Using blood as paint is to paint from the inside.

Influenced by Santeria, Mendieta used animal blood or red tempura paint as a symbol for sacrifice and rebirth. In many of her siluetas, she also added these elements to represent the blood of Christ in transubstantiation. Mendieta mixed Christian and pagan symbols in her art, since both held deeply sacred meaning for her. Thanks to Breder,

Mendieta became familiar with bloody works, including animal sacrifices, known in Vienna Aktion artists' works, like those of Hermann Nitsch. Paint that resembled blood had also been smeared on the participants in Carolee Schneemann's 1964 performance piece, *Meat Joy*.

Mendieta traced her body's outline in blood, created a bloody heart on top of her naked body, and made repeated prints of her bloody hands. In one performance piece, Mendieta wrapped herself in a white bed sheet and laid in various poses while Brader sprinkled blood onto the sheet that covered her body. The result was a bright, blood-stained silhouette of her form. In another, he placed a bloodied animal heart on top of her own. Recalling Christ's Shroud of Turin, Mendieta established her role as symbolic of eternal themes of martyrdom. The bloody outline of her body and heart, the bright silhouette on the sheet, these are the essential traces she leaves of her body, her heart, her life. Mendieta's blood, the invisible fluid coursing in her darkest depths, is made visible while Mendieta herself is absent, invisible, as if to say "Mendieta is here and yet not here at all (see Plates 13 and 15)."

On a more personal level, it is important to recall that Mendieta came close to dying in infancy. It was her father's blood, transfused into her body that revived her and kept her alive. Incorporating blood in many of her works recreates the act of sacrifice and resurrection present in Catholicism, Santeria, and her own childhood. By smearing or dripping blood onto her body or its silhouette, Mendieta created a ritual of sacrificial healing and rebirth. She thus became one with her absent father.

Fire

"Fire has always been a magical thing for me . . . fusion . . . its transformation of materials," Mendieta once said.[30] Incorporating candles, gunpowder, and fireworks into her art, Mendieta infused fire with multiple meanings. The light produced by the fire invokes a sense of ritualized spirituality or enlightenment, an illumination of form sacrificed to flame, the fire of life consuming its own material in a glorious blaze, sometimes slowly with candles, sometimes in explosive transformations, sometimes with dazzling pyrotechnic display. Mendieta's use of fire in her art is symbolic of awareness, existence, and sacrifice, suggesting consciousness of the human situation, inherently poignant and tragic. She favored the powerful posture of the human form with arms upraised, beckoning upward for release, recalling the Catholic tradition of a soul burning in purgatory, or the innocent and holy witch's surrender to the fire while being burned at the stake. Few things astonish us more than a body on fire, arms raised, both feeding and being eaten by the flame. We are life and yet life devours us. We are the fire and what it consumes; we burn and our smoke rises to the heavens. Small wonder Mendieta revived alchemy and created her own recipe for gunpowder using sulfur (representing the soul), sugar, and saltpeter.[31] Some of her figures were set in mounds or raised "containers" of earth resembling volcanoes waiting to erupt. In contrast to the slow changes the Siluetas underwent when left to natural decaying processes, gunpowder and fireworks siluetas transformed rapidly, dramatizing the suddenness and speed of change occurring in life's often seemingly slow march to the end.

And yet it is always to the land which she returned, not merely because she loved it, but also because she raged against her exile, the expulsion from her mother's bosom, the gnawing sense of rejection that she attempted to overcome. Her love for what she missed and her fury at losing it while still so innocent permeates her art. She once remarked, "Art for me has been a way to sublimate rage. In fact it has been necessary to have such rage to free myself from confinement and the fury of confinement."[32] This statement casts further light on her use of explosives in some of her silhouettes. After becoming one with the elements, a number of her forms were set on fire and left to smoke and simmer until all that remained was a blackened cavity filled with the ashes of what had once been a benign union.

Santeria

Santeria became a major source of inspiration for Mendieta, showing her a way to use natural elements to enact her spiritual quest. Derived from the Spanish *Santo*, Santeria connotes the worship of saints. Mendieta preferred the teachings of Santeria, with its view of the earth as a living thing from which one

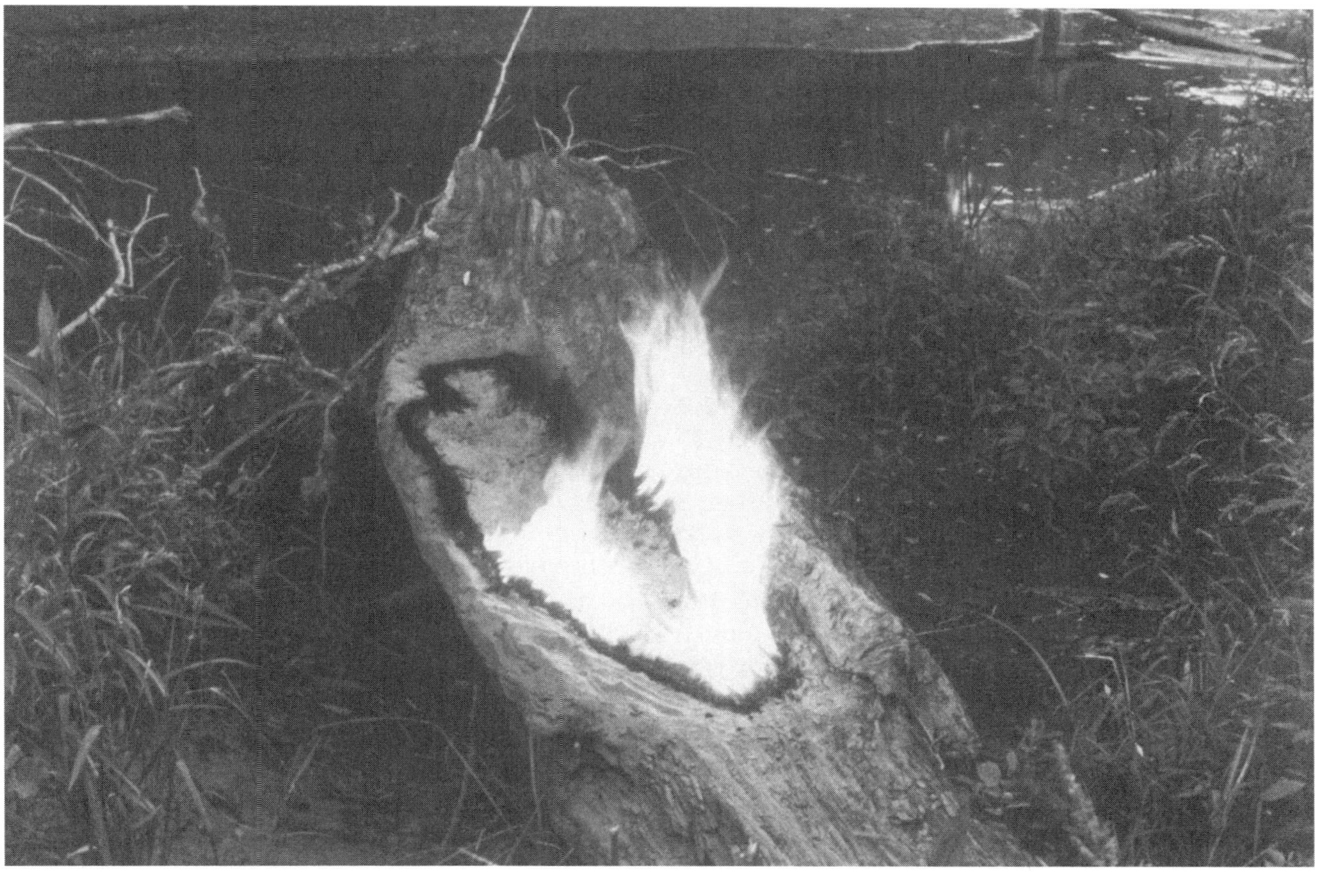

42. Ana Mendieta, *Untitled* (Silueta Series, Iowa), 1977. Lifetime color photograph. 13½ × 20 in (33.7 × 50.8 cm). © The Estate of Ana Mendieta Collection. Courtesy Galerie Lelong, New York.

gains power, over Catholicism's emphasis on distant, heavenly forces. Catholicism, the religion in which she was raised in Iowa orphanages, reminded her of the pain of exile and difference while Santeria connected for her the natural and spiritual realms. Santeria also brought back fond memories of her lost childhood because it was the religion of the black servants and nannies with whom she grew up. She is known to have spent many afternoons with these servants listening attentively to their tales of the powers and magic of the *orisha* gods, each of whom is identified with a force of nature.[33] In her exiled adulthood, Mendieta sought to reestablish connections with some of her secondary maternal figures from early life. She found affirmation and comfort in Santeria's holistic belief in the harmony of the universe which, in turn, found expression in her art. She once said: "It was during my childhood in Cuba that I first became fascinated by primitive art and cultures. It seems as if these cultures are provided with an inner knowledge, a closeness to natural resources. And it is this knowledge which gives reality to the images I have created. The sense of magic, knowledge and power found in primitive art has influenced my personal attitude toward art-making."[34]

Santeria influenced Mendieta's transition from the personal use of her body in art to the creation of more generalized female archetypes. In 1975, she replaced her actual body with the arrangement of natural elements in the shape of her silhouette.[35] Later, she used a cardboard form of her body to make the form of her silhouette. In the 1980s, she abandoned her body shape entirely and replaced it with universal feminine forms. The movement from body, to natural element, to cardboard form, to archetype suggests the gradual disappearance of Mendieta's immanence from her work, a soft and slow exile of her flesh gradually replaced by universal symbols, again Mendieta addressing the trauma of exile and loss, but now from the transcendent viewpoint as if to say, "I am the mother I seek whose home is everywhere." Her fade from view is thus all the more poignant and the delicate beauty of her journey toward the ephemeral generated a continuum of artistic self-representation that speaks to and of the human condition for which exile, loss, and grief are guaranteed.

Goddess

As Mendieta's art evolved over the years, the theme of her work remained closely tied to the mother; however it eventually became Mother with a capital M. Because they were once worshipped for their association with fertility, fecundity, and agricultural bounty, goddesses supplied the perfect catalyst for Mendieta's movement away from the personal to more universal themes. She first employed the Mayan goddess, Ixtel, as inspiration for several pieces she made in 1977; however, it was not until the 1980s that she created plentiful goddess images.

Interestingly, psychoanalyst Otto Rank believed that all artistic form, from the primitive to the modern, can be traced to the maternal vessel.[36] He argued that the human need for form originates from the will to overcome the first separation from the mother: the trauma of birth. Rank believed that birth was our first major trauma because it represents death of unity with the mother. Considering the first body art—in the form of tattoos or self-ornamentation—Rank demonstrated how artists have always been tied to nature both in their will-to-form and in their desire to assert their own independence and immortality.

Mendieta's goddess works use minimalist lines to represent the female form. They are delicate images in which the lone figure is carved or burned into the surface of cave interiors, tree trunks, paper, or leaves. Some divide the female form into three oval—limbless—shapes; some include large breasts; some have a deep gash denoting the female sex. Several have mud coils that curve about inside the body to create a labyrinth effect with no discernible beginning or ending. In one, Mendieta carved a goddess shape around a thick vine that moves through its entire body. She used the mother-child metaphor, with its "umbilical cord" attaching the woman to the earth, to prove the obvious connection among goddess, mother, and earth.

Goddess mythology embraces notions of fertility, creation, and symbiosis and exhibits the universal female principle in its most arcane conception. It contrasts with traditional male hero mythology which denotes the hero's endeavor to transcend boundaries along his path *away* from the mother. Through acts of heroism, the hero completes his differentiation and distinction from the female mystery; he stands alone and apart, becoming his own man, an entity who may have emerged from the female, but now transcends her. Goddess mythology does not have this aim: rather, one becomes great by seeking to merge with the "Great Mother," by becoming the willing form through which her creative principle is expressed. Thus this mythology is highly sensitive to the cycles of Mother Nature and the mysteries of her creatures. Destructive forces, in addition to creative and nurturing ones, are necessary elements in goddess mythology. Mendieta was naturally drawn to Goddess lore because it helped her apply universal symbolism to convey her personal experiences and gave her the elements necessary to express her need and desire for transcendence. In the end, she seemed to be saying that while art is temporary, earth and sky (nature) are everlasting and we belong to them—they are our true home, they are our primordial parents. This unification of the personal and the cosmic, with immanence and transcendence, with time and the eternal, is what makes Mendieta's oeuvre essentially spiritual. She once wrote that "the greatest value" of art is the "spiritual role" it plays.[37]

Mendieta joined second-wave feminist artists, Mary Beth Edelson, Betsy Damon, and Jane Ellen Gilmore, all of whom belonged to the Goddess Movement in art of the 1970s. These feminist artists summoned goddess symbolism from multiple sources to express female solidarity and to impart a sense of hope and empowerment to women who felt erased or harmed by patriarchal oppression. Thus, the reclamation of matristic values took on a form of exorcism in several of Mendieta's performance pieces. Here, her images of women posed with arms uplifted are not a sign of hope-

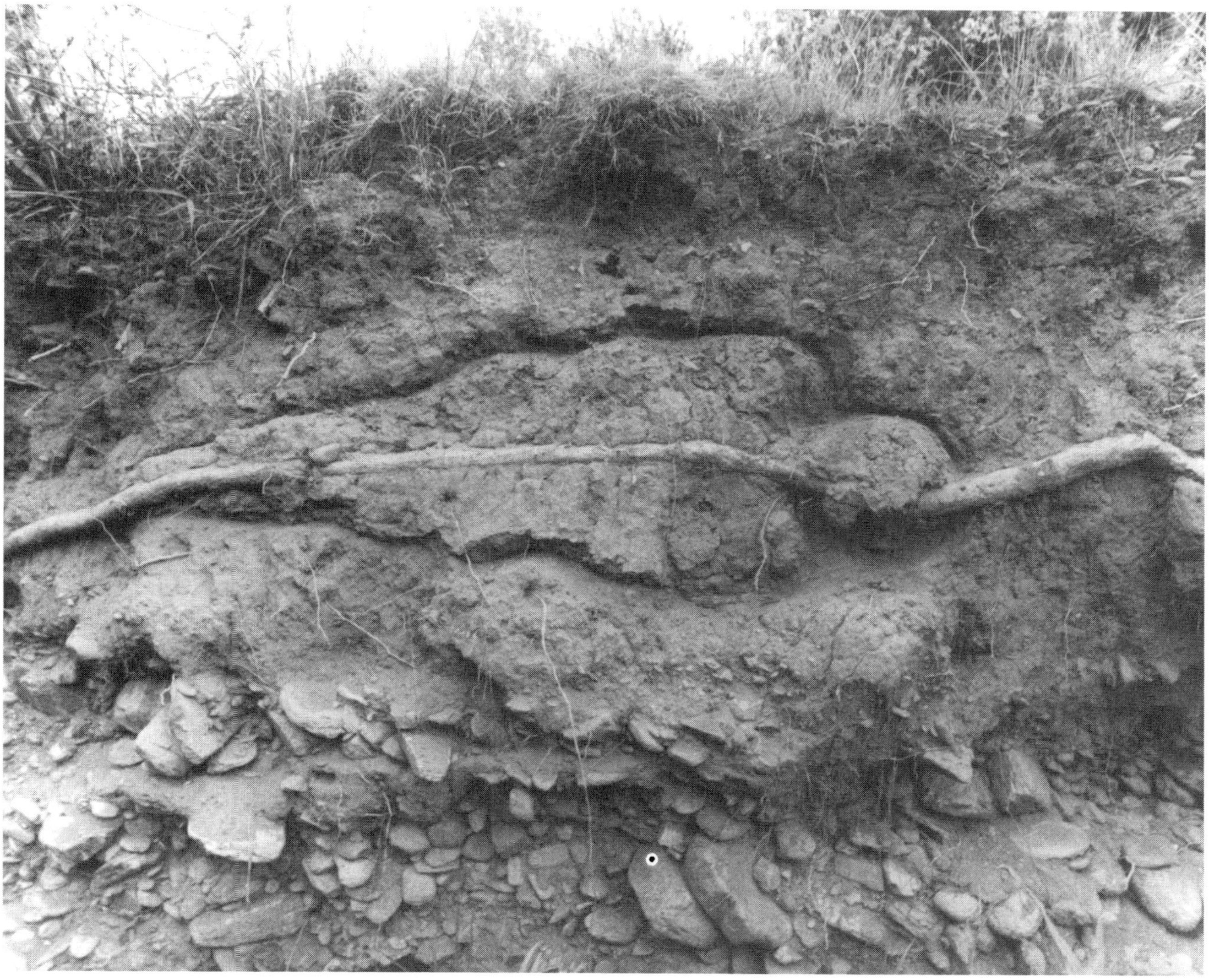

43. Ana Mendieta, *Untitled,* 1980. Lifetime black-and-white photoraph. 40 × 55 in (101.6 × 139.7 cm). © The Estate of Ana Mendieta Collection. Courtesy Galerie Lelong, New York.

less surrender but, rather, a symbol of spiritual reception: "Everywoman recovering Goddess energy from the Cosmos."[38] Works like these became emblems of transformation, empowerment, and rebirth.

The Goddess movement celebrated and emphasized innate feminine qualities believed to be passed down through history. Such a claim clearly flies in the face of postmodern views which regard gender as a social construct. Mendieta's style, perhaps more than any other artist in this book, assumes a recognizable feminine (not merely feminist) aesthetic that is more in line with feminists Gilligan, Irigaray, Cixous than with Butler and Garber. Mendieta was attracted to the goddess culture because she felt it united women to a universal source and transcended differences among them.

For years, Mendeita was obsessed with returning to Cuba. Between 1980 and 1983, she took seven trips to Cuba and was once even invited by the Castro government. Her best-known goddess earthworks were executed in her native land. By making works on Cuban landscape, she claimed that she was bringing her Silueta series back "to its source."[39] In 1981, Mendieta carved what she called her *Rupestrian Sculptures,* feminine images of Taínan goddesses, into the limestone rock of the womb-like caves of Jaruco, a mountainous region west of Havana. Mendieta's choice of the "cavern of Lost Space" was significant because it had served as a refuge for runaway slaves and independence fighters as well as a hospital site during the battle of 1895. The cave became a symbol for freedom and healing in Mendieta's art.

Mendieta named her images for the pre-Columbian goddesses in the language of the Tíano Indians. Her attraction to the Tíans is clear: she identified with this extinct people whose culture was lost because they had been overpowered by the Spanish and decimated by hunger and disease.[40] Once again Mendieta employed her art to give life to what had formerly been destroyed. Unsurprisingly, in her motherland—the land of her mother(s)—the place where she had once been mothered—many of Mendieta's titles refer to the Mother Goddess (e.g., *Mother of Waters, Old Mother Blood, First Woman,* or simply *Mother*). The themes of exile, separation, absence, dislocation, and loss infuse Mendieta's work with her personal pain. The parallel focus on reunion, regeneration, ancient fertility cults, and archetypal mother and goddess imagery points to the healing and mastery of that pain.

Although Mendieta identified with feminist causes, like Wilke, she critiqued certain aspects of the feminist movement and kept her distance from what she called "white feminism."[41] Also, like Wilke, she chose to transform the Venus goddess into a more personal and ethnically diverse symbol. Seeking to empower women through identification with primordial female archetypes, she proposed a project in 1981 called *Venus Negra* (Black Venus) for the feminist art journal, *Heresies.* Mendieta provocatively adopted Venus, the Western goddess of love, to make a statement about the dark female body. Along with a black-and-white image of one of her gunpowder *Siluetas* executed outside of Iowa City in 1980, Mendieta wrote a text about the Cuban legend of Venus Negra, a black Indian woman who was believed to be the sole inhabitant of the island. Venus Negra's bond to nature and to natural ways was emphasized by her nakedness as well as her refusal to be enslaved or colonized by the Spanish settlers in the 1800s. Mendieta's admiration for and identification with the tale of this "noble savage" derived from the goddess's primitivism, victimization, solitude, resistance to Western domination and, perhaps most of all, her condition of exile.

Exile

Despite the private nature of Mendieta's oeuvre, it resonates with larger themes possessing universal appeal not merely because it includes goddesses but, also, because our world has increasingly become one teeming with exiles, refugees, and émigrés. In fact, much of modern Western culture—think of Joyce, Nabokov, Beckett, Pound, Einstein, Marcuse, or Conrad, to name only a few—has been shaped by those who were estranged from their homes in one way or another. Therefore, exile and displacement might easily be considered the tragedy of our time.[42] Adorno wrote in his memoir, *Minima Moralia: Reflections on a Damaged Life:* "The house is past. . . . The best mode of conduct, in the face of this, still seems an uncommitted, suspended one: to lead a private life, as far as the social order and one's needs will tolerate nothing else, but not to attach weight to it as something socially substantial and individually appropriate. 'It is even part of my good fortune not to be a house-owner,' Nietzsche already wrote in *The Gay Science.* Today we should have to add: it is part of morality not to be at home in one's home."[43]

The exile's anxiety unequivocally embraces homelessness, orphanhood, dislocation, and alienation. I believe this anxiety is largely responsible for having nurtured the postmodern emphasis on multiple, shifting identities and perspectives. The notion of a decentered self in a fragile home that is vulnerable to a largely indifferent, and often destructive, environment has become the norm in our conscious and unconscious minds. Self-invention and reinvention, popular tools of the contemporary art scene (see chapters on Cindy Sherman and Orlan), develop naturally from such a precarious scenario.

Like anyone forced into exile, the artist has the option, and more often the necessity, to use her exile as inspiration and muse for her work. Mendieta sought to replace a fluid existence with a stable one, a rootless life with rootedness, wandering with a home. Her work involved compromises made between her native land and that of her hosts; it created an intermediary place to live on the hyphen between Cuban and American. She wrote: "There is an African custom which I think . . .

is analogous to my work. . . . The men from Kimberly go outside their village to seek their brides. When a man brings his new wife home, the woman brings with her a sack of earth from her homeland and every night she eats a little bit of that earth. The earth will help her make the transition between her homeland and her new home."[44]

Some of Mendieta's *Siluetas*, built up in sand and surrounded by water, or made to float in water, created miniature islands, like the island of Cuba, and assumed the shape of the female body. This adds a feminist reading to the works: the exile of the female from the patriarchal texts that have dominated Western culture. Interestingly, Freud used a land metaphor when referring to women as "the dark continent." He admitted to having a blind spot for the significance of the mother in early development when he wrote that "everything in the sphere of this first attachment to the mother seemed to me so difficult to grasp . . . so grey with age and shadowy and almost impossible to revivify . . . it was as if it had succumbed to an especially inexorable repression."[45] In fact, women analysts, most notably Melanie Klein and Margaret Mahler, have shifted the psychoanalytic focus from the oedipal father to the mother by uncovering and elaborating the insufficiently explored territory of pre-oedipal (mother-infant) relations, with the emphasis on early maternal bonding.[46]

As with psychoanalysis, it has taken the work of women artists to recover and represent the "shadowy" stage of early development that Freud found so impenetrable. It is difficult to find an artist who has done more than Ana Mendieta to represent the archaic union between mother and child, or what Mahler called the *milieu interieur.* Mendieta's art surfaced and underscored the crucial significance of early states of merger with the mother for the development of one's body ego. She thereby captured the indissoluble yet fragile nonverbal bond with the mother in the form of art-making.

Violence Against Women

Mendieta considered colonization violent, claiming that ruling classes uproot persons from their traditions and beliefs, and exploit them for greedy benefit.[47] She also moved easily between the orbits of culture and gender, and therefore felt troubled by cultural violence and violence against women. In 1973, college student, Sara Ann Otten, was brutally murdered on the campus of the University of Iowa where Mendieta was an art student. Soon afterward, Mendieta staged a performance to which she invited an unsuspecting audience of fellow students. When they entered her apartment, whose door was left ajar, they were aghast to discover Mendieta's bloody, motionless, half-naked body tied to a table amid a panorama of disarray. She later explained that she had conceived this work, the first in a series of rape pieces, in reaction against the idea of violence against women.

Mendieta's rape piece is reminiscent of Kahlo's fascinatingly gruesome 1934 painting, *A Few Small Nips,* which the artist painted in response to a newspaper account she read of a drunken man who threw his girlfriend on a cot and stabbed her twenty-three times. When arrested, he protested, "But I only gave her a few small nips!"[48] In Kahlo's painting, blood pours from the canvas onto the frame, expressly entering the world outside of art. Mendieta, who was certainly familiar with Kahlo's work, took the theme of violence against women further by playing the role of the victim herself and by presenting the drama in her actual environment. Like Kahlo, Mendieta fearlessly blurred the boundary between life and art.

Mendieta staged additional tableaux of rape and violence scenes that year. She did not announce these works but, rather, left them to be discovered by unsuspecting passersby. In one, she spread animal blood on the sidewalk next to a door and sat in a nearby car, while filming the pedestrians who invariably noticed the blood but did not stop and inquire about it, thus demonstrating casual voyeurism and indifference to violence. Mendieta's "rape" art was a precursor for some of the works Cindy Sherman photographed in the 1980s depicting thanatopsistic scenes suggesting crimes against women. One of Mendieta's rape performances (1973) shows her half-naked body lying exposed and bloody on a tree trunk, her pubis elevated for all to see (see Plate 11). This work is reminiscent of Duchamp's *Etant Donnés,* Wilke's *I Object,* and Orlan's *The Head of Medusa.*

Continuing this theme, Mendieta created a powerfully economical piece, *Blood Writing,* (1973), in which she faced a white wall with her back to the camera (see Plate 15). She left traces of her bloodstained hands on the wall as she leaned against it and slid down to her knees from a standing position. Two wide lines of blood move toward her body and onto the floor. When she finished marking the wall, Mendieta physically disappeared leaving the pair of her hand prints to stand alone in supplication, surrender, and testimony. Later artists, including Nancy Spero, Carolee Schneemann, and Hope Sandrow, deliberately borrowed from Mendieta's hand gestures and incorporated her imagery into their art as a way of memorializing Mendieta's powerful statement and, more importantly, keeping her and her art alive.

Mendieta's signature handprints, as well as the numerous Siluetas with hands upraised, were the perfect symbol for her helplessness, on the one hand, and for her victory on the other. In one unforgettable piece in which she departed from the familiar horizontal pose, Mendieta mounted the figure vertically high on a pole.[49] *Anima, Silueta de Cohetes* [Soul, Silhouette of Fireworks], created in Oaxaca, Mexico in 1976, shows the Goddess with arms raised toward the sky on a burning pyre (see Plate 16). The piece, made of bamboo armature, was constructed with the help of a local fireworks maker and set on a vacant expanse of land with a mountain view. The periphery of the figure and its heart were ignited creating a burning effigy that assumed the shape of a cross. Yet here, as in Kahlo's "martyr" works, it is not a man who is being sacrificed but Mendieta—Woman—Mother—Artist—Goddess. The heart continued to burn when the flames encircling the body extinguished, ash falling back to the earth. This work is one of the most sublime in Mendieta's entire oeuvre, its aesthetic form revealing a simple beauty and a natural elegance. The martyred woman who is empowered by her martyrdom creates a testimonial, both intimate and grand, that is deeply felt more than understood.

Mendieta's martyrdom, so powerfully articulated in her "fireworks *Silueta,*" came back to haunt her legacy twelve years later during the trial accusing her husband, artist Carl Andre, of her murder. Andre's defense attorney tried to use Mendieta's art, especially its use of blood, its affinity for death and martyrdom, and, in his words, "the wedding of the human body with the earth," to justify his claim that she had committed suicide rather than been murdered.[50] He went so far as to suggest that the flattened shape her body had assumed from the fall was, after all, no different than her death-enamored *Siluetas* and, in fact, could have been her final—fatal—work of art.

Surely, Mendieta's art showed a fascination and ease with the forces of death. The countless images of her body positioned flat on the ground readily call to mind burial rites and undoubtedly relate to Mendieta's working through death-like processes in her art. The outrageously shocking allegation that Mendieta's art exposed her suicidal tendencies, however, neglects the very obvious connection Mendieta always had to life. Also, suicide by leaping out a window would hardly be the choice of someone terrified of heights. Death, to her, was an inseparable part of the life cycle, a cycle in which all of nature and humans invariably partake. Mendieta confronted loss, decay, abandonment, and exile by showing these processes in her repetitive cycle of creation-death-rebirth and regeneration. I would argue that her attempts to *master* loss, exile, and death are the most pronounced messages in Mendieta's oeuvre. She regenerated herself again and again like the legendary phoenix, and she brought the dead back to life by reviving even the most buried civilizations. Mendieta's spirit continues to live on through her art in defiance of its ephemeral quality and in defiance of her own death.

8
Adrian Piper: Plain as Black and White

So no matter what I do or do not do about my racial identity, someone is bound to feel uncomfortable. But I have resolved that it is no longer going to be me.
—Adrian Who-The-Hell-Does-She-Think-She-Is Piper

SINCE RACISM IS FIRST AND FOREMOST A REACtion to visual difference, the perceptible nature of art renders it an ideal vehicle to engage in the politics of vision. "The negro's color throws him into a drama of race that is never hidden," wrote Franz Fanon, in *Black Skin, White Masks*.[1] Adrian Piper, artiste provocateuse nonpareil,* was confronted with a very different predicament than the one Fanon speaks of, and most blacks encounter in their daily lives.[2] Unlike blacks whose physical appearance might be sufficient cause to invite specific racist behavior, Piper appears white although she is black. As such, she capitalizes on her unique circumstance by presenting us with the perfect challenge to the security we feel when basing our reactions on visual cues alone. Her art demonstrates the illusory and deceptive nature of appearance as it simultaneously delves into the depths and complexities of racism and xenophobia.

Piper, born in 1948, is a very light-skinned woman of African descent who grew up in Harlem. Rather than pass for white, as did some members of her family, she made an issue of her racial identity. Her art is innovative and revolutionary in its use of self-representation and autobiography to directly address racism and racial stereotyping.

This chapter clarifies the psychological, historical, and aesthetic reasons for Piper's creation of an art that is as personal as it is political. It additionally focuses on the reasons for the powerful and disturbing effect her oeuvre has on her audience. I intend to show the ways in which her work deals with states of hostility and fear between people, between men and women, between reality and fantasy, and between each person and him or her self. Piper's art beautifully illustrates the psychological mechanisms enlisted to cope with the aggression and violation of self and other in the quest for identity and a sense of wholeness.

THE BLACK FEMALE BODY IN ART

Whereas the feminist movement of the 1970s can be said to have had the largest impact on art from that time onward, the Civil Rights (and Gay Rights) movement(s) informed not only the direction of American social and political life but, also, activist-inspired art.[3] Unlike the white female body, which has long been the object of the voyeuristic gaze, the nonwhite body has largely remained peripheral and, therefore, obscure.[4] Judith Wilson writes of the "legions of black servants who loom in the shadows of European and European-American aristocratic portraiture,[5] and bell hooks argues that black women in Western art have assumed the roles of "mammies, whores, or sluts. Caretakers whose bodies and beings are empty vessels to be filled with the needs of others . . . [telling the world that] the black female is born to serve—a servant—maid—made to order."[6] Indeed, the black maid in Edouard Manet's *Olympia* (see Fig. 1) is perhaps the most famous example of the

*Ms. Piper denied permission to include images of her work in this book. I strongly encourage readers to view her artwork (found at Google Images) while reading this chapter.

marginal use of the black woman in art. In it, a young white female's naked body assumes center stage; her black servant, careful not to upstage her mistress, emerges from the dark background of which she is part to present her with a bouquet of flowers. Lorraine O'Grady claims that "The black female body needs less to be rescued from the masculine 'gaze' than to be from a historic script surrounding her with signification while at the same time, and not paradoxically, it erases her completely."[7] Piper's art provides a potent commentary to the claims of the stereotypical black female roles, on the one hand, and the invisible black female body, on the other.

Piper was strongly influenced by Sol LeWitt's theories on conceptual art and gave up object-based art in the seventies to become a conceptual artist, one for whom "the idea or concept is the most important aspect of the work."[8] The "ideas" Piper wished to address in her work centered on issues of racism and xenophobia. Influenced by feminist consciousness raising practices that were fashionable at the time, Piper designed a concept-based art aimed at raising consciousness on racism, thereby linking "the personal, the political and the aesthetically concrete."[9] Although she espoused the tenets of conceptualism, Piper was the sole black and one of only two women (the other being Christine Kozlov) associated with the movement. As a result, she felt marginalized and took the decision to temporarily drop out of the art world.[10]

Retaining the concept as central to her art but removing it from its usual venues, Piper began to incorporate performance into her work. Tricia Rose claims that performance is "the obverse of black invisibility in a society of white privilege."[11] In *Catalysis*, a series from the early 1970s, Piper walked New York streets, Central Park, rode elevators, subways and buses, and entered the Plaza hotel as a provocative presence impossible to ignore. For example, she wore clothing that had been soaked in vinegar, milk, codliver oil, and eggs. Or she attached balloons to her ears, nose, teeth, and hair. In *Catalysis No. 4*, she wandered the streets and rode public transportation with a towel stuffed in her mouth.

Piper's subversive performances clearly forced passersby to confront their reactions to an alien Other in a setting quite unlike the museum or gallery wherein the boundaries between art object and audience had been clearly delineated. When referring to these works, she states, "in violating my body, I was making it public. I was turning myself into an object."[12] Perhaps one reason Piper objectified herself in this manner was to acknowledge and solidify herself as a subject. Being recognized by the other, even as an Other, represented a first step toward forcing public recognition for black women.

Piper broke more ground with *Food for the Spirit*, a 1971 performance piece involving her naked body. Although the female nude had always been one of high art's major themes, the naked black woman had been curiously avoided in Western art, even by North American black artists. In a private loft performance that lasted two months, Piper fasted on a liquid diet while reading Kant's *Critique of Pure Reason* and practicing yoga, all the while photographing herself in the nude. Fourteen photographs depict her in the dark and show her image becoming progressively less visible. It seems that Piper wished to record herself in the process of dematerializing in order to reflect her experience of feeling overwhelmed by the enormity of Kant's ideas. Like Wilke who, in *So Help Me Hannah* (1979–85), forced a recontextualization of famous men's words when spoken by a beautiful, naked feminist artist, Piper, too, demanded that she be seen as possessing both body and mind for her nude pose does not preclude her engaging in intellectual discourse.[13]

Piper's use of her mirror in this piece further recalls Cahun's and Kahlo's incorporation of the maternal mirroring function in their art. Piper explains, "To anchor myself in the physical world, I ritualized my frequent contacts with the physical appearance of myself in the mirror . . . every time the fear of losing myself overtook me and drove me to the 'reality check' of the mirror."[14] The more she felt she was losing her sense of self, the more Piper turned to her mirror to find the assurance she needed that she existed and to provide her with the concrete boundaries of that existence.

Piper's mirror differs from that of Cahun and Kahlo, however, in its engagement with the problem of black female visibility. Piper's self-starvation, in literal terms, accounts for her decreased visibility. Yet, by displaying the nude black female body, along with its vague, nearly invisible, borders, Piper made a bold statement about its lack of a place in the visual lexicon of the historical tradition of Western art.[15] Michele Wallace called this piece a "revolution in vision." Like Piper, Lorna Simpson's photographs emphasize the black woman as invisible or interchangeable; her women are masked, headless, faceless bodies or women with their backs turned away from the camera. Conversely, Carrie Mae Weems has created several photography series—*Family Pictures and Stories* (1978–83) and *Kitchen Table* (1990)—in which she documents situations that make visible the black female experience. Her women are shown in their encounter with both politics and emotions.

Piper plays with black female visibility and invisibility all at once. She can be thought of as the antithesis of Michael Jackson who, through cosmetic surgery and skin bleaching, has gone out of his way to erase his racial features and become, as psychiatrist Franz Fanon put it, "lactified." Despite his conspicuous efforts, Jackson repeatedly claims that race, for him, is a nonissue. Piper, on the other hand, states that race is *the* issue for her and that it should be one of the key issues for society in general. To make her point, she magnifies the traits reflecting her African heritage in *Self-Portrait Exaggerating my Negroid Features* (1981).

Erasing one's ethnic signifiers or pointing them out at every turn ("I am black," "I am black O.K.?") constitutes an extreme reaction to personal and political meanings of race, power, and identity. These complementary reactions not only demonstrate the lengths to which people go in order to "fit in" with their desired group; they also highlight the inordinate difficulty inherent in the establishment of a positive black self-image. As someone frequently mistaken for white, Piper's portrait represents a wish fulfillment on her part. If she were more visibly black, perhaps she could have avoided the pain of feeling like an imposter, or continuously having to explain her race. This becomes clear in *My Calling (Card) #1*, on which she writes:

Dear Friend,

I am black.

I am sure you did not realize this when you made/laughed at/agreed with that racist remark. In the past, I have attempted to alert white people to my racial identity in advance. Unfortunately, this invariably causes them to react to me as pushy, manipulative, or socially inappropriate. Therefore, my policy is to assume that white people do not make these remarks, even when they believe there are no black people present, and to distribute this card when they do.

I regret any discomfort my presence is causing you, just as I am sure you regret the discomfort your racism is causing me.

Sincerely yours,
Adrian Margaret Smith Piper
My Calling Card #1, 1986

Although Piper expresses regret at causing others, particularly whites, discomfort, this nevertheless seems to be the *raison d'être* of her art. The calling card format, with its superficial polite tone, in fact, assails the very "civilized" people she aims to enlighten. Lippard aptly characterizes Piper's art as "fusing rage with extraordinary cool."[16] Aware of her bite, Piper copyrighted her calling cards on the back as "Angry Art" and described them as "reactive guerilla performances."[17]

An example of Piper's self-consciousness regarding her white appearance is *Self-Portrait as a Nice White Lady* (1995) which consists of a photograph of the artist with a cartoon strip bubble containing her thoughts, "*Whutchoo lookin at mofo,*" on a bright red background. Though posing as a nice white lady, she is really angry and black. External and internal worlds are in collision and appearances are indeed deceiving. Titles of works like *Pretend,* and *Decide Who You Are* reflect her dilemma and ask us to face it as well. She shows us her divide—the cool, light-skinned exterior juxtaposed with the angry black interior. We introject this divide and feel it as the opposition/conflict between our politically correct exterior and our deeply conditioned prejudicial interior. This confuses us but also constitutes a choice we must make: either exile the image to the camp of repression/alienation and further distance ourselves from our brutality or feel that brutality within and perhaps be transformed by remorse.

Double Consciousness

Since childhood, Piper found herself in an in-between state with the costs and benefits of a double consciousness. Her art serves to depict these two sets of consciousness as well as to bridge them: "perhaps the real point of it for me has to do with the ways in which it enables me to overcome my own sense of alienation, both from white and black culture."[18] A piece that clearly attempts to bring together her two sides is *Paleface* (1978), the second of three *Political Self-Portraits.* Text overwrites a self-portrait drawing that is vertically split down the middle, one half black and one half white. This is a very significant work in Piper's oeuvre because it is one of the few in which she shows herself as both black *and* white. It is also the only work that recounts racist and discriminatory reactions she suffered at the hands of *both* whites and blacks.

Piper existed in two worlds from an early age. Although she lived in Harlem as a child, she gained admission to an exclusive private school where most of the students were white and privileged. All her life, she was made to feel ambivalent because of her racial identity. In the three *Political Self-Portraits,* perhaps her most obvious autobiographical works, she enumerates the contradictions she lived, attempting to resolve them by dispassionately recounting personal information that further provides a critique on American racism, sexism, and classism. For instance, in *Political Self-Portrait #2,* Piper tells the history of her racial awareness. At age five, a counselor of an all-white summer camp informed her she was black; she was called "Paleface" by neighborhood children in Harlem; accepted as exotic at art school (New York School of Visual Arts which she attended from 1966 to 1969); and envied in graduate school (Harvard) for affirmative action opportunities her minority status supposedly afforded her. Piper continued to live a double life as artist and professor of philosophy, first at the University of Michigan and then at Wellesley College. She currently resides in Berlin.

Tension exists in Piper's work between symbiosis and separateness, me and not-me, artist and audience, white and black, male and female. She repeatedly disassociates from either side of her personality at a given time and, paradoxically, at the same time, tries to bring these two sides together, the sides she represents as black and white, but which evidently stand for much more. On one hand, she wishes to rid herself of her history, to create a "device to relieve me of the weight of the unshared intimacy of my own past (ascribe it to another, make it public)."[19] On the other hand, she expresses the desire that "eventually the twain shall meet."[20] She is determined to merge the two, if necessary by force: "we've got to overcome the divisive illusion of Otherness."[21]

One source of Piper's experience of duality arises from an early split in her family between those who lived as blacks and those who passed for white. Though Piper emphasizes her blackness, there exists a part of her that wishes to deny it, the part that says: "Sometimes what we observe hurts so much that we want more than anything else to disappear, disembody, disinherit ourselves and our consciousness from our black identity."[22] And it is when she experiences this part that she projects her dark, angry, prejudiced side onto her audience. We are called in to hold it for her and to render it less harmful.

At the same time, she identifies with her black side, exaggerates its features, and metamorphoses into the angriest and most frightening of blacks: the angry, violent male. Piper's alterations between black and white, male and female, aggressor and victim force the audience to alternate along with her because we are expected to represent the other side of the dialectic she conveys. The two sides are necessary and reciprocal. Ultimately, Piper tries to collapse the difference between self and other by putting herself in our place and us in hers. She repeatedly informs us that we are like her. Taking her up on her own logical argument, then she is also like us. She too is inclined to prejudice, racism, xenophobia and, yes, being white.[23]

Aggression and Identity

Piper's art is about aggression, violation, and identity. Identity affirms one thing and, at the same time, denies or negates another. "I am this" carries with it "I am not that." This inherent divisiveness creates an Other who inspires fear because he or she threatens the safety felt within the boundaries we carve out for ourselves. In our anti-essentialist, post-identity, postmodern times, these very boundaries are believed to be fluid, constructed, and mutable.[24] Cultural theorists like Franz Fanon, Homi Bhabha, and Stuart Hall attempt to de-essentialize blackness and treat race solely as a social construction.[25] Piper, too, employs her art to disrupt the conventionally accepted division separating blacks from whites and, in doing so, turns a mirror toward the viewer. However, she does this not from a postmodern position but, rather, from the presentation of facts about miscegenation, facts that are meant to startle: "The fact is, however, that the longer a person's family has lived in this country, the higher the probable percentage of African ancestry that person's family is likely to have . . . the fact of African ancestry among whites ranks up there with family incest, murder, and suicide, as one of the bitterest and most difficult pills to swallow."[26]

Piper aims, through her art, to make American whites face their racism but, more, to own their black ancestry. She is like the concerned mother who coerces her child to swallow foul tasting medicine, all the while insisting "It's for your own good!" Piper gets under our skin because she tells us who we are, what's wrong with us, and what we need to do to become better human beings. Her art purports to know us better than we know ourselves. And just as children reject adults who behave as if they know what their needs are without asking them, so too we resist Piper's all-knowing attitude regarding our views and feelings.

As a light-skinned black woman, Piper claims: "I embody the racist's nightmare, the obscenity of miscegenation, the reminder that segregation has never been a fully functional concept, that sexual desire penetrates social and racial barriers, and reproduces itself. I am the interloper, the alien spy in perfect disguise, who slipped through the barricades by mistake."[27] Feeling she must trumpet her blackness lest she be taken for white leaves Piper no choice: she is cornered. In 1988, she created a multimedia piece titled *Cornered* in which her prim image is projected onto a video monitor screen strategically placed in the corner of a gallery space boxed in by chairs and an overturned table. Two framed documents flank her from either side. These are her father's birth certificates, one identifying him as white and one identifying him as black. Her voice fills the room and calmly challenges the viewer with her black heritage:

> I'm black. . . . if I don't tell you who I am, I have to pass for white. And why should I have to do that? . . . the problem is not simply my personal one, about my racial identity. It's also your problem, *if* you have a tendency to behave in a derogatory or insensitive manner toward blacks when you see none present. . . . some researchers estimate that almost all purportedly white Americans have between 5% and 20% black ancestry. Now, this country's entrenched conventions classify a person as black if they have any black ancestry. So, most purportedly white Americans are, in fact, black. . . . What are you going to do about it?

Piper's question recalls Wilke's (1978–84) "What does this represent? What do you represent?" words she borrowed from Ad Reinhart to question the audience's (mostly male) gaze of her naked body. Both Piper and Wilke sit in their respective "corners"—one because of sexism and the other racism—interrogating the aesthetic response as they engage us and force us into the role of active participant. Piper continues: "I represent the loathsome possibility that all of you are 'tainted' by black ancestry. If someone can look and sound like me and still be black, who is safely white?"

Indeed, in recent years, Piper has created media installations that increasingly aim for interactive confrontation between the object (often herself) and the viewer. Her control and intrusiveness are part of what make her art so effective. We cannot help but react to her work, not simply because it is often didactic and moralistic, but also because we are literally put in her place, the place of someone for whom basic freedom cannot be taken for granted. There is no white privileging here. Our gaze is co-opted and we are forced to feel divided like imposters, filled with anger, even rage, at our confusion and at the brutality that surrounds us and ultimately resides in us. Whether we like it or not, we leave the work of Adrian Piper with an inner sense of what it is like to be frightened, persecuted, and angry.

Black and White Spaces

To be sure, Piper is acutely aware of spaces in which racism and racist violence take place.

She views the gallery or museum space as restrictive and therefore creates spaces of her own, spaces that ironically resemble claustrophobic cells from which escape is difficult. *Art for the Art World Surface Pattern* (1976), for instance, consists of a white container which opens up to a wallpapered interior filled with newspaper clippings of slaughter and devastation from Cambodian atrocities. Large red letters—"NOT A PERFORMANCE"—are meant to confuse the viewer about the boundaries between life and art. Likewise, *Four Intruders Plus Alarm System* (1980) is a very powerful piece that takes place in a cell, this time a rounded black booth. After entering the booth, viewers are confronted with projections of four black men staring directly at them. The backlighting of the photographs makes the subjects' eyes glow, lending them an uncanny appearance. The images are placed higher than eye level forcing us to look up at them. Piper not only projects these dark and mysterious male faces onto our consciousness in her inescapable booth; she projects four sets of voices, each expressing different prejudicial reactions with which she expects her audience to identify. We are inhabited by her images, thoughts, and voice in this prison-like container of her making. *Cornered* (1980), mentioned earlier, depicts Piper's projected image literally cornered behind an overturned table. But we too become cornered by Piper's words in the restricted gallery space; she lures us into the darkness of her inner and outer world and forces us to confront as well as incorporate its menacing properties. Like psychoanalysts, Piper adheres to the conviction that only those who are able to face their darkest thoughts and emotions will emerge on a higher moral plane. If we are able to survive in such a world, perhaps so will she.

I-Thou: Piper and her Audience

Piper's attempts to communicate with her audience are highly complex. Since 1970, she has employed the I-you textual mode of address in her works in order "to build intimacy and confrontational intimacy."[28] Austrian Jewish philosopher, Martin Buber, employed the terms "I" and "Thou" when referring to the relationship between oneself as subject and the Other who is experienced as alive and separate and who recognizes the self as a subject.[29] For Buber, the I-Thou relationship is based on mutuality and respect; it is also the way we experience God's presence in the world. He distinguished the I-Thou relationship from the I-It relationship, the latter referring to ways of relating to others as objects, functions, members of categories, or instruments of achievement. As we have already seen, relationships in Piper's world are exploitative and sadomasochistic; there is no concern, empathy, safety, or trust. Her use of the I-you mode more suitably recalls Sartre's 1963 essay, "Black Orpheus," in which he, a white man, interprets *négritude* in Hegelian-Marxist categories. His essay opens with a direct address to his uncomprehending white audience: "What then did you expect when you unbound the gag that had muted those black mouths? That they would chant your praises? Did you think that when those heads that our fathers had forcibly bowed down to the ground were raised again, you would find adoration in their eyes?"[30] Piper states that "Language is a weapon of power"[31] and, like Sartre, she employs it in such a way when addressing *her* unenlightened audience. For example, in *Art for the Art-World Surface Pattern* (1978), a voice is heard as the viewer faces a photograph of black South Africans descending steps into a subway: "In looking at this picture, you carefully monitor any subliminal or undisciplined reactions you have to this image of assertive, aggressive, angry-looking blacks . . . all your reactions, all your thoughts about what you're now experiencing, might be part of this piece." She continues to quiz the viewer about his or her reactions: "How do the images in this picture relate to each other? . . . What's the significance of all the people in the photo being black? Of their looking angry or sullen? Of your emotional distance from them? . . . What exactly is the aesthetic content of this work? What is it trying to tell you?"[32] Even Fanon recognized that black pride and Afrocentrism are necessary to reverse white racial values but he argued that they must do so as action rather than reaction. Piper's art often seems to respond to white racism with an "antiracist racism." Whereas her audience is humanity at large, it seems clear that white Americans are meant to be the targets of her unapologetic political messages. On one level, this makes sense since most gallery and museum goers are white. On another level, she rarely addresses the ways racism and the distrust of difference moves in both directions. She also avoids dealing with reactions among blacks to herself as a light-skinned black.[33] Yet, through her aggressive confrontations and interrogations with her audience, she invites self-analysis and, more importantly, seeks transformation—both for herself and others.

One objective of Piper's art, then, is to establish a relationship of mutual respect between blacks and whites, and between the black and white parts of herself. Yet, her "I" and "you" become confused because thoughts and feelings fly this way and that and it is not always clear where they come from and to whom they belong. In *Some Reflective Surfaces* (1975), for example, Piper wears thick white makeup and draws a thin mustache above her lip, transforming herself into a white male. Her texts in this piece are interspersed with statements apparently intended to clarify, yet which end up confusing. " 'You' here is us" and " 'I' here is you," she states as she collapses the distinction between herself and her audience. Projections and dissociations abound in her art with her audience rendered "black" (because she says so, supporting her statements with statistics) and she white (because she speaks for her "white" audience in its voice). Her coercive incursions into our belief and emotional systems are sometimes experienced as "not me." She says (and we think), "I am not who you [the viewer] think I am" and "You are not who you think you are."

One could think of Piper's work as operating on multiple levels, all of which include the ways she finds to address racism. First, she highlights the history of racism by accentuating the difference between black and white as well as the rage, hatred, and otherness it engenders. Second, she demonstrates the continuance of racism by showing the admixture of black and white as well as the denial of it, leading to the separation of black and white into distinct categories. Finally, and perhaps most importantly, she shows the calamity and ignorance of racism by focusing on the ultimate existential unity of black and white. Piper moves among these three levels and mixes them at will.

Splitting, Projection, and Containment

Piper does much more than create a work of art; she creates an audience. She has even said, "I want simply to look outside myself and see the effect of my existence on the world at large."[34] Her work often defines the viewer's reaction and that very definition becomes a major part, and even the central purpose, of her art. For Piper, racist fear is "the loss of self through coercive interpenetration by an omnipotent alien invader."[35] Piper becomes this very invader in order to elicit such fears in us as well as to contain her own.

The fact that Piper is one of those unusual artists who is as verbally articulate about her artistic intentions as she is visually astute is both refreshing and complicated. In her comprehensive and highly informative two-volume collection of writings, her motivation for the creation of specific works is clarified in a way that is rarely encountered among artists. On the surface, it seems that everything is spelled out and little is left for the critic to evaluate or appraise. Yet, predictably, a vast residuum for psychological and social critique remains.

Whereas Piper has said that "artists do not have privileged access to the significance of what they are doing,"[36] she has also stated that her aim is "to retain control over the cultural interpretation of her work."[37] One way she accomplishes this is to incorporate the most extreme forms these interpretations take (as voices or texts in one part of a piece reacting to another) into the work itself. Controlling the interpretative aftermath of her art has increasingly become an integral part of Piper's work. Kuspit's biting critique of Piper's need for control in her work addresses this aspect of her art.[38] Yet, Kuspit misses the point because he does not seem to grasp the meaning of Piper's "thought control" as deliberate and representing one of the ways she has her audience feel what she feels to better identify with her plight. More importantly, she uses her audience to heal herself while offering healing to the audience. The dynamic goes something like this: "I—Piper—show myself as I believe I appear in your eyes. I therefore show you how you appear to me so that you may see yourself as I see you and perhaps change yourself so that I may be changed."

Here is the continuous reflection and paradox encompassed in the self-referential aspect of her art. Piper transforms her art into a social phenomenon which invites personal change that is impossible without engaging in an intentionally painful, conscious encounter.

The significance of the audience for Piper cannot be underestimated. She has said, "I exist simultaneously as the artist and the work. *I define the work as the viewer's reaction to it*" (my emphasis).[39] The logical consequence of this statement is that Piper is also defined by that very reaction which leaves only two choices: deeper alienation or collective healing. Piper creates a relationship with her audience filled with splitting, projection, and control. She needs to have us think her thoughts and feel her feelings. There is no escaping her, no ridding ourselves of her. Melanie Klein referred to this type of projection as projective identification to distinguish it from simple projection.[40] Klein understood projective identification as a defense mechanism in which a part of the self (not merely a feeling or attitude) is projected into another. It is in exactly this manner that we serve not only as blank screens for what Piper projects *onto* us; we unwittingly identify with what is being projected *into* us. As a result, we are better able to comprehend the profound experience of violation among blacks. We feel constricted, stifled, violated, offended, misjudged, and lacking a sense of individuality. The best example of this dynamic is *Four Intruders Plus Alarm System* (1980), in which viewers are transmitted four monologues, complete with hesitations and stutters, to express their conjectured reaction to the piece:

1.) "Yes, well . . . well . . . I . . . I suppose this is . . . it's . . . it's an interesting attempt to disrupt my composure as an art viewer . . ."
2.) "Well, personally, . . . I'm simply antagonized by the hostility of this piece."
3.) "Oh, this is . . . this is really right on. Yeah, this is really boss, you know."
4.) "Well, I . . . I must say this [sigh], this certainly doesn't bring me any closer to the uh, the so-called black experience."

Klein's followers have enlarged the concept of projective identification to include a form of interactive communication.[41] The projector evacuates a part of him or herself into another person and the recipient of the projection is induced to feel or act in ways that originate with the projector, rendering a mutual process of unconscious communication. Projective identification indicates that we play a role in, and serve as author of, someone else's unconscious fantasy. Bion, for instance, conceived of projective identification as a method of control not simply of unmanageable feelings but, also, of the object/Other, and even as a process underlying empathy.[42]

It is true that projection is an integral part of every creative act, and that art which directly portrays or uses the self necessarily results in a complex dynamic characterized by mechanisms of externalization and internalization. African American artist Lorraine O'Grady has written that in order to reclaim black female subjectivity, the artist must "project the inside onto the outside long enough to see and take possession of it."[43] But Piper is doing much more than this; she is taking possession of her audience too. Although she informs her (white) audience, "I want to understand what it is like to be you . . . by voicing your . . . thoughts, by depicting your visions . . . by entering your psyche . . . empathy[zing] with you";[44] the art is *her* creation, a product of *her* thoughts, visions, and psyche. Thus, it is we who are invited—no, forced—to understand and empathize with Piper's plight. In the end, however, Piper desires more than empathy from her audience. She wants us to serve a containing function for her projection of unbearable thoughts and painful feelings, her racial conflict and personal prejudice. Bion elaborated the concept of the container and showed how both mother and therapist contain malignant projections for children and patients to "detoxify" them and give them back in a more benign form.[45] Piper, too, wishes her audience to perform the task of container. We are the Other who become inhabited and taken over from within by the child/artist, to own and render her darkest fears bearable and to give shape to her physical and psychological being.

The Black Male

When whites are exposed to Piper's work, they cannot avoid confronting the inescapable presence of blacks as well as their stereotypical responses to them. The black male, in particular, is omnipresent: an uninvited and inexorable being that invades and intrudes. In her *Vanilla Nightmare* series (1986), Piper draws menacing, erotic images of black people over popular advertisements. Here, the black man is not confined in the ghetto or warehoused in prison, but in attendance at white clubs (American Express), around the necks (like Poison perfume) of white women, and in the underwear (Calvin Klein) of white men. Desires and fears merge as Piper simultaneously presents the infiltrator as sexually potent, ominous, and threatening. She takes fantasies that usually do not find their way to print and imposes them on the *New York Times*, a newspaper whose motto prides itself in its commitment to write "all the news that's fit to print." Contemporary artist Kara Walker has followed in Piper's footsteps by superimposing silhouetted black figures, many of them unruly characters, onto the sanitized version of history most people are exposed to. Walker's figures seduce us with their playfulness yet they are as serious as Piper's in their implication of her audience.

The fear of the black male as Other assumes a sexual meaning in Piper's art. Her phallic males invade and penetrate the vaginal openings of the curved containers she creates. A symbolic intercourse takes place and is experienced as a rape. An example of this is *Four Intruders Plus Alarm System* (1980) in which the audience enters a black cylinder and surrenders to four black men and four voices. Another is her *Vanilla Nightmare* series in which highly charged charcoal drawings are superimposed on newspaper advertisements. A sea of black, androgynous, naked, hairless, zombie-like faces force their way into the exclusive American Express club and nearly drown out its logo "Membership has its Privileges." Art has often been compared to a dream, yet Piper wants us to experience her art as if it were a nightmare. And these "nightmares" represent the purported dark erotic fantasies of white men and women, and also the artist.

Yet, Piper's art is not only about whites and blacks; it is also about men and women. Through her art, she attempts to make the black male less frightening, partly by confronting him and partly by *becoming* him. Piper creates cartoon-like photographic posters of a smiling white female who, as a result of having been hurt and betrayed, transforms into a progressively sinister and increasingly African male persona. The final balloon's message in this series is the most ominous and one that blurs the boundaries between male-female and victim-aggressor: "*I hate you for doing this to me, and myself for allowing it to happen.*" Piper identifies the male part of her as that which violates convention and announces "in your face, here-I-am aggressivity."[46] It is finally as this male *Mythic Being*— the "permanently hostile object"[47]— that Piper enables herself to experience not only a cross-sexual, androgynous identity, but also one that is angry and threatening. It is her male *Mythic Being* who personifies black rage when he declares, "*I embody everything you most hate and fear*" (1975).

Piper's admission of a strong male identity joined with the trend (from the 1950s to the 1970s) to redeem the black male.[48] Thus, it is also necessary to place her didacticism within the context of texts on white racism that, until the last twenty years, were written primarily by black men. Authors like Franz Fanon, Malcolm X, James Baldwin, and W. E. B. Du Bois allotted a primary place to educating white men on the politics of oppression and exploitation. They accomplished this from the position of authority gained as a result of their experiences as black men. Young-Bruehl conceives of this stage of black writing thus: "Black witnessing and truth telling . . . appears to be the only route to redemption for whites, the only cure for their sickness, as well as the mainstay of Black integrity and moral superiority."[49]

Racism appeared to be a predominantly white pathology in relation to black men in 1960s America. African American women had little influence on the social sciences at that time.[50] It is not surprising, therefore, that Piper's art often resembles the concerns of black men when it addresses American racism. The black male often becomes her alter ego as well as the prime subject matter of much of her art, and stereotypes toward black males are presented and confronted in many of her pieces.

Thelma Golden has written that "One of the greatest inventions of the twentieth century is the African-American male—'invented' because black masculinity represents an amalgam of fears and projections in the American psyche . . ."[51] In her *Mythic Being* series

(1974–76), Piper created street performances in which she appeared as a young, angry, afro-coiffed, cigar-smoking, third world male who wears glasses and sports a mustache. (Some are tellingly titled *Get Back.*) It is interesting that Piper more easily owns the aggressive side of her self when it is masqueraded as the male/Other. She plays with the media personification of the black male as a rampant, promiscuous criminal who rapes, abuses, and harasses. She takes this construction of social imagination and seems to enjoy becoming a dangerous presence capable of evoking such fear.

Piper not only masquerades as a male ("the masculine version of myself; myself in drag");[52] she masquerades as one who is demonized according to popular racist media as an oversexed, violent, "unhuman or dangerously superhuman."[53] Integrating what C. G. Jung would call her shadow (unconscious aspects denied in the self), or animus (the male within), she attempts to assimilate it into her conscious life. As a result, she seems to avoid the negative stereotypes associated with black women, summarized by bell hooks and Cornel West as "sexual savages, sluts, or prostitutes . . . the 'mammy' stereotype."[54] Even in *Food for the Spirit,* Piper's naked body is far from being erotic or sexual.

Ur-Mutter

One work that attempts, at least superficially, to oppose the fear-inducing tactics usually encountered in Piper's works is her 1990 *Pretend* series. In it, we are presented with enlarged black-and-white photographs, some from newspapers, showing silk-screened panels. Once again, Piper informs her audience that they are inhabited: "We are around you." "We are among you." "We are within you." This time, however, she takes over the reassuring function: "You are safe." "We don't want what you have." "Pretend not to know what you know," she announces repeatedly. Piper uses Peter Turnley's image of a Somalian mother, "Ur-Mutter," a woman excruciatingly thin from starvation cradling a (dying?) infant in her arms. Her African *Pieta* recalls Kollwitz's grieving mothers and carries the additional message: "We made you." Indeed, this work is about creation and mothering. Additional images depict Vietnamese boat people—mother and children seeking refuge. Despite her reassuring words—"You are safe"—one gets the feeling that there is no safety, perhaps not even, or especially, in a mother's arms. Mother and child are not safe; both could die, and happiness and freedom are illusory and at the expense of another's suffering. Atrocities take place under our noses and before our eyes. One piece from this series shows a graphic picture of the lynching of a black man hanging dead from a tree, with accompanying text "Land of the free." A second picture of two policemen forcing a black man onto the ground, his eyes filled with fear and anger, carries the text "Home of the brave."

Notwithstanding her pictures of smiling black faces and her manifest messages to relax, Piper seems determined to discourage feelings of complacency and comfort when coming face to face with her art. In her own words, she asks us to say "goodbye to easy listening."[55] In Piper's world, people and places —even those like mother and home, and, yes, art too—which we ordinarily think of as providing basic safety and nurturance, are in essence frightening, hazardous, and unsettling.

Therapy and Art: Is Change Possible?

Piper's stated aim is more than artistic; it is therapeutic: to effect change in her audience (and herself). However, her art cannot be further from what we ordinarily envision as therapeutic. The strong didactic element in Piper's oeuvre becomes understandable when we consider that she is not only a professor but also a philosopher. Piper puts us in a situation in which we are expected to face our fears as well as the defenses we have constructed to protect ourselves. Yet, she does much more than this. She displaces and projects her pain onto her spectators, wishing to unload it on them and have them own it instead of her. In her words, her desire is to "free myself of the past."[56] Rather than thinking of her art as therapeutic, one can envision it as playing an important role in exposing sad, tragic truths regarding differences, specifically racial differences that divide us and make us hurt each other. Her art is like being thrown headlong into situations, both painful and discomforting. In that way it is not like therapy; Piper is a "real-life" artist.

Indeed, it is Piper's belief that we are all xenophobic and that only by publicly acknowledging this fact can we begin to overcome it. It is rather curious, nonetheless, that whereas she deals with powerful, emotionally laden material, she does so in a seemingly logical and dispassionate manner. She reveals the origins of this approach when describing her early childhood in an extended family of four adults. She learned quickly that "reasoning rationally and logically was the best way to command attention, authority, and respect for what I had to say"[57] In the final analysis, Piper believes that racism is a psychological problem and that to cure such a problem, one must be prepared to endure painful and discomforting reactions. She explains: "I'm not interested in doing subtle, understated work. I'm not interested in an ambiguous message. . . . racism has to be dealt with individually. And I'm committed to using my work as a catalytic tool of political change."[58]

Although her goals are admirable, I believe that Piper is a bit psychologically naive in her belief that making the unconscious conscious through reasoning and confrontation is sufficient to rid one of a complex problematic symptom—in this case, racism. By forcing her audience to feel fear, anger and identification with the "other side," she may actually distance people from change. Yet, Piper is acutely aware of healing spaces, especially those that serve a containing function. For example, *Black Box/White Box* (1992) is a mixed media installation that creates a healing space. The black leather chair and tissue box inside the black and white cubes are not coincidentally universal to a therapist's office, a space where one confronts one's demons in order for healing to take place. We are invited to sit in the chair, to become emotional, and to use the box of tissues at our side, all the while watching the brutal beating of Rodney King during the Los Angeles Rebellion.

In addition to challenging therapeutic approaches, Piper clearly confronts traditional notions of aesthetics in terms of visual appeal and good taste, yet she is not alone in doing so. Arthur Danto, in his book, *After the End of Art,* claims that "artists from the seventies onward have ceased being concerned with pressing the limits of art or extending the history of art."[59] Piper's stated goals are unmistakably political: "to target higher order racial discrimination."[60] Yet, her personal goals are also discernible within the political. In what is perhaps her most private essay, "On wearing three hats," she claims that her primary activities (art, philosophy, and yoga) are for her ways of "transforming pain into meaning."[61] Despite her expressions of personal pain, Piper's art is concerned with political consciousness raising and is meant to aspire toward truth through confrontation rather than visual pleasure. Pleasure, if there is any to be had from experiencing her art, hardly derives from visual stimulation, color, composition, or texture. Indeed, her art is often burdensome to the viewer. In addition to its provocative qualities, the viewer is often called upon to read long texts in small print that accompany, or are superimposed on, visual images.

It is not surprising, then, that Piper's aesthetics have been debated. Some believe her art lacks aesthetic sensibility. Ken Johnson wrote that Piper's work does not have "a very compelling way with form" and even went so far as to compare the artist's touch to that of a sledgehammer![62] It is true that a great deal of Piper's work packs a wallop of a Muhammad Ali punch; although some may take pleasure in her art, there is limited sense of enjoyment in the aesthetic experience. This is because Piper employs techniques of manipulative persuasion and intimidation and does so with an attitude of irreverance and antagonism. Furthermore, she leads us into an unsafe world where our freedom cannot be taken for granted because we are repeatedly invaded, intruded upon, and controlled. Nevertheless, if an artist's work is powerful—and no one would deny that Piper's is—can it not transcend and redefine the meaning of aesthetic?

Piper's art does not offer facile answers to the issues she addresses regarding race, fear of the Other, and rejection of parts of the self. She does however raise important questions concerning how we can make the world safe, build relationships while dealing with fear of persecution and, most importantly, come to accept, or at least know, the dark social parts of ourselves, a feat that ultimately allows us to accept and know others. Piper raises these questions in ways that cannot be easily ignored or forgotten. What we do about them is left to us.

9

Cindy Sherman: Dressing Up and Make-Believe

Be what you would seem to be—or, if you'd like it put more simply—Never imagine yourself not to be otherwise than what it might appear to others that what you were or might have been was not otherwise than what you had been would have appeared to them to be otherwise.

—Alice's Adventures in Wonderland

NEW YORK BASED ARTIST CINDY SHERMAN dresses up and masquerades as others; she plays peek-a-boo and hide-and-seek games, games of loss and retrieval. She clowns around and plays with dolls. Sherman's art depicts a theater in which she manipulates her favorite toy—her own body—to play out an infinite number of roles. Indeed, child's play begins with and centers on the body.[1] The body is the first object of play, found as hands and feet, found in bits and pieces, a self assembled and a self that assembles, manipulates, connects, and creates. This differentiation/integration is already an act of both seriousness and frivolous play.

Sherman (b. 1954) literally makes a spectacle of herself as she becomes innocent girl, seductress, man, woman, hermaphrodite, historical figure, old, young, rich, poor, monster, beast, and clown. In her tragic comedy, she sets the stage on which her infantile and adult selves, as well as figures she has loved and hated in the past, become acquainted and reacquainted, merge and separate, morph and fragment, and in which various ambivalences and contradictions come together in an attempt to assume a more cohesive identity all the while defying the notion of identity altogether. After all, if she can become everyone, then she is really no one at all. Her magic consists in inviting us to view a kaleidoscope filled with multiple selves and the worlds that they inhabit while leaving the question "Who is Cindy Sherman?" entirely open.

Like Alice in Wonderland, Sherman is extremely elusive and evasive both in her art and in person. She grants few interviews and, when she does, evades many of the questions. She does not want to be pinned down, identified, or boxed in. Yet she wishes to be seen, as is evident in her oeuvre which consists primarily of photographs of herself in endless guises and disguises. Her art reflects this fundamental paradox: on the one hand she is searching for an identity and, on the other, she seems to be saying that identity is an illusion, a dynamic shifting composite of outside and inside that functions as both mask and mirror. It masks the terror of change and decay, of violence and strife, and most importantly of doom. It mirrors the weird and the ugly and reflects back to culture its need for stability and security. A human being cannot help but quest to be someone; the need for identity cannot be avoided by a creature highly conscious of its self-existence, one who can articulate that existence in voice, letter, figure, and number. Yet, one thing is certain: Sherman tells us that we are stories, not selves, and that the most central fact of our stories involves some very grim and tragic elements. She explains that she likes "to fantasize about this person's life or what they're thinking or what's inside their head, so I guess that's like telling a story."[2]

Like Scheherezade, who made up stories in order to stay alive, Sherman's fictional narratives continuously take life and death into her hands as she weaves story after story in a lively panorama of psychic scenarios. She "plays" with images appropriated from pop culture (film, television, advertising) and history (art masterpieces), gender stereotypes, myths, fairy tales, dreams, and nightmares.

Everything is permitted; and nothing is off-limits. Yet, despite—or because of—her emphasis on illusion and make-believe, Sherman confronts powerful emotional realities. Her art can be viewed as progressively peeling off layers in order to arrive at deeper truths, more frightening wishes, and archaic anxieties. Working through ambiguities in her "artistic play," Sherman searches out meanings and answers to the following basic questions: Who am I? What does it mean to be a woman? What should a woman look like? What is my role? What am I made of? What is my relation to the past? and How do I relate to others?

Unsurprisingly, Sherman ranks among today's most successful contemporary artists. Her oeuvre has provoked questions of alienation, female identity, disguise, and transformation. Some art historians have labeled her narcissistic due to her self-consciousness and overemphasis on self-portraiture.[3] Contrarily, postmodernists have believed her work to be self-abnegating for they insist it is fiction, about representation and, therefore, about nobody in particular.[4] Feminists have perceived her art in terms of the de-individualization of women in society and claimed that in a patriarchal culture, woman is nothing more than "image."[5] It is not my intention to dispute any of these views; I think all three have offered valuable insights into the multidimensional fabric of Sherman's work. In this chapter, I hope to demonstrate that Sherman's art takes place in an arena existing within us, between the self-knowing and the self it knows, between external and internal reality, a space like that between mother and child, a place where conditions are created for the growth of authentic agency. Play begins in the space between freedom and anxiety, and Sherman's art spans the range between these two extremes.

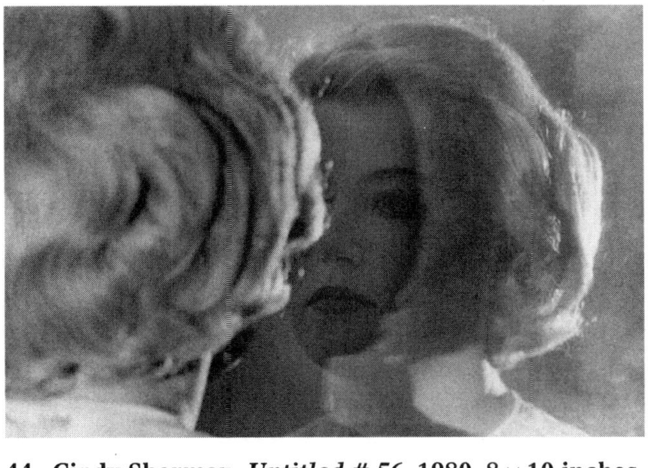

44. Cindy Sherman, *Untitled # 56*, 1980. 8 × 10 inches. Courtesy of the artist and Metro Pictures.

Play and Creativity

It is perhaps necessary to state at the outset that I do not equate the art of Cindy Sherman with the play of a child. Nevertheless, play and creativity do overlap, and Sherman's playfulness is impressive in her artistic work. Like the child who, in her imaginative play, is preoccupied with questions such as: "What will happen to my body if I succeed in my wish to be big and have power over people?"[6] Sherman both entertains and keeps in suspension all possibilities involving her body and identity.

One obvious difference between the play of a child and the play of Sherman concerns the fact that Sherman's art is directed at an audience. An additional difference entails the amount of control the artist exercises over the games she plays. Sherman assumes the roles of director, actor, cinematographer, lighting designer, makeup artist, and costumer; simultaneously behind and before the camera. She sets the rules, limits what takes place, and has the power to stop the game whenever she wishes. She also employs her camera as an instrument through which she examines, plays with, and works through questions of representation and identity. In her own words, Sherman has exclaimed, "I want to play with what's real." As Kramer has noted, art makes more stringent demands on the ego and is more lasting than play.[7]

After sifting through the grammatical labyrinth of the opening quotation from *Alice in Wonderland*, we discover it means simply this: imagine yourself always as beyond the capture of other minds. It means we are always "otherwise." It implies that there is an abyss existing between the way we see ourselves and the way others see us. But that perceptual abyss does not simply exist between the subjective and the so-called objective. That abyss infuses both with incompleteness and mystery. We are not completely present to ourselves as a grasped object, nor do others grasp us as such. There is no place the abyss is not! Both sides—the view from within and the view from without—leave something forever absent from the scene of categorization, analysis, and the understanding of ourselves and others. And what is the nature of that unreality, that space left untouched by verbal capture? It is only this: play. In that inherent incompleteness we are free and what is felt freedom if not play, invention, and the infinite potential of supplementation? Play is what defines us beyond the grinding fatigue of self-definition. Therefore, let us play!

Dressing Up (1977–80)

In the late seventies, Sherman became known for a series of black-and-white *Untitled Film Stills* in which she photographed herself in a variety of 1940s and '50s Hollywood B-movie situations, particularly of the *film noir* (Godard, Hitchcock) genre. The photographs are single frames, frozen moments from a larger implied fictional narrative. Together they tell the story, previous versions of which were told by Cahun and Kahlo: the story of femininity as masquerade. Alternately resembling a European film starlet (of the Brigitte Bardot, Jeanne Moreau, Sophia Loren, Anna Magnani types), an ingénue, a worn-out housewife, a playboy bunny, a prostitute, a woman on the run or waiting in anticipation, she dresses up and poses as one stereotyped female after another. Besides the clothing, which varies from one photograph to another, Sherman set her nameless women in mysteriously ambiguous environments both outdoors and indoors. Some resemble hotel rooms, others angles of deserted buildings, all of them places she said "looked as if they could be anywhere."[8] The single constant in Sherman's photographs of this period is her solitary figure; throughout her chameleon metamorphoses, she is always alone. Recalling the lone figures in Edward Hopper's paintings, Sherman, too, presents us with women intensely alone in isolated and impersonal settings. She seems to have been trying to establish the constancy of self in the face of her changing appearance, a lone self surrounded by anxious ambiguity.

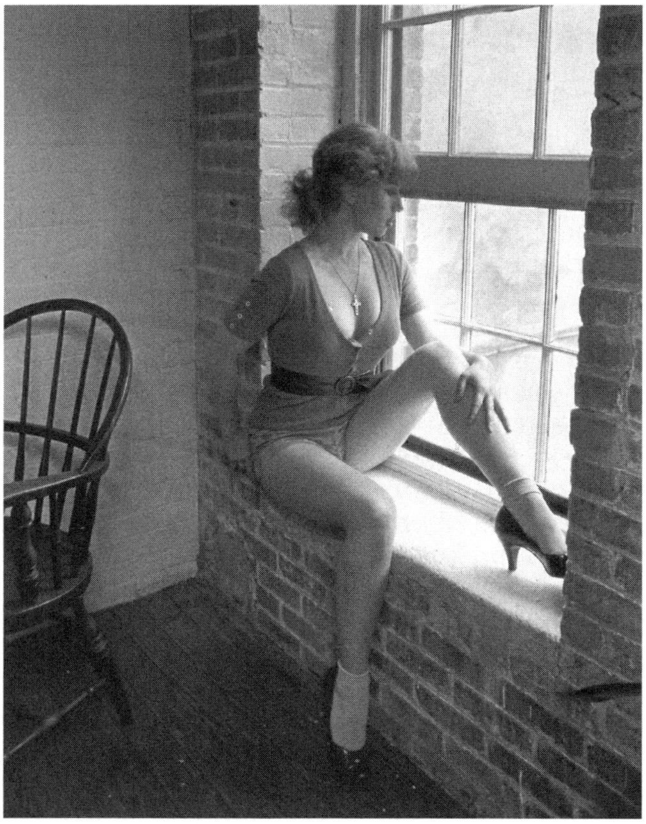

45. Cindy Sherman, *Untitled # 15*, 1978. 10 × 8 inches. Courtesy of the artist and Metro Pictures.

Naturally, postmodernist and feminist commentary on Sherman's oeuvre interpret her exchangeable feminine guises in terms of a lack of a set feminine identity in modern life, a construction of femininity as opposed to the essentialist female images in Mendieta's oeuvre. While this may be valid, from the psychoanalytic perspective of play, Sherman's dressing up as a woman (or women) reveals a game of playing with identity by manipulating one's exterior much the way children do when they play house and dress up in their parents' clothing. It is known that children's play is dominated by an unconscious desire to be grown up and to do what adults do.[9] Similarly, play functions to prepare the child for adult roles and societal expectations. As such, it allows children to try on adult functions and alter these roles as they become aware of "society's version of reality."[10] Sherman herself recalls how she dressed up in the clothes of her mother and grandmother when growing up. She even rolled up socks and stuffed them under her blouse to simulate breasts.[11] She admits, too, that she always had a love for make-up.[12] In an essay she wrote on the making of her film stills, Sherman commented, "I didn't know what I was doing at the time, I was playing."[13] Indeed, Sherman playacted by wearing the mask of grownup female stereotypes. In one of her *Film Stills* (#11, 1978), she lies on a bed dressed up in her mother's actual wedding dress, as Kahlo did before her.[14]

Behind the feminine costumes, however, Sherman's gaze remains remarkably empty; exchangeable exteriors do not fill an inner vacuum. One can dress up as a grown-up woman, but to be a grown up, one must have lived life. Children make use of "dressing up" games to create the illusion of assuming the identity of someone they admire.[15] Recall how Kahlo employed femininity as somewhat of a masquerade when she dressed in the clothes of Tehuantepec women, partly for defensive purposes.[16] Sherman accomplishes this objective in the name of play, yet she too demonstrates the distinction between imitation and identification.[17] Trying to bypass the process of maturation, she holds onto the magical and wishful thinking that she can *be someone* without having to *become like* her. A fundamental confusion exists between superficial imitation of a person and real identification. Here, Sherman suggests role-playing is either a substitute for or interchangeable with self-knowledge, for it is clothing that conveys female identity. The emotional vacancy exhibited in her blank facial expression has the effect of creating affective distance in the viewer. It discourages a stereotypical reaction and makes us see these derivative images in a new and unsettling way. We recognize the configuration of the stereotype, but somehow are deprived of it, and so we experience a sense of the uncanny.

Only a handful of her *Film Stills* stand out in their expression of emotion and serve as a preview for what is yet to come. The "crying girl (#27, 1979)," as Sherman calls it, is a close-up shot of her face after a good cry which caused her eye makeup to run down her cheeks. Despite Sherman's frequent denials that her work contains anything personal, she explains that when filming this image, she was looking at herself in the mirror calling out "I hate you, I hate you," all of which felt very cathartic.[18] In a number of other *Stills*, she resembles a mental patient trapped in an asylum and in the confines of her own mind. Besides these obvious cracks in her dispassionate façade, what we see in Sherman's *Film Stills* is a female body, but no indication of a living subject, no shadow of an inner life. Here, image *is* everything and nothing appears to lie below the surface. The culture's stunning superficiality is reflected back to us and the question as to whether the artist will quest for an inner, psychological identity is still open.

As we watch Sherman assume the roles of isolated women who engage in intimate dialogue with themselves in private settings, we inadvertently take on the role of voyeur. According to classic psychoanalytic theory, the desire to look derives from the primal scene, the child's observation of parental sex. Although not all children actually witness their parents having sex, we all develop fantasies about what our parents are doing behind closed doors.[19] One reason the primal scene has traditionally been considered traumatic is traced to the child's narcissistic injury at feeling excluded, rejected, or treated like an unwelcome intruder. Visual artists "play" with their primal scene experiences and fantasies (recall Salomon) by taking control of a situation in which they were once passive observers.[20] In the new scenario, the artist assumes the roles of creator, director, and actor(s), thereby turning the tables and relegating the spectator to the role of excluded outsider or voyeur. The power relations provoked by the act of looking are reversed. In an interesting twist on her primal scene, Sherman had her father, who collected cameras and took family pictures as a hobby, photograph her in several of her *Film Stills* (see Fig. 3). Illustrating the complex and multilayered dynamics of seeing and being seen, she states, "I liked watching my father in the face of what I was doing."[21] In one mysterious, purposely blurry shot taken by her father (#82, 1980), whose head is visible in the larger uncropped print, she sits in a chair by a window, barefoot and dressed in a white nightgown, at the far end of a long corridor behind two sets of partially opened doors. Like Sherman's father who took this picture, we have the uncomfortably exciting sensation that we are sneaking a peek on a very private moment in a woman's life.

Later, while living in New York City, Sherman had her then boyfriend, Robert Longo, photograph her in different venues. Like Wilke before her, this was one way she incorporated the male gaze into her works.[22]

Sherman's *Film Stills* are the smallest in her oeuvre (8 x 10 inches), and they have no titles; they are numbered, as are all of her works. Sherman says that she deliberately chose not to title her works to allow viewers to draw their own conclusions, to make up their own narratives, to be more about them than her. The artist averts her gaze, looking off into the distance, avoiding direct eye contact. Yet although these photographs are ambiguous and mysterious, there is nevertheless something familiar about them that evokes a sense of *déjà vu* and allows the viewer to project meaning onto them and interpret them in a variety of personal ways. Their ambiguity is structured by the shifted context in which they reside. We've seen them before. *But now we see ourselves seeing them and so they appear different.* They accuse us of being as shallow as they appear to be and they refer to us as much as they refer to the artist, and they also refer to themselves because they recall the contexts in which they had previously appeared. The erotic function of these stereotyped images is now in open conflict with their subtle accusation aimed at the viewer. To the man, they say: *This is what you want.* To the woman, they say: *This is what you are willing to become. And so, what are you both, really? A mere surface pretending depth and inwardness? A number, like me, perhaps?* What is important thus far in Sherman's work is her statement that she is a woman; the kind of woman she will become is not yet clear.

Masquerade (1980–85)

In the early eighties, Sherman turned to color. Although she continued to dress up in feminine clothes and to pose in a variety of situations, her photographs of this phase appear to delve deeper than the black-and-white *Stills* of the seventies. The colors are vivid and the lighting powerful, possessing a glossy veneer and lending her image a sense of reality previously denied it. In this phase, the work questions the previous superficial identities and asks us to question them as well. What does it mean to be a woman? What does a real woman look like? What is the relationship between a woman's external appearance and her internal world?

Employing the technique of backlighting which produces a candlelight effect, Sherman enhances the erotic exploration of her image. This technique makes her body boundaries become clearly delineated. The Rembrandtian glow further suggests a greater awareness of her inner world and the beginning of an introspective process. She now appears absorbed in thought, and though her facial expression remains somewhat empty, there is increased emotional subtlety that suggests interior space.[23] For instance, there are clues that indicate she is anxious, dependent, and yearns to escape loneliness, as she glances at a telephone that doesn't ring (#90, 1981) or fantasizes about something related perhaps to the torn newspaper ads she holds in her hands (#96, 1981). A noteworthy development involves the gradual disappearance of environment; background becomes superfluous and dispensable. Previously defined primarily by her setting, she now has the camera zoom in on her figure, and more specifically, on her facial features. As the distance lessens between Sherman and the camera, so does that between the viewer and the image. Sherman's photographs now invite the spectator to approach and enter. Many of the photographs in this phase are horizontal, which also lends them an increasingly intimate, close-up (as well as centerfold) quality.

The final "self-portraits" of this phase mark an important shift in Sherman's self-representation and intimate what is yet to come. The photographs become increasingly bizarre, as they portray a woman examining her own vulnerability and sanity. The unwavering scrutiny of surface and superficiality has broken down as a defense. The problem of fronting to hide the fear of looking more deeply, of openly facing the problem of emptiness, of recognizing how much of what we are is merely derivative, has led to disassembly. Dressing up eventually turns into masquerade as "normal" clothes are replaced with Halloween-type costumes and garish makeup. One almost expects her to shriek "Trick or Treat! (#125, 1983)" These portraits clearly portray Sherman as deranged; her clothes are bizarre, she wears oddly cut wigs, and she either grins eerily and inappropriately (#138, 1984), or appears lost in a catatonic reverie (#133, 1984). Clearly, playing with one's boundaries, as Sherman begins to do in these photographs, involves a certain danger. She toys with the simultaneous excitement and risk involved in self-knowledge and the interplay between psychic reality and object control. Who said all games have to be fun?

A Grim Fairy Tale (1985–89)

A major alteration in Sherman's self-representation took place in the mid-1980s. No longer using her photography to create changing images of herself, she now began to use appearance as a means of expressing the contents of her inner world, fantasy life, and unconscious thinking (see Plate 17). The first part of this phase involves Sherman's use of material from fairy tales, dreams, mythology, and fantasy, all of which represent a more marked transition from external to internal world. The world Sherman presents is hardly a friendly one; it is terrifying and awful, albeit somewhat comical as well. It is reminiscent of the atmosphere created by preadolescent children who gather around a campfire at night and compete with one another to determine who can tell the most horrifying tale. Laughter and screams combine in their expressions of horror and excitement. Sherman, however, competes only with herself; each photograph attempts to surpass the previous one in its sole capacity to frighten and delight.

The artist adds false body parts to her own for the first time, suggesting how we make ourselves by borrowing and incorporating external cultural artifacts. Thus, though the boundary between inner and outer seems clearly demarcated, it is actually blurry. The alluring, vulnerable females in Sherman's *Film Stills* are replaced with a motley cast of grotesque, scarred, pock-marked, cow-tongued, pig-snouted, wart-chinned, blemished-derrière images of the artist. Sherman transforms herself into a giantess in the land of Lilliputians or the child-devouring witch from "Hansel and Gretel." Whereas she sometimes flirts with danger and perhaps takes matters too far, there is both pleasure and relief in being reassured that it isn't real after all.

Bruno Bettleheim illustrated the importance of fairy tales as symbolic depictions of the "essential steps of growing up and achieving independent existence."[24] He elucidated the ways children intuitively know that fairy tales are *unreal*, but not *untrue*. As Sherman's audience, we are made aware of a similar distinction. These photographs bring to the surface the hidden dimensions of human experience, the dark and sometimes terrifying figures that roam the human sub-terrain: ghouls, monsters, or as we now know them: impulses, desires, and obsessions not yet integrated into one's ego. Once the surface is broken, the beast must have its day. In one (156), she gets down on hands and knees to pick pebbles from the beach. She looks up to the camera and we discern a dark face with a bizarre smile filled with rotting teeth. In another (99), she dons a short black wig and plays with an enormous tongue while little people wander in the background. In yet another (104), both inner and outer worlds appear dark as she grins with evil glee and mysteriously pats her naked belly.

Whereas these pictures are dark in color and in spirit (Sherman's camera lighting simulates sunlight, moonlight, and firelight) and more monstrous and nightmarish than those that preceded them, they continue to play with the erotic, although the play becomes more dangerous as it is now accompanied with disease, infection, and mutilation. Seduction turns into rape; playfulness into crime and sin. Oedipal guilt and fear of punishment are clearly at work in these pictures that, at six feet tall, are large enough to threaten the viewer with their size as well as their content. Sherman describes her turn to the grotesque: "I began reading the fairy tales and found that I was going in the direction anyway. The grotesque. I read Aesop's fables, the brothers Grimm, the *Arabian Nights*, and some Chinese folktales, which I liked best, because it wasn't always a story leading to some happy ending. I liked it when things got weird or ugly."[25]

And things did get weird and ugly in the latter half of this stage during which Sherman regressed to "gross out" games. The photographs—some of which do not include her own likeness for the first time—are filled with images of excremental matter: vomit, debris, trash, and fungus. Her motive here is clearly to make the most repulsive and disgusting scenes possible. Indeed, she seems to be creating a monster child (see #186, 187, 1989) or to give representation to the ugly, bizarre parts of herself through these repulsive pictures. Overwhelmed with primal angry impulses, Sherman attempts to cope with the disgust and fear of the anal child. She tries to take control of the tendency to make a mess and partly accomplishes this by turning the viewer into an unwilling participant in a regressive state in which there is no control over one's body fluids. The "weird" and "ugly" Sherman shows us is infrequently expressed by the "normal" or "healthy" self. Yet, there is so much about life that is both weird and ugly: war, hatred, and ongoing strife, disease, loss, castration, deformity, garbage, fungus, infection, snot, shit, piss, blood, puke, and of course death. Death is in life's face at every moment. Death, the spoiler of all hope and dreams. Death, the queen of all fears. The weird and the ugly is part of a truth that must be somewhat denied in order for us to live. Sherman uncovers what the static image conceals.

Julia Kristeva's concept of abjection is relevant here: "There looms, within abjection, one of those violent, dark revolts of being, directed against a threat that seems to emanate from an exorbitant outside or inside, ejected beyond the scope of the possible, the tolerable, the thinkable."[26] When applied to women, the concept of abjection reveals the monstrous feminine, the uncanny, the transgressive, the grotesque, and the alien, inevitably bringing to mind associations of woman as vampire, witch, hideous mother, or possessor of a monstrous womb.[27] Sherman's vision in these works offers ample examples of Kristeva's abject.

The abject is rampant in children's play. Indeed, many have mistakenly believed children's play to consist solely in pleasure or fun. This parallels outdated views about art as depicting only what is beautiful. Yet we know that play reflects the child's attempts to "compensate for anxieties and deficiencies in order to obtain pleasure at minimum risk of danger and/or irreversible consequences."[28] Winnicott addressed the precarious nature of play when he explained that "playing is always liable to become frightening [since] it is always on the theoretical line between the subjective and that which is objectively perceived."[29] Erikson was also aware that not all play is pleasurable when he commented on children's "anxiety play." In fact, he viewed play as taking place "on the border of dangerous alternatives" and always "beset both with burdening consequences and with liberating choices."[30] Play objects that cause fear have been called "chimeric objects" to differentiate them from transitional objects (e.g., teddy bears) whose purpose is to alleviate anxiety.[31] Finally, games in which children pretend to be blind or crippled have been labeled "damage play."[32]

Sherman's art of this phase easily fits into the categories of anxiety or damage play. At every turn, we almost expect the artist to jump out from a hidden corner squealing, "Boo! I scared you!" The photographs are dark in content and replete with references to disease, death, and the abject. The game she plays now resembles children's game of "statues," in which they strike poses and remain immobile for extended periods, or, at times, the more macabre "playing dead" (153). In fact, when Sherman does make an appearance in these photographs, it is as a corpse, a dead body, or simply a body part. The pictures at least partially represent an inner state of emptiness and deadness.

Taken in temporal context, Sherman's photographs display the inevitable trajectory of the image: the movie starlet and pinup queen will age, degrade, decompensate, and die. The artist seems to be saying that her self is made of time and the things of her time. Its body conceals excrement. Its character conceals monsters. Its fate is decay. Its destiny is to become a story. The whole of her art will tell this story, her story and ours too, without flinching from the truth. Sherman's humanity, her true beauty, her true self, which is never a clearly bounded individual entity, is a story. Her awareness of the way her art prepares her, and us, for the unthinkable is evident when she says, "My biggest fear is a horrible, horrible death, and I think this fascination with the grotesque and with horror is a way to prepare yourself psychically if, God forbid, you have to experience something like that."[33]

This quote is very telling in that it hides the impossible, yet universal, hope that everyone will die but me. It implies that Sherman's "biggest fear" is and was the driver for much of her art. Even the early film stills can be reinterpreted keeping this in mind. Perhaps she longed to become one of those characters —eternally frozen in time and place—a nice safe literal two-dimensional stereotype whose stasis and meaning is eternally ensured. Being an artist, however, she could not and her photographs show the gap between her desire to be an eternal form and the reality of impermanence.

In contrast to the grim subject matter in these works, Sherman's lush colors are almost shockingly vivid and glowing. The colors lend a sense of reality and even an uncanny attractiveness to these photographs that can easily be considered the most difficult to view to date. Donald Kuspit describes the manner in which Sherman saturates her images with color to lure us into what he calls her "vomited fantasies": "We sift the ruins of Sherman's pictures in search of her identity, and we find it in the tension between the erotic, glamorized pleasure of color that is part of the ingeniousness of artistic construction, and the thanatopsistic scene."[34] What Kuspit refers to as Sherman's "thanatopsistic scene" can also be interpreted as the artist's projection of the interior of the female body. No longer using external appearance as a means of trying on feminine roles, she now reveals the monstrous "other" hidden behind the carefully crafted cosmetic facade of her *Film Still* beauties, and displays a wounded body that essentially disappears into a mass of vomit and body fluids. As bulimic women know well, behind the mask of the "perfect female," there is an abundance of turmoil and debris to be evacuated. It is no coincidence, then, that these pictures are replete with images of food and vomit. No longer masking the sense of herself as a wounded creature, she expresses her anger and control by vomiting onto the viewer, so to speak. Repelled by these scenes, we are nonetheless compelled by the power and forcefulness they project. It is difficult to avert our gaze in the same way that we find ourselves staring at a car accident or a disfigured person. These images project onto us something we deny to ourselves in our blind search for beauty and perfection; they are the forms of reality that are denied by culture. How soothing and poignant is the pinup, by contrast, pleading for a moment with the figure of doom. Sherman is aware of the two ends of this reality continuum when she states, "I like making images that from a distance seem kind of seductive, colorful, luscious and engaging, and then you realize what you're looking at is something totally opposite."[35]

Many of these photographs seem to depict scenes of a crime; and the crime appears to be sexual. One is able to discern a destroyed bed, a fallen head, bloody underwear, a woman's hand, condoms, buried body parts, and a partially inflated sex doll. These images are clearly scenes of destruction. In addition to portraying crimes against women, as feminist critics correctly interpret, however, they also depict the dissolution of Sherman's made-up images. We are self-conscious creatures who, because we cannot bear the thought of death, imagine immortality. And yet, we are "raped" by time, alteration, and decay; we are nature's victims and our fate is to feed underground insects. These are therefore pictures of fragmentation of the figure in which the boundaries of identity have become erased. We are faced with part-objects: shreds of hair, fingers protruding from the ground under which they have been buried, scraps of clothing, and disconnected body parts. There is no longer a whole, not even a fake whole. Sherman seems to be saying that this mess is what was hidden behind the masks she wore in the previous stages; the "shell" has vanished and in its place are disintegrated remains, bits and pieces torn apart and scattered about.

A further clue to these scenes of destruction is to be found in the tormented pair of eyes discernible in several of the photographs. These eyes are reflected in the lenses of a discarded pair of eyeglasses, a small mirror, and a piece of broken glass. Through these images, Sherman seems to be depicting the kind of fragmentation that takes place in one's self image when one has experienced inadequate mirroring, or when one sees oneself in the mirror of death. Through her art, however, Sherman compels the audience not only to witness her disintegration, but also, to mirror her ugly, distorted image. Jessica Benjamin has noted that "The act of violation of the body becomes a way of representing the struggle to death for recognition."[36] Sherman portrays her fears of disintegration, and simultaneously brings them under aesthetic control by establishing containment for a fragmented image.

Playing House (1988–90)

As in Freud's famous *fort-da* game, or the classic drama of destruction and survival, Sherman reemerges whole, but this time in full body costume. While living in Rome, the artist's genius for acting, makeup, and costume climaxed in her *History Portrait* series. She leaves behind the realm of popular culture, fairy tales, and horror movies, and turns to art history by adopting the genre of portraiture that was popular during the Renaissance. Coming forth from the self-destructiveness of the previous stage, Sherman enters a "renaissance," a rebirth, in which she turns to the past—the world of her ancestors—her parents (see Plate 18). It is no coincidence therefore that many of these portraits represent mother with child (the largest is an 8 x 10 foot Madonna). This is also the first phase in which Sherman takes on the appearance of men as well as women.[37] She dramatically depicts a blending of past and present, fantasy and reality in the child's relationship to the parents through her multiple and shifting identifications.[38] Thus playing with the family romance, the fantasy that one's parents are other than who they are, Sherman dons the costumes of her predecessors and retells the story of the past in her own unique way. Most importantly, she begins to explore her identity in relation to others. And in order to fully realize one's identity as well as its inherent transience and incompleteness, one must necessarily come to terms with one's relation to significant figures from the past.

Sherman claims that she "never did terribly well in art history: I could never memorize the slides."[39] Just as the film stills of the seventies did not refer to specific films, the portraits of this phase merely recall master painters and portraits. Goya, Ingres, Titian, Caravaggio, Raphael, Holbein, David, and others are suggested but never identically copied. Sherman and Orlan (see next chapter) thus reinvent classical high art. Jarring the spectator's recall of portrait masterpieces from the past, Sherman encourages personal memories to play a crucial part in the way we respond to these works. As she did in her *Film Stills*, she also challenges the reality of distinct masters producing distinct works. Again, we have here no independent markers along the clean highway of art history but, rather, elements emerging in the complex story of art, a story with multiple profiles and cross-connected influences too complex to map, a story where, as with any interesting story, one thing can become another just by turning away from it for a moment before you look at it again.

As we follow Sherman's physical and psychological transformations in her game of "cultural charades,"[40] we question: "Where is she now? Who is she now?" She practically has the viewer demanding to him/herself, "Will the real Cindy Sherman please stand up!" Through her chameleon-like incarnations and reincarnations, she becomes in turn a Madonna, a Renaissance prince, a scholar, a bald monk, a hairy-chested Romantic rake, a lord, a lady, and more. Both Sherman and her audience obtain pleasure from the *illusion* she creates—an illusion that is presently recognized as such. Yet this illusion covers an even greater illusion; and that is the illusion that something is distinct, concrete, independent and real. She is calling attention to the greatest magic of all: *the illusion of permanence and stability in a universe of constant, dynamic flux*. She does not hesitate, therefore, to reveal the overlapping lines of a false nose or oversized prosthetic breasts. No longer attempting to convince the viewer that the clothes she wears are her own, she allows the seams to show; disguise is even flaunted rather than merely implied. "It's all in the game," she seems to be saying, amused. Thus, these portraits are the most playful of all and those easiest to take lightly. This does not detract from their seriousness however, for Sherman's blatant aesthetic illusion gives the game away.

On the one hand, Sherman idealizes her figures and places them in elaborate frames of varying shapes and sizes. On the other hand, she playfully expresses her anger by poking fun at them. For example, a bulbous false nose is added to an otherwise virginal young lady (#197, 1989), or a visible sagging breastplate is attached to an elderly woman (#222, 1990). Sherman thus caricatures the methods and subjects her "parent artists" employed between 1600 and 1800 through her creation of mood, character, class, status, gender, and occupation. She demonstrates how ridiculous this world of adults appears from a child's point of view. In this phase, Sherman singles out the maternal figure as an object of ridicule. "I collect breasts,"[41] claims Sherman, who here exposes a Madonna's prosthetic breasts which are awkwardly placed or squirt milk aimlessly into the air; the baby's features are not discernible (#216, 1989). This blending of idealization with the grotesque illustrates Sherman's coming to terms with a more realistic view of her parents. Whereas these adults remain idealized figures in many ways, they are literally depicted with the warts and imperfections of everyday human beings. Furthermore, she does not allow them to cover up their sexuality and makes certain that they flaunt it instead. This little girl refuses to be left out of the adult world and, as the *enfant terrible* that she is, reveals a child who knows all the things an adult knows but does not hide from them, a child who does not conceal the absurdity of life but flings it in our face like a baby throwing food.

Doll Play (1992–99)

In her next phase, Sherman aggressively, yet playfully, explores issues of sexuality, gender, and relationships with life-size plastic and rubber dolls. Like the child who plays the game "Show me yours and I'll show you mine," Sherman is curious about her sexuality as well as that of others—especially her parental figures. In her art of this phase, she experiments with the most basic sexual issues related to body integrity and the difference between the sexes. Sherman claims that she turned to dolls because she was tired of using her own image in her photographs.[42] I believe her doll play allowed her to enter territory that would have remained inaccessible had she restricted herself to the use of her own body. Dolls permitted her to delve further in her exploration of sexuality and gender and to take greater risks as she dealt with psychically loaded material. With dolls she leaves human beings behind. And, importantly, dolls don't die.

Resembling children who play the game "Doctor" to examine the difference between the sexes, Sherman sets up her anatomically correct and hyper-realistic male and female dolls, ordered from medical supply companies, in pornographic poses. Explicit close-ups of sexual organs invest the photographs with a genital intensity. The photographs are additionally enlarged to such a degree that one can not always tell if they show dolls or humans. In one, a gigantic penis dripping semen could be mistaken for a nose dribbling mucous. Sherman's art, having run the gamut of existential truth and the inevitable sense of despair it brings, has entered the *cul-de-sac* of the perverse. Although the viewer knows this is doll play, the boundaries between make believe and reality break down and the line between the two becomes blurred. These pictures, therefore, hit close to home and create intense discomfort in viewers, perhaps because they show the hell we must enter when there are no more creative illusions.

The perverse or fetishistic quality of a number of these works derives from the many poses Sherman borrows from hard-core pornography. She credited the impetus for these "Sex Pictures" to some of Jeff Koons's sexually explicit art as well as the NEA's decision to cut funding for and censor the artwork of photographers Robert Mapplethorpe and Andres Serrano. Her response was "to make work that could never be funded. Having had some success, I could afford to take that risk."[43] Sherman's work of this phase is also considered perverse because she essentially represents a child's vision of gender and sexuality. Irene Fast proposed that children's primary identifications are with both mother and father. She coined the term *bisexual completeness* to describe the young child's gender consciousness as both undifferentiated and over-inclusive before becoming aware of the difference between the sexes.[44] Thus, many of Sherman's photographs display crossbreeds of male and female combinations. She detaches, then mixes and matches, the dolls' numerous body parts, and sometimes adds masks, makeup, and artificial body parts. The end result is often jarring as in the case (#263, 1992) of a limbless male torso attached with a ribbon to a limbless female torso, creating the effect of a hybrid amputated hermaphrodite.

Bernstein observed that women's experiences of their bodies generate singular anxieties (i.e., access, penetration, and diffusivity) which result in unique defenses for mastery. She claimed that unlike the boy, who can rely on direct sensory experience, the developing girl relies instead on proprioceptive experiences, symbolization, and other people to help her define her "elusive" genital experience.[45] Sherman deals with these bodily anxieties by magnifying them, and demonstrating their inescapable nature. Exemplifying penetration anxiety, for example, one photograph (#258, 1992) shows a doll posed from behind, spreading her buttocks to expose an enormous gaping hole which we penetrate with our vision and imagination. A rape is thus created as the spectators become unwilling perpetrators in a drama forced upon them. It important to note that the hole is in the shape of a heart. Like the pervert, who turns intimacy into rape, objectification, and dehumanization, Sherman moves the heart to the place of the anus, thereby turning the world backwards and violating and shitting on romantic notions of love and intimacy.

Macabre humor abounds in these photographs. Take, for instance, Sherman's twist on an artist's model in the traditional odalisque pose (#250, 1992). A composite of doll parts lies on a bed of wigs and wears a mask of an ambiguously gendered wrinkled elderly person who smiles enigmatically (see Plate 19). Showing off her naked breasts—although one can see she wears a chest plate with nothing on underneath—she poses with artificial arms behind her head. A pelvis, devoid of limbs, lies in a spread-eagle position, its wide-open vagina stuffed with an enormous sausage, conjuring a disgusting and disruptive image reminiscent of Freud's notorious "fecal penis."[46] Sherman collapses the difference between the sexes and the generations in this photograph, thus it comes as no surprise that Wallach has branded it "Olympia from Hell."[47]

A later exhibition (1995) of doll photographs shows bruised and damaged dolls, some of which bear a remarkable resemblance to Mr. Potato Head. Despite the pervasive expression of violence and destructiveness, parallel attempts at reparation are discernible as well. Sherman uses bandages which she wraps around several of the figures. At once destructive and seductive, these works use dolls to play with decomposition and recomposition and to illustrate highly condensed stories, not unlike perverse *mise-en-scènes*, that signal hidden meanings in their symbolism.

In 1999, Sherman's doll perversion reached new frontiers in her first black-and-white photographs since the 1970s *Film Stills*. This collection of mutant dolls posed in blatant pornographic poses possesses a Surrealist ambiance that offers homage to Hans Bellmer's 1932 *Poupée* photographs, many of which, like Sherman's, suggest child abuse, subjugation, violation, and dismemberment. The dolls she uses are familiar ones—Barbie, GI Joe, Aladdin and Hercules (from Disney), Billy and Carlos (gay dolls)—yet uncanny not only because the inanimate seems to become animate but, also, because the dolls now display slashed faces, severed and castrated limbs, enlarged or misshapen genitalia, and they are framed in pornographic poses. Although the artist admits that these photographs "allude to pornography or X-rated photos," she also insists that "they are just dolls."[48] Yet, Sherman's "sex play" in these works can be considered pornographic for several reasons. First, common perverse practices involving sadomasochism, dolls, or amputees are played out in them. Second, they dehumanize the sexual act and blur the boundary between children and adults, playthings and intimacy. Third, there is no relationship between the dolls; they pose for the cameras, not for each other, recalling the Marquis de Sade's statement that "it is *easier* every time to fuck a man than to try to understand him."[49] Finally, they summon a voyeuristic and sadomasochistic gaze related to peep shows or sexual acts performed or fantasized about in private quarters. Yet, unlike pornography, Sherman's photographs are not limited to the narrow purpose of instant sexual gratification. Instead, they play with the ambiguous boundaries between dolls and humans, children and adults, desire and danger, pornography and art in order to raise crucial questions about human desire and the status of the naked body in our culture.

Acting Up and Clowning Around (2000–2004)

In the year 2000, Sherman put together a series of photographs of herself in the guise of

West Coast middle-aged women with day jobs (secretaries, real estate saleswomen, housewives, or gardeners) who aspire to be actresses. These "Hollywood types," as she calls them, can be viewed as the characters in her *Film Stills* who have arrived at a certain age and who now rely on a different kind of artifice for the image they wish to portray. This is the dark side of Hollywood movies, the wannabees who never made it or who made it but continue to cling to faded illusions and idealized visions of their lost glamour days. Sherman combines comedy and tragedy once more in the exaggerated makeup she applies—lipstick that extends far beyond the lips or thin penciled eyebrows drawn on top of larger, still visible, original ones. Fake tans, cosmetic surgery, and push-up bras reveal desperate attempts to cling to one's youth in the face of encroaching signs of aging.

The women are posing for headshots to get acting jobs. Thus, Sherman here is an artist who masquerades as an actor who, in turn, puts on an act for the camera. Multiple, layered masquerades offer endless possibilities for self-invention and self-concealment. All of these pseudo-portraits show her characters' illusions at the same time that she strips them of these same illusions. Reality and fantasy merge once more as the gap between a character's real features and her unrealized potential are revealed; her dreams and aspirations appear to have been greater than her talent. These photographs are those in Sherman's oeuvre most filled with pathos as they bring into relief a painful narcissistic moment in the lives of women, a reckoning with one's gains and achievements but, more often with one's losses and failures, the assaults to one's vanity that necessarily accompany age.

As a natural extension of what Sherman has been doing in her art all along, and as a logical outcome of her previous photographs, Sherman turned to a series of photographs (2003–4) of herself in the role of clown. In these photographs, the most colorful of her oeuvre, due also to the digitally created psychedelic backgrounds, she is costumed in gaudy clothing and flamboyant makeup. Sherman faces us from within a world of artificial gaiety and buffoonery, a world she deliberately turned to after the September 11 disaster. "My clowns are anything but funny," she exclaims.[50]

Clowns are artists who use makeup and costume to create a unique face that becomes their trademark. Like Sherman, they have a bag of tricks and poke fun at themselves and at the human condition. Most of Sherman's clowns are white-faced, traditional aristocratic clowns. Some are August clowns, who show some natural skin tones, and present with impish, gregarious, or slapstick humor. It is these clowns who often get the brunt of jokes as they make fools of themselves next to the white-faced straight men. Some of Sherman's clowns take on the roles of vagabonds or loners; others play with their sexuality; still others reveal a menacing figure which underlies the outward glee. When discussing this series, Sherman said, "What attracted me to clowns was . . . the possibility . . . of being sad, disturbed, a psycho killer."[51] Indeed, like many children, Sherman did not like clowns when she was young. What is clear from all of her clowns is the comic slant they propose to lend to the human condition. The clown and the artist provide entertainment while they remind us that we too are on a fool's journey through life.

As always, Sherman denies any connection to the clown characters she portrays: "The greatest challenge for me was to allow a personality to emerge from behind the clown make-up: a personality that has nothing to do with my own."[52] Her protests notwithstanding, one unforgettable portrait stands out as the most striking of the bunch (#413). There is a commonly held assumption that the clown, despite its painted cheery mask, conceals a deep sadness. Yet, what can one say when faced with a deliberately painted sad faced clown? The portrait in question has brown shaggy hair, a fake red-tipped nose, and false bulbous cheeks which hover over a distinctly downwardly curved white and red mouth (see Plate 20). Most jarring are the eyes, especially since they are the most genuine and the saddest of any in her entire body of work. Encircled in white, Sherman's eyes here speak to us beseechingly amid profound pain and weariness; the bright vibrating blues, greens, and violets in the background serve as an emphatic frame for the blue mood she exudes. This androgynous—but not anonymous—clown notably wears a black satin jacket with a daintily embroidered pink name over its chest: "*Cindy.*"

The Artist at Play

Cindy Sherman creates a safe space, akin to a children's playground, in which to work through issues of self-image, identity, gender, and object relations. Clearly, play is as important for the adult as it is for the child because life never stops being a problem. Erikson's theory of play focuses on the child's creation of model situations to master reality through experimenting and planning.[53] Winnicott, describes play not in opposition to reality, but rather, as a bridge to it.[54] Other studies support these views and describe the socially adaptive and organizing, as well as self-regulating and problem-solving, functions of pretend or play.[55] When Sherman says of her later work, "The pictures are fake, yet real," she is addressing these very points and referring to the authentic nature of the issues being dealt with in her art.[56]

Sherman adopts in her art the practice of solutions and adaptations to difficult situations. One can enact, in play or through art, a position of control with respect to a situation over which one has no control. One can similarly enact wishes that would otherwise be repudiated by a harsh conscience or invite dangerous consequences from the real world.[57] Imaginative play can serve as a trial, a rehearsal (a "dress rehearsal" in Sherman's case) for solutions to reality, or as preparation for future roles in adulthood.[58] Therefore, Sherman's work can be understood as a recreation of past experiences for the purpose of active response and mastery and, as such, it furnishes a blueprint for future experiences.

Importantly, her work attacks the illusory idea of the unitary self and plays instead with a multiplicity of selves, especially as they are manifest in the spectrum of gender identity. Rather than perceive her multiple identifications as narcissistic or pathological, one can understand her work as an attempt to bear them all, granting her greater freedom of being. Everyone (in her) gets a say and a chance to take the stage.

Sherman's art changed over time, revealing a deepening of her explorations into the self. Initially assuming the identities of women she impersonated, she played off them but remained empty inside. Then she reversed the game by replacing superficial feminine beauty with the menacing contents of her internal world. Taking on the family romance in her *History Portraits,* she broadened her world to include others and exposed her ambivalent feelings toward her parents as well as her parent artists. Sherman turned to doll play to probe the world of sexuality, perversion, and gender difference. In her most recent work, she plays with what it means to be a middle-aged woman and to face the illusions we construct to live a bearable life. Finally, she plays the clown—goofy, broken-hearted, menacing—who entertains us with games of artifice and whose antics highlight the seriousness and dark complexity of what we consider fun.

Like Alice who traverses her looking glass and meets numerous creatures along her *Adventures in Wonderland* who help her come to terms with the puzzling process of attaining an adult identity, so too Sherman takes us on a daring and dramatic journey to what often resembles a carnival, complete with its house of horror and freak show. We encounter leering masks, mocking jeers, and familiar characters from the likes of a wax museum. Inevitably, we end up in the circus with its house of mirrors. No matter where we turn, we confront our own reflection; it is sometimes distorted, and often frightening, but always familiar.

It will be terribly interesting to see what Cindy Sherman does next.

10
Orlan: Monster Beauty

> Art that interests me has much in common with—belongs to—resistance. It must challenge our preconceptions, disrupt our thoughts; it is outside the norms, outside the law, against bourgeois order; it is not there to cradle us, to reinforce our comfort, to serve up again what we already know. It must take risks; at the risk of not being immediately accepted or acceptable. It is deviant, and in itself a social project. Art can, art must change the world, it is its only justification.
>
> —Orlan

SEVERAL YEARS AGO, FRENCH MULTIMEDIA artist Orlan spent the night at my place. Before retiring for the night, she asked me if I had any makeup remover. I shall never forget how we stood shoulder to shoulder before the bathroom mirror, each removing the masks we used to face the world, two middle-aged women, me with wrinkles around the eyes and creases at the sides of my mouth and she with her horned implants, swollen lips, and translucent skin, the results of her many cosmetic surgeries. As she wiped the dark purple from her lips and the silver glitter from her horns, I couldn't help thinking about Freud's concept of the uncanny—*umheimlich,* unhomey—and its opposite—*heimlich,* familiar and of the home. We were engaged in a very conventional female bonding experience, and yet the difference between our faces *was* uncanny. Mine was the result of aging, the surrender to time and gravity, while hers the result of unbending intent. Horns do not normally grow out of the human head nor do faces inherit a disparate collection of features from classical art.

I wondered how my then three-year-old son might react to Orlan in the morning. Would he recoil in fear at her two-colored head, hair half black and half bright yellow? Would the matching thick round black and yellow glasses remind him of an owl's eyes? Would he want to touch the horns on the sides of her head? I reflected, too, on how many of my colleagues and attendees at lectures I'd given on Orlan seemed stuck on the issue of whether she was a revolutionary and groundbreaking artist or simply "sick" and her "art" an expression of sheer pathology. I'd always found this issue tedious, for just as a system of reasoning depends on its axioms for the path to its conclusions, so, too, the response to the question of Orlan and her art depends on the presuppositions of the viewer; and it is precisely our assumptions about art, art history, female beauty, gender politics, and technology that Orlan seeks to disrupt and even overturn. If one is willing to bear the disruption imposed by Orlan's art and subvert the defensive response it engenders, one is rewarded with a radically provocative vision that consistently defies either/or definitions. Nothing in a once familiar world is as it seems and everything is open to re-arrangement, reinterpretation, and re-creation.

When I awoke the next morning I found the two of them talking playfully, my son unbothered by her appearance. I thought again of Orlan's powers—female powers—of seduction and repudiation. She had invited my son into a play space, a space alive with possibility and contradiction, a space not unlike the one opened to us through her world of art, whose physical center is her very own body—play most serious indeed.

What is most amazing about Orlan (b. 1947) is that unlike any artist before her, she has transformed herself into a living work of art, one that questions not only the history of Western art, but human history as well. She enters her passion to create, assert, and disrupt so deeply that there is no more space between her and it. Unlike other artists, she cannot walk out of the studio to return to some "normal" aspect of her life. For her there is nothing but self-representation at the service of an art meant to get under our skin. Some might not like what she does and may wish to avoid it and even dismiss it as madness; but none can encounter it and remain unaffected.

In this chapter I explore Orlan's mind-body theater to highlight the many psychological dynamics at play in the complicated process she has initiated in her revolutionary art form. In addition to her artistic, feminist, and social agenda, I clarify the personal psychology of someone who has undertaken a complete identity transformation in the name of art and how the process of that metamorphosis affects her audience and challenges our theories of self, identity, sexual difference, and castration.

Self-Creation

About to give a performance in Lyons in 1978, an ectopic pregnancy sent Orlan to the hospital. With her life at risk, she had the brilliant idea while in the ambulance of filming the dangerous surgery and sending the film back to take the place of her performance. This moment highlights the multiple functions and meanings present in Orlan's oeuvre. Orlan immediately appreciated the possibilities involved in moving her studio to the operating room, thereby equating the surgical act with that of creation. She noted the theatricality of surgery: the lights, the rituals, the surgeon who is God the father, the crew around him, the risk of life and death—a moment to be seized.[1]

"My body was a sick body that suddenly needed attention,"[2] Orlan has said in a provocative statement about surgery as performance. Her transformation of deathly emergency into artistic opportunity reveals the manner in which she creatively came to terms with loss—the loss of a child—by replacing it with birth—the birth of a new art form which incorporates medical technology. It also highlights her unity with her work, that zero distance between what she is and what she does. Perhaps most importantly, Orlan's imaginative gesture suggests the healing potential of art.

Orlan has taken up a formidable task. She states it simply: "I fight against God and DNA."[3] (Note well that if one is fighting God and DNA, religion and science, one is challenging the very foundations of Western culture.) She wants to completely control the process of self-creation and self-definition. "I hate nature. Because I don't know where the switch is that forces me to die . . . Life is a killer. . . . Nature represents everything that locks me in, that applies force to me, that bothers me."[4] Orlan's rejection of nature initially involved rejection of her own budding femininity. She recalls how, as a young adolescent, she could not halt her breasts and pubic hair from growing. She despised what was happening to her: "I couldn't stop it; it was against my will."[5]

Whereas Orlan rebels against the restrictions of her natural-given skin, at the same time, she appreciates its many aesthetic possibilities. Her art is born between nature's grim reality and the poignant desire for transcendence throbbing in the heart of imagination. It struggles against finality and seeks to surpass limitation, gender, position, and circumstance to forge from her own flesh a formula for immortality. It is from the fury of her rebellion that she creates, sparing neither safety nor convention.

One of Orlan's earliest works (1964) recalls Frida Kahlo's painting *My Birth,* in that both artists employ their art literally and figuratively to give birth to themselves. Orlan rejects her mother's "natural" position as the person who gave birth to her by depicting the artist giving birth to herself—here, a mannequin, a nonhuman creature. The French title, *Orlan accouche d'elle m'aime* (Orlan gives birth to herself), plays on the homonym, *elle meme* (herself) and *elle m'aime* (she loves me). Eerily predicting what she would do throughout her artistic career, Orlan gives birth to herself as a way of loving herself. The difference between Kahlo and Orlan is obvious; the former used paint while the latter her own flesh and blood.

Orlan's repeated representations of the birth process culminated in her best-known, most ambitious and controversial project, *The Reincarnation of Sainte Orlan:* ten cosmetic surgery operations to date, the first initiated on the artist's forty-third birthday, May 30, 1990. These painful alterations engage in a literal and often ironic dialogue with (art) history because they have shaped on her face the features from female models, most of whom

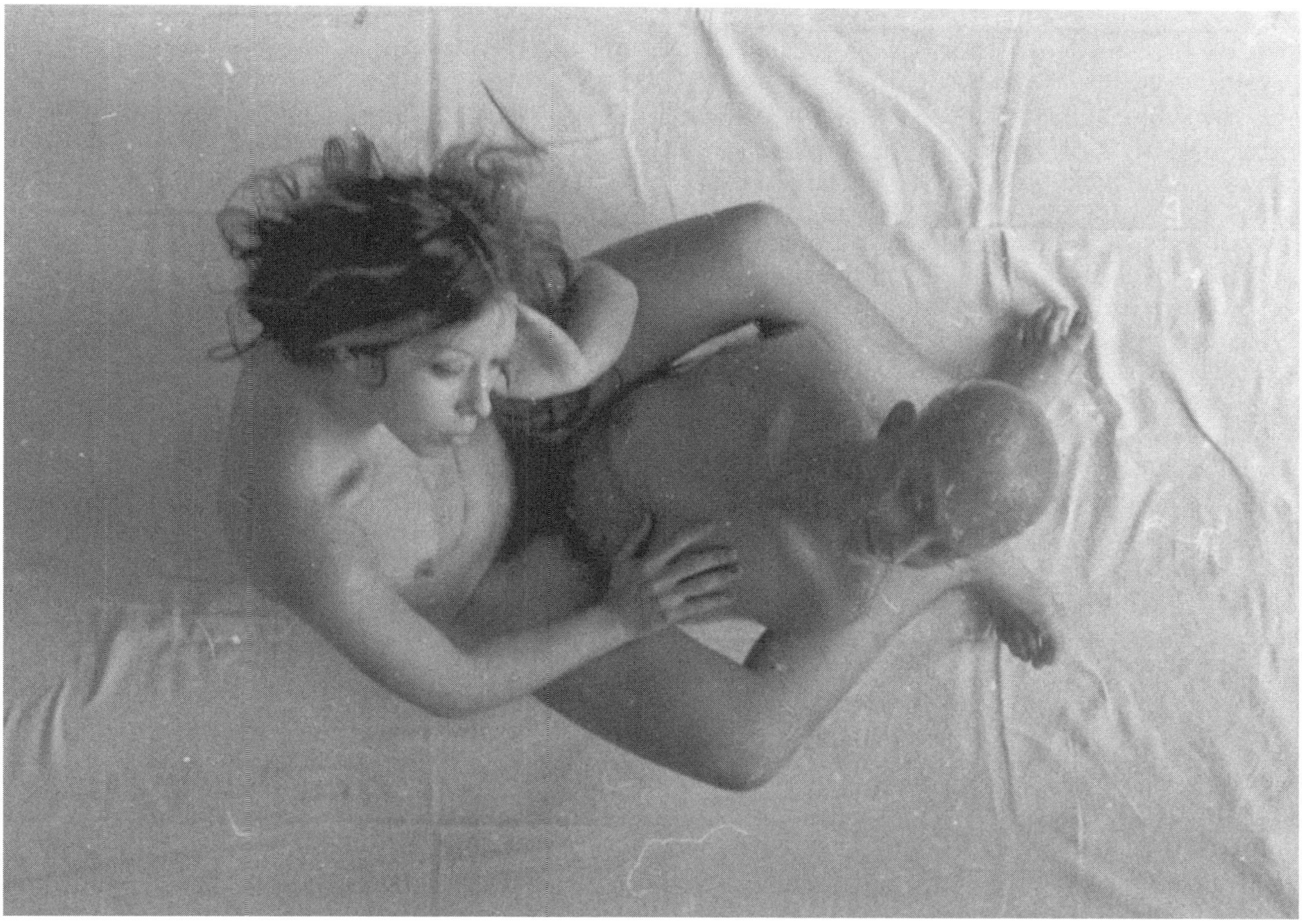

46. Orlan, *Orlan Accouche d'elle M'aime [Orlan gives birth to her loved self]*, 1964. 81 × 76 cm. Black-and-white photograph. © 2009 Artists Rights Society (ARS), New York/ASAGP, Paris. Photo: Courtesy Galerie Michel Rein.

are Greek goddesses in art historical masterpieces. She has taken the chin of Botticelli's *Venus*, the nose from the school of Fontainbleau's *Diana*, the mouth of Boucher's *Europa*, the eyes of Gerome's *Psyche*, and the forehead of Leonardo da Vinci's *Mona Lisa*. Incredibly, under her direction, Orlan's doctors mold these classic features from iconic women into her own, forever altering both her appearance and our perception of those great works. Anyone who has seen Orlan can never look at a classical masterpiece of a beautiful model in the same way again. She has destroyed our naiveté forever.

Orlan reacts angrily when critics accuse her project of masking a desire to be more beautiful. She insists that she chose these icons for their personal qualities rather than because they embody an ideal of beauty. Diana, the adventuress, denies herself to men; Europa allows herself to be carried off to an uncertain future and the painting of her by Moreau remains unfinished; Psyche, beloved of Eros, is the embodiment of the life force; Venus is equated with fertility and creativity; and the Mona Lisa is the quintessence of androgyny since it is said to be a self-portrait of the artist, Leonardo da Vinci. To further prove her rejection of the claim that she was aspiring toward ideal beauty, Orlan had two silicone implants inserted in her temples. These swellings, often referred to as [Dionysian] "horns," clearly mark her face as grotesque and otherworldly. They also turn it into a phallic visage like Cahun's elongated head. Most importantly, Orlan argues, the horns "protrude . . . like volcanoes erupting against the dominant ideology."[6]

During the surgeries producing her self-hybridizations, the artist remains awake and reads from psychoanalytic or philosophical texts. For example, at the onset of each of her surgical operations, Orlan quotes from Lacanian psychoanalyst, Eugenie Lemoine-Luccioni's *La Robe:* "Skin is deceiving . . . in life, one only has one's skin . . . there is a bad exchange in human relations because one never is what one has . . . I have the skin of an angel, but I am a jackal . . . the skin of a crocodile, but I am a puppy, the skin of a black person, but I am white, the skin of a woman, but I am a man; I never have the skin of what I am. There is no exception to the rule because I am never what I have."[7] Many questions arise from Orlan's use of texts in her art. Could they somehow mirror what she does with the surgery, borrowing from texts the way she borrows the features of historic artistic models? Is this the staging of irony she purchases with her body and blood, the impossible female heaping herself upon the postmodern altar to plumb the depths (the texts) as she plays with the surface (the face and skin)? Is she, at the same time, mocking the Patriarchy, thumbing her modified nose at its values and history, while turning it inside out by injecting herself into it? Is she the ultimate cultural foil, the beautiful monster, who crashes through the edifice of Western culture to remind us that we got it wrong to begin with because we subverted, appropriated, and marginalized the woman? Interestingly, Orlan brings something both sacred and precious into her oeuvre—her personal quest for transcendence expressed as art carved into her flesh. What is sacred about this is that she is reaching beyond the limitations of our culture and history, even finding "God" in herself; after all, she is Saint Orlan. And what is precious is again that there is no reserve between her and her project, no space of safety. She has put into it her entire life and body.

Orlan alters the medical environment by having surgeons and assistants attired in designer wear, and adds props and music as she choreographs and directs the surgery, turning it into a theatrical production. Posters of the painting from which she has chosen a body part are on display to guide the surgeons' hands. Interestingly, the computer-generated composite images of her face joined with the painting are not static pictures but change even as we look at them. Revealing the layering of both women's features, the images she calls *Entre-Deux* [between the two] are semi-transparent, shadowy, and deceptive renderings that cause our gaze to move back and forth between shifting figure and ground representations (see Plate 21). Orlan focuses on the gap between illusion and representation, the real and the imaginary. She demonstrates, through these hybrid depictions, that the outcome of this process is always indefinite and that who she is and what she becomes is largely a play of creation and projection.

Medusa and Castration

Orlan's evolution as a Medusan female has its artistic origin in 1981 when she produced *Documentary Study: The Head of Medusa* at the Musée S. Ludwig in Aix-la-Chapelle. In this performance piece, spectators were invited to gaze, through a large magnifying glass, at the artist's colorfully painted genitals glimpsed through a hole at the center of sheets taken from her trousseau. Orlan's *Documentary Study* is meant as a reference to Marcel Duchamp's famous *Etants Donnés* (see Plate 10), in which the viewer peers through a crack in a barnyard door to witness the splayed body of a woman who appears to have been raped and killed. (Recall that the art of both Wilke and Mendieta referred to this seminal work.) At the end of Orlan's piece, the artist handed out a text taken from Sigmund Freud's "The Head of Medusa," in which he wrote: "At the sight of the vulva even the devil runs away."[8] Freud was referring to the moment in which boys (and girls) come to the realization of the mother's absent penis which, he believed, forces a reckoning with the reality of gender difference and, more traumatically, the possibility of castration.

Orlan's self-named "carnal art" very explicitly deals with castration fantasies and gender differences. Her surgeries, as in her Medusa performance piece, recreate the notorious Freudian moment by traumatizing her viewers with unforgettable visual scenes of mutilation that horrify and repel but, more importantly, attack the schisms of male-female, inside-outside, real-artificial, art-life, and castrated-castrating, all of which challenge our normative and restricted understanding of gender and identity.

Interestingly, the burgeoning of "body art" has its parallel in growing numbers of those who suffer from eating disorders, body dysmorphic disorders, and gender identity disorders, all of which share the common conviction that there is something wrong with one's body. It is in this vein that I speak of castration, that is as referring to a sense of incompleteness in one's physical self, a sense that can be experienced by both genders. In general, castration is about the restrictions set by one's body and the desire to transcend one's physical limitations. It is not only about cutting or being cut; as in Lemoine-Luccioni's quote, it is about the gap between what one is and what one would like to be. It is about lack, loss, and fantasies of wholeness.[9] Cosmetic surgery and cyberspace, two media employed by Orlan in her art, allow such fantasies to become reality.

Orlan's choice of Medusa in her performance is an apt one.[10] Even after her death, Medusa continued to petrify those who dared to gaze at her decapitated head. Like Medusa, Orlan is both fascinating and dreadful. We wish to gaze at her as she engages in body mutating and life-threatening practices, yet we are aghast at the slicing of her flesh, frozen by the literal confrontation with bloody castration, mortality, and the uncanny encounter between reality and fantasy. In her Medusa piece, Orlan filmed her spectators' faces as they entered and left the performance, rendering them an integral part of the artwork.

Menstrual blood, a blood of loss and gain, is among the most privileged signifiers of abjection cited by Julia Kristeva in her book *Powers of Horror*.[11] Unsurprisingly, Medusa has been tied to menstruation and Orlan performed her Medusa piece displaying her vulva while she was menstruating, her crimson blood blending in with the painted genital hair. The bloody wound from Medusa's castrated neck acted as a womb that brought life to Pegasus and Chrysaor, the Golden Child. Orlan has also created self-portraits using the blood (and fat) taken from her surgeries. Perhaps more important than its abject quality, therefore, is the female blood's relation to procreativity and creativity.[12]

Thus, although Medusa appears tragic, her myth highlights our notions about castration and gender difference, the relationship between wound and womb, the abject and the maternal, the monstrous and the beautiful, the mirror and mirroring. In his paper on the uncanny, Freud spoke of the inscription of the female genitals as "blinding."[13] Likewise, Orlan has said: "I make images which almost make us blind. My work stands between the folly of seeing and the impossibility of seeing."[14] She forces us to recognize what we do not recognize and the effect is blinding.

The juxtapositions of the many paradoxes inherent in Orlan's art—castrated/castrating, victim/abuser, sacrificed/sacrificing, woman/artwork—are what make it so compelling and impossible to dismiss. An inevitable sense of female empowerment emerges from her daring use of her self and her body. She repeatedly gives birth to a new art form as well as a new self. Orlan's art is, in essence, an art of self-creation and, as such, it demonstrates female generativity.

Monster Beauty

Orlan's *Reincarnation* project has been explained by herself and by others as a feminist critique of Western standards of beauty and the male gaze.[15] Her fantasies of power, control, and reversal are shoved in our face as she shows us her insides both literally and through her artistic performance.

She becomes the grotesque body, Kristeva's abject body, whose boundaries are unstable, ambiguous, open, excessive, and out of control.[16] It is a body whose owner is regarded as impolite and aggressive, subversive albeit ironic and humorous. Whereas classic bodies are elevated on pedestals to distance themselves from the baser human realm, Orlan's body lies down as its materiality is dissected and scrutinized. Hers is a body intimate with bleeding transgression, a body conversant with pain and shock, a body that utilizes the frozen ideals of classical beauty in order to mock them, because they are false and steeped in denial. "Carnal art loves parody and the baroque, the grotesque and the extreme," she asserts in her *Manifesto*.[17]

Orlan shows us that the concepts of beauty, the grotesque, and castration are more closely related than we would otherwise presume. If we consider woman's need to deal with her body, which is constantly deemed lacking or incomplete (e.g., never hairless, odorless, fashionable, or thin enough)—that is, "castrated"—then we can grasp her need to make that body beautiful in order to attain a sense of wholeness associated with classical beauty, even if it means putting herself through pain and torture. It is not a penis that woman covets, but, rather, beauty, or at least the illusion of completeness that ideal beauty represents.

Pacteau has drawn a parallel between the significance castration anxiety holds for men with that beauty holds for women: "Freud observes that no man escapes castration anxiety; . . . it seems to me that, at least within the so-called Western world in which I am situated, no woman escapes 'beauty.'"[18] Although I agree with Pacteau, I would add my belief that the two anxieties are interconnected. Woman is preoccupied with beauty, whether she considers herself, or is considered, beautiful or not. She is raised to seek beauty at any cost, to suffer for it, and to lament it when it diminishes. Orlan's art, by simultaneously dealing with issues of castration (surgeries) and beauty (features lifted from classical art), exposes the plight of contemporary women. They are (1) considered incomplete—"castrated"—and seeking perfection; (2) monstrous and grotesque, castrating and frightening; and, therefore finally, (3) challenged to establish a new and more fluid standard of beauty, one constantly recreated.

Interestingly, feminists have recently begun to write about female beauty as monstrous. Moreover, they are proudly beginning to own terrifying aspects of femininity—"monster beauty"—in ways that simultaneously embrace and challenge Freud's notions of the castrated woman. Frueh describes monster beauty as expressing male projections while simultaneously revealing the authentic, rather than ideal, dimensions of woman:

> Monstrousness is an unnamed and implicit feminine condition . . . The Western tradition is populated by terrifically exciting female monsters, whose threat to men or male dominance is so great that they must be killed: Tiamat, the Sphinx, Medusa. Woman has been constructed as a hormonal and sexual monster whose physical attractions lure man into the *vagina dentata*, where he will be emasculated; whose femininity must be controlled through the administration of estrogen and progesterone and through dieting, the constriction of appetite. Female monsters in film can be monsters whose protectiveness of their spawn and whose procreative powers are both deadly to the human species—witness female villainy in the *Alien* films.[19]

Frueh celebrates the notion of monstrous femininity and illustrates the real and erotic potential it possesses. She claims that "becoming *visibly* different from normative beauty will prove women's powers in self-love and transformation."[20]

Indeed, it can be said that Orlan's reincarnation gives birth to a type of she-monster. She has explicitly compared her artistic aim with the creation of a monster; and even had herself photographed as the Bride of Frankenstein in 1990. The difference between the two "monsters" is that she is the creator as well as the final product: the *sacré monstre*.

Concurrent and oddly coincidental with the attention to monster beauty is the virtual disappearance of the female as the subject of beauty in the art of recent decades.[21] Certainly the feminist movement encouraged artists to record and explore women's inner experiences and challenged the importance of outward beauty. When classical traces of beauty appear in the works of artists like Hannah Wilke, Cindy Sherman, or Orlan, it speaks as social commentary, rather than bristle with its own aesthetic energy. As beauty has become ironic, the female body is most frequently depicted as grotesque or fragmented, calling attention to body parts (e.g., Louise Bourgeois, Mona Hatoum, Kiki Smith) and/or women's violation and victimization (e.g., Sue Williams, Nan Goldin). Trauma and humor combine to make points about the female's experiences and the violence that is an ever-present threat to her. Encountering Orlan's carnal art, our minds easily imagine the countless nameless women who have been carved up in the world, in the street and the home, on the movie screen, or between the pages of books. Her work naturally draws our attention to our own voyeuristic participation in the dissection of the female body.

Part of Orlan's "monstrosity" entails her use of technology and media to advance her argument that "the body is obsolete." Like Stelarc, the Australian-based performance artist who extends the concept of the body and its relationship with technology through human-machine interfaces, Orlan is indebted to telecommunication, artificial intelligence, and the creation of virtual realities; both artists draw inspiration from medical technological advances and cybernetics, such as cloning and genetic programming. In the virtual world of cyberspace, the physical body is absent; it is gender-free, age-free, race-free, and siteless. Media theorist Derrick de Kerckhove predicts the dissolution of the boundary of our skin: "Through interactive media . . . we will no longer be sure where our body begins and where it ends."[22] In *Omnipresence*, Orlan's seventh surgery, the physical reality of the live body was less relevant than the mediatized reality in which electronic signals transmitted the surgery by satellite to galleries around the world.

Orlan's ongoing series of *Self-Hybridizations* (begun in 1998) consists in virtual images created by computer technology to morph her image with non-Western (e.g., pre-Columbian, African, and Native American) representations of beauty, thereby making of her a hybrid of past and present, self and other (see Plate 22). Orlan speaks of these works as "entering into the skin of the other."[23] The aim of her refashioned body, then, is not only designed to transcend gender limitations; it is meant to rise above the body itself, to become pure image, in the brave new world of posthumanity. For Orlan, "the body is no longer adequate for the current situation . . . We are on the threshold of a world for which we are neither mentally or physically ready."[24] It is in this vein that the artist titled a traveling exhibit, *This is my body . . . This is my software.*

Altering the body and self through medical technology is a contemporary phenomenon; yet, for Orlan, such acts also challenge classical conceptions of a core identity presupposed in religion and psychoanalysis while making use of both systems. In assuming an eternal, unchanging soul, religion assumes a core spiritual identity, the foundation of one's human personality. Psychoanalytic theories that posit a core self[25] and relational writings that discuss true and false aspects of the self[26] imply that individuals have one genuine self and that changing or altering that self is a sign of alienation, narcissism, mental illness, and impostordom. For example, McDougall has described the developmental mourning process we must all go through when relinquishing a particular gender identity or sexual preference.[27] Orlan dismisses these theories as primitive, ancestral, anachronistic concepts. Instead, she refuses to accept her body's limitations—its difference and/or lack—which place her in a state of castration.

Catholicism, the religion Orlan was born into, is also rife with taboos, many of which center around the body and self-sacrifice. Using her art to make intentional parallels to religious martyrdom, she says: "The vision of my body being opened painlessly was extremely seductive aesthetically . . . I found it similar to the light coming through the windows of a church illuminating the religious imagery inside."[28] Orlan's fantasy of self-liberation from the shackles of her body leads to the fantasy of rebirth, a Christlike attempt to transcend the body and mortality.

For the culmination of *Reincarnation*, Orlan has expressed her intention to commission an advertising agency to create a new name for her as it would for a commercial product. She then plans to go to court to change her name legally to the one chosen by the agency. Although Orlan may appear to passively hand her naming to another, she is, in fact, an active agent in the transformation of herself into a product for market consumption. "I have given my body to Art," she exclaims again and again.[29] Orlan has also declared the wish to have her body embalmed after death and donated to a museum, thereby becoming the first living/dead work of art. In so doing, she will not only wrap herself in an eternal skin to attain immortality; she will transform the museum into a womb/tomb, a skin for the dead, the ultimate dwelling for a "body of art."[30]

Origins

Orlan claims that the idea for her "reincarnation" first occurred to her when she realized that she had mistakenly signed her name "morte" (death) on a check to her psychoanalyst. At that moment, she says, she appreciated the need to kill off her old self, Mireille Porte (rhymes with morte) and reincarnate as Saint Orlan, a person whose outer layering matters only so far as it becomes a site for public debate.

Clearly entering into a power struggle with her analyst over a sudden change in policy that had her pay cash rather than by check, Orlan wrote the check signed as "Morte." Orlan's aggression toward her analyst turned into an internalized death wish, yet she acted out her anger and sublimated it all at once by deciding to retain "or" (gold/light), the only positive part of the signature, and expand it into Orlan. There are many names that might have inspired the artist in her choice of name. Like the artificial self she creates, orlon is a synthetic fabric. Virgina Woolf's Orlando is a character who exists between male and female worlds. French heroine and martyr, Joan of Arc, is also known as the maid of Orleans. And, finally, Pauline Réage's *Story of O* comes to mind because of its sadomasochistic themes.[31]

Parallel to the relationship women have with their plastic surgeon, people often enter psychoanalytic therapy with the intention of refashioning themselves into the kind of person they would prefer to be. It is interesting that Orlan informed me that when she phoned her analyst to share her novel idea of employing cosmetic surgery in her art, the analyst expressed shock and admonished her not to go through with it. At that moment, Orlan, a savvy analysand, knew that if she had succeeded in getting her analyst to depart from her characteristically neutral therapeutic stance, then she must be onto something—in her words, she had "hit a nerve."[32] Her relationship with her analyst (she has undergone at least two analyses, both classical and Lacanian) is significant both for its catalytic function in her art and, also, because that relationship, in its transference manifestations, takes the place of the parent-child relationship and, therefore, informs us about the origins of her character formation and object relationships. Aware of the dynamic function of her art, Orlan has said, "I am in the process of creating a psychological self-portrait."[33] Indeed, Orlan has helped change the definition of art, which was previously concerned with a final external product, to a practice, not unlike psychoanalysis, that is in constant flux and emphasizes process rather than outcome. Both activities highlight identity and the self as never ending processes of construction.

Orlan's rebelliousness in relation to her analyst most probably reflects the ways she was with her family of origin, of whom little is known. What we do know is that she was born to a Catholic family in the industrial town of St. Etienne, France on May 30, 1947. She was close to her father, an electrician for the local theater, a man she called an "anarchist and libertarian.[34] She had a strained relationship with her mother, a woman who seemed only to pay attention to her when she was sick. Her sister, eight years her senior, apparently got along better with the mother as she too was always preoccupied with physical illness. In fact, Orlan described her household as containing two couples: mother and sister; father and Orlan. In an interview, she depicts the troubled relationship she had with both mother and sister:

> The search for dust, that's all. Chronic mental crises, screams and chronic hysteria. She was a housewife, married, two children, normal . . . We were always very distant. I used to assert myself when she used to telephone asking how it was going, only as she was hanging up . . . It was necessary for me to tell her, "I'm sick," for her to become interested in me. My sister always followed her example. She was always sick and is still *always* sick. When I call her, the only thing she talks about is her illness.[35]

On one level, Orlan's art, with its emphasis on the hysterical female body, can be read as a direct response to French neurologist Jean-Martin Charcot, who theatrically paraded female hysterics before medical students and high society at the Salpètrière, the Parisian hospital where he worked and Freud trained, in the late 1880s. On another level, it could be said that Orlan became the "sick child" her mother needed her to be, the child who is repeatedly placed in a medical environment where her body is surgically manipulated and then allowed to heal. Like Kahlo and Wilke, Orlan uses the hospital setting to expose the medical objectification of female bodies. However, unlike these artists, whose work brought physical and emotional private pain into the public domain by baring their scars from the ravages of physical illness and injury, Orlan was not physically wounded. Rather, like the hysteric, she takes a healthy body and turns it into a sick body, one that requires medical attention and one that alters the way she perceives herself and we perceive her. She rejects her mother for only attending to her when she is ill, yet she gains enormous attention by flaunting her wounded body and having us all react with horror, shock, and concern for her.

Orlan's seventh surgical performance is titled *Omnipresence* because it was sent by satellite to galleries around the world. Orlan *has* become omnipresent; she is everywhere, not to be ignored or forgotten. She is tended to by doctors and nurses and we, her audience, look on anxiously while she endures the knife. The repetitive quality of these performances reveals Orlan's attempts at mastery over what appears to have been an original situation with some traumatic significance. It is as if she asks us to engage in a reciprocal relationship patterned after the one she had with her mother. She seems to test the limits of whether she is lovable even—or especially—with her wounds.

Thus, despite her multiple conscious attempts to disown her biological family, Orlan's unconscious familial connection remains strong. In essence, she has created her own family romance through her art, a novel narrative in which she replaces her family of origin with another that better suits her. She changed her name from Porte to Orlan and chose parents from art history rather than her family of origin. Orlan's father is now the artist and her mother is the subject. Step-by-step, she removes features genetically inherited from her parents and substitutes them with those from famous female art icons. She in effect rewrites her story, her face, and her self. These are her new parents whose features she literally inscribes onto her skin. She is now the daughter of Leonardo da Vinci and Mona Lisa; that of Botticelli and Venus. Both creator and created, masculine and feminine, unite in her, on her body, to produce its offspring: Saint Orlan, whom many believe to be monstrous but whom she has anointed a saint, a holy child.

Talking Heads

Although she likens her surgery to woman-to-woman transexualism, Orlan has stated that she is a manwoman or a womanman ("*Je suis une homme et un femme*"). Significantly, one of her early works (1989) involves her alteration of Courbet's well-known painting, *L'Origine du Monde* [The Origin of the World], to which Frida Kahlo's *My Birth* also referred (see Plates 7 and 8). Courbet's painting is a close-up view of a woman's genitals. It is interesting, in the context of castration anxiety triggered by the sight of the female genital, that Lacan once owned this painting and had a special cupboard made for it to keep it hidden from view. Orlan cunningly changed Courbet's original title to *L'Origine de la Guerre* [The Origin of War] and inserted an erect penis into what was once a uniquely female genital site (see Plate 9).

As sociological and historical commentary, Orlan emphasizes the contrast between female creativity and male destructiveness. On a psychological level, however, the artist replaces the female genitals with the male phallus, thereby literally undoing—or reversing—castration. The naked woman with a large, erect penis declares her war with male theorists and artists who have deprived her of the power of aggression and the possibility to be all things at once.

Like the transsexual who feels himself or herself to have been born in the wrong body, Orlan, too, acknowledges a deep divide between her outward appearance and her inner self: "When I was young, I had a very different image of myself from my reflection. I was very rebellious yet, in the mirror, I resembled a cute, normal, banal girl. I was confused. I didn't understand."[36] She has expressed her belief that the surgeries succeeded in closing the gap between her inner and outer selves. Orlan describes how she transformed not only her external appearance but also her gentle, fragile, and fearful character traits into stronger, more aggressive, even violent, ones.[37]

Orlan's transformation is therefore more extensive than that of the transsexual, for her aim has been to change not only her sex but her identity in its entirety. It demonstrates a new version of castration anxiety. Orlan is not striving to deny her femininity and become male, as the transsexual would; she is rebelling against all recognition of her bodily limits. Unwilling to accept the narcissistic loss, symbolically represented by castration, she strives for a state of limitlessness, narcissistic completion, omnipotence, and primary creativity.[38] "I have always sought to erase the limits," she says, "to transform reality into virtuality and vice-versa."[39]

Thus, whereas most transsexual surgery focuses on genital reconstruction; Orlan's surgeries are performed primarily on her face. Because the face is the key site of identity, it is not surprising that it is such a critical focal point in her art. When the skin is pulled away from her face (*Omnipresence*, Nov. 21, 1993), it appears like a mask and highlights the perspective that we are all veiled creatures and that exteriority is a mere shell, a costume. It is also significant that Orlan's face, like that of Medusa, with its dissections and transformations, is the body part that most frightens us. When he analyzed the terrifying aspect of woman, Freud focused on her "castrated" genitals rather than her face, the locus of her identity.[40] Thus, whether we gaze at Medusa's head, the head of Frankenstein's Bride, or the composite images of Orlan's face with those of pre-Columbian, African, or Native American origin, we come tête-à-tête with the artist's hybrid images in an intimate yet bizarre reciprocal mirroring of her own devising. Who is this woman of transforming heads? And who are we who cannot escape the nagging questions she raises regarding the relationship between what we look like and who we are.

In 1996, Orlan collaborated with magician, Paul Kieve, and video artist, Robin Rambau, to create *Woman with Head . . . Woman without Head*, a performance piece in which tech-

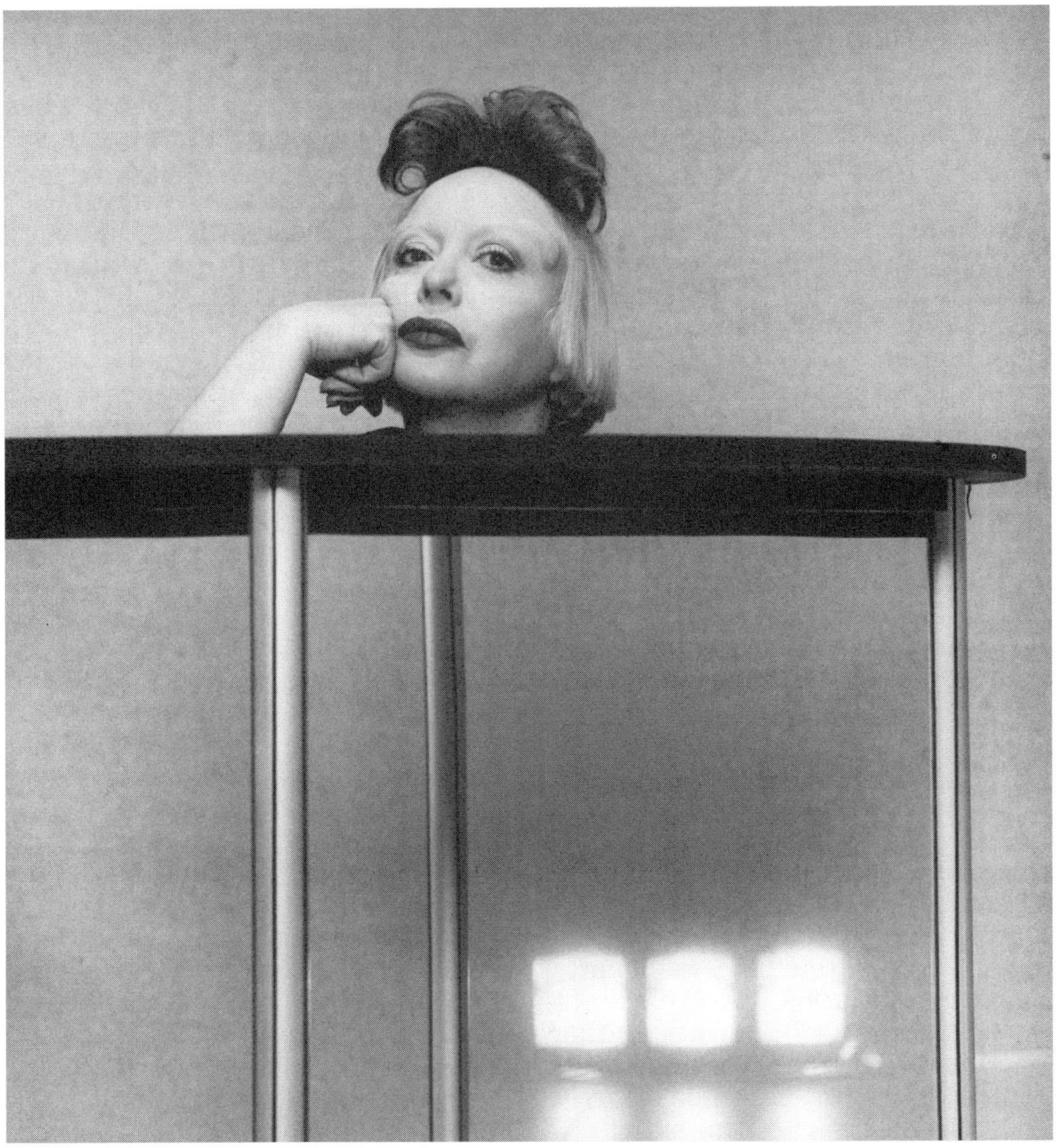

47. Orlan, *Femme Avec Tête, no. 8: [Close-up of hand on cheek]*, 1996. Performance during Totally Wired show, curated by Lois Keidan at ICA, London, with Paul Kieve (magician), Dean Bramnagann (videomaker), and Robin Rambau (musician). 50 × 60 cm. Photo: Peter Sinclair. Courtesy of the artist. © 2009 Artists Rights Society (ARS), New York/ASAGP, Paris.

niques of illusion were employed to project Orlan's disembodied head on a table. Questioned by her audience about who she is—whether she is mad—an original or a copy—she responds by reading from texts, including some by Antonin Artaud, the French artist whose writings on the *Theater of Cruelty* and a body without organs had a profound influence on her. Orlan literally becomes the woman who is only head, thereby subverting the traditional dichotomy characterized in Western philosophy and art associating mind with masculine and matter with feminine. She has us never forget that she is an intelligent and eloquent woman who controls what she is doing to herself and to us. The issue of castration, she appears to be saying, is about who we are and what we know. In the end, *it is all in our heads!*

And from her head emanates her voice, perhaps the single feature that has remained unaltered throughout all of her surgeries. Despite her claims that she has painlessly adapted to her shifting selves, she nonetheless asserts, "My voice is my security, I know that I can accept any failure because my voice will always remain with me . . . "[41] As a woman who once dreamt of becoming an opera singer, it is interesting that Orlan changes her outward appearance but does not relinquish her voice. Yet, she reads from texts and adopts the voices of others, both men and women. Interestingly, she confessed that her mother had tried to inhabit her voice ("she put her tongue inside of me") by making her lie.[42] Preserving her own voice was therefore an important act of survival and defiance for her.[43] By reading and speaking the words of others, one might think that she is repeating her past, yet Orlan puts a new spin on things while retaining complete control. She chooses the words and changes what they mean by placing them within the unique context of her artistic practice, even including within her surgical entourage a person who translates the words into sign language. Orlan explains this inclusion as a reminder that we are all deaf at times.

The Pain of Absence and the Absence of Pain

It is difficult to avoid viewing Orlan's art without reinforcing the stereotype connecting women with pain, masochism, and illness.[44] Orlan has said, "I want to make visual work for which one has a strong bodily reaction."[45] It is easy to confirm that Orlan succeeds in her goal of producing brutally visceral work. During her surgeries, she performs with a Medusan vengeance.

We suffer an assault on our need to conceive of the body as a whole, sanitized, coherent, sealed entity when we watch Orlan's skin pulled away from her face or new orifices being created during her surgeries. We are confronted with what Vivian Patraka calls "binary terror," the panic unleashed when people are faced with the dissolution of illusory binaries, such as mind-body, sacred-profane, interior-exterior, subject-object, male-female, active-passive, and identity-alterity.[46] Orlan's body is open, incomplete, and excessive in its flaunting of materiality and orifices. It is the end result of the unmirrored body that Lacan referred to as *le corps morcelé* (the body-in-pieces).[47]

It is the juxtaposition of images that is most disturbing: Orlan's body in repose and being cut on the operating table, while she remains awake and conscious, reading her texts aloud and smiling with an air of insouciance and histrionic *belle indifférence.* The artist claims that an impression of an autopsied corpse that continues to speak is created when she reads or answers questions while being operated upon.[48] This disconnect between the violence we witness to her body and her self-possession, produces a disjointed and ambivalent response in us. More important, it invokes in us the reaction we imagine she should be experiencing. It is her audience rather than Orlan who responds with terror, repulsion, rage, fear, and anxiety, all inspired not only by the cutting but also by the graphic and concrete alteration of identity. Kauffman suggests that Orlan functions like the psychoanalyst as a screen onto which we project our loves and hatreds.[49] I would add that, like Piper, she employs the mechanism of projective identification, inducing in us what she avoids experiencing.[50] Furthermore, we not only identify with Orlan who is cut and bleeding; we also identify with the doctor performing the violence of the surgery.

Orlan seems to believe that she is not masochistic as long as she does not experience physical pain. Yet, some would regard

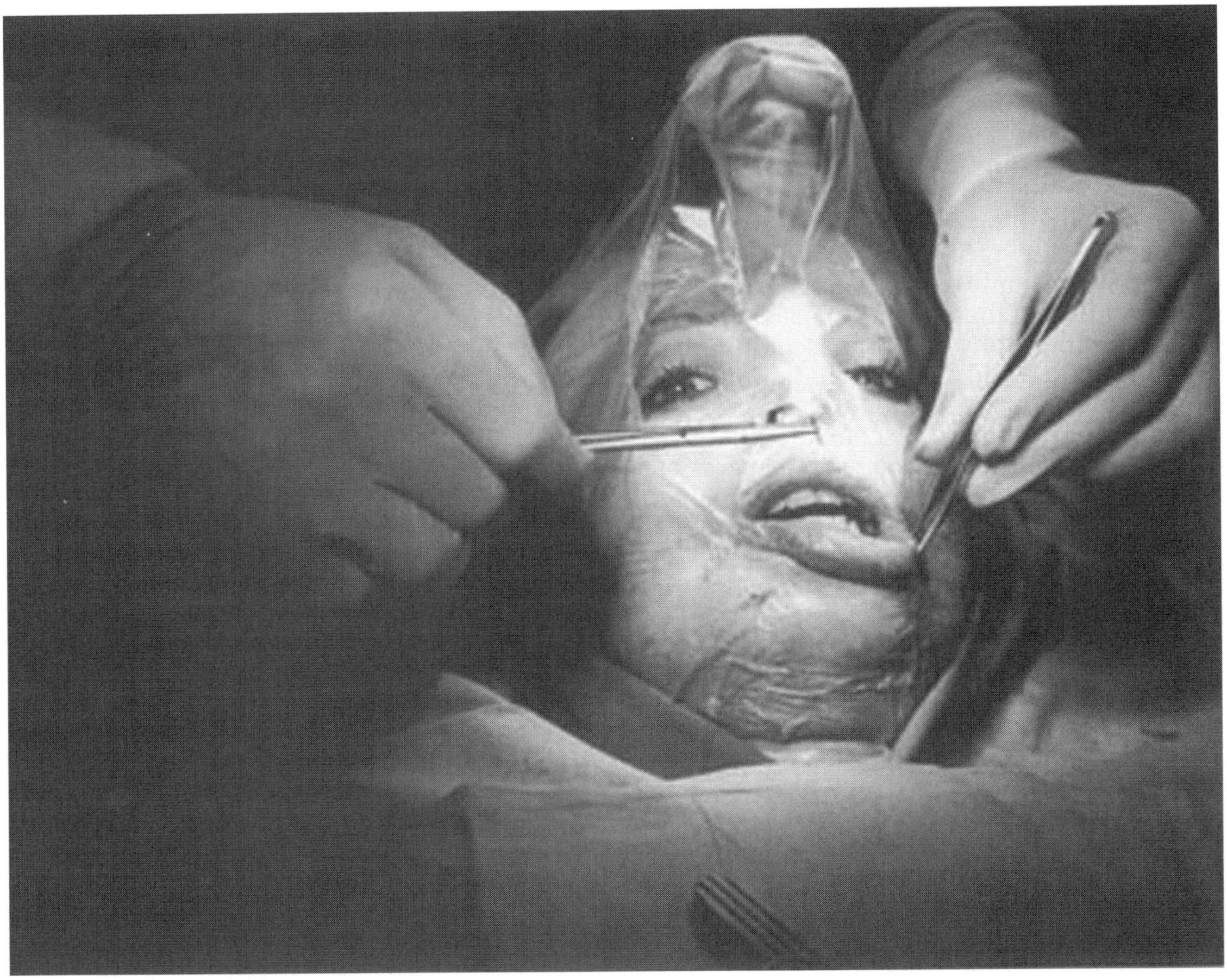

48. Orlan, *The Reincarnation of Saint Orlan, or Pic new[s] Pics,* the "unicorn" operation with transparent sheets and grimacing lips, 1990. 60 × 80 cm. Black-and-white photograph. © 2009 Artists Rights Society (ARS), New York/ ASAGP, Paris. Photo: Courtesy Galerie Michel Rein.

her surgery theatricals as publicly humiliating situations and the suffering she imposes on her audience as sadomasochistic. Even some of her early works convey a masochistic message. Long before her cosmetic artwork, Orlan performed *Mésurages* (Measurements) in which she literally crawled on the ground to use her body as a measuring stick for the lengths of streets named after famous men. How many Orlans would it take to measure Rue Victor Hugo, for example? After she finished measuring, Orlan washed her sweaty clothes in public and bottled the dirty water. Comparing her petite body to those of men considered larger-than-life could be interpreted as Orlan contrasting what men have (long streets, public acclaim, and, yes, penises) with what females have (apertures and sullied bodily fluids).

Whereas she denies that she experiences pain or that her work is masochistic or self-mutilating, Orlan does, nevertheless, emphasize that its focus is pain: "My work is not about standards of beauty alone; it is also on physical pain . . . Carnal Art is not self-mutilation."[51] Notwithstanding her comments, Orlan quite deliberately makes her body the instrument of pain and a site of recognition evoking Christian iconography of martyrdom. If she does this in order to present a critique of it, it nonetheless involves a masochistic stance. Furthermore, Orlan's claim that she experiences no pain is highly untenable. It is impossible to accept that anyone could endure surgery after surgery without extreme physical discomfort and pain. More importantly, Orlan denies that she experiences emotional pain related to the repeated psychological adaptation she necessarily has to make to her newly constructed visage. She adopts Rimbaud's paradoxical formula, "*Je est un autre*" (I is an other), to show how the seemingly contradictory poles of subjectivity and objectivity become subverted in an identity as scrutinized as hers. Hers is indeed an amazing ability to detach herself from her physicality. She has said that "being a narcissist isn't easy when the question is not of loving your own image, but of re-creating the self through deliberate acts of alienation."[52] I once pressed Orlan on the topic of emotional pain to which she finally acknowledged that her emotional pain is to be found in her art: "My symptom is my art."[53] And certainly the practice of her art has worn her. She alleges that she no longer wishes to undergo cosmetic surgery and has ceased this aspect of her art. "My work has always been hard on me. It's difficult to sustain because it is a form of aggression against myself. Other people perceive it as a form of aggression against them and are therefore frequently very aggressive towards me. You have to be strong to withstand the reactions I get."[54]

As in her Medusa project, audience reactions form an integral part of Orlan's work. Her art would not be what it is without them. Yet, our reactions of horror and disgust, even concern and awe, it could be argued, all entail the contained projections of the mirroring response she seeks to the 'monster beauty' she has created.

Is she Mad? Is it Art?

Is Orlan inspired or mad? Is her art a vehicle to illustrate her psychopathology or is she an artist ahead of her time? Is she a hysteric, a narcissist, a fetishist, a scalpel slave and masochist, a sufferer of body dysmorphic disorder? Or is she a radical who is literally on the "cutting edge" of art?

Orlan's art conveys serious messages about the many contradictory meanings assigned to the female body and self by art, religion, and medicine. Instead of debunking psychoanalytic theories of gender, castration anxiety, penis envy, and female development, she flaunts them, and plays with them. Most importantly, she challenges them, adds to them, and makes them her own. Explicitly enacting her fantasies of transcendence, Orlan ensures that her sacred child is attended to, down to its last drop of blood and ounce of fat.

Assessing psychopathology in a creative person such as Orlan is not easy and, in my opinion, is undesirable. She herself has stated, "We often have to do crazy things without necessarily being crazy."[55] Orlan agreed to be assessed by a team of psychiatrists who found her lacking in severe pathology and devoted an issue of their scientific journal to their observations and conclusions.[56] I believe that it is crucial, when examining the art of someone as innovative and controversial as Orlan, to be aware of both the defensive *and* the transformative functions of her art. Orlan's is clearly an individual as well as a social project. Some go so far as to regard her as one of the most important artists of the twentieth century.[57]

Orlan's art is fundamentally about crossing boundaries and breaking down binaries. She molds past and present and creates herself in forms that point toward the future. She prefers to replace the word "or" with "and," which allows her to be all things in all places at one time: "All of my work is based on the notion of 'and': the good and the bad, the beautiful and the ugly, the living and the artificial, the public and the private."[58] Her man-woman, mutant, cyborg, posthuman body—a body that connects the maternal, the monstrous, and the machine—far exceeds the traditional conception of the castrated female. Orlan is what Ince calls the "millennial female."[59] Besides representing our fears around the issues of body, self and change, Orlan is what we find unnerving about the future possibilities offered by technological and medical advancements to transform our bodies (think of the controversial new procedure, the face transplant) as well as the fate of embodiment in an information age. Orlan's body, and the fears and anxieties we project onto it, takes a monstrous form that Jacques Derrida ties to its futuristic leaning: "A future that would not be monstrous would not be a future; it would be already a predictable, calculable and programmable tomorrow. All the experience open to the future is prepared or prepares itself to welcome the monstrous *arrivant*."[60] Orlan *is* the monster of our future; she is the epitome of the project of transhuman transcendence. Her motto "Remember the Future" captures her insistence that we relentlessly move forward, no matter the pain, toward a posthuman stage that at present we can only barely glimpse.

Epilogue
In Her Own Image

It now seems like another lifetime since I first embarked on my doctoral dissertation. At that time, I wished to write about ten artists whose oeuvres were primarily self-representational. My committee members thought I was being overly ambitious and they directed me to choose a single artist. I chose the Austrian Expressionist artist Egon Schiele and focused on his many self-portraits. My professors added jokingly that I could one day write a book on the self-portraits of more than one artist. Well, here is that book.

It took me a long time to finish this book, which I worked on, taking extended breaks in between, over the last fifteen years. In some ways, I am glad that it has taken me this long. I have learned so much about women over these years, having treated many more women in my clinical practice and taught scores of young women in classrooms and supervisory settings. Over the expanse of years I have watched, with each new generation, the changes in their relationships to their bodies and sensibilities, to men, to feminism, and to life. I have also been aware of my own evolution as a woman as I became a mother, moved back and forth between continents and relationships, coped with my parents' aging as well as my own, and faced life-threatening illness. All of these experiences have deepened my understanding of and appreciation for the female experience.

Over the years I have felt progressively closer to each artist appearing between these pages, feeling as if their lives and personalities reflect aspects of my own psyche. Each artist, it now seems, has told me something central about myself, about being a woman and facing the things a woman must face, not only by virtue of her gender but also because she is a human being living in a cultural time and place. So, I see their lives and work as tracing a scintillating trajectory not only through female self-representational art but also through the last century of our history.

Influenced by Expressionist self-portraiture as a genre and the newly forged psychoanalytic views of Freud that had begun to seep into the culture, Käthe Kollwitz broke new ground by calling attention to the feminine interior, shifting the focus from the idealized female body to the female face as it confronted the terrible difficulties of its time: war, poverty and the tragic aspect of human life. She created women who were strong, loving and protective mothers, but transcended domestic life, for they were socially aware and politically active, though often victims of social circumstance. Hers were women who found their power in stoic perseverance amidst the bewilderment and sadness of their time. With her chisel she chopped away the artifice of the shallow to reveal the throbbing, sentience below the skin.

French-born artist, Claude Cahun (1894–1954) challenged and expanded the constrictive boundaries of her gender, adamantly refuting the reductive definitions of woman by distorting and fragmenting her androgynous image on stages both grotesque and surrealistic. Not to be pinned down in gender or role, she played with being both genders as well as something in between. Her photographic self-portraits express classical notions like the uncanny, and reflect the unconscious where nothing is defined with finality and all possibilities, however contradictory or paradoxical, are simultaneously alive. She reminds us of our absurd yet undying passion to be all things at once, to contain and express everything, and to break free from cultural constraints imposed upon us. Cahun introduced the mirror, mask, and masquerade as well as monster beauty—psychological and aesthetic devices adopted in the art that followed. Her work is one of the first to pose the question of whether anything real or permanent exists within the mirror and behind the mask, while eloquently arguing that because it demands the reduction of an identity, perhaps social life can never be more than a masquerade. A woman far ahead of her time, she responded to Freud's question, "What do women want?" with her own: "What do you want from me?" to which she offered a veritable parade of answers while dismissing them at the same time.

Surrealism encouraged artists like Cahun and Mexican-born Frida Kahlo (1907–54) to express complex, multilayered visions of women in their art. Their experimentation with gender identity and self-reinvention prefigured what would later take place in postmodern art. Although Kahlo adamantly rejected the designation of Surrealist, still her classification within the movement remains justified because the dream, the vision, and the mystery and mystique of the unconscious mind permeate her work. Indeed, Kahlo dazzled with a new art that boldly depicted her profound experience with physical injury, infidelity, and miscarriages, thus paving the way for women to represent their unique experiences. She shows us pain, human pain and especially woman's pain around issues of castration—not the loss of a penis but, rather, the gap between what one has and what one wishes to be. Kahlo's harrowing losses and betrayals were followed by her reparative attempts, those in which she doubled herself and contextualized her suffering within a larger vision of life. Her art reflects in nearly equal parts a resplendent beauty and an inherent detachment. Kahlo created a bridge between the material and the spiritual.

Charlotte Salomon (1917–43), a German-born artist killed in Auschwitz at the age of twenty-six, showed us how she transformed trauma into creativity in her coming-of-age opus, *Life or Theater.* Salomon fought against madness and suicide with every resource she could muster in this autobiographical epic. Using bold colors in repetitive scenes marked by narration both profound and humorous, and setting her story in a musical context, she defied the downward pull of her family in a poignant and courageous battle to illuminate her inner life and hold it up as a torch against the oncoming and terrible night of her time. Due to the interweaving of text, music, and image, Salomon's oeuvre is impossible to confine to one genre. Yet, clearly it shows us her courage to keep creating in the face of destruction, to uphold life and find its good even when there is every reason to despair. Her work directly addresses the distinctive way a woman approaches her autobiography.

The feminist movement of the 1960s and 1970s had a profound effect on women's self-portrayals. Feminist "body art" offered women a set of aesthetic and ideological tools to give shape to their concerns about gender issues. Women sought to reclaim sole authority over their bodies and part of this process entailed the rejection of certain psychoanalytic and patently patriarchal assumptions about female development. The Freudian theory of sexual development used boys as models and girls were reduced to "little men" and defined in terms of envy for what they lacked: a penis.[1] American artists Carolee Schneemann (b. 1939) and Hannah Wilke (1940–93) espoused a feminist agenda to redress the previously omitted aspects of women's consciousness and sexuality.

Schneemann left painting to pioneer feminist performance art, leading the way for generations of women artists to literally put their own bodies in their work. She championed the rights of the female body in a sex-phobic and misogynist culture, all the while showing that body in a dialogue with the social body. Schneemann boldly advanced the legitimacy and authenticity of female sensual pleasure as a compelling reality to be acknowledged and responded to. Her work illustrates Freud's purified pleasure ego as well as the French concept of *jouissance.* The origin of Schneemann's artistic preoccupation with the erotic body can be found in her curiosity about her physician father's goings-on, and her mother's pregnancies.

When she created vaginal iconography, Hannah Wilke made the invisible visible and turned the female body inside out. She suggested that woman's experience—diffuse, receptive, and exquisitely sensitive—is infused with a womb-like embodiment and sensibility. Wilke also brought the centrality of relationships to the forefront of her work—her relationship to the men in her life and her relationship to her mother. By exposing their beautiful, naked bodies in their art, Schneemann and Wilke both illustrated and challenged theories of female narcissism and exhibitionism. For many, it wasn't until Wilke fell ill that her work was appreciated as more than an expression of her vanity. It is for this reason I believe that of all the artists in this book, Wilke's art was that most misunderstood and misinterpreted. In the 1960s and '70s, she covered her flawless, naked torso with miniature vulvae made of chewing gum; in the 1990s, she unabashedly displayed her transformation into a woman ravaged by cancer and chemotherapy as she courageously confronted illness and death. Both Kahlo and Wilke face the viewer with the effects of illness on the female body. Although they took pride in their beauty and sexuality, they refused to be perceived solely in those terms.

In the 1980s the Great Goddess movement divided feminists into opposing camps: those who assumed that sexuality and gender are culturally produced in the service of ideology and those, like Cuban-born Ana Mendieta (1948–85), who believed in an innate, immutable essence of femininity. Mendieta combined personal imagery with universal symbols of femininity, fertility, and maternity, often drawn from ancient rituals. She stamped her silhouette into the earth, sketched its outline in the sand, and carved its allegorical form into rock. Separated from her mother and her motherland at a young age, Mendieta created art from the earth to cope with loss, exile, and dislocation. Her works highlight symbiosis with the mother and the mourning process that is an integral part of separation and loss. In addition to her sublime earth art, Mendieta was one of the first artists whose work brought attention to violence against women. How ironic, then, that she is believed to have met her untimely and brutal death as a result of her husband's violent act of throwing her out of the thirty-fourth floor of a building.

Adrian Piper (b. 1948), like Wilke and Schneemann, developed a visual and performance language to address political issues—in her case, racism and xenophobia. She aggressively used her face and body in her work to make visible the body and self of black women in our society. She fostered awareness of racial difference and the marginalization of black men as well as black women. She transformed herself into an inescapable provocative presence to elicit and confront the viewer's conscious as well as subliminal racist and xenophobic attitudes. In the mirror of her art, the white person is invited to see and feel his or her prejudice, fear and hatred. Piper's work illustrates splitting and projective identification, psychological mechanisms from object relations theory enlisted to cope with the aggression and violation of self and other in the quest for identity and a sense of wholeness. Her audience not only becomes intellectually aware of racism and xenophobia; we literally feel what it is like to be taken over and invaded. We react with fear and anger both in our identification with her position and in our having been forcefully put in it. Thus, Piper's art creates a complex intersubjective dynamic that forces us to escape the solipsism of our own separate psychological existence.

In our postmodern times, women have become skeptical of feminism. To my dismay, many of my students consider feminism extremist, reductionistic, and simply passé. Just when women thought they knew who they were, the question of who they are arose again. Thus, multiple and ambiguous representations in the postmodern age are used to confront social stereotypes of gender. Postmodernists deny the existence of an essential "feminine" nature, since femininity is considered a social construct, along with the concept of a stable self or reality.

Postmodern artist Cindy Sherman (b. 1954) critically examines media-enforced images and stereotypes to challenge the notion of a single, fixed female identity. She appropriates images from pop culture, history, gender stereotypes, myths, and fairy tales as she engages in numerous games of make-believe and "dress up." Sherman's art reveals woman as an ambiguous, complex, and fluid being whose identity is impossible to pin down. She shows that aspect of woman capable of continuous shape-shifting and transformation. Her endless disguises illustrate psychoanalytic theories of play as well as the endless play of self-referential acts. Yet, her play is not all fun as her images show, sometimes in graphic detail (though usually tongue in cheek), the carnival of life's dark side—the worm at the core of human existence in repulsive excremental forms and monstrous deformity, and the perversion and madness that frequently and perhaps necessarily inform human behavior.

Contemporary French multimedia artist Orlan (b. 1947), like Sherman, plays with her external appearance to show its fluidity and exchangeability. Unlike Sherman, Orlan has undertaken a complete and literal identity alteration in the name of art by undergoing multiple plastic surgery operations and engaging in a corporeal dialogue with the features of female models from art historical masterpieces. As such, she has transformed herself into an *objet d'art* as well as a site for public debate while injecting a new female sensibility not only into all of Western art but its history as well. Orlan has disrupted everything we thought we knew and believed. Of all the artists covered in these pages, she is the most radical and subversive, not simply because she has literally sacrificed her body and self to her work, but also because that sacrifice and its results profoundly challenge our notions of art, history, beauty, gender and, yes, even sanity. Orlan's surgeries revisit Freud's castration theory, in which the child's discovery of sexual difference leads to exploration of solutions to problems of difference and identity. Yet the artist refuses to offer simple answers to the questions: Who am I? What does it mean to be a boy or a girl? What does it mean to be human? What is right and what is wrong? Her world and work offer us a mind-boggling complexity of motivation, definition, and dialogue while daring to imagine a post-human future that must be both frightening and exciting.

I sometimes like to think of these ten artists as one artist who lived for a hundred years, one artist who wished to express herself and truly be heard and then, by necessity of that desire, took an oppositional but creative stance to the problems confronting her. How could she reach those who not only did not want to hear her, but whose assumptions about reality, gender, social roles, and morality precluded an understanding of what she needed to say? My mythical artist began by showing her reticent audience the suffering throbbing in her interior. She presented images of herself that make it impossible to delight solely in her body as a site for carnal desire and pleasure. She expanded her body beyond its fleshy and semipermeable boundary. She displayed her pain, her wounds, and her desire for real contact. She told the story of her life, her decidedly female life, whether shaped by biology or society or a vectorial sum of both, her childhood, her relationships, her need to be seen and loved, her need to create, her fear of violence, her freedom to transform herself by forging the possibilities that enrich her life. She offered a journey through bright day and dark night, leaving nothing out —the good, the bad, the unthinkable—until at last her viewers are deeply affected by what they witness. In short, she told us the truth about herself and that truth necessarily changed us.

What most unites the very different work of these ten artists is that each one, in her own way and *in her own image,* shifts our gaze away from seeing what we've always seen, to appreciating new and expanded visions of the experiential female body. Each one sought mirroring in her art and ended up mirroring to us some hard truths and hidden pleasures about women's lives and inner worlds and about ourselves. Thus, these women are not alone in becoming empowered in the process of their artmaking. Through their rich and varied oeuvres, they empower us to see differently and to be different.

We leave here with the question of the future of women's art, especially its self-representational aspect. Certainly this issue is wide open to speculation. What will women artists do with the explosive scientific and technological advancements that are taking place in our time in the fields of physics, cosmology, psychology, biology, medicine, and communication? How will they respond to the crisis of meaning in our own culture? How will they dialogue with the new war of the twenty-first century, one without borders and abounding in the ever-insidious threat of global terrorism? My own feeling is that what they will do next is highly unpredictable. Could anyone have predicted Orlan? Certainly this much seems true: many more surprises are in store.

Notes

Introduction

1. Wendy Steiner, *Venus in Exile: The Rejection of Beauty in 20th Century Art* (New York: The Free Press, 2001), 35.
2. John Berger, *Ways of Seeing* (London: British Broadcasting Corporation and Penguin Books, 1972), 47; Laura Mulvey, "Visual Pleasure and Narrative Cinema," *Visual and Other Pleasures (Theories of Representation and Difference)* (Bloomington: Indiana University Press, 1989), 14–26; Luce Irigaray, quoted in Janice Lieberman, *Body Talk: Looking and Being Looked At in Psychotherapy* (Northvale, NJ: Jason Aronson, 2000), 225; Griselda Pollack, "Modernity and the Spaces of Femininity," in *Vision and Difference* (London: Routledge, 1989), 67.
3. Frances Borzello, *Seeing Ourselves: Women's Self-Portraits* (New York: Abrams, 1998), 167.
4. Marsha Meskimmon, *The Art of Reflection: Women Artists' Self-Portraiture in the Twentieth Century* (New York: Columbia University Press, 1996), 11.
5. Adrienne Harris. *Gender as Soft Assembly* (Hillsdale, NJ: Analytic Press, 2005), 19–20.
6. Linda Nochlin, *Women, Art, and Power and Other Essays* (New York: Harper & Row, 1988); Whitney Chadwick, *Women, Art, and Society* (London: Thames & Hudson, 1990); Lucy Lippard, *The Pink Glass: Selected Feminist Essays on Art* (New York: The New Press, 1995); Griselda Pollack, *Vision and Difference.*
7. Laura Cottingham, *Seeing Through the Seventies: Essays on Feminism and Art* (Amsterdam: G&B International, 2000); Maura Reilly and Linda Nochlin, eds., *Global Feminisms: New Directions in Contemporary Art* (London: Merrell, 2007) have begun to redress this imbalance.
8. Jessica Benjamin, *The Bonds of Love: Psychoanalysis, Feminism, and the Problem of Domination* (New York: Pantheon, 1988); Muriel Dimen, *Sexuality, Intimacy, Power* (Hillsdale, NJ: Analytic Press, 2003); Dorothy Dinnerstein, *The Mermaid and the Minotaur* (New York: Harper & Row, 1976); Virginia Goldner, "Toward a Critical Theory of Gender," *Psychoanalytic Dialogues* 1 (1991), 249–72; Adrienne Harris, *Gender as Soft Assembly* (Hillsdale, NJ: Analytic Press, 2005).
9. Muriel Dimen and Virgina Goldner, "Gender and Sexuality," in the *American Psychiatric Association Publishing Textbook of Psychoanalysis,* ed. Arnold Cooper, Glen Gabbard, and Ethel Person. (Washington, DC: American Psychiatric Publishing, 2008), 93–114.
10. It is interesting to note that a parallel process has taken place in the evolution of psychoanalytic thinking. See Mendieta chapter for more on this.
11. Donald Woods Winnicott coined the term "good enough mothering."
12. Linda Nochlin, "Why Have There Been No Great Women Artists?" *Women, Art, and Power and Other Essays* (New York: Harper & Row, 1988) 169.
13. Raquelin Mendieta, Personal interview, Jan. 11, 1996.
14. Hans Breder, Personal interview, Jan. 15, 1996.
15. Hayden Herrera, *Frida: A Biography of Frida Kahlo* (New York: Harper Colophon Books, 1983), 95.
16. Hans Breder, Personal interview, Jan. 15, 1996.
17. Christopher Bollas, *The Shadow of the Object: Psychoanalysis of the Unthought Known* (London: Free Association Books, 1987) wrote of the mother as 'transformational object." The mother, in his view, is less experienced as a separate object than as "a process that is identified with cumulative internal and external transformations" (14).
18. Sigmund Freud, "On Narcissism: An Introduction," *The Standard Edition of the Complete Psychological Works of Sigmund Freud* 14 (1914) 88. Hereafter referred to as *Standard Edition.*
19. Naomi Wolf, *The Beauty Myth: How Images of Beauty Are Used Against Women* (New York: Anchor, 1991).

Chapter 1. Käthe Kollwitz

1. Sigmund Freud, "Screen Memories," *Standard Edition* 3 (1899) 301–22.
2. Peter Selz, *German Expressionist Painting* (Berkeley: University of California Press, 1957), 3.
3. Danielle Knafo, *Egon Schiele/A Self in Creation: A Psychoanalytic Study of the Artist's Self-Portraits* (Rutherford, NJ: Fairleigh Dickinson University Press, 1993), 29.
4. Martha Kearns, *Käthe Kollwitz: Woman and Artist* (New York: Feminist Press, 1976), 137.
5. Russian-born Werefkin was financially wealthy and supported her protegé, Alexej Jawlensky, and even gave up painting for a period of ten years in order to avoid competing with him. Her writings on color, abstraction, and spirituality are certain to have substantially influenced Kandinsky's well-known aesthetic theories. Münter, who was Kandinsky's lover, has often been dismissed as a second-rate artist whose work is merely derivative.
6. Kearns, *Käthe Kollwitz,* 81
7. Alessandra Comini, "Kollwitz in Context: The Formative Years," in *Käthe Kollwitz,* ed. Elizabeth Prelinger (New Haven: Yale University Press, 1992), 100.

8. Käthe Kollwitz, *The Diary and Letters of Käthe Kollwitz* (Evanston, IL: Northwestern University Press, 1988), 72.
9. Comini, "Kollwitz in Context," 96.
10. Kollwitz, *Diary,* 439.
11. Estelle Weldon, *Mother, Madonna Whore: The Idealization and Denigration of Motherhood* (New York: Guilford Press, 1988), 7.
12. Elizabeth Prelinger, "Kollwitz Reconsidered," in *Käthe Kollwitz,* ed. Elizabeth Prelinger (New Haven: Yale University Press, 1992), 40.
13. Kollwitz, *Diary,* 20.
14. Ibid., 17.
15. Ibid., 20.
16. Ibid., 18.
17. Ibid., 21.
18. Ibid., 23.
19. Ibid., 125.
20. Ibid., 71.
21. André Green, "The Dead Mother," in *On Private Madness* (London: Hogarth Press, 1986), 142–73.
22. Kollwitz, *Diary,* 99.
23. Otto Nagel, *Käthe Kollwitz* (Old Greenwich, CT: New York Graphic Society, 1971), 80.
24. Hanna Segal, *Introduction to the Work of Melanie Klein* (New York: Basic Books, 1964), 37.
25. Kollwitz, *Diary,* 59.
26. Hans Kollwitz, "Introduction," in *The Diary and Letters of Käthe Kollwitz,* trans. Richard and Clara Winston (Evanston, IL: Northwestern University Press, 1988), 2.
27. Survivor guilt with regard to the death of significant others creates a fear of one's own death as well as a feeling that life has been purchased at the cost of others.
28. Kearns, *Käthe Kollwitz,* 217.
29. Ibid., 134.
30. Kollwitz, *Diary,* 116–17.
31. Ibid. 72.
32. Italian artist Rosalba Carriera (1675–1757) painted several portraits of herself as an old woman (*Self-Portrait as Winter,* 1731; *Self-Portrait as an Old Woman,* 1746). Sofinisba Anguissola (1532–1625) painted self-portraits at age eighty and ninety.
33. Kollwitz, *Diary,* 96.
34. Ibid., 100.
35. Ibid., 97.
36. See Joanna Frueh, "Visible difference: Women artists and aging," in *New Feminist Criticism: Art, Identity, Action,* ed. Joanna Frueh, Cassandra Langer, and Arlene Raven (New York: Icon, 1991), 264–88, for more on this subject.

Chapter 2. Claude Cahun

1. Pierre Apraxine, and Xavier Demange, *La Divine Comtesse: Photographs of the Countess de Castiglione* (New Haven: Yale University Press and The Metropolitan Museum of Art, 2000). The Countess de Castiglione (1837–1899), mentioned in the introduction, is known for the more than four hundred photographs taken of herself in collaboration with Pierre-Louis Pierson. Unlike Cahun, she costumed herself rather than disguised herself.
2. Whitney Chadwick, *Women Artists and the Surrealist Movement* (New York: Thames and Hudson, 1985), and Mary Ann Caws, Rudolf Kuenzli, and Gwen Raaberg, *Surrealism and Women* (Cambridge: MIT Press, 1995) do not mention Cahun. Whitney Chadwick, *Mirror Images: Women, Surrealism and Self-Representation* (Cambridge: MIT Press, 1998), 19, corrects this oversight.
3. Judith Butler, *Gender Trouble: Feminism and the Subversion of Identity* (New York: Routledge, 1990), 46–51.
4. Claude Cahun, *Aveux non Avenues* (Paris: Editions du Carrefour, 1930), 66. All translations are mine unless otherwise noted.
5. Shelley Rice, *Inverted Odysseys* (Cambridge: MIT Press, 1999), 77.
6. Chris Townsend, *Francesca Woodman* (London: Phaidon, 2006), 88. Woodman's brief life (1958–81) ended in suicide.
7. François Le Perlier's *Claude Cahun: L'Ecart et la Metamorphose* (Paris: Jean Michel Place, 1992), and "Claude Cahun: La gravités des apparances," in *Rêve D'une Ville: Nantes et le Surrealisme* (Nantes: Musée des Beaux Arts, 1994), provide the biographical data on Cahun's life unless otherwise noted.
8. LePerlier, *Rêve D'une Ville,* 289.
9. Ibid., 19.
10. Cahun's beheaded man could be her response to the male Surrealists' plethora of images of faceless females.
11. The Dreyfus affair divided France in the 1890s and early 1900s as it involved the wrongful conviction of a Jewish French artillery officer.
12. LePerlier, *Rêve D'une Ville,* 263.
13. Georges Bataille, "The Language of Flowers," in *Visions of Excess,* ed. Allan Stoekl (Minneapolis: University of Minnesota Press, 1985), 10–14.
14. Julie Cole, "Claude Cahun, Marcel Moore, and the Collaborative Construction of a Lesbian Subjectivity," in *Reclaiming Female Agency: Feminist Art History After Postmodernism,* ed. Norma Broude and Mary Garrard (Berkeley: University of California Press, 2005), 349.
15. Another photograph exists in which Cahun photographed Moore in front of the same mirror. The pictures are dramatically different in that Moore's is less staged, she smiles shyly, and one hand touches the wall. Cahun's, on the other hand, is a work of art with many possible meanings. I refer to these two photographs later in the chapter.
16. Havelock Ellis, *Psychology of Sex* (London: Pan Books, 1933), 195.
17. Marjorie Garber, *Vested Interests: Cross-dressing and Cultural Anxiety* (New York: Routledge, 1992), 133.
18. Donald Woods Winnicott, "The Place Where We Live," in *Playing and Reality* (London: Tavistock, 1971), 107.
19. Thomas Ogden, "The Analytic Third: Working with Intersubjective Clinical Facts," in *Subjects of Analysis* (Northvale, NJ: Aronson, 1994), 64.
20. Cahun, *Aveux non Avenues,* 137.
21. Julia Kristeva, *Powers of Horror: An Essay on Abjection,* trans. L. Roudiez (New York: Columbia University Press, 1982), 47.
22. Francois LePerlier, *Claude Cahun: L'Ecart et la Metamorphose* (Paris: Jean Michel Place, 1992), 129.

23. Cahun, *Aveux non Avenues,* 148.
24. Louis Aragon and André Breton, "Le Cinquantenaire de l'Hystérie," *La Révolution Surréaliste* 11 (1928): 20–22.
25. Sigmund Freud, "The Uncanny," *Standard Edition* 17 (1955), 241.
26. Ibid., 234.
27. LePerlier, *Rêve D'une Ville,* 128.
28. Heinz Kohut, *The Analysis of the Self* (New York: International Universities Press, 1971), 3–6.
29. Ibid., 115.
30. Otto Rank, *The Double: A Psychoanalytic Study,* trans. and ed. Harry Tucker Jr. (New York: New American Library, 1971), 83.
31. Cole, "Lesbian Subjectivity," 351.
32. Heinz Lichtenstein, "Narcissism and Primary Identity," in *The Dilemma of Human Identity* (New York: Aronson, 1977), 207–22.
33. Jacques Lacan, "The Mirror Stage as Formative of the Function of the I as Revealed in Psychoanalytic Experience," in *Ecrits,* trans. Alan Sheridan (New York: Norton, 1977), 93–100.
34. Donald Woods Winnicott, "Mirror Role of Mother and Family in Child Development," in *Playing and Reality* (London: Tavistock, 1971), 118.
35. René Spitz, *The First Year of Life* (New York: International Universities Press, 1965).
36. Margaret Mahler, "On Human Symbiosis and the Vicissitudes of Individuation," *Journal of the American Psychoanalytic Association* 15 (1967): 740–64.
37. Danielle Knafo, *Egon Schiele: A Self in Creation: A Psychoanalytic Study of the Artist's Self-Portraits* (Rutherford, NJ: Fairleigh Dickinson University Press, 1993), 30.
38. Honor LaSalle and Abigail Solomon-Godeau, "Surrealist Confession: Claude Cahun's Photmontages," *Afterimage* 19.8 (1992): 12.
39. Walter Benjamin (1936), "The Work of Art in the Age of Mechanical Reproduction," in *Art in Theory 1900–2000. An Anthology of Changing Ideas,* ed. Charles Harrison and Paul Wood (Oxford: Blackwell, 2003), 520–27.
40. Tirza True Latimer, "Acting Out: Claude Cahun and Marcel Moore," in *Don't Kiss Me: The Art of Claude Cahun and Marcel Moore,* ed. Louise Downie (New York: Aperture and Jersey Heritage Trust, 2006), 58.
41. Therese Lichtenstein, "A Mutable Mirror: Claude Cahun," *Artforum* 30.8 (1992), 67.
42. Cahun, *Aveux non Avenues,* 231.
43. Penelope Rosemont, ed., *Surrealist Women: An International Anthology* (Austin: University of Texas Press, 1998), 52.
44. Joan Rivière, "Womanliness as Masquerade," *International Journal of Psychoanalysis* 10 (1929): 303–13.
45. Ibid., 306.
46. Claude Cahun, "Heroines," trans. Norman MacAfee, in *Inverted Odysseys: Claude Cahun, Maya Deren, Cindy Sherman,* ed. Shelley Rice (Cambridge: MIT Press, 1999), 43–94. Cahun was very interested in female heroines from Western history and even produced a work entitled "Héroïnes" in which she wrote a fictional series of monologues spoken by the women, who included Delilah, Cindarella, Sappho, the Virgin Mary, etc.
47. Cahun, *Aveux non Avenues,* 236.
48. Therese Lichtenstein, *Behind Closed Doors: The Art of Hans Bellmer* (Berkeley: University of California Press, 2001), 138.
49. Cahun, *Aveux non Avenues,* 62.
50. Claire Follaine, "Lucy Schwob and Suzanne Malherbe—Résistantes," in *Don't Kiss Me: The Art of Claude Cahun and Marcel Moore,* ed. Louise Downie (New York: Aperture and Jersey Heritage Trust, 2006), 84.
51. Their efforts were signed "The soldier with no name." Although the signature's intent was to camouflage, it is nonetheless revealing that Cahun, who, along with Moore, finally reverted to her given name after moving to Jersey, now signed the propaganda as someone who has "no name."
52. Therese Lichtenstein (1992) quotes from Baron von Aufsess's *Occupation Diary:* "There are very few Jews in the islands. The two Jewish women who have just been arrested belong to an unpleasant category. . . . A search of their house, full of ugly, cubist painting, brought to light a quantity of pornographic material of an especially revolting nature. One woman had had her head shaved and been thus photographed in the nude from every angle. Thereafter she had worn men's clothes. Further nude photographs showed both women practicing sexual perversion, exhibitionism and flagellation" (65).
53. Ibid., 93.
54. Ibid., 94.
55. Irene Fast, *Gender Identity: A Differentiation Model* (Hillsdale, NJ: Analytic Press, 1984). More will be said about Fast's theory in the chapter on Orlan.
56. Katy Kline, "In or Out of the Picture: Claude Cahun and Cindy Sherman," in *Mirror Images: Women, Surrealism, and Self-Representation,* ed. Whitney Chadwick (Cambridge: MIT, 1998), 74.

Chapter 3. Charlotte Salomon

1. Mary Lowenthal Felstiner, *To Paint Her Life: Charlotte Salomon in the Nazi Era* (New York: HarperCollins, 1994). All biographical information on Salomon's life is taken from Felstiner's biography of the artist unless otherwise noted.
2. Judith Herzberg, *Charlotte: Life or Theater: An Autobiographical Play by Charlotte Salomon,* trans. Leila Venewitz (New York: Viking, 1981). The numbers in parentheses refer to images or texts from this version of *Life or Theater.*
3. Christine Conley, "Memory and Trauerspiel: Charlotte Salomon's *Life? or Theater?* and the Angel of History," in *Reading Charlotte Salomon,* ed. Michael P. Steinberg and Monica Bohm-Duchen (Ithaca: Cornell University Press, 2006), 89.
4. Nanette Salomon, "On the Impossibility of Charlotte Salomon in the Classroom," in Steinberg and Bohm-Duchen, *Reading Charlotte Salomon,* 220.
5. Herzberg, *Charlotte: Life or Theater,* vii.
6. Donald Woods Winnicott wrote of the holding environment as a psychical and physical space within which the infant is protected, made to feel safe, allowed to develop a self and grow.
7. Sigmund Freud, "The Interpretation of Dreams," *Standard Edition* 3 (1900): 5.

8. Felstiner, *To Paint Her Life,* 21. Paula Lindberg worked with Käthe Kollwitz in Berlin to create a speaking chorus of a thousand workers.

9. The primal scene is commonly referred to as the oedipal tableau. It involves the child's witnessing or fantasizing about sexual acts between the parents and the relationship between the young child and the adult couple. In negotiating primal scene issues, the child comes to terms with the difference between the sexes and the difference between the generations. For more on this, see: Danielle Knafo and Kenneth Feiner, *Unconscious Fantasies and the Relational World* (Hillsdale, NJ: Analytic Press, 2005), 33–55.

10. Felstiner, *To Paint Her Life,* 14.

11. Darcy Buerkle, "Historical Effacements: Facing Charlotte Salomon," in Steinberg and Bohm-Duchen, *Reading Charlotte Salomon,* 73–87.

12. Evan Imber-Black, *The Secret Life of Families* (New York: Bantam, 1998), 9.

13. Felstiner, *To Paint Her Life,* 21, 26, 64, 102.

14. In 1940, while she was facing the decision of whether to commit suicide herself or to create something wildly eccentric, Walter Benjamin, the Jewish philosopher from Berlin, took his life on the French-Spanish border while trying to flee from the Nazis.

15. See http://www.personalmd.com/news/a1996061806.shtml for more on "Suicide Linked to Sexual Abuse."

16. Felstiner, *To Paint Her Life,* 125.

17. Herzberg, *Charlotte: Life or Theater,* xi.

18. Later in London, where he developed a cult-like following, Wolfsohn chose to be called by his initials, AW, recalling the unspoken Jewish God's name.

19. Felstiner, *To Paint Her Life,* 55.

20. Ibid., 53.

21. The positive oedipal complex refers to the child who is enamored by the parent of the opposite sex and in competition with the parent of the same sex; the negative oedipal complex refers to the child who is enamored by the parent of the same sex and competitive with the parent of the opposite sex. Freud believed that the complete oedipal complex involved both its positive and negative aspects.

22. Kristine Stiles, "Survival Ethos and Destruction in Art," *Discourse: Journal for Theoretical Studies in Media and Culture* 14 (1992): 71–102.

23. Gilbert Rose, *Necessary Illusions: Art as "Witness"* (New York: International Universities Press, 1995), 1–11.

24. Stiles, "Survival Ethos and Destruction in Art," 77.

25. Robert Jay Lifton, *The Future of Immortality and Other Essays for a Nuclear Age* (New York: Basic Books, 1987), 256.

26. Phyllis Greenacre [1957], "The Childhood of the Artist," in *Emotional Growth 2* (New York: International Universities Press, 1971), 479–504. Greenacre wrote about the heightened sensitivity in children who become artists.

27. Hanna Segal, "Art and the Depressive Position," in *Dream, Phantasy and Art* (London: Tavistock and Routledge, 1991), 92.

28. Nagler was twelve years Salomon's senior and also experienced childhood trauma. He burned the side of his face and remained sensitive to his obvious physical flaw, even wearing a toupee to conceal it. Interestingly, Nagler was Ottilie Moore's lover before she left for America. Once again, Salomon found herself in a love triangle with an older man who was involved with a mother figure.

29. Felstiner, *To Paint Her Life,* 141.

Chapter 4. Frida Kahlo

1. Frida Kahlo, *Frida by Frida: Selection of Letters and Texts,* trans. Gregory Dechant (Mexico: Editorial RM, 2003), 47.

2. Laura Mulvey and Peter Wollen, *Frida Kahlo and Tina Modotti* (London: Whitechapel Art Gallery, 1982), 7–27. Alice Adams, "Frida Kahlo's Passion," *Art and Antiques* (1989): 58–98. Anne Horton, "Fridamania," *Art and Antiques* 14, no. 4 (1991): 126–78.

3. Hayden Herrera, *Frida Kahlo: The Paintings* (New York: Harper Collins, 1991), 18.

4. Ibid., 18.

5. Ibid.

6. Ibid., 12–13.

7. Ibid.

8. René Spitz, *The First Year of Life* (New York: International Universities Press, 1965); Jacques Lacan, (1949), "The Mirror Stage as Formative of the Function of the I as Revealed in Psychoanalytic Experience. In *Ecrits,* trans. Alan Sheridan (New York: Norton, 1977), 93–100.

9. Erika Billeter, "Frida and Maria," in *Images of Mexico* (Dallas: Dallas Museum of Art, 1987), 134.

10. Herrera, *Paintings,* 14.

11. Kahlo, *Letters.*

12. Sigmund Freud, "Recommendations to Physicians Practicing Psycho-analysis," *Standard Edition* 12 (1912): 109–20.

13. Donald Woods Winnicott, "Mirror Role of Mother and Family," in *Playing and Reality* (London: Tavistock, 1971), 117.

14. Heinz Kohut, *The Restoration of the Self* (New York: International Universities Press, 1977), 30.

15. Danielle Knafo, "Egon Schiele's Self-Portraits: A Psychoanalytic Study in the Creation of a Self," *The Annual of Psychoanalysis* 19 (1991): 59–90. Danielle Knafo, "Egon Schiele and Frida Kahlo: The Self-Portrait as Mirror," *Journal of the American Academy of Psychoanalysis* 19, no. 4 (1991): 629–46. Danielle Knafo, *Egon Schiele: A Self in Creation* (Rutherford, NJ: Fairleigh Dickinson University Press, 1993), 30.

16. Herrera, *Paintings,* 135.

17. Frida Kahlo, *The Diary of Frida Kahlo: An Intimate Self-Portrait* (New York: Harry Abrams, 1995; Mexico: La Vaca Independiente S.A. de C.V., 1995), 228.

18. Donald Cordry, *Mexican Masks* (Austin: University of Texas Press, 1980), 4.

19. Hayden Herrera, *Frida: A Biography of Frida Kahlo* (New York: Harper and Row, 1983), 75–76.

20. Anna Freud, "The Role of Bodily Illness in the Mental Life of Children," in *Physical Illness and Handicap in Childhood,* ed. Kurt Eissler, Anna Freud, Marianna Kris, and Albert Solnit (New Haven: Yale University Press, 1977), 1–12.

21. Herrera, *Biography,* 156.

22. Ibid., 138.

23. Kahlo, *Diary*, 246–47.
24. Herrera, *Biography*, 8.
25. Sarah M. Lowe, "Essay" in *The Diary of Frida Kahlo*, 26.
26. Kahlo, *Diary*, 278.
27. Ibid., 234.
28. Herrera, *Biography*, 148.
29. Ibid., 410.
30. Ibid., 347.
31. Ibid., 109.
32. William Niederland, "Narcissistic Ego Impairment in Patients with Early Physical Malformations," *The Psychoanalytic Study of the Child* 20 (New Haven: Yale University Press, 1965), 518–34.
33. Anna Freud, *Normality and Pathology in Childhood*, (New York: IUP, 1965) describes how children make use of "dressing up" games as a means of creating an illusion of assuming the identity of someone they admire. George Zavitzianos, "Homeovestism: Perverse Form of Behavior Involving the Wearing of Clothes of the Same Sex," *International Journal of Psycho-Analysis* 53 (1972): 471–77, and "The Object in Fetishism, Homeovestism and Transvestism," *International Journal of Psycho-Analysis* 58 (1977): 487–95; Joan Riviere, "Womanliness as a Masquerade," *International Journal of Psycho-Analysis* 10 (1929): 303–13; and Louise Kaplan, *Female Perversion* (New York: Doubleday, 1991), 237–83 have differentiated among transvestism, fetishism, and homeovestism and have written about women who use femininity as a masquerade and who dress in the clothes of their own sex for defensive purposes.
34. Kahlo, *Diary*, 205.
35. Herrera, *Biography*, 401.
36. Kahlo, *Diary*, 225.
37. Herrera, *Paintings*, 3.
38. Herrera, *Biography*, 266.
39. Kahlo, *Diary*, 235.
40. Ibid., 274.
41. Claudia Schafer, *Textured Lives: Women, Art, and Representation in Modern Mexico* (Tucson: University of Arizona Press, 1992), 5–28.
42. Diego Rivera, *My Art, My Life: An Autobiography* (New York: Dover Publications, 1991), 285–86. Rivera belatedly realized the significance of his loss. In his autobiography, he wrote: "July 13, 1954, was the most tragic day of my life. I had lost my beloved Frida, forever. . . . Too late now, I realized that the most wonderful part of my life had been my love for Frida." When the time came, Rivera asked that he be cremated and his ashes be mixed together with those of Frida. The wish was not honored.

Chapter 5. Carolee Schneemann

1. I used several sources to research Schneemann's work to prepare for my interview with her: Carolee Schneemann, *More than Just Meat Joy, Performance Works and Selected Writings*, ed. Bruce R. McPherson (Kingston, NY: McPherson, 1979); Carolee Schneemann, *Up to and Including her Limits*, ed. Dan Cameron (New York: The New Museum of Contemporary Art, 1996); and Carolee Schneemann, *Imaging her Erotics* (Cambridge: MIT Press, 2002).

Chapter 6. Hannah Wilke

1. Joanna Frueh, "The Body Through Women's Eyes," in *The Power of Feminist Art*, ed. Norma Broude and Mary Garrard (New York: Abrams, 1994), 192.
2. Marvin Jones, "Hannah Wilke's Art, Politics, Religion, and Feminism," *The New Common Good* 1 (1985): 9–11.
3. Ibid., 201.
4. Louise Bourgeois's well-known *Torso/Self-Portrait* (1963–64) similarly alludes to both female and male genitalia.
5. Hannah Wilke, "Intercourse with . . ." in *Hannah Wilke: A Retrospective*, ed. Thomas H. Kocheiser (Columbia: University of Missouri Press, 1976). Text used in videotape performance and lecture at the London Tate Gallery, London, Ontario, Canada, February 17, 1977; text originally written for Guggenheim Memorial Foundation Grant, p. 139.
6. Amelia Jones, "The Rhetoric of the Pose: Hannah Wilke and the Radical-Narcissism of Feminist Body Art," in *Body Art: Performing the Subject* (Minneapolis: University of Minnesota Press, 1998), 177.
7. In a letter to boyfriend, Donald Goddard's ex-wife, Wilke expounds on the importance of childhood sexuality: "What is natural behavior in the development of a child's personality is often embarrassing behavior to an adult . . . culture does not teach instinctive behavior. It exists, and yet can easily be damaged during the formative years of a child's life. What is natural to a three year old is a healthy interest in his or her own body parts. To make one aware that they should not be talked about or exposed at this age is unhealthy and often damaging to the child's later healthy sexual behavior." Courtesy Donald Goddard.
8. Lucy Lippard, "The Pains and Pleasures of Rebirth: European and American Women's Body Art," in *From the Center: Feminist Essays on Women's Art* (New York: Dutton, 1976), 135.
9. A. Jones, "The Rhetoric of the Pose," 153.
10. "I must admit I may never have had the courage to insist upon my life as an artist without having lived with Oldenburg for eight years." From Wilke's answers to a questionnaire to contemporary artists who create wall sculpture. Courtesy Donald Goddard.
11. Saundra Goldman, "Too Good Lookin' to be Smart: Beauty, Performance and the Art of Hannah Wilke" (PhD diss., University of Texas, Austin, 1999). 196. Wilke wrote a letter to the *Village Voice* in which she expressed her thoughts on this idea: "Art does not exist without its creator although it is often an unacknowledged collaboration of ideas and the efforts of more than the individual artist that transform a conceptual idea into a work of art. Just as art critics could not exist had they nothing to bitch about, many male artists might not have endured without the support of women." It is interesting to note that, after his experience with Wilke, Oldenberg did give credit to his wife, Coosje van Bruggen, for her collaboration in his work.
12. Ibid., 201–2.
13. Ibid., 207–8.
14. Ibid., 212.
15. M. Jones, "Hannah Wilke's Art," 11.
16. Judy Siegel, "Between the Censor and the Muse?

Hannah Wilke: Censoring the Muse?" *Women Artists News* 4 (1986): 47.

17. A. Jones, "The Rhetoric of the Pose," 184.

18. Joanna Frueh, "Hannah Wilke," in *Erotic Faculties* (Berkeley: University of California Press, 1996), 144.

19. Joanna Frueh, "Hannah Wilke," in *Hannah Wilke: A Retrospective,* ed. Thomas H. Kochheiser (Columbia: University of Missouri Press, 1989), 35.

20. Frueh, *Erotic Faculties,* 144.

21. Hannah Wilke, "Memoirs of a Sugargiver," in *Hannah Wilke: A Retrospective,* 148.

22. Frueh, "Hannah Wilke," in *Hannah Wilke: A Retrospective,* 79.

23. Margaret Mahler, Fred Pine, and Anni Bergman, *The Psychological Birth of the Human Infant: Symbiosis and Individuation* (New York: Basic Books, 1975).

24. It is significant that as an adult Wilke began to use her middle name, Hannah, rather than Arlene, the name she grew up with. She retained the name Wilke from the last name of her first husband, rather than Butter, her father's last name.

25. Amelia Jones (1998) quotes Goddard as saying that Wilke originally included some quotations from women too (Lucy Lippard, Eleanor Antin) but later removed them, p. 300, note 23.

26. Frueh, *Hannah Wilke: A Retrospective,* 30.

27. Hannah Wilke, "Artist Hannah Wilke Talks with Ernst," *Oasis d'Neon* 1, no. 3 (1978): no page numbers.

28. Frueh, *Hannah Wilke: A Retrospective,* 51.

29. Norman Kleeblatt, *Too Jewish? Challenging Traditional Identities* (New York: The Jewish Museum and Rutgers University Press, 1995), 8.

30. Hannah Wilke, "Intercourse with . . ." in *Ubrigens Sterben Immer die Anderen,* ed. Alfred M. Fischer and Dieter Daniels (Cologne: Museum Ludwig, 1977), 266.

31. Judy Siegel, "Between the Censor and the Muse?" 47.

32. "Wilke Talks with Ernst," n.p.

33. Joanna Frueh, *Erotic Faculties,* 143.

34. A. Jones, "The Rhetoric of the Pose," 300, n. 15.

35. Laura Cottingham, "Hannah Wilke: Some Naked Truths and Her Legacy in the 1990s," in *Hannah Wilke: A Retrospective,* ed. Elizabeth Delin Hansen, Kirsten Dybbol, and Donald Goddard (Nikolaj: Copenhagen Contemporary Art Center, 1998), 59.

36. Susan Paul, "The Just Desserts: 'Dinner Party,' Now Closed Draws Praise and Attack," *The Phoenix* 12 (1981): 19.

37. M. Jones, "Hannah Wilke's Art," 1.

38. Donald Goddard, personal interviews, 1996.

39. Goldman, "Too Good Lookin' to be Smart," 36.

40. Lippard, "The Pains and Pleasures of Rebirth," 103.

41. M. Jones, "Hannah Wilke's Art," 9.

42. Hannah Wilke, "Seura Haya," *New Observations* 58 (1988): 13.

43. I believe that, despite her portrayals of the female body in illness, Wilke would not agree with the trend among some recent feminist writers who see the mother's body as Julia Kristeva's exemplary abject body.

44. Goldman, "Too Good Lookin' to be Smart," 219.

45. A. Jones, "The Rhetoric of the Pose," 169.

46. Janet Wichenhaver, "Hannah Wilke Soho Artist Does 'About Face,' " *The West Side Spirit* 1 (1989): 5.

47. Goldman, "Too Good Lookin' to be Smart," 242.

48. Ibid., 240.

49. Ibid., 246–47.

50. Frueh, *Erotic Faculties* 154.

51. Goldman, "Too Good Lookin' to be Smart," 234. Wilke apparently expected to recover from her cancer and therefore initially wished the exhibition to be titled "Cure."

52. In the 1980s, several other women artists—Jo Spence, Matuschka, and Nancy Fried—documented their battles with breast cancer in their art.

53. Goldman, "Too Good Lookin' to be Smart," 234, n. 483. It is perhaps important to note that this was not Wilke's choice.

54. Carol Diehl, "Hannah Wilke," *Art News* 93/4 (1994): 164.

55. Goldman, "Too Good Lookin' to be Smart," 243. Wilke even considered showing her early work together with her new work to help viewers make this connection but perhaps decided against it due to the obvious reading it would invite as "before" and "after" pictures.

56. Donald Goddard, Personal interviews, New York, 1999.

57. Ibid.

58. Wilke's dying words were "Help me" (Donald Goddard, personal interview, Aug. 21, 1996).

Chapter 7. Ana Mendieta

1. Raquel Mendieta, personal interview, Jan. 13, 1996.

2. Heidi Rauch and Federico Suro, "Ana Mendieta's Primal Scream," *Americas* 45, no. 4 (1992): 45.

3. Robert Katz, *Naked by the Window: The Fatal Marriage of Carl Andre and Ana Mendieta* (New York: Atlantic Monthly Press, 1990), 39.

4. Julia Ann Herzberg, "Ana Mendieta, The Iowa Years: A Critical Study, 1969 Through 1977" (PhD diss., CUNY Graduate Center, 1998), 16–17.

5. Diana Montane, "The Rise and Fall of TropicAna," *Miami Herald Tropic* , Sept. 15 1991, 11.

6. Nancy Spero, "Tracing Ana Mendieta," *Artforum* 30 (1992): 75. Mendieta wrote: "My orphanhood I live." See poem at beginning of this chapter.

7. Ana Mendieta: "Fuego de Tierra," VHS, directed by Kate Horsfield, Branda Miller, and Nereyda Garcia-Ferraz, 1988.

8. In 1979, she attended a party in which those invited were asked to come dressed as their favorite artist. Mendieta dressed as Frida Kahlo.

9. Bonnie Clearwater, *A Book of Works,* ed. Ana Mendieta (Miami Beach: Grassfield Press, 1993), 11.

10. Katz, *Naked by the Window,* 143.

11. Clearwater, *Works,* 41.

12. Nancy Spero, "Tracing Ana Mendieta," *Artforum* 30 (1992): 77.

13. Gloria Feman Orenstein, "Recovering Her Story: Feminist Artists Reclaim the Great Goddess," in *The Power of Feminist Art: The American Movement of the 1970's, History and Impact,* ed. Norma Broude and Mary Garrard (New York: Abrams, 1994), 174–89.

14. Sigmund Freud, "The Aetiology of Hysteria," *The Standard Edition* 3 (1896): 192.

15. Linda Montano, "An Interview with Ana Mendieta," *Sulfur* 22 (1988): 67.
16. Sigmund Freud, "Beyond the Pleasure Principle" *The Standard Edition* 18 (1920) 7–64.
17. Petra Barreras del Rio and John Perrault, *Ana Mendieta: A Retrospective* (New York: The New Museum of Contemporary Art, 1988), 10.
18. Sigmund Freud, "Civilization and Its Discontents," *The Standard Edition* 21 (1930): 68.
19. Jane Bloker, *Where is Ana Mendieta? Identity, Performance, Exile* (Durham: Duke University Press, 1999), 18.
20. Beatrice Beebe and Daniel Stern, "Engagement-Disengagement and Early Object Experiences," in *Communicative Structures and Psychic Structures,* ed. Milton Freedman and Stanley Grand (New York: Plenum, 1977), 35–55.
21. Sigmund Freud, "Mourning and Melancholia," *The Standard Edition of the Complete Psychological Works of Sigmund Freud* 14 (1917): 237–58.
22. Raquel Mendieta Harrison, personal interview, Jan. 11, 1996.
23. Hans Breder, personal interview, Jan. 15, 1996.
24. Ibid.
25. Olga M. Viso, "The Memory of History," in *Ana Mendieta, Earth Body: Sculpture and Performance, 1972–1985* (Hirshhorn Museum and Sculpture Garden, Smithsonian Institute: Hatje Cantz Publishers, 2004), 61.
26. Ana Mendieta, "Personal Writings," in *Ana Mendieta,* ed. Gloria Moure (Barcelona: Ediciones Polígrafa, 1996), 216.
27. Coco Fusco, "Traces of Ana Mendieta," *Poliester* 4 (1992): 61.
28. Hans Breder, personal interview, Jan. 15, 1996.
29. Charles Mereweather, "From Inscription to Dissolution: An Essay on Expenditure in the Work of Ana Mendieta," in *Ana Mendieta,* ed. Gloria Moure (Barcelona: Ediciones Polígrafa, 1996), 90.
30. Guy Brett, "One Energy," in *Ana Mendieta, Earth Body: Sculpture and Performance, 1972–1985,* ed. Olga M. Viso (Hirshhorn Museum and Sculpture Garden, Smithsonian Institute: Hatje Cantz Publishers, 2004), 186.
31. Julia Ann Herzberg, "Ana Mendieta's Iowa Years, 1970–1980," in *Ana Mendieta, Earth Body: Sculpture and Performance, 1972–1985,* ed. Olga M. Viso (Hirshhorn Museum and Sculpture Garden, Smithsonian Institute: Hatje Cantz Publishers, 2004), 170.
32. Spero, "Tracing Ana Mendieta," 77.
33. Mary Jane Jacob, *Ana Mendieta: The "Silueta" Series, 1973–1980* (New York: Galerie Lelong, 1991), 4.
34. Clearwater, *Works,* 41.
35. Ibid.
36. Otto Rank, *Art and Artist* (New York: Agathon, 1932); Otto Rank, *The Trauma of Birth* (New York: Dover, 1924/93).
37. Mendieta, "Writings," 167.
38. Orenstein, "Feminist Artists Reclaim the Great Goddess," 181.
39. Viso, "The Memory of History," 99.
40. Clearwater, *Works,* 17.
41. Bloker, "Where is Ana Mendieta?" 62. In a catalog essay, Mendieta expressed her disappointment and anger at feminism's racist bias: "During the mid to late sixties as women in the United States politicized themselves and came together in the Feminist Movement with the purpose to end the domination and exploitation by the white male culture, they failed to remember us. American Feminism as it stands is basically a white middle class movement."
42. Edward Said, *Reflections on Exile* (Cambridge, MA: Harvard University Press, 2000).
43. Theodor Adorno, *Minima Moralia: Reflections on a Damaged Life* (London: New Left Books, 1974), 38–39.
44. Mendieta went to Rome in 1983, a city that represented a viable compromise between Cuba and America. She quickly adapted to Rome, making many friends and showing her work.
45. Sigmund Freud, "Female sexuality," *The Standard Edition* 21 (1931): 226. See Andre Green, "The Analyst, Symbolization and Absence in the Analytic Setting," in *On Private Madness* (New York: International Universities Press, 1987), 30–59; Heinz Kohut, *The Restoration of the Self* (New York: International Universities Press, 1977), 296; Hans Loewald, "The Waning of the Oedipus Complex," in *Papers on Psychoanalysis* (New Haven: Yale University Press, 1980), 384–404; and Janine Chasseguet-Smirguel, *Sexuality and Mind: The Role of the Father and Mother in the Psyche* (New York: New York University Press, 1986), who have all discussed Freud's blind spot regarding female sexuality and motherhood.
46. It should be mentioned that Otto Rank and Sandor Ferenczi were among the early male psychoanalysts who were alert to the importance of the mother. Significantly, Freud broke off with both men over their differences.
47. Mendieta, "Writings," 171.
48. Hayden Herrera, *Frida Kahlo: The Paintings* (New York: Harper Collins, 1991), 81.
49. After 1984, Mendieta began to create vertical sculptures, mostly freestanding upright tree trunks with fire engravings. She also began to make lasting transportable sculptures that lent themselves to exhibition in gallery spaces.
50. Katz, *Naked by the Window,* 331.

Chapter 8. Adrian Piper

1. Franz Fanon, *Black Skin,White Masks* (New York: Grove Press, 1952), 115.
2. I will use the term "black" rather than "African American" in this chapter, both because Piper does so and because her art evokes the visual/color connotations associated with race.
3. Laura Cottingham, "The Feminist Continuum: Art After 1970," in *The Power of Feminist Art: The American Movement of the 1970s, History and Impact,* ed. Norma Broude and Mary Garrard (New York: Abrams, 1994), 276–85.
4. Lorraine O'Grady, "Olympia's Maid: Reclaiming Black Female Subjectivity," in *New Feminist Critisicm: Art, Identity, Action,* ed. Joanna Frueh, Cassandra Langer, and Arlene Raven (New York: HarperCollins, 1994), 152–70.
5. Ibid., 153.
6. bell hooks, *Art on My Mind: Visual Politics* (New York: The New Press, 1995), 97.

7. O'Grady, "Olympia's Maid," 160.

8. Sol LeWitt, "Paragraphs on Conceptual Art," *Artforum* 5, no. 10 (1967): 79–83.

9. Adrian Piper, "The Metaphysics of Conceptual Art," in *Out of Order, Out of Sight 1968–1992,* vol. 1, (Cambridge: MIT Press, 1996), 10. Hereafter referred to as *Out of Order,* vol. 1.

10. Piper, "Some Very Forward Remarks" (1973–74), in *Out of Order,* vol. 1, xxxvi.

11. Tricia Rose, "Rap Music and the Demonization of Young Black Males," in *Black Male: Representations of Black Masculinity in Contemporary American Art,* ed. Thelma Golden (New York: Abrams and the Whitney Museum, 1994), 162.

12. Adrian Piper, quoted in Lucy Lippard, "Catalysis: An Interview with Adrian Piper," *NYU Drama Review,* March 1972, 76.

13. Amelia Jones, *Body Art/Performing the Subject* (Minneapolis: University of Minnesota Press, 1998), 162.

14. Piper, "Talking to Myself: The Ongoing Autobiography of an Art Object," (1981), in *Out of Order,* vol. 1, 55.

15. Carrie Mae Weems's *Mirror, Mirror,* a photograph in her series *Ain't Jokin'* (1987–88), also plays with the unique relationship the black female has with her mirror. She looks into the mirror and asks, "Who's the fairest of them all?" only to have the mirror respond: "Snow White you black bitch and don't you forget it!!!"

16. Lucy Lippard, *Mixed Blessings: Art in a Multicultural America* (New York: Pantheon, 1990), 236.

17. Piper, "My Calling (Cards) #1 and #2," (1990), in *Out of Order,* vol. 1, 219.

18. Piper, "Racism, Racial Sterotyping, and Xenophobia (1983–1984)," in *Out of Order, vol. 1,* 204."

19. Piper, "Performance Catalysis on the Street and in the World (Preparatory Notes for the Mythic Being)," (1973–74), in *Out of Order,* vol. 1, 114.

20. Piper, "Racism," (1983), 204.

21. Maurice Berger, "The Critique of Pure Racism: An Interview with Adrian Piper," in *Adrian Piper: A Retrospective,* ed. Maurice Berger (Baltimore: Fine Arts Gallery, 1999), 77.

22. Piper, "Racism," 230.

23. Piper, *Out of Order,* vol 1, xxxx. In the foreword to her 1996 (vol. 1) book, Piper openly identifies with white males and explains, "my writing feeds my white male's sense of entitlement even as it locates me as a subject relative to an audience. And this enhances my confidence, my epistemic insecurity, my interiority."

24. See Judith Butler, *Gender Trouble: Feminism and the Subversion of Female Identity* (New York: Routledge, 1990) as well as the chapter on Cindy Sherman's art for more on identity construction in postmodern thinking and art.

25. Franz Fanon, *Black Skin, White Masks* (New York: Grove Press, 1952); Homi Bhabha, *The Location of Culture* (New York: Routledge, 1994); Stuart Hall, "The After-Life of Franz Fanon: Why Fanon? Why Now? Why Black Skin, White Masks?" in *The Fact of Blackness: Frantz Fanon and Visual Representation,* ed. Alan Read (Seattle: Bay Press, 1996), 13–31.

26. Piper, "Passing for White, Passing for Black," (1992), in *Out of Order,* vol. 1, 289.

27. Lippard, *Mixed Blessing,* 180.

28. Berger, "The Critique of Pure Racism," 96.

29. Martin Buber, [1923] *I and Thou,* trans. Walter Kaufman (New York: Scribner, 1970).

30. Jean-Paul Sartre, quoted in Elisabeth Young-Bruehl, *The Anatomy of Prejudices* (Cambridge: Harvard University Press, 1996), 493.

31. Piper, "Racism," (1992) 265.

32. Piper, "Object Catalysis and Political Self-Awareness (Aspects of the Liberal Dilemma)," (1978), in *Out of Order,* vol. 1, 169–70.

33. See Addette Williams, "Skin Color in Psychotherapy," in *Reaching Across Boundaries of Culture and Class,* ed. Rose Marie Perez Foster, Michael Moskowitz, and Rafael Art Javier (Northvale, NJ: Aronson, 1996), 211–24, for a discussion and review of the literature on prejudice among African Americans based on skin color.

34. Piper, "Talking to Myself," (1970), in *Out of Order,* vol. 1, 35.

35. Piper, "Racism," (1990) 254.

36. Jones, *Body Art/Performing,* 303, n. 43.

37. Adrian Piper, "Performance: The Problematic Solution," in *Out of Order, Out of Sight 1967–1992,* vol. 2 (Cambridge: MIT Press, 1984), 93. Hereafter referred to as *Out of Order,* vol. 2.

38. Donald Kuspit, "Adrian Piper: Self-Healing Through Meta-Art," *Art Criticism* 3 (1987): 9–16.

39. Piper, "Talking to Myself" (1970), in *Out of Order,* vol. 1, 42.

40. Melanie Klein, "Notes on Some Schizoid Mechanisms," in *Envy and Gratitude and Other Works 1946–1963 (The Writings of Melanie Klein),* vol. 3 (New York: Delta, 1984), 1–24.

41. Paula Heimann, "On Countertransference," *International Journal of Psycho-Analysis* 31 (1950): 81–84; Leon Grinberg, "On a Specific Aspect of Countertransference Due to the Patient's Projective Identification," *International Journal of Psycho-Analysis,* 43 (1962): 436–40; Thomas Ogden, "On Projective Identification," *International Journal of Psycho-Analysis* 60: 357–73.

42. Wilfred Ruprecht Bion, "Language and the Schizophrenic," in *New Directions of Psychoanalysis,* ed. Melanie Klein, Paula Heimann, and Roger Money-Kyrle (London: Tavistock, 1955), 220–39.

43. O'Grady, "Olympia's Maid," 166.

44. Adrian Piper, "Art-World Practice and Real-World Politics (Ways of Averting One's Gaze)" (1988), *Out of Order, Out of Sight,* in vol. 2, 130.

45. Wilfred Ruprecht Bion, "Attacks on Linking," in *Second Thoughts* (London: Karnac Books, 1993), 93–109.

46. Personal interview New York City, March 8, 1996.

47. Piper, "Performance Catalysis on the Street and in the World (Notes on the Mythic Being I-III)," (1976), in *Out of Order,* vol. 1, 138.

48. Ibid., 123, in which Piper wrote: " I feel my masculinity to be very nearly fully articulated in me."

49. Young-Bruehl, *The Anatomy of Prejudices,* 509.

50. Ibid.

51. Thelma Golden, ed., *Black Male,* 19.

52. Adrian Piper, "Notes on the Mythic Being I-III," (1974–76), *Out of Order,* in vol. 1, 117.

53. Rose, "Black Male," 52–53.

54. bell hooks and Cornel West, *Breaking Bread: Insurgent Black Intellectual Life* (Boston: South End Press, 1991), 154.
55. Piper, "Goodbye to Easy Listening," (1990), *Adrian Piper: Out of Order,* in vol. 2, 175–87.
56. Piper, "Performance Catalysis," *Out of Order,* in vol. 1, 114.
57. Adrian Piper, "On Wearing Three Hats," unpublished draft April 27, 1996, 12.
58. Adrian Piper, quoted in Mary Anne Staniszewski, "Race Against Time," in *Adrian Piper: PRETEND* (New York: John Weber Gallery, 1990).
59. Arthur Danto, *After the End of Art: Contemporary Art and the Pale of History* (Princeton, NJ: Princeton University Press, 1997), 15.
60. Personal interview, March 8, 1996.
61. Piper, "On Wearing Three Hats,"12.
62. Ken Johnson, "Art in Review: Adrian Piper," *New York Times,* Nov. 17, 2000, E41.

Chapter 9. Cindy Sherman

1. Erik Erikson, *Childhood and Society* (New York: Norton, 1950), 213.
2. Cindy Sherman, *Studio: Cindy Sherman (Interview with Betsy Berne),* in *Tate Magazine* 5, http://www.tate.org.uk/magazine/issue5/sherman.htm.
3. Kay Larson, "Who's That Girl?" *New York Magazine,* Aug 13. 1987, 52–53; Arthur Danto, *Cindy Sherman: History Portraits* (New York: Rizzoli, 1991), 8.
4. Rosalind Krauss, *Cindy Sherman 1975–1993* (New York: Rizzoli, 1993), 20.
5. Laura Mulvey, "A Phantasmagoria of the Female Body: The Work of Cindy Sherman," *New Left Review* 188 (1991): 136–51.
6. E. Kirsten Dahl, "Play and the Construction of Gender in the Oedipal Child," in *The Many Meanings of Play: A Psychoanalytic Perspective,* ed. Albert Solnit, Donald Cohen, and Peter Neubauer (New Haven: Yale University Press, 1993), 130.
7. Edith Kramer, *Childhood and Art Therapy* (New York: Schocken Books, 1979), 63.
8. Cindy Sherman, *The Complete Untitled Film Stills* (New York: Museum of Modern Art, 2003), 13.
9. Sigmund Freud "Creative Writers and Day-Dreaming," *The Standard Edition of the Complete Psychological Works of Sigmund Freud,* 9 (1908): 141–53.
10. Erik Erikson, *Play and Development* (New York: Norton, 1972), 127.
11. *Nobody's Here But Me,* dir. Mark Stokes, pro. Robert McNab, Cinecontact Production for BBC and the Arts Council of England, 1994.
12. Sherman, *Film Stills,* 11.
13. Ibid., 7.
14. The numbers used throughout this chapter refer to Sherman's works, all numbered but untitled.
15. Anna Freud, *Normality and Pathology in Childhood* (New York: International Universities Press, 1965), 80.
16. Joan Riviere, "Womanliness as a Masquerade," *International Journal of Psychoanalysis* 10 (1929): 303–13; George Zavitsianos, "Homeovestism: Perverse Form of Behavior Involving the Wearing of Clothes of the Same Sex," *International Journal of Psycho-Analysis* 53 (1972): 471–77; George Zavitsianos, "The Object in Fetishism, Homeovestism and Transvestism," *International Journal of Psycho-Analysis* 58 (1977): 487–95; Louise Kaplan, *Female Perversions: The Temptations of Madame Bovary* (New York: Doubleday, 1991); Danielle Knafo, "The Mirror, the Mask and the Masquerade in the Art and Life of Frida Kahlo," *The Annual of Psychoanalysis* 21 (1993): 277–99 have written about women using feminine dress or femininity as masquerade.
17. Annie Reich, *Psychoanalytic Contributions* (New York: International Universities Press, 1973), 213.
18. Sherman, *Film Stills,* 8.
19. See chapter 3, note 9.
20. Danielle Knafo, "What You See is Not Always What You Get: Voyeurism and the Primal Scene in Art," *New Observations* 12 (1996): 7–9.
21. Sherman, *Film Stills* 14.
22. Mark Stevens, "How I Made it: Cindy Sherman on her 'Untitled Film Stills,' " *New York Magazine,* April 14, 2008, 78.
23. Mulvey, "A Phantasmagoria of the Female Body," 142–43.
24. Bruno Bettleheim, *The Uses of Enchantment: The Meaning and Importance of Fairy Tales* (New York: Vintage, 1972), 73.
25. Gerald Marzorati, "Self-Possessed," *Vanity Fair,* October 1985, 112–3.
26. Julia Kristeva, *Powers of Horror: An Essay on Abjection,* trans. Leon S. Roudiez (New York: Columbia University Press, 1982), 1.
27. Barbara Creed, *The Monstrous-Feminine: Film, Feminism, Psychoanalysis* (London: Routledge, 1993), 1; Tabitha Goode, "Abstract Representational Space: Uncanny Aliens and Others (Pandora, or Prometheus's Return)," *Camera Obscura* 40, no. 4 (1997): 244–74.
28. Lili Peller, "Libidinal Phases, Ego Development, and Play," The *Psychoanalytic Study of the Child* 9 (1954): 180.
29. Donald Woods Winnicott, *Playing and Reality* (London: Tavistock, 1971), 50.
30. Erikson, *Play and Development,* 127.
31. Matthew Cohen, "Chimeric Objects and Playthings," *The Psychoanalytic Study of the Child* 42 (1987): 85–104.
32. Jacob Arlow, "Trauma, Play and Perversion," *The Psychoanalytic Study of the Child* 42 (1987): 31–44; Matthew Cohen, "Chimeric Objects and Playthings," *The Psychoanalytic Study of the Child* 42 (1987): 85–104.
33. Cohen, "Chimeric Objects and Playthings," 85–104.
34. Donald Kuspit, "Inside Cindy Sherman," in *The New Subjectivism: Art in the 1980s* (Ann Arbor: U.M.I., 1991), 396.
35. Noriko Fuku, "A Woman of Parts—Artist Cindy Sherman—Interview," *Art in America* 6 (1997): 80.
36. Jessica Benjamin, *The Bonds of Love: Psychoanalysis, Feminism, and the Problem of Domination* (New York: Pantheon, 1988), 55.
37. She did take a roll of film of herself dressed as a man for the Film Stills series but she never displayed them claiming they were unsuccessful because "I wasn't

really in touch with my masculine side." Sherman, *Film Stills*, 9.

38. Danielle Knafo and Kenneth Feiner, *Unconscious Fantasies and the Relational World* (Hillsdale, NJ: Analytic Press, 2005), 33.

39. Glenn Collins, "A Portraitist's Romp through Art History," *New York Times*, February 1, 1990, C12, C22.

40. Brooks Adams, "Cindy Sherman at Metro Pictures," *Art in America*, June 1990, 172.

41. Sherman, *Studio*, 2.

42. Amei Wallach, "Tough Images to Face," *Los Angeles Times*, June 7, 1992, 80.

43. Fuku, "A Woman of Parts," 125.

44. Irene Fast, *Gender Identity* (Hillsdale, NJ: The Analytic Press, 1984), 4; Irene Fast, "Aspects of Early Gender Development: Toward a Reformation," *Psychoanalytic Psychology* 7 (1990): 105–17.

45. Doris Bernstein, *Female Identity Conflict in Clinical Practice* (Northvale, NJ: Jason Aronson, 1993), 209.

46. Sigmund Freud, "Anal Erotism and Castration." *Standard Edition* 17 (1918): 84. Freud believed that feces, baby, and penis were equated in the unconscious, symbolizing "a little one' that can be separated from one's body."

47. Wallach, "Tough Images to Face," 80.

48. Therese Lichtenstein and Cindy Sherman, "Cindy Sherman," *Journal of Contemporary Art*, http://www.jca-online.com/sherman.html.

49. Sheldon Bach, "Sadomasochistic Object Relations," in *The Language of Perversion and the Language of Love* (Northdale, NJ: Jason Aronson, 1994), 3.

50. Cindy Sherman, "No Make-Up. An Interview with Isabelle Graw," in *Cindy Sherman: Clowns*, (Hannover: Schirmer/Mosel & Kestnergesellschaft, 2004), 55.

51. Sherman, *Clowns*, 54.

52. Ibid., 54.

53. Erikson, *Childhood and Society*, 214.

54. Donald Woods Winnicott, "Transitional Objects and Transitional Phenomena," *International Journal of Psycho-Analysis* 34 (1953): 89–97.

55. Nancy Moore, Carolyn Everston, and Jere Brophy, "Solitary Play: Some Functional Considerations," *Developmental Psychology* 10, no. 6 (1974): 830–34; Jerome Singer, "Affect and Imagination in Play and Fantasy," in *Emotions in Personality and Psychopathology*, ed. Caroll Izard (New York: Plenum, 1979), 13–34; Greta Fein, "Pretend Play: An Integrative View," *Child Development* 52 (1981): 1095–1118.

56. Collins, "Art History," C22.

57. Steven Marans, Linda Mayes, and Alice Colonna, "Psychoanalytic Views of Children's Play," in *The Many Meanings of Play: A Psychoanalytic Perspective*, ed. Albert Solnit, Donald Cohen, and Peter Neubauer (New Haven: Yale University Press, 1993), 18–19.

58. Peter Neubauer, "The Many Meanings of Play: Introduction," The *Psychoanalytic Study of the Child* 42 (1987): 3–10; Dahl, *Play and the Construction of Gender*, 130.

Chapter 10. Orlan

1. *VST, Revue Scientifique et Culturelle de Santé Mentale* "Issue devoted to Orlan," 23/24 (1991): 16.

2. Jill O'Bryan, *Carnal Art: Orlan's Refacing* (Minneapolis: University of Minnesota Press, 2005), 14.

3. Orlan and Stéphane Place, "Sujet Objet," in *Orlan: De l'Art Charnel au Baiser de l'Artiste* (Paris: Editions Jean-Michel Place, 1997), 2–3.

4. Peg Zeglin Brand, "Bound to Beauty: An Interview with Orlan," in *Beauty Matters*, ed. Peg Zaglin Brand (Bloomington: Indiana University Press, 2000), 301.

5. Orlan, Personal interview, Tel-Aviv, Mar. 29, 1999.

6. O'Bryan, *Carnal Art*, 135.

7. Eugénie Lemoine-Luccioni, quoted in Orlan, "Conference," in *This is My Body . . . This is My Software . . .*, trans. Tanya Augsburg and Michael A. Moos, ed. Duncan McCorquondale (London: Black Dog, 1996), 88.

8. Sigmund Freud, "The Medusa's Head," *Standard Edition* 18 (1922): 273–74. This is a misquotation attributed to Freud who actually wrote, "We read in Rabelais of how the Devil took flight when the woman showed him her vulva."

9. For more on this, see Danielle Knafo, "Castration Fantasies, Sexual Difference, and Mind-Body Matters," in *Unconscious Fantasies and the Relational World*, Danielle Knafo and Kenneth Feiner (Hillsdale, NJ: Analytic Press, 2005), 125–42.

10. Medusa was the mortal Gorgon who, because she was raped by Poseidon in Athene's temple, was punished by the angered goddess. Athene converted Medusa's beautiful locks into snakes that could turn men who gaze at her into stone. Perseus killed Medusa by chopping off her head. He avoided looking directly at her by using his shield as a mirror.

11. Julia Kristeva, *Powers of Horror: An Essay on Abjection*, trans. Leon S. Roudiez (New York: Columbia University Press, 1982), 71.

12. See Irene Fast, *Gender Identity: A Differentiation Model* (Hillsdale: Analytic Press, 1984), 7–22 and Danielle Knafo (2005) in *Unconscious Fantasies and the Relational World*, 125–142 for a more expanded and updated view of castration theory. Interestingly, Freud and his followers nearly always neglect mention of the envy males experience for the female's genital capacities—in particular, her ability to give birth. Whereas for Freud, it is primarily the male genital that is envied; today's castration complex more accurately refers to the difficulties *each* sex has in adapting to its own bodily limitations.

13. Sigmund Freud, "The Uncanny," *Standard Edition* 17 (1919): 217–56.

14. Peg Zeglin Brand, "Disinterestedness and Political Art," in *Aesthetics: The Big Questions*, ed. Carolyn Korsmeyer (Oxford: Basil Blackwell, 1998), 289.

15. See: John Berger, *Ways of Seeing* (London: British Broadcasting Corporation and Penguin Books, 1972), 47; Laura Mulvey, "Visual Pleasure and Narrative Cinema," in *Visual and Other Pleasures (Theories of Representation and Difference)* (Bloomington: Indiana University Press, 1989), 14–26.

16. Kristeva, *Powers of Horror*, 4.

17. Orlan, http://www.fdcw.unimaas.nl/cwsiot/shopwindow/art/persoons,%20van%20der%20leeuw%20(orlan)/page%204,%20manifesto.htm.

18. Francette Pacteau, *The Symptom of Beauty* (Cambridge: Harvard University Press, 1994), 14.

19. Joanna Frueh. *Monster Beauty: Building the Body of Love* (Berkeley: University of California Press, 2001), 18–19.
20. Ibid., 22.
21. See Wendy Steiner, *Venus in Exile: The Rejection of Beauty in Twentieth-Century Art* (New York: The Free Press, 2001), 1.
22. Derrick de Kerckhove, "Touch versus Vision: Aesthetik neuer Technologien," in *Die Aktualität des Asthetischen,* ed. Wolfgang Welsch (Munich: Fink, 1993), 231.
23. Robert Ayers, "Serene and Happy and Distant: An Interview with Orlan," in *Body Modification,* ed. Mike Featherstone (London: Sage, 2000), 177.
24. Orlan, *Conférence,* 91.
25. See Heinz Kohut, *The Analysis of the Self* (New York: International Universities Press, 1971).
26. See Donald Woods Winnicott, "Ego Distortion in Terms of True and False Self," in *The Maturational Processes and the Facilitating Environment* (New York: International Universities Press, 1965), 140–52.
27. Joyce McDougall, *Plea for a Measure of Abnormality* (New York: Basic Books, 1980).
28. David Gale, "Knife Work," *Gentlemen's Quarterly* [London], February 31, 1995, 31.
29. Orlan, *Conférence,* 92.
30. Danielle Knafo, "Skin and Psyche: From the Womb to the Tomb," in *Skin-Deep: Surface and Appearance in Contemporary Art* (Jerusalem: The Israeli Museum, 1999), 15–19.
31. Kate Ince, *Orlan: Millennial Female* (Oxford: Berg, 2000), 1.
32. Orlan, personal interview, Mar. 29, 1999.
33. *VST,* "Issue devoted to Orlan," 17.
34. Orlan, personal interview, Mar. 29, 1999.
35. *VST,* "Issue devoted to Orlan," 14.
36. Orlan, personal interview, Mar. 29, 1999.
37. *VST,* "Issue devoted to Orlan," 17.
38. Fast, *Gender Identity,* 128–29.
39. Orlan, http://www.orlan.net.
40. Sigmund Freud, "Some psychical consequences of the anatomical distinction between the sexes." *The Standard Edition* 19: 248–58.
41. Ince, *Millennial Female,* 132.
42. Personal interview, March 29, 1999.
43. Orlan, Personal interview, Mar. 29, 1999.
44. Marie Bonaparte, "Passivity, Masochism and Femininity," *International Journal of Psychoanalysis* 16 (1934): 325–33; Helena Deutsch, "Sur Genese des Familienromans," *Internationale Zeitschrift für Psychoanalyse* 16 (1930): 249–53.
45. Carey Lovelace, "Orlan: Offensive Acts," *Performance Arts Journal* 49 (1995): 18.
46. Vivian Patraka, "Binary Terror and Feminist Performance: Reading Both Ways," *Discourse* 14, no. 2 (1992): 163–85.
47. Jaques Lacan, "La state du miroir comme formateur de la function du Je, telle qu'elle nous est révelée dans l'éxperience psychanalytique," in *Ecrits* (Paris: Editions du Seuil, 1996), 93–100.
48. Orlan, www.orlan.net.
49. Linda S. Kauffman, *Bad Girls and Sick Boys: Fantasies in Contemporary Art and Culture* (Berkeley: University of California Press, 1998), 65.
50. Projective identification refers to a complex, two-part defense mechanism. Firstly, a person aims to project one's inner feelings into another person. Secondly, that person identifies with the projection and owns it as his or her own. In this way, the unconscious minds of two people communicate and create a new reality that includes both of their experiences.
51. Brand, "Bound to Beauty," 302–3.
52. Kauffman, *Bad Girls and Sick Boys,* 67.
53. Orlan, personal interview, New York City, July 9, 2005.
54. Jim McClellan, "The Extensions of Women," *Observer "Life" Magazine 17,* April 17, 1994, 42.
55. Orlan, www.orlan.net.
56. See: *VST,* "Issue devoted to Orlan," 44–45.
57. Ayers, "Interview with Orlan," 171.
58. Ibid., 184.
59. Ince, *Millennial Female.*
60. Jacques Derrida, "Passages—From Traumatism to Promise," in *Points . . . Interviews 1974–1994,* ed. Elisabeth Webster (Stanford, CA: Stanford University Press, 1995), 307.

Epilogue

1. Sigmund Freud, "New Introductory Lectures on Psycho-Analysis." *Standard Edition* 22 (1933): 118.

Bibliography

Adams, Alice. "Frida Kahlo's Passion." *Art and Antiques* 6, no. 1 (1989): 58–98.

Adams, Brooks. "Cindy Sherman at Metro Pictures." *Art in America*, June 1990, 172.

Adorno, Theodor. *Minima Moralia: Reflections from a Damaged Life*. London: New Left Books, 1974.

Apraxine, Pierre, and Demange Xavier. *La Divine Comtesse: Photographs of the Countess de Castiglione*. New Haven: Yale University Press and the Metropolitan Museum of Art, 2000.

Aragon, Louis, and André Breton. "Le Cinquantenaire de l'Hystérie." *La Révolution Surréaliste* 11 (1928): 20–22.

Arlow, Jacob. "Trauma, Play and Perversion." *The Psychoanalytic Study of the Child* 42 (1987): 31–44.

Ayers, Robert. "Serene and Happy and Distant: An Interview with Orlan." In *Body Modification*, edited by Mike Featherstone. London: Sage, 2000, 171–84.

Bach, Sheldon. "Sadomasochistic Object Relations." In *The Language of Perversion and the Language of Love*. Northvale, NJ: Jason Aronson, 1994, 3–25.

Barrerras del Rio, Petra, and John Perrault. *Ana Mendieta: A Retrospective*. New York: The New Museum of Contemporary Art, 1988.

Bataille, Georges. "The Language of Flowers." In: *Visions of Excess*, edited by Allan Stoekl. Minneapolis: University of Minnesota Press, 1985, 10–14.

Beebe, Beatrice, and Daniel Stern. "Engagement-Disengagement and Early Object Experiences." In *Communicative Structures and Psychic Structures*, edited by Milton Freedman and Stanley Grand. New York: Plenum, 1977, 35–55.

Benjamin, Jessica. *The Bonds of Love: Psychoanalysis, Feminism, and the Problem of Domination*. New York: Pantheon, 1988.

Benjamin, Walter. "The Work of Art in the Age of Mechanical Reproduction." In *Art in Theory 1900–2000: An Anthology of Changing Ideas*, edited by Charles Harrison and Paul Wood. Oxford: Blackwell, 2003, 520–26.

Berger, John. *Ways of Seeing*. London: British Broadcasting Corporation and Penguin Books, 1972.

Berger, Maurice. "The Critique of Pure Racism: An Interview with Adrian Piper." In *Adrian Piper: A Retrospective*, edited by Maurice Berger. Baltimore: Fine Arts Gallery, 1999, 76–98.

Bernstein, Doris. *Female Identity Conflict in Clinical Practice*. Northvale, NJ: Jason Aronson, 1993.

Bettleheim, Bruno. *The Uses of Enchantment: The Meaning and Importance of Fairy Tales*. New York: Vintage, 1972.

Bhabha, Homi. *The Location of Culture*. New York: Routledge, 1994.

Billeter, Erika. "Frida and Maria." In *Images of Mexico*. Dallas: Dallas Museum of Art, 1987.

Bion, Wilfred Ruprecht. "Language and the Schizophrenic." In *New Directions of Psychoanalysis*, edited by Melanie Klein, Paula Heimann, and Roger Money-Kyrle. London: Tavistock, 1955, 220–39.

———. "Attacks on Linking." In *Second Thoughts*. London: Karnac Books, 1993, 93–109.

Blocker, Jane. *Where is Ana Mendieta?* Durham: Duke University Press, 1999.

Bollas, Christopher. *The Shadow of the Object: Psychoanalysis of the Unthought Known*. London: Free Association Books, 1987.

Bonaparte, Marie. "Passivity, Masochism and Femininity." *International Journal of Psychoanalysis* 16 (1934): 325–33.

Borzello, Frances. *Seeing Ourselves: Women's Self-Portraits*. New York: Abrams, 1998.

Brand, Peg Zeglin. "Disinterestedness and Political Art." In *Aesthetics: The Big Questions*, edited by Carolyn Korsmeyer. Oxford: Basil Blackwell, 1998, 155–71.

———. "Bound to Beauty: An Interview with Orlan." In *Beauty Matters*, edited by Peg Zaglin Brand. Bloomington: Indiana University Press, 2000, 289–314.

Breder, Hans. Personal interview, Jan. 15, 1996.

Brett, Guy. "One Energy." In *Ana Mendieta, Earth Body: Sculpture and Performance, 1972–1985*, edited by Olga M. Viso. Hirshhorn Museum and Sculpture Garden, Smithsonian Institute: Hatje Cantz Publishers, 2004, 181–203.

Buber, Martin. [1923] *I and Thou*. Translated by Walter Kaufman. New York: Scribner, 1970.

Buerkle, Darcy. "Historical effacements: Facing Charlotte Salomon." In *Reading Charlotte Salomon*, edited by Michael Steinberg and Monica Bohm-Duchen. Ithaca: Cornell University Press, 2006, 73–87.

Butler, Judith. *Gender Trouble: Feminism and the Subversion of Identity*. New York: Routledge, 1990.

Cahun, Claude. *Aveux non Avenues*. Paris: Editions du Carrefour, 1930.

Caws, Mary Ann, Rudolf Kuenzli, and Gwen Raaberg. *Surrealism and Women*. Cambridge: MIT Press, 1995.

Chadwick, Whitney. *Women Artists and the Surrealist Movement*. New York: Thames and Hudson, 1985.

———. *Women, Art, and Society.* London: Thames and Hudson, 1990.

———. *Mirror Images: Women, Surrealism, and Self-Representation.* Cambridge: MIT Press, 1998.

Chasseguet-Smirguel, Janine. *Sexuality and Mind: The Role of the Father and the Mother in the Psyche.* New York: New York University Press, 1986.

Clearwater, Bonnie. *Ana Mendieta: A Book of Works.* Miami Beach: Grassfield Press, 1993.

Cohen, Matthew. "Chimeric Objects and Playthings." *The Psychoanalytic Study of the Child* 42 (1987): 85–104.

Cole, Julie. "Claude Cahun, Marcel Moore, and the Collaborative Construction of a Lesbian Subjectivity." In *Reclaiming Female Agency: Feminist Art History After Postmodernism,* edited by Norma Broude and Mary Garrard. Berkeley: University of California Press, 2005, 343–59.

Collins, Glenn. "A Portraitist's Romp through Art History." *New York Times,* February 1, 1990.

Comini, Alessandra. "Kollwitz in Context: The Formative Years." In *Käthe Kollwitz,* edited by Elizabeth Prelinger. New Haven: Yale University Press, 1992, 89–114.

Conley, Christine. "Memory and Trauerspiel: Charlotte Salomon's *Life? or Theater?* and the Angel of History." In *Reading Charlotte Salomon,* edited by Michael P. Steinberg and Monica Bohm-Duchen. Ithaca: Cornell University Press, 2006, 88–104.

Cordry, Donald. *Mexican Masks.* Austin: University of Texas Press, 1980

Cottingham, Laura. "The Feminist Continuum: Art after 1970." In *The Power of Feminist Art: The American Movement of the 1970s, History and Impact,* edited by Norma Broude and Mary Garrard. New York: Abrams, 1994, 276–87.

———. "Hannah Wilke: Some Naked Truths and her Legacy in the 1990s." In *Hannah Wilke: A Retrospective,* edited by Elizabeth Delin Hansen, Kirsten Dybbol, and Donald Goddard. Nikolaj: Copenhagen Contemporary Art Center, 1998, 56–62.

———. *Seeing Through the Seventies: Essays on Feminism and Art.* Amsterdam: G&B International, 2000.

Creed, Barbara. *The Monstrous-Feminine: Film, Feminism, Psychoanalysis.* London: Routledge, 1993.

Dahl, E. Kirsten. "Play and the Construction of Gender in the Oedipal Child." In *The Many Meanings of Play: A Psychoanalytic Perspective,* edited by Albert Solnit, Donald Cohen, and Peter Neubauer. New Haven: Yale University Press, 1993, 117–34.

Danto, Arthur. *Cindy Sherman: History Portraits.* New York: Rizzoli, 1991.

———. *After the End of Art: Contemporary Art and the Pale of History.* Princeton, NJ: Princeton University Press, 1997.

Derrida, Jacques. "Passages—From Traumatism to Promise." In *Points . . . Interviews 1974–1994,* edited by Elisabeth Webster. Stanford, CA: Stanford University Press, 1995, 385–87.

Deutsch, Helena. "Sur Genese des Familienromans." *Internationale Zeitschrift für Psychoanalyse* 16 (1930): 249–53.

Diehl, Carol. "Hannah Wilke." *Art News* 93, no. 4 (1994): 164.

Dimen, Muriel. *Sexuality, Intimacy, Power.* Hillsdale, NJ: Analytic Press, 2003.

Dimen, Muriel, and Virginia Goldner. "Gender and Sexuality." In *American Psychiatric Association Publishing Textbook of Psychoanalysis,* edited by Arnold Cooper, Glen Gabbard, and Ethel Person. Washington, DC: American Psychiatric Publishing, 2008, 93–114.

Dinnerstein, Dorothy. *The Mermaid and the Minotaur.* New York: Harper & Row, 1976.

Ellis, Havelock. *Psychology of Sex.* London: Pan Books, 1933.

Erikson, Erik. *Childhood and Society.* New York: Norton, 1950.

———. *Play and Development.* New York: Norton, 1972.

Fanon, Franz. *Black Skin, White Masks.* New York: Grove Press, 1952.

Fast, Irene. *Gender Identity: A Differentiation Model.* Hillsdale, NJ: Analytic Press, 1984.

———. "Aspects of Early Gender Development: Toward a Reformulation." *Psychoanalytic Psychology* 7 (1990): 105–17.

Fein, Greta. "Pretend Play: An Integrative View." *Child Development* 52 (1981): 1095–1118.

Felstiner, Mary Lowenthal. *To Paint her Life: Charlotte Salomon in the Nazi Era.* New York: HarperCollins, 1994.

Follaine, Claire. "Lucy Schwob and Suzanne Malherbe—Résistantes." In *Don't Kiss Me: The Art of Claude Cahun and Marcel Moore,* edited by Louise Downie. New York: Aperture and Jersey Heritage Trust, 2006, 83–95.

Freud, Anna. "The Role of Bodily Illness in the Mental Life of Children." In *Physical Illness and Handicap in Childhood,* edited by Ruth Eissler, Anna Freud, Marianne Kris, and Albert Solnit. New Haven: Yale University Press, 1977, 1–12.

———. *Normality and Pathology in Childhood.* New York: International Universities Press, 1965.

Freud, Sigmund. "The Aetiology of Hysteria." *The Standard Edition of the Complete Psychological Works of Sigmund Freud* 3 (1896): 191–221.

———. "Screen Memories." *Standard Edition* 3 (1899): 301–22.

———. "The Interpretation of Dreams." *Standard Editions* 5 (1900).

———. "Creative Writers and Day-Dreaming." *Standard Edition* 9 (1908): 141–53.

———. "Recommendations to Physicians Practicing Psycho-Analysis." *Standard Edition* 12 (1912):109–20.

———. "On Narcissism: An Introduction." *Standard Edition* 14 (1914): 73–102.

———. "Mourning and Melancholia." *Standard Edition* 14 (1917): 237–58.

———. "Anal Erotism and Castration." *Standard Edition* 17(1918): 72–88.

———. "The Uncanny." *Standard Edition* 17 (1919): 217–56.

———. "Beyond the Pleasure Principle." *Standard Edition* 18 (1920): 7–64.

———. "Civilization and its Discontents." *Standard Edition* 21 (1920): 64–145.

———. "The Medusa's Head." *Standard Edition* 18 (1922): 273–74.

———. "Some Psychical Consequences of the Anatomical Distinction Between the Sexes." *Standard Edition* 19 (1925): 248–58.

———. "Female Sexuality." *Standard Edition* 21(1931): 225–43.

Frueh, Joanna. "Hannah Wilke." In *Hannah Wilke: A Retrospective,* edited by Thomas H. Kochheiser. Columbia: University of Missouri Press, 1989, 11–151.

———. "Visible Difference, Women Artists and Aging." In *New Feminist Criticism: Art, Identity, and Action,* edited by Joanna Frueh, Cassandra Langer, and Arlene Raven. New York: Icon, 1991, 264–88.

———. "The Body through Women's Eyes." In *The Power of Feminist Art,* edited by Norma Broude and Mary Garrard. New York: Abrams, 1994, 190–207.

———. "Hannah Wilke." In *Erotic Faculties.* Berkeley: University of California Press, 1996, 141–54.

———. *Monster Beauty: Building the Body of Love.* Berkeley: University of California Press, 2001.

Fuku, Noriko. "A Woman of Parts—Artist Cindy Sherman—Interview." *Art in America* 6 (1997): 80.

Fusco, Coco. "Traces of Ana Mendieta." *Poliester* 4 (1992): 61.

Gale, David. "Knife Work." *Gentlemen's Quarterly* (London), February, 31, 1995.

Garber, Marjorie. *Vested Interests: Cross-Dressing and Cultural Anxiety.* New York: Routledge, 1992.

Goddard, Donald. *Interviews and Private Communications.* New York City, 1996–99.

Goldman, Sandra. "Too Good Lookin' to be Smart: Beauty, Performance and the Art of Hannah Willke." PhD diss., University of Austin, Texas, 1999.

Golden, Thelma. (1994). *Black Male: Representations of Masculinity in Contemporary American Art.* New York: Whitney Museum of Art.

Goldner, Virginia. "Toward a Critical Theory of Gender." *Psychoanalytic Dialogues,* 1: 249–72, 1991.

Goode, Tabitha. "Abstract Representational Space: Uncanny Aliens and Others (Pandora, or Prometheus's Return)." *Camera Obscura* 40, no. 4 (1997): 244–74.

Green, André. *On Private Madness.* Madison, CT: International Universities Press, 1986.

———. "The Analyst, Symbolization and Absence in the Analytic Setting." In *On Private Madness.* New York: International Universities Press, 1987, 30–59.

Greenacre, Phyllis. "The Childhood of the Artist." In *Emotional Growth 2.* New York: International Universities Press, 1971, 479–504.

Grinberg, Leon. "On a Specific Aspect of Countertransference due to the Patient's Projective Identification." *International Journal of Psycho-Analysis* 43 (1962): 436–40.

Hall, Stuart. "The After-Life of Franz Fanon: Why Fanon? Why Now? Why Black Skin, White Masks?" In *The Fact of Blackness: Franz Fanon and Visual Representation,* edited by Alan Read. Seattle: Bay Press, 1996, 12–37.

Harris, Adrienne. *Gender as Soft Assembly.* Hillsdale, NJ: Analytic Press, 2005.

Heimann, Paula. "On Countertransference." *International Journal of Psycho-Analysis,* 31 (1950): 81–84.

Herrera, Hayden. *Frida: A Biography of Frida Kahlo.* New York: Harper Colophon Books, 1983.

———. *Frida Kahlo: The Paintings.* New York: Harper Collins, 1991.

Herzberg, Judith. *Charlotte: Life or Theater: An Autobiographical Play by Charlotte Salomon.* Translated by Leila Venewitz. New York: Viking, 1981.

Herzberg, Julia Ann. 1998. "Ana Mendieta, The Iowa Years: A Critical Study, 1969–1977." PhD diss., City University of New York, 1998.

———. "Ana Mendieta's Iowa Years, 1970–1980." In *Ana Mendieta, Earth Body: Sculpture and Performance, 1972–1985,* edited by Olga M. Viso. Hirshhorn Museum and Sculpture Garden, Smithsonian Institute: Hatje Cantz Publishers, 2004, 137–80.

hooks, bell, and Cornel West. *Breaking Bread: Insurgent Black Intellectual Life.* Boston: South End Press, 1991.

———. *Art on my Mind: Visual Politics.* New York: The New Press, 1995.

Horsfield, Kate, Branda Miller, and Nereyda Garcia-Ferraz. writer/director. *Ana Mendieta: Fuego de Tierra.* VHS, 1988.

Horton, Anne. "Fridamania." *Art and Antiques* 14, no. 4 (1991): 126–78.

Imber-Black, Evan. *The Secret Life of Families.* New York: Bantam, 1998.

Ince, Kate. *Orlan: Millennial Female.* Oxford: Berg, 2000.

Jacob, Mary Jane. *Ana Mendieta: The "Silueta" Series, 1973–1980.* New York: Galerie Lelong, 1991.

Johnson, Ken. "Art in Review: Adrian Piper." *New York Times,* November 17, 2000, E41.

Jones, Amelia. "The Rhetoric of the Pose: Hannah Wilke and the Radical-Narcissism of Feminist Body Art." In *Body Art: Performing the Subject.* Minneapolis: University of Minnesota Press, 1988, 151–96.

———. *Body Art/Performing the Subject.* Minneapolis: University of Minnesota Press, 1998.

Jones, Marvin. "Hannah Wilke's Art, Politics, Religion, and Feminism." *The New Common Good* 1 (1985): 9–11.

Kahlo, Frida. *The Diary of Frida Kahlo: An Intimate Self-Portrait,* New York: Harry Abrams, and Mexico: La Vaca Independiente S.A. de C.V., 1995.

———. *Frida by Frida: Selection of Letters and Texts.* Translated by Gregory Dechant. Mexico: Editorial RM, 2003.

Kaplan, Louise. *Female Perversions: The Temptations of Madame Bovary.* New York: Doubleday, 1991.

Kauffman, Linda S. *Bad Girls and Sick Boys: Fantasies in Contemporary Art and Culture.* Berkeley: University of California Press, 1998.

Katz, Robert. *Naked by the Window: The Fatal Marriage of Carl Andre and Ana Mendieta.* New York: Atlantic Monthly Press, 1990.

Kearns, Martha. *Käthe Kollwitz: Woman and Artist.* New York: Feminist Press, 1976.

Kerckhove, Derrick de. "Touch versus Vision: Aesthetik Neuer Technologien." In *Die Aktualität des Ästhetischen,* edited by Wolfgang Welsch. Munich: Fink, 1993, 137–68.

Kleeblatt, Norman. *Too Jewish? Challenging Traditional Identities.* New York. The Jewish Museum and Rutgers University Press, 1995.

Klein, Melanie. "Notes on Some Schizoid Mechanisms." In *Envy and Gratitude and Other Works 1946–1963 (The Writings of Melanie Klein, Vol. 3).* New York: Delta, 1984.

Kline, Katy. "In or Out of the Picture: Claude Cahun and Cindy Sherman." In *Mirror Images: Women, Surrealism, and Self-Representation,* edited by Whitney Chadwick. Cambridge: MIT Press, 1998, 66–81.

Knafo, Danielle. "Egon Schiele's Self-Portraits: A Psychoanalytic Study in the Creation of a Self." *The Annual of Psychoanalysis* 19 (1991): 59–90.

———. "Egon Schiele and Frida Kahlo: The Self-Portrait as Mirror." *Journal of the American Academy of Psychoanalysis* 19, no. 4 (1991): 629–46.

———. *Egon Schiele/A Self in Creation: A Psychoanalytic Study of the Artist's Self-Portraits.* Rutherford, NJ: Fairleigh Dickinson University Press, 1993.

———. "The Mirror, the Mask and the Masquerade in the Art and Life of Frida Kahlo." *The Annual of Psychoanalysis* 21 (1993): 277–99.

———. "What You See is Not Always What You Get: Voyeurism and the Primal Scene in Art." *New Observations* 12 (1996): 7–9.

———. "Skin and Psyche: From the Womb to the Tomb." In *Skin-Deep: Surface and Appearance in Contemporary Art.* Jerusalem: The Israeli Museum, 1999, 15–19.

———. "Castration Fantasies, Sexual Difference, and Mind-Body Matters." In *Unconscious Fantasies and the Relational World,* edited by Danielle Knafo and Kenneth Feiner. Hillsdale, NJ: Analytic Press, 2005, 125–42.

Knafo, Danielle, and Kenneth Feiner. *Unconscious Fantasies and the Relational World.* Hillsdale, NJ: Analytic Press, 2005.

Kollwitz, Käthe and Hans Kollwitz. *Diary and Letters of Käthe Kollwitz.* Translated by Richard and Clara Winston. Evanston, IL: Northwestern University Press, 1988.

Kohut, Heinz. *The Analysis of the Self.* New York: International Universities Press, 1971.

Kohut, Heinz. *The Restoration of the Self.* New York: International Universities Press, 1977.

Kramer, Edith. *Childhood and Art Therapy.* New York: Schocken Books, 1979.

Krauss, Rosalind. *Cindy Sherman 1975–1993.* New York: Rizzoli, 1993.

Kristeva, Julia. *Powers of Horror: An Essay on Abjection.* Translated by L. Roudiez. New York: Columbia University Press, 1982.

Kuspit, Donald. "Adrian Piper: Self-Healing through Meta-Art." *Art Criticism* 3 (1987): 9–16.

———. "Inside Cindy Sherman." In *The New Subjectivism: Art in the 1980s.* Ann Arbor: U.M.I., 1991, 391–96.

Lacan, Jacques. [1949]. "The Mirror Stage as Formative of the Function of the I as Revealed in Psychoanalytic Experience." In *Ecrits,* trans. Alan Sheridan. New York: Norton, 1977, 93–100.

Larson, Kay. "Who's that Girl?" *New York Magazine,* August 3, 1987, 52–53.

Lasalle, Honor, and Abigail Solomon-Godeau. "Surrealist Confession: Claude Cahun's Photomontages." *Afterimage* 19, no. 8 (1992): 10–13.

Latimer, Tirza True. "Acting Out: Claude Cahun and Marcel Moore." In *Don't Kiss Me: The Art of Claude Cahun and Marcel Moore,* edited by Louise Downie. New York: Aperture and Jersey Heritage Trust, 2006, 56–71.

LePerlier, François. *Claude Cahun: L'Ecart et la Metamorphose.* Paris: Jean Michel Place, 1992.

———. "Claude Cahun: La Gravités des Apparances. "In *Rêve D'une Ville: Nantes et le Surrealisme,* edited by Henry-Claude Cousseau. Nantes: Musée des Beaux Arts, 1994, 263.

LeWitt, Sol. "Paragraphs on Conceptual Art." *Artforum* 5, no. 10 (1967): 79–83.

Lichtenstein, Heinz. "Narcissism and Primary Identity." In *The Dilemma of Human Identity.* New York: Aronson, 1977.

Lichtenstein, Therese. "A Mutable Mirror: Claude Cahun." *Artforum* 30, no. 8 (1992): 64–67.

———. *Behind Closed Doors: The Art of Hans Bellmer.* Berkeley: University of California Press, 2001.

Lichtenstein, Therese, and Cindy Sherman. "Cindy Sherman." *Journal of Contemporary Art,* http://www.jca-online.com/sherman.html.

Lieberman, Janice. *Body Talk: Looking and Being Looked At in Psychotherapy.* Northvale, NJ: Jason Aronson, 2000.

Lifton, Robert Jay. *The Future of Immortality and Other Essays for a Nuclear Age.* New York: Basic Books, 1987.

Lippard, Lucy. "Catalysis: An Interview with Adrian Piper." In *From the Center: Feminist Essays on Women's Art.* New York: Dutton, 1976, 167–71.

———. "The Pains and Pleasures of Rebirth: European and American Women's Body Art." In *From the Center: Feminist Essays on Women's Art.* New York: Dutton, 1976, 121–38.

———. *Mixed Blessings: Art in a Multicultural America.* New York: Pantheon, 1990.

———. *The Pink Glass: Selected Feminist Essays on Art.* New York: The New Press, 1995.

Loewald, Hans. "The Waning of the Oedipus Complex." In *Papers on Psychoanalysis.* New Haven: Yale University Press, 1980, 384–404.

Lovelace, Carey. "Orlan: Offensive Acts." *Performance Arts Journal* 49 (1995): 18.

Lowe, Sarah. “Essay.” In *The Diary of Frida Kahlo: An Intimate Self-Portrait.* New York: Harry Abrams, and Mexico: La Vaca Independiente S.A. de C.V., 1995, 25–29.

Mahler, Margaret. “Human Symbiosis and the Vicissitudes of Individuation.” In *Selected Papers of Margaret Mahler,* vol. 2. New York: Aronson, 1979, 77–97.

Mahler, Margaret, Fred Pine, and Anni Bergman. *The Psychological Birth of the Human Infant: Symbiosis and Individuation.* New York: Basic Books, 1975.

Marans, Steven, Linda Mayes, and Alice Colonna. “Psychoanalytic Views of Children's Play.” In *The Many Meanings of Play: A Psychoanalytic Perspective,* edited by Albert Solnit, Donald Cohen, and Peter Neubauer. New Haven: Yale University Press, 1993, 9–28.

Marzorati, Gerald. “Self-Possessed.” *Vanity Fair,* October 1985.

McClellan, Jim. “The Extensions of Women.” *Observer “Life” Magazine.* April 17, 1994.

McDougall, Joyce. *Plea for a Measure of Abnormality.* New York: Basic Books, 1980.

Mendieta, Ana. *Fuego de Tierra.* Directed by Kate Horsfield, Branda Miller, and Nereyda Garcia-Ferraz. VHS, 1987.

Mendieta, Raquelin. Personal interview, Jan. 11, 1996.

———. Personal interview, New York, Jan. 13, 1996.

Mereweather, Charles. “From Inscription to Dissolution: An Essay on Expenditure in the Work of Ana Mendieta.” In *Ana Mendieta,* edited by Gloria Moure. Barcelona: Ediciones Polígrafa, 1996, 83–134.

Meskimmon, Marsha. *The Art of Reflection: Women Artists' Self-Portraiture in the Twentieth Century.* New York: Columbia University Press, 1996.

Montane, Diana. “The Rise and Fall of TropicAna.” *Miami Herald Tropic,* Sept. 15, 1991, 8–21.

Montano, Linda. “An Interview with Ana Mendieta.” *Sulfur* 22 (1988): 67.

Moore, Nancy, Carolyn Everstson, and Jere Brophy. “Solitary Play: Some Functional Considerations.” *Developmental Psychology* 10, no. 6 (1974): 830–34.

Moure, Gloria. *Ana Mendieta.* Barcelona: Ediciones Polígrafa, 1996.

Mulvey, Laura. “Visual Pleasure and Narrative Cinema.” In *Visual and Other Pleasures (Theories of Representation and Difference).* Bloomington: Indiana University Press, 1989, 14–26.

———. “A Phantasmagoria of the Female Body: The Work of Cindy Sherman.” *New Left Review* 188 (1991): 136–51.

Mulvey, Laura, and Peter Wollen. *Frida Kahlo and Tina Modotti.* London: Whitechapel Art Gallery, 1982.

Nagel, Otto. *Käthe Kollwitz.* Old Greenwich, CT: New York Graphic Society, 1971.

Neubauer, Peter. “The Many Meanings of Play: Introduction.” *Psychoanalytic Study of the Child* 42 (1987): 3–10.

Niederland, William. “Narcissistic Ego Impairment in Patients with Early Physical Malformations.” *The Psychoanalytic Study of the Child* 20 (1965): 518–34.

Nochlin, Linda. “Why Have There Been No Great Women Artists?” In *Women, Art, and Power and Other Essays.* New York: Harper & Row, 1988, 145–78.

———. *Women, Art, and Power and Other Essays.* New York: Harper & Row, 1988.

Ogden, Thomas. “On Projective Identification.” *International Journal of Psycho-Analysis* 60 (1979): 357–73.

———. “The Analytic Third: Working with Intersubjective Clinical Facts.” In *Subjects of Analysis,* Northvale, NJ: Aronson, 1994, 61–96.

O'Bryan, Jill. *Carnal Art: Orlan's Refacing.* Minneapolis: University of Minnesota Press, 2005.

O'Grady, Lorraine. “Olympia's Maid: Reclaiming Black Female Subjectivity.” In *New Feminist Criticism: Art, Identity, Action,* edited by Joanna Frueh, Cassandra Langer, and Arlene Raven. New York: HarperCollins, 1994, 152–70.

Orenstein, Gloria Feman. “Recovering Her Story: Feminist Artists Reclaim the Great Goddess.” In *The Power of Feminist Art: The American Movement of the 1970s, History and Impact,* edited by Norma Broude and Mary Garrard. New York: Abrams, 1994, 174–89.

Orlan website. http://www.orlan.net.

Orlan. “Conférence.” In *This is My Body . . . This is My Software . . .* Translated by Tanya Augsburg and Michael A. Moos, edited by Duncan McCorquondale. London: Black Dog, 1996, 81–93.

Orlan, and Stéphane Place. “Sujet Objet.” In *Orlan: De l'Art Charnel au Baiser de l'Artiste.* Paris: Editions Jean-Michel Place, 1997, in side corner and 2–3.

Pacteau, Francette. *The Symptom of Beauty.* Cambridge: Harvard University Press, 1994.

Patraka, Vivian. “Binary Terror and Feminist Performance: Reading Both Ways.” *Discourse* 1, no. 2 (1992): 163–85.

Paul, Susan. “The Just Desserts: “Dinner Party,” Now Closed Draws Praise and Attack.” *The Phoenix* 12 (1981): 19.

Peller, Lili. “Libidinal Phases, Ego Development, and Play.” *Psychoanalytic Study of the Child* 9 (1954): 178–98.

Piper, Adrian. *Out of Order, Out of Sight, Vol. I. Selected Writings in Meta-Art 1968–1992.* Cambridge: MIT Press, 1996.

———. *Out of Order, Out of Sight, Vol. II. Selected Writings in Art Criticism 1967–1992.* Cambridge: MIT Press, 1996.

———. “On Wearing Three Hats.” Unpublished Draft, 1996.

Pollack, Griselda. *Vision and Difference: Femininity, Feminism, and the Histories of Art.* London: Routledge, 1988.

———. “Modernity and the Spaces of Femininity.” In *Vision and Difference.* London: Routledge, 1989, 50–90.

———. http://www.personalmd.com/news/a1996061806.shtml.

Prelinger, Elisabeth, ed. *Käthe Kollwitz.* New Haven: Yale University Press, 1992.

Rank, Otto. *The Trauma of Birth.* New York: Dover, 1924/93.

———. *Art and Artist*. New York: Agathon, 1932.

———. *The Double: A Psychoanalytic Study.* Translated and edited by Harry Tucker Jr. New York: New American Library, 1971.

Rauch, Heidi, and Federico Suro. "Ana Mendieta's Primal Scream." *Americas* 45, no. 4 (1992): 44.

Reich, Annie. *Psychoanalytic Contributions.* New York: International Universities Press, 1973.

Reilly, Maura, and Linda Nochlin. *Global Feminisms: New Directions in Contemporary Art.* London: Merrell, 2007.

Rice, Shelley. *Inverted Odysseys.* Cambridge: MIT Press, 1999.

Rivera, Diego. *My Art, My Life.* New York: Dover, 1991.

Rivière, Joan. "Womanliness as Masquerade." *International Journal of Psychoanalysis* 10 (1929): 303–13.

Rose, Gilbert. *Necessary Illusions: Art as "Witness."* New York: International Universities Press, 1995.

Rose, Tricia. "Rap Music and the Demonization of Young Black Males." In *Black Male: Representations of Black Masculinity in Contemporary American Art,* edited by Thelma Golden. New York: Abrams and the Whitney Museum, 1994, 149–58.

Rosemont, Penelope. *Surrealist Women: An International Anthology.* Austin: University of Texas Press, 1998.

Said, Edward. *Reflections on Exile.* Cambridge: MA: Harvard University Press, 2000.

Salomon, Charlotte. *Life or Theater? An Autobiographical Play by Charlotte Salomon.* Translated by Leila Vennewitz. New York: Viking, 1981.

Salomon, Nanette. "On the Impossibility of Charlotte Salomon in the Classroom." In *Reading Charlotte Salomon,* edited by Michael Steinberg and Monica Bohm-Duchen. Ithaca: Cornell University Press, 2006, 212–22.

Schafer, Claudia. *Textured Lives: Women, Art, and Representation of Modern Mexico.* Tucson: University of Arizona Press, 1992.

Schneemann, Carolee. *More than Just Performance: Works and Selected Writings,* edited by Bruce R. McPherson. Kingston, NY: McPherson, 1979.

———. *Up To and Including her Limits.* Compiled by Dan Cameron. The New Museum of Contemporary Art, New York, 1996.

———. *Imaging her Erotics.* Cambridge: MIT Press, 2002.

Segal, Hanna. *Introduction to the Work of Melanie Klein.* New York: Basic Books, 1964.

———. "Art and the Depressive Position." In *Dream, Phantasy and Art,* edited by Elizabeth Bott Spillius. London: Tavistock & Routledge, 1991, 85–100.

Selz, Peter. *German Expressionist Painting.* Berkeley: University of California Press, 1957.

Sherman, Cindy. *Cindy Sherman: The Complete Untitled Film Stills.* New York: The Museum of Modern Art, 2003.

———. "No Make-Up. An interview with Isabelle Graw." In *Cindy Sherman: Clowns.* Hannover: Schirmer/Mosel & Kestnergesellschaft, 2004, 53–60.

———. "Studio: Cindy Sherman" (Interview with Betsy Berne). In *Tate Magazine* 5, http://www.tate.org.uk/magazine/issue5/sherman.htm.

Siegel, Judy. "Between the Censor and the Muse? Hannah Wilke: Censoring the Muse?" *Women Artists News* 4 (1986): 46–48.

Singer, Jerome. "Affect and Imagination in Play and Fantasy." In *Emotions in Personality and Psychopathology,* edited by C. Izard. New York: Plenum, 1979, 13–34.

Spero, Nancy. "Tracing Ana Mendieta." *Artforum* 30 (1992): 75–77.

Spitz, René. *The First Year of Life.* New York: IUP, 1965.

Staniszewski, Mary Anne. "Race Against Time." In *Adrian Piper: PRETEND.* New York: John Weber Gallery, 1990.

Steinberg, Michael P., and Monica Bohm-Duchen. *Reading Charlotte Salomon.* Ithaca: Cornell University Press, 2006.

Steiner, Wendy. *Venus in Exile: The Rejection of Beauty in 20th Century Art.* New York and London: The Free Press, 2001.

Stevens, Mark. "How I Made It: Cindy Sherman on her 'Untitled Film Stills.' " *New York Magazine,* April 14, 2008, 78.

Stiles, Kristine. "Survival Ethos and Destruction in Art." *Discourse: Journal for Theoretical Studies in Media and Culture* 14 (1992): 74–102.

Stokes, Mark, director, McNab, Robert, producer. *Nobody's Here But Me* (documentary). Cinecontact Production for BBC and the Arts Council of England, 1994.

Townsend, Chris. *Francesca Woodman.* London: Phaidon, 2006.

Viso, Olga M. "Ana Mendieta, Earth Body: Sculpture and Performance, 1972–1985." Hirshhorn Museum and Sculpture Garden/Smithsonian Institute: Hatje Cantz Publisher, 2004.

Von Oehsen, Kristine. "The Lives of Claude Cahun and Marcel Moore." In *Don't Kiss Me: The Art of Claude Cahun and Marcel Moore,* edited by Louise Downie. New York: Aperture and Jersey Heritage Trust, 2006, 10–23.

VST: Revue Scientifique et Culturelle de Santé Mentale 23/24 (1991): 16. Issue devoted to Orlan.

Wallach, Amei. "Tough Times to Face." *Los Angeles Times,* June 7, 1992, 80.

Weldon, Estelle. *Mother, Madonna, Whore: The Idealization and Denigration of Motherhood.* New York: Guilford, 1988.

Wickenhaver, Janet. "Hannah Wilke Soho Artist does 'About Face.' " *The West Side Spirit* 1 (1989): 5.

Wilke, Hannah. "Intercourse with . . ." In *Hannah Wilke: A Retrospective,* edited by Thomas H. Kocheiser. Columbia: University of Missouri Press, 1976. Text used in videotape performance and lecture at the London Tate Gallery, London, Ontario, Canada, February 17, 1977; text originally written for Guggenheim Memorial Foundation Grant, 139.

———. "Intercourse with . . ." In *Übrigens Sterben Immer die Anderen,* edited by Alfred M. Fischer and Dieter Daniels. Cologne: Museum Ludwig, 1977, 226.

———. "Artist Hannah Wilke Talks with Ernst." *Oasis d'Neon*, v.1 (3). 1978. Branford, CT.

———. "Stand up" (1982). Words for song written and performed by Hannah Wilke for *Revolutions Per Minute: The Art Record.* Ronald Feldman Fine Art and Charing Cross Co.

———. "Seura Haya." *New Observations* 58 (1988): 13.

———. "I OBJECT. Memoirs of a Sugargiver (Edition Coup de Couteau)." In *Hannah Wilke: A Retrospective,* edited by Thomas H. Kochheiser. Columbia: University of Missouri Press, 1989, 143–49.

Williams, Addette. "Skin Color in Psychotherapy." In *Reaching Across Boundaries of Culture and Class,* edited by Rose Marie Perez Foster, Michael Moskowitz, and Rafael Art. Javier. Northvale, NJ: Aronson, 1996, 211–24.

Winnicott, Donald Woods. "Transitional Objects and Transitional Phenomena." *International Journal of Psycho-Analysis* 34 (1953): 89–97.

———. "Ego Distortion in terms of True and False Self." In *The Maturational Processes and the Facilitating Environment.* New York: International Universities Press, 1965.

———. "Mirror-Role of Mother and Family in Child Development." In *Playing and Reality.* London: Tavistock, 1971, 111–18.

———. *Playing and Reality.* London: Tavistock, 1971.

Wolf, Naomi. *The Beauty Myth: How Images of Beauty Are Used Against Women.* New York: Anchor, 1991.

Young-Bruehl, Elisabeth. *The Anatomy of Prejudices.* Cambridge: Harvard University Press, 1996.

Zavitzianos, George. "Homeovestism: Perverse Form of Behavior Involving the Wearing of Clothes of the Same Sex." *International Journal of Psycho-Analysis* 53 (1972): 471–77.

———. "The Object in Fetishism, Homeovestism and Transvestism." *International Journal of Psycho-Analysis* 58 (1977): 487–95.

Index

abandonment, 76, 109
abject, 150, 161. *See also* Kristeva, Julia
Abramovic, Marina, 89
Adams, Alice, 178 n. 2

Adorno, Theodor, 130; *Minima Moralia: Reflections on a Damaged Life*, 130
affirmative action, 136
Afrocentrism, 138
alienation, 163, 169
alter ego, 61, 68, 80, 87, 99, 141
Andre, Carl, 121, 132
androgyne, 37
androgynous, 68, 104, 171
androgyny, 159
Anguissola, Sofinisba, 15, 176 n. 32
anorexia, 41
Anti-semitism, 37, 39, 45, 70
Antoni, Janine, 89, 104
Anzieu, Didieu, 90
Apraxine, Pierre and Demange, Xavier, 176 n. 1
Aragon, Louis and Breton, André, 177 n. 24
archeology, 125
Arlow, Jacob, 183 n. 32
art: feminist, 53, 59, 69, 72; history of, 18; self-representational, 16, 18; women's, 18
art-making, 21, 127, 131
art objects, 69, 121
art of multiple selves, the, 56
artistic transference, 48
Artuad, Antonin, 167; *Theater of Cruelty*, 167
Ashton, Lyle, 57
attachment, 120
Auschwitz, 58, 60, 70, 72, 172. *See* Salomon, Charlotte
autonomy, 107, 110
Ayers, Robert, 185 nn. 23, 57, and 58

Bach, Sheldon, 184 n. 49
Barbie doll, 154
Barreras del Rio, Petra and Perrault, John, 181 n. 17
Baldwin, James, 141
Barnes, Djuna, 41
Barney, Matthew, 57, 104
Bataille, Georges, 42; theory of the *informe*, 42, 55
Beach, Sylvia, 39
Beauvoir, Simone de, 96
Beebe, Beatrice and Stern, Daniel, 181 n. 20
Bellmer, Hans, 42, 55, 154; *Die (La) Poupée*, 42, 55, 154; *Unica*, 42
Bemelman, Ludwig, 63; *Madeline*, 63
Benglis, Lynda, 112
Benjamin, Jessica, 18, 151
Benjamin, Walter, 53, 178 n. 14
Berger, John, 15, 100, 184 n. 15
Berger, Maurice, 182 n. 21, 182 n. 28
Bergman, Anni, 110
Berlin Academy of Art, 60, 70
Bernstein, Doris, 153
Bettleheim, Bruno. 149
Beuys, Josef, 112
Bhabha, Homi, 137
Billeter, Erika, 178 n. 9
Bion, Wilfred Ruprecht, 140
birth, 80, 102, 104, 109, 158, 161; -death, 22; imagery, 19; process, 158
black: female, 133; female body, 134; female subjectivity, 140; female visibility, 135; identity, 136; invisibility, 134; maid, 133; masculinity, 141; pride, 138; servant, 133, 134; woman, 22, 133, 134, 173
Bloker, Jane, 181 nn. 19 and 41
blood, 78–80, 83–84, 89, 92, 98, 120, 125, 161, 169
bodily: defect, 83; damage, 83
body, 73, 74, 79, 80, 87–89, 91, 97, 101, 102, 104, 107, 109, 114, 121, 124, 125, 127, 132, 144, 153, 168, 171; -art, 22, 121, 128; -art-making, 125; broken-, 84, damaged-, 73; female, 84; -fragmentation, 76; fragmented-, 86; imagery, 93, inferior, 84; integrity, 153; male-, 85; naked-, 93, 126, 154; naked female-, 125, woman's-, 85, 104
body dysmorphic disorder, 160, 169
Boiffard, Jacques-André, 42
Bollas, Christopher, 21
Bonaparte, Marie, 185 n. 44
Bourgeois, Louise, 162, 179 n. 4
Brand, Peg Zeglin, 184 nn. 4 and 14, 185 n. 51
Bravo, Lola Alvarez, 87
Breder, Hans, 19, 121, 124, 125
Breton, André, 41, 42, 46, 55, 56, 87. *See also* Surrealism
Brett, Guy, 181 n. 30
Bride of Frankenstein, 162
Brothers Grimm, the, 149
Brooks, Adams, 184 n. 40
Buber, Martin, 138
Buerkle, Darcy, 66
Butler, Judith, 37, 39, 56, 129, 182 n. 24
Butter, Selma (Hannah Wilke's mother), 113

Cage, John, 94
Cahun, Claude: 18, 19, 22, 37–57, 72, 76, 120, 134, 135, 146, 159, 171, 172; Claude Courlis, 37, 45; Daniel Douglas, 37, 45; death of, 56; Jersey Resistance, 55–56, masquerade, 54–55; and the mirror, 51–54;

Cahun, Claude (*continued*)
Paris and Surrealism, 41–45; self-creation, 45–46; the uncanny double, 46–51. *See also* Schwob, Lucy
—Works of: *Aveux non Avenus* (autobiography-Disavowed Confessions), 46, 53–56; *Le Chemin des Chats,* 56; *Le Père* (The Father), 45; *Poupée,* 55; *Que me veux-tu?,* 49; *Self Pride (IOU),* 39–41, 54
Cahun, George, 41
Cahun, Leon, 45
Calderon, Mathilde (Frida Kahlo's mother), 74
Cannes Film Festival, 94
Caravaggio, Michelangelo Merisi da, 152
Carnal Art, 160, 168. *See also* Orlan
Carriera, Rosalba, 176 n. 32
Castiglione, Countess de, 16
castration, 78, 83–84, 158, 160, 161, 163, 165–67, 172: anxiety, 162, 165, 169; fantasies, 160; female, 169; final-, 87; male, 39; symbolic-, 84
Castro, Fidel, 120, 129
catharsis, 147
Catholicism, 21, 39, 74, 126–27, 163
Chadwick, Whitney, 18, 176 n. 2
Chagall, Marc, 61
Charcot, Jean-Martin: 46, 164; *Salpetrière,* 46
Chicago, Judy, 83, 112; *Dinner Party,* 112; *Menstruation Bathroom,* 83; *Red Flag,* 83
Chodorow, Nancy, 18
Christ, Jesus, 28, 67, 110–11, 125
Christian, 125; iconography, 28, 168
Civil Rights Movement, 133
Cixous, Helene, 91, 129
Clark, Kenneth: 15; *The Nude,* 15
Clearwater, Bonnie, 180 nn. 9 and 11, 181 nn. 34, 35, and 40
clitorectomy, 97, 107
Cocteau, Jean, 55; *enfants terribles,* 55
Cohen, Matthew, 183 nn. 31 and 33
Cole, Julie, 176 n. 14, 177 n. 31
Collins, Glenn, 184 nn. 39 and 56
Comini, Alessandra, 175 n. 7, 176 n. 9
Communism, 74, 83
Conley, Christine, 177 n. 3
Conrad, Joseph, 130
Constructionism, 22, 129
container(s): 140; -of earth, 126; -of isolation, 124
containment, 19, 76, 139, 152
"convulsive beauty," 46
Cordry, Donald, 178 n. 18
cosmetic: artwork, 168; surgery, 22, 107, 135, 157, 161, 169
Côte d'Azur, 60, 61
Cottingham, Laura, 18, 180 n. 35, 181 n. 3
Courbelaise, Marie-Antoinette (Claude Cahun's mother), 39
Courbet, Gustav: 79, 165; *L'Origine du Monde,* 79, 165
creation, 69, 70, 96, 118, 123, 125, 128, 133, 140, 142, 158, 160
creative, 21, 90, 91, 93, 103, 128, 169; equity, 96; history, 96; process, 21, 89, 94, 95, 123
creativity, 18–20, 22, 45, 58, 66, 69, 70, 80, 86, 145, 159, 172; artistic, 30–33; inhibition of, 33
creator, 22, 106, 165
Creed, Barbara, 183 n. 27
cross-dressing, 56
cross-sexual, 141
Cuba, 118, 124, 127, 129, 131
"cunt-positive art," 102
"cunt-positiveness," 103
cyber space, 161, 163
cybernetics, 162

da Vinci, Leonardo, 159, 165; *Mona Lisa,* 159, 165. *See also* Orlan
Dali, Salvador, 42
Damon, Betsy, 128
Danto, Arthur, 143; *After the End of Art,* 143
David (Michelangelo), 152
Day of the Dead, 125
dead, 60, 114, 125; bird, 83; child, 24, 27, 28; children, 30; dread of, 31; girl, 24, grandson, 24, 31, 32; psychically, 30; siblings, 24, 30; son, 24, 31, 32; tree stump, 83
"dead mother," 24, 28–33, 35, 36, 79. *See* Green, André
death, 21, 35, 69, 70, 78, 85, 87, 88, 95, 106, 114, 115, 118, 125, 132, 150, 151, 161, 163, 173; -drive, 122; object, 150; premature-, 22; ship, 83; wish, 163
defense mechanism, 140
DeKerchove, Derrick, 163
De Maria, Walter, 122
Delvaux, Paul, 42
DeMaria, Walter, 122
depression, 27, 30, 85
Derrida, Jacques, 169, 185 n. 60
Deutsch, Helena, 185 n. 44
Dhal, Kirsten, 183 n. 6
Diehl, Carol, 116
Dimen, Muriel, 18
Dinnerstein, Dorothy, 18
Dix, Otto, 25
doppelgänger, 51
double, 48, 51, 57, 78, 80, 87; -entendre, 93, 109; -images, 78; play, 111; portrait, 113; -self-portraits, 48, 49; -is uncanny, 48
Drancy, 60, 72
dream, 90, 93–95, 97–99; -content, 93; -drawings, 92; menstrual dream, 98; -notes, 92
"dressing up games," 147. *See also* Sherman, Cindy
Dreyfus Affair, 41
duality, 136
DuBois, W.E.B., 141
Duchamp, Marcel, 45, 104, 109, 114, 131, 160; *Etant Donnés,* 109, 131, 160; *Large Glass,* 109; Levy, 45; marchand du sel, 109; Sélavy, Rrose, 45
Dürer, Albrecht, 15

earth, 126, 128, 131, 132, 173; art, 19, 22, 173; works, 121, 122, 129
Edelson, Mary Beth, 122, 128
ego, 64, 90, 124, 145, 149; body ego, 28, 90, 131; pleasure ego, 91
Ellis, Havelock, 45
Erikson, Erik, 150, 156, 183 nn. 1 and 10
Ernst, Max, 42
Eros, 95, 102, 122, 159; and Thanatos, 95
erotic: 89, 90, 92–94; objectification, 105
Erro, 90
Essentialism, 22
Eurydice, 68

exhibitionism, 22, 90, 94, 117
exile, 118, 120, 126, 128, 130, 132, 173; and loss, 127; pain of, 127; self-imposed, 125; tragedy of, 124
Expressionism, 21, 24, 25, 111, 171; Artists, 24, movement, 24
—Groups: *Der Blaue Reiter,* 25; *Die Brücke,* 25
ex-voto, 79

family romance, 39, 61, 125, 152, 156, 165
Fanon, Franz: 133, 135, 137, 138, 141; "lactified," 135
Fast, Irene, 56, 153, 184 n. 12, 185 n. 38
Father, the, 19, 45–46, 109, 147
Fein, Greta, 184 n. 55
Felstiner, Mary Lowenthal, 66, 177 n. 1, 178 nn. 8, 10, 13, 16, 19, 20, and 29
female, 25, 45, 91, 99, 100, 104, 131; archetypes, 127; artist, 17; body, 15, 17, 18, 25, 42, 92, 93, 98, 100, 102–4, 109, 117, 123, 131, 147, 151, 162, 164, 169, 172–74, beauty, 157; bonding, 157; creativity, 165; development, 18, 102, 169, empowerment, 161; experience, 22, 104, 171; generativity, 161; genital sexuality, 90; genitalia, 96, 98, 102, 103; genitals, 83, 102, 161, 165; iconography, 104; identity, 18, 22, 56, 145, 147, 173; "inner space," 102; life, 17, 174; martyr, 84; narcissism, 21; narcissism and exhibitionism, 173; nude, 100; pain, 86, pleasure, 93; power, 112, 157; pronouns, 96; psyche, 18; representation, 25, 116, self representation, 15, 18, 21, 22; self-representational art, 171; sensual pleasure, 89; sex, 97, 128; sexual pleasure, 91; sexuality, 96, 102; torso, 42; vanity, 42
feminine: -body, 115; -dress, 85; experience, 103; -forms, 127; glorification of, 28; iconography, 25; identity, 146; interior, 171; mythology, 18; roles, 151; self, 85
feminine, 16, 37, 39, 42, 55, 73, 79, 85, 129, 147, 148, 150, 156, 127
femininity, 21, 46, 54, 74, 78, 84, 104, 146, 147, 158, 162, 165, 173; as masquerade, 146, Mexican-, 76
feminism, 18, 95, 96, 112, 145, 146, 171, 173; white-, 130
feminist, 105, 130, 131, 134, 146, 158; art, 102, 112; artists, 57, 95, 110; -awareness, 111; "body art," 172; constructivist semiotics, 98; critics, 151; critique, 18, 161, icon, 73; issues, 96; movement, 122, 133, 162, 172; pre-, 96; performance art, 96, 172; performance artists, 104, 128; scholars, 96; thinkers, 18
feminists, 27, 90, 91, 102, 104, 105, 109, 129, 145, 162, 173; art projects: 53; *Woman House,* 53.
Ferenczi, Sandor, 181 n. 46
film noir genre, 146
Finley, Karen, 89, 100, 104
Follaine, Claire, 177 n. 50
fragmentation, 69, 151
Frank, Anne (*The Diary of-*), 69
Freud, Anna, 79, 179 n. 33, 183 n. 15
Freud, Sigmund, 18, 21, 24, 25, 41, 46, 48, 53, 56, 64, 76, 89–91, 95–98, 102, 122–25, 131, 152, 157, 160–62, 164, 166, 171, 172, 174, 183 n. 9; the castrated woman, 162; castration theory, 174; "The Dark Continent," 131; *fort-da game,* 123, 152; "The Head of Medusa," 160; *Interpretation of Dreams,* 41, "little men," 172; *oceanic feeling,*123; pleasure ego, 172; *repetition compulsion,* 123; "secondary revision," 64; theory of sexual development, 172
Fried, Nancy, 180 n. 52
Frueh, Joanna, 103, 162, 176 n. 36, 179 n. 1, 180 nn. 18, 19, 20, 22, 26, 28, 33, and 50
Fuku, Noriko, 183 n. 35, 184 n. 43
Fusco, Coco, 181 n. 27

Gale, David, 185 n. 28
Garber, Marjorie, 45, 129
Gauguin, Paul, 28.
Gay Rights Movement, 133
gaze, 25, 37, 51, 53, 75, 80, 103, 105, 113, 115, 137, 147, 148, 151, 174; the female-, 22, male-, 20, 104, 106, 107, 125, 147; voyeuristic-, 133; a woman's, 42
gender, 21, 22, 37, 39, 42, 56, 90, 97, 104, 111, 131, 152, 153, 156, 158, 169, 171, 173, 174; bending, 39, 56; difference, 42, 156, 160, 161; and ethnic stereotype, 22, identity, 37, 156, 163, 172; integration, 96; limitation, 107, 163; politics,157, psychological-, 18; roles, 54; as a social construct, 129; stereotypes, 173, theoretical-, 18
Gilligan, Carol, 129
Gilmore, Jane Ellen, 128
Goddard, Donald, 19, 105, 106, 109, 115–17, 146, 179 n. 7, 180 nn. 25 and 38
Goddess, 128–30, 132; Mayan, 128; movement, the-, 128, 129, 173; Tainan-, 129; Venus-, 130
Goethe, Johann Wolfgang von, 31
Golden, Thelma, 141
Goldin, Nan, 162
Goldman, Saundra, 179 n. 11–14, 180 nn. 39, 44, 47, 48, 49, 51, 53, and 55
Goldner, Virginia, 18
"good enough mothering," 19. *See also* Winnicott, Donald Woods
Goode, Tabitha, 183 n. 27
Goya, Francisco, 152
Green, André, 24, 30; *"The Dead Mother,"* 30. *See also* Kollwitz, Käthe
Greenacre, Phyllis, 178 n. 26
Grinberg, Leon, 182 n. 41
Grosz, George, 25
Gurs (French Transit camp), 67, 69, 71

Hall, Stuart, 137
Hamilton, Richard, 19, 102, 106, 109
Harris, Adrienne, 17, 18
Hatoum, Mona, 162
Hauptmann, Gerhart, 27
Heimann, Paula, 182 n. 41
Heizer, Micheal, 122
Heresies, 130
hermaphrodite, 51, 144, 153
Herrera, Hayden, 19, 178 n. 3–7, 178 n. 10, 178 n. 16, 178 n. 19, 178 n. 21–22, 179 nn. 24, 28–31, 35, 37, and 38, 181 n. 48
Herzberg, Judith, 177 n. 2, 177 n. 5, 178 n. 17
Herzberg, Julia Ann, 180 n. 4, 181 n. 31
Hitchcock, Alfred, 146
Hitler, Adolf, 60
Hoch, Hannah, 53
Holbein, Hans, 152
holding environment, 64

Holocaust, 70, 111
homeland, 121, 123, 131
homo: erotism, 41; phobia, 37, 42; sexuality, 56
hooks, bell (a.k.a. Gloria Jean Watkins) and West, Cornel, 142
Hopper, Edward, 146
Horton, Anne, 178 n. 2
Höss, Rudolf (ruler of Sachsenhausen), 71
human psyche, 24, 42
hysteria, 19, 46, 74, 164, 167

id, 89
ideal: beauty, 159; body, 94
idealization, 65, 153, 155
identification, 75, 124, 130
identity, 21, 22, 37, 39, 42, 45, 51, 56, 72, 133, 144, 151, 152, 156, 158, 164–67, 169, 172–74; androgynous, 141; male-, 141; mythological-, 74; personal-, 111, 120; psychological, 147; transformation, 158
illness: 102, 114, 167, 173; life-threatening-, 171; physical, 164
Imber-Black, Evan, 178 n. 12
immortality, 158, 163
Ince, Kate, 169, 185 nn. 31, 41, and 59; "millennial female," 169
incest, 41
infidelity, 73, 121, 172
Ingres, Jean-Auguste-Dominique, 152
inner space, 19, 39, 102, 148
intimacy, 41, 154
invisibility, 33, 36
Irigaray, Luce, 15, 91, 102, 129

Jackson, Michael, 135
Jacob, Mary Jane, 181 n. 33
Janson, H. W., 15; *The History of Art*, 15
Jawlensky, Alexej, 175 n. 5
Jersey Resistance, 37
Jesus Christ Super Star, 107
Jew(s), 60, 61, 69, 70–72
Jewish: 39, 45, 66, 70; contamination, 70; identity, 72
Jewishness, 37, 55, 111
Johnson, Ken, 143
Jones, Amelia, 114, 179 nn. 6 and 9, 180 nn. 17, 25, 34, and 45, 182 nn. 13 and 36
Jones, Marvin, 179 nn. 2, 3, and 15, 180 nn. 37 and 41
Joyce, James, 96, 130
Jung, Carl G., 142; animus, 142

Kabbalah, 70; *Tikkun Olam*, 70
Kaddish, 60
Kafka, Franz, 96
Kahlo, Frida: 18–20, 22, 57, 73–88, 121, 125, 131, 132, 134, 135, 146, 147, 158, 164, 165, 172, 173; "ancient concealer," 78–84; "daughter of the revolution," 74; death of, 87–88; the heroic sufferer, 79; "martyr" works, 132; and the mirror, 74–78
—Works of: *The Broken Column*, 80, 81, 84, 86; *The Deer*, 80, 84; *Diego and Frida*, 84; *Diego on My Mind*, 82; *The Dream*, 87; *A Few Small Nips*, 131; *Henry Ford Hospital*, 84; *The Little Deer*, 86; *Little Girl with Death Mask*, 78; *The Love Embrace of the Universe, the Earth (Mexico), Diego, Me and Seòor Xolotl*, 86, *My Birth*, 76, 79, 80, 85, 86, 158, 165; *My Dress Hangs There*, 85; *My Grandparents, My Parents and I*, 79; *My Nurse and I*, 74, 75, 76, 79, 86; *Remembrance*, 83; *Roots*, 87; *Ruina*, 84; *Self-Portrait with Cropped Hair*, 84, *Self-Portrait as Tehuana*, 79, 86; *Thinking of Death*, 85; *Tree of Hope*, 83; *Tree of Life, Stand Firm*, 85; *The Two Fridas*, 77, 78, 83; *What the Water Gave Me*, 82–84; *Without Hope*, 85
Kahlo, Guillermo, 74
Kaiser Wilhelm II, 27
Kant, Immanuel, 134; *Critique of Pure Reason*, 134
Kaplan, Louise, 179 n. 33, 183 n. 16
Katz, Robert, 180 nn. 3 and 10, 181 n. 50
Kauffman, Angelica, 15
Kauffman, Linda S., 167, 185 n. 52
Kearns, Martha, 175 nn. 4 and 6, 176 nn. 28 and 29
Kelly, Mary, 35; *Interim*, 36
Kerckhove, Derrick de, 163
Kirchner, E. L., 24
Kleeblatt, Norman, 180 n. 29
Klein, Melanie: 30, 70, 131, 140; the depressive position, 70
Klein, Yves, 104
Klimt, Gustav, 28
Kline, Katy, 177 n. 56
Klinger, Max, 27
Knafo, Danielle: 175 n. 3, 177 n. 37, 178 n. 15, 183 n. 16, 183 n. 20, 184 n. 12, 185 n. 30; and Kenneth Feiner, 178 n. 9, 184 nn. 38 and 9 (chap. 10)
Kohut, Heinz, 48, 53, 77, 185 n. 25
Kokoshka, Oskar, 24
Kollwitz, Hans, 24, 176 n. 26
Kollwitz, Karl, 19, 30
Kollwitz, Käthe: 18, 19, 22, 24–36, 48, 68, 70, 76, 113, 142, 171; aging and death, 33–36, and Expressionism, 24–25; motherhood, 27–28; Social Realism, 25–27. *See Also* dead mother
—Works of: *Attack*, 27; *Call of Death*, 35; *Carmagnole*, 27; *Death Series*, 35, *Death, Mother and Child*, 28; *The Mothers*, 28, 31; *Pieta*, 28; *Poverty*, 27, 28, *Protecting Mother*, 31; *Run Over*, 28; *The Sacrifice*, 31; *Seed for the Planting Must not be Ground*, 31; *The Sick Child*, 27; *Self Portrait*, 33; *Self-Portrait on the Balcony*, 33; *Self-Portrait with Karl Kollowitz*, 30; *Self Portrait en face, Laughing*, 33; *Self-Portrait in Profile Facing Right*, 35; *Self Portrait Seated at Table*, 35; *Tower of Mothers*, 31; *Unemployment*, 28; *War*, 30, 31; *Weaver's Revolt*, 27; *Woman with Dead Child*, 28; *Woman Lost in Thought*, 33; *Young Couple*, 30
Kollwitz, Peter, 28, 32
Koons, Jeff, 153
Kozlov, Christine, 134
Kristallnacht, 71
Kristeva, Julia,150, 161, 176 n. 21, 180 n. 43; abject body, 161; concept of abjection, 150, 161; *Powers of Horror*, 161
Kramer, Edith, 183 n. 7
Krauss, Rosalind, 183 n. 4
Kulturbund, 60, 61, 70
Kuspit, Donald, 139, 151

Lacan, Jacques, 51, 54, 56, 76, 96, 97, 167; "the mirror phase," 51, 76; *le corps morcelé*, 76, 167
"land artists," 121

Landsman, Stanley, 106
Larson, Kay, 183 n. 3
LaSalle, Honor and Solomon-Godeau, Abigail, 177 n. 38
Latimer, Tirza True, 177 n. 40
Le Perlier, Francois, 176 nn. 7, 8, 9, 12, and 22, 177 n. 27
Lemoine-Luccioni, Eugene, 160, 161; *La Robe*, 160
lesbian, 18, 37, 41
LeWitt, Sol, 134
Lichtenstein, Heinz, 177 n. 32
Lichtenstein, Therese, 177 nn. 41, 48, 52, 53, and 54; and Cindy Sherman, 184 n. 48
Lifton, Robert J., 70
Lindberg, Paula, 60. *See also* Salomon, Charlotte
Lippard, Lucy, 18, 104, 112, 135, 182 n. 27
Longo, Robert, 19, 147
Lovelace, Carey, 185 n. 45
Lowe, Sarah M., 179 n. 25
Ludwig Museum, 109

"mad woman," 46
madness, 80, 172
Madonna, 28, 67, 86, 115, 152, 153; -of Sorrows, 84
Magdalene, Mary, 107
Magritte, René, 42
Mahler, Margaret: 51, 110, 131; *milieu interieur*, 131
male, 91; artists, 21, 96; gaze, 15, 19, 161; phallus, 165
Malherbe, Suzanne (a.k.a. Moore, Marcel), 41, 42, 51
Mammen, Jeanne, 27
Manchot, Melanie, 113
Manet, Edouard, 16, 133; *Olympia*, 16, 133
Mann, Thomas, 27, 96
Mapplethorpe, Robert, 153
Marans, Steven, Mayes, Linda, and Colonna, Alice, 184 n. 57
Marcuse, Herbert, 130
Marx, Karl, 74, 83, 110
martyr, 84, 88, 107, 111, 164; martyrdom: 126, 132, 164, 168; religious-, 163
Marzorati, Gerald, 183 n. 25
masculine, 53, 55, 84, 85; gaze, 134
masculinity, 46, 84, 85; gay-, 100
mask, 37, 39, 41, 54, 56, 73, 74, 76, 78–80, 83, 85, 144, 166, 171, 172; of iron, 75; steel-, 76; -of pain, 80; masking, 93
masochism, 167; masochistic, 167–69
masquerade, 22, 39, 54–57, 85, 148, 171, 172
"mater dolorosa," 76, 84. *See also* Kahlo, Frida
mastery, 84, 130, 153, 156, 165
maternal, 45, 46, 161; body, 48; bonding, 131; care, 18; depression, 30, 31, 76; failure, 74; figure(s), 127, 153; function, 78; identification, 80; -images, 76; loss, 118, mirroring, 134; -objects, 76; universe, 76; vessel, 128
maternidad, la, 79
maternity, 28, 33, 173
Matuschka, 85, 180 n. 52
McCombe, Maedbhina, 108; *Clitoris Allsorts*, 108; *Appetites*, 108
McDougall, Joyce, 163
McClellan, Jim, 185 n. 54
medical: technology, 158; objectification, 164
Medusa: 161, 162, 166, 167; Pegasus and Chrysaor, the Golden Child, 161; Project, 169
Meidner, Ludwig, 30
Mendieta, Ana: 18–20, 22, 48, 83, 88, 89, 118–32, 146, 160, 173; death of, 121, 132, exile, 130–31; goddess, 128–30; Mother Earth, 121–24; Siluetas, 124–28, violence against women, 131–32
—Works of: *Anima, Silueta de Cohetes*, 132; *Blood Writing*, 132; *Burial Pyramid*, 122; *Fetish* Series, 118; "fireworks *Silueta*," 132; *First Woman*, 130, *Old Mother Blood*, 130; *On Giving Life*, 122, 123; *Mother*, 130; *Mother of Waters*, 130; *Rape Pieces*, 83, 131; *Siluetas Series*, 48, 83, 124–28; *Untitled*, 119, 124, 127; *Untitled (1980)*, 129; *Venus Negra*, 130
Mendieta, Carlos, 120
Mendieta, Ignacio, 120, 124
Mendieta Harrison, Raquelin (Ana Mendieta's older sister), 19, 120, 180 nn. 1 and 22
menstruation: 78, 83, 161; -leaves, 99
mental: breakdown, 39; illness, 41, 46, 163
Mereweather, Charles, 181 n. 29
Meskimonn, Marsha, 16
metamorphosis, 54, 158
Mexican: Communist Party, 88; folk art, 74; iconography, 125; Mexican Revolution, 74; *Mexicanidad*, 79
Mickey Mouse, 104, 109. *See also* Oldenburg, Claes
mind-body theater, 158
Minimalism, 89
mirror: 19–21, 42, 51, 53, 73, 74, 76–78, 83, 111, 112, 114, 124, 134, 137, 144, 151, 160, 161, 165, 171, 172; of death, 151; image, 87; reflection, 37
"mirror phase, the," 51. *See* Lacan, Jacques
mirroring, 19, 51, 53, 74–78, 134, 137, 144, 161, 166, 169, 171–72, 174; faulty-, 76, inadequate-, 151
miscarriage, 79, 83, 84, 172
miscegenation, 137
mise en scène, 54, 154
Modersohn-Becker, Paula, 28
Monnier, Adrienne, 41
"monster beauty," 162, 169, 171. *See also* Orlan
Montane, Diana, 180 n. 5
Montano, Linda, 181 n. 15
Moore, Marcel, 42, 48, 51, 53, 55, 56, 120. *See also* Malherbe, Suzanne
Moore, Nancy, Everston, Carolyn, and Brophy, Jere, 184 n. 55
Moridis, Georges, 58
Morimora, Yasuma, 57
Mother, 19, 24–36, 98, 110, 111, 112, 117, 118, 124, 128, 131, 132, 140, 142, 153, 158, 164, 165, 171, 173; archetypal, 130; and child, 76, 79, 142, 145, 152; -child relationship, 18, 33, 76–77, 79, 128; creator versus mother destroyer, 78; "dead," 24, 30, 31; earth, 19, 48, 86, 113, 118, 121, 123, 125; goddess, 130; "great," 128; grieving, 27, 30, 33, 68, 79, 142; -hood, 19, 27, 28, 46, 80, 84, 86, 113, identification with the-, 18; -infant dyad, 78; land, 61, 130, 173; lost, 33; mad, 46; masks of, 76; nature, 123, 128; nurturing, 76; "symbolic," 75; as universal mirror, 79; and infant: 124; bond, 124; dyad, 124; merger, 124; mother's: bosom, 126; role, 18; womb, 123;
mourning; 124; process, 163, 173
Mulvey, Laura: 15, 183 nn. 5 and 23, 184 n. 15; and Wollen, Peter, 178 n. 2
Munch, Edvard, 27, 55, 61
—Works of: *The Sick Child*, 27; *Vampire*, 28

Münter, Gabriele, 25, 175 n. 5
murder, 132
Musée S. Ludwig, 160
mutilation, 160
mutuality, 124
mythology, 55, 149

Nagel, Otto, 176 n. 23
Nagler, Alexander, 72
naked body, 80, 83, 93, 102, 104, 111, 154, 165, 172
narcissism, 21, 22, 42, 48, 74, 77, 111–13, 115, 163
narcissistic: 90, 94, 104, 116, 155, 156; completion, 165; injury, 20, 147; loss, 165; -type love, 21
Nazi(s): 33, 55, 56, 67, 69, 71, 111; invasion, 58; oppression, 58; persecution, 58
NEA (National Endowment for the Arts), 153
Neel, Alice, 36
Neubauer, Peter, 184 n. 58
New York City, 90, 107, 110, 112, 121, 134, 144, 147
New York School of Visual Arts, 136
New York Times, the, 141
Niederland, William, 179 n. 32
Nietzsche, Friedrich, 130; *The Gay Science,* 130
Nitsch, Hermann, 126
Nochlin, Linda, 18, 19
Noggle, Ann, 36; *Face Lift,* 36
Noguchi, Isamu, 74
nude: body, 94; female, 94; female performance art, 89
nudity, 104–5, 111

object: 108, 109, 112, 123, 133, 134, 137, 145; -based art, 134; lost, 124; relational matrix, 18; relations, 156; relations theory, 173; relationships, 164
objet d'art, 174
objectification, 21
O'Bryan, Jill, 158n2, 184 n. 6
Oedipal: 20; complex, 68; drama, 39; father, 131; guilt, 149; search, 121; tension, 65, triangle, 20, 68
Ogden, Thomas, 45, 182 n. 41
O'Grady, Lorraine, 181 n. 4 and 5, 134, 140
Oldenburg, Claes: 105–7, 109, 110, 112, 113; *Upside Down City,* 105
Oppenheim, Meret, 104; *Spring Feast,* 104
Orenstein, Gloria Feman, 180 n. 13, 181 n. 38
orgasm, 91–92
Orlan, 18, 19, 22, 46, 83, 107, 130, 131, 152, 157–70, 174; "Carnal Art," 160; and beauty, 159, 168; Dionysian "horns," 159; living work of art, 157; *Manifesto,* 161; Medusa and Castration, 160; Mireille Porte, 163, 165; monster Beauty, 161–63; and Stephane Place, 184 n. 3; pain, 167–69; *sacré monstre,* 162, self-creation, 158–60; "sick child," 164; theatricality of surgery, 158
—Works of: *Documentary Study: The Head of Medusa,* 131, 160; *Entre-Deux,* 160; *L'Origine de la Guerre* [The Origin of War], 165; *Mésurages,* 168, *Omnipresence,* 163–65; *Orlan accouche d'elle m'aime,* 158, 159; *The Reincarnation of Sainte Orlan,* 158, 161, 163, 168; *Self-Hybridizations,* 163; *This is my body . . . This is my software,* 163; *Woman with Head . . . Woman without Head,* 166
orphan, 125; -hood, 130; orphanage, 121
Orpheus, 68
other, 134, 136, 151
otherness, 136
Other, the, 49, 53; the mad, 46

Pacteau, Francette, 162
pain, 74–76, 78, 80, 82–85, 87, 112, 114, 118, 121, 161, 167–70, 172, 174; emotional, 113, 114, 169; physical, 81, 114, 167
Pandora's Box, 53, 89
Paris, 41, 51, 55–56, 72, 93
Patraka, Vivian, 167; "binary terror," 167
patriarchy, 160
Paul, Susan, 180 n. 36
Paula Cooper Gallery, 112
Pechstein, Max, 30
Peller, Lili, 183 n. 28
penetration anxiety, 154
penis, 39, 83, 153, 162, 168, 172
penis envy, 96, 102, 169
"perfect body, the," 55
"perfect female," 151
perversion, 154, 156
phallic, 99, 104; forms, 105; male, 141; power, 28; prop, 110; woman, 46, 96
phallus, 84, 96, 97
Pierson, Pierre-Louis, 16, 176 n. 1
Pine, Fred, 110
"pinup," 104, 107
Piper, Adrian Margaret Smith: 18, 22, 57, 107, 133–43, 167, 173; aggression and identity, 136; "Angry Art," 135; art and therapy, 142–44; black female body in art, 133; black male, 140; conceptual art, 134; double consciousness, 136; I-Thou, 138; "paleface," 136; "real-life" artist, 143; "thought control," 139;
—Works of: *Art for the Art World Surface Pattern,* 138; *Black Skin, White Masks,* 133; *Catalysis,* 134; *Cornered,* 137, 138; *Decide Who You Are,* 135; *Food for the Spirit,* 134, 142; *Four Intruders Plus Alarm System,* 138, 140, 141; *Get Back,* 142; *My Calling (Card) #1,* 135; *Mythic Being,* 141; *Paleface,* 136; *Political Self-Portraits,* 136; *Pretend,* 135, 142; *Self-Portrait Exaggerating My Negroid Features,* 135; *Self-Portrait as a Nice White Lady,* 135; *Some Reflective Surfaces,* 139; *Vanilla Nightmare,* 141
play, 145, 146, 150; space, 157
Playboy, 104, 108
pleasure principle, 113
polio, 73, 80, 87
Pollack, Griselda, 15, 18; *flaneur,* 15
Pollock, Jackson, 89
pop art, 89
pop culture, 144
pornography, 90, 93, 104–5, 115, 153, 154
portraiture, 24, 63, 80
post-human stage, 170
Postmodernism: 37, 39, 129, 130, 137, 146, 160, 173; art, 107, 172
potential space, 45. *See also* Winnicott, Donald Woods
Pre-Columbian: goddess, 86, 130; statues, 79
pre-oedipal relations, 131
prejudice, 136
Prelinger, Elizabeth, 176 n. 12
primal scene, 20, 48, 55, 65, 147
primary identifications, 153
projection, 96, 139, 140, 160

projective identification, 140, 167, 173
proletarian women, 27
Prussian Academy of Art, 33
P.S. 1, 105
psyche, 18, 20, 21, 74, 83, 93, 140, 158, 171
psychic reality, 149
psychoanalysis, 18, 24, 25, 41, 53, 65, 68–69, 76, 90, 124–25, 131, 147, 164
psychopathology, 20–21, 169
purified pleasure ego, 91, 172
Pygmalian, 102

Queer theory, 56

race, 133, 135, 137
racial, awareness, 136; conflict, 140; difference, 173; identity, 133, 135–37, stereotyping, 133
racism, 22, 133–39, 141, 143, 173
racist, 133, 136; fear, 139
Rank, Otto, 51, 128, 181 n. 46
rape, 131, 149, 151, 154, 160
"rape" art, 131. *See* Mendieta, Ana
Rauch, Heidi and Suro, Federico, 180 n. 2
Ray, Man, 42
Réage, Pauline: 164; *Story of O*, 164
rebirth, 152, 163
Reich, Annie, 183 n. 17
Reich, Wilhelm, 91
Reinhardt, Ad, 104, 137
Rembrandt, van Rijn, 15, 24, 35, 148
Renaissance, the, 15, 152
repression, 48, 131, 135
retablo, 79
Rice, Shelley, 176 n. 5
Rimbaud, Arthur, 169
Rivera, Diego, 19, 73, 74, 76, 78, 83–88; *Dream of a Sunday Afternoon in Alameda Park*, 86
Riviere, Joan, 54, 56, 179 n. 33, 183 n. 16; *Womanliness as Masquerade*, 54
Rodin, Auguste, 33; *The Thinker*, 33. *See Also* Käthe Kollwitz
role-playing, 147
Rorschach blot, 48
Rose, Gilbert, 69n23
Rose, Tricia, 134, 182 n. 53
Rosemont, Penelope, 177 n. 43
Rousseau, Henri, 74
Rubenstein, Ida, 54
Rupestrian sculptures, 129. *See* Mendieta, Ana

Sachsenhausen, 71
Sade, Marquis de, 154
sadomasochism, 154 sadomasochistic, 138, 154, 164, 168
safe space, 156
Said, Edward, 118, 181 n. 42
Saint Orlan, 163, 165
Salomon, Albert, 60, 67, 71
Salomon, Charlotte: 18, 19, 22, 58–72, 114, 147, 172; art of trauma, 69; Auschwitz, 60, 72; Charlotte Grunwald (Charlotte Salomon's aunt, renamed Charlotte Knare in the play), 58; Franze Grunwald (Charlotte Salomon's mother), 60, 66; Charlotte Kahn, 61; Grandfather Knare, 67; Grandmother Knare, 67–69; L'Ermitage (the Hermitage), 58; Paula Lindberg (Charlotte Salomon's stepmother, renamed Paulinka Bimbaum in the play), 60, 61, 64, 65, 67, 68, 71; Ottilie Moore, 68, murder of, 60; Alexander Nagler (Charlotte Salomon's husband), 60, 72, psychoanalysis and Orpheus, 67; secrets and suicide, 66; Kurt Singer (renamed Dr. Singsong in the play), 61, 70; Singespiel (Operetta), 64; text and image: love and healing, 64; Alfred Wolfsohn (a.k.a. Amadeus Daberlohn or "The Prophet of Song"), 60, 61, 63–69, 71
—-Works of: *Death and the Maiden*, 71; Dreifarben Singespliel (three-color opera), 60; *Leben? oder Theater?* (Life? or Theater?), 58, 60–66, 69, 70, 72, 172, *The Meadow with the Yellow Buttercups*, 71; *Self-Portrait, 1940*, 59
Salomon, Nanette, 63
Salpètriere, 46, 164
Sandrow, Hope, 132
Santeria, 118, 125–27
Santi, Raffaello (a.k.a. Raphael), 152
Sartre, Jean-Paul: 138; "Black Orpheus," 138; *negritude*, 138
scarification, 107–8, 113. *See* Wilke, Hannah
Schafer, Claudia, 179 n. 41
Schiele, Egon, 24, 171
schizoid, 67
Schmidt, Karl, 30
Schneemann, Carolee, 18, 19, 22, 57, 89–103, 126, 132, 172, 173; and dreams, 94, 97–99; and feminism, 96; and Freud, 89, 91; performance, 89, 93, 100–101
—Works of: "Anti-Dementer: The More I Give The More You Steal," 99; *Eye Body*, 90, 94; *Fresh Blood-A Dream Morphology*, 98, 99; *Fuses*, 91, 93, 94, *Interior Scroll*, 95–98, 102; *Meat Joy*, 89–93, 95, 126; *The Message*, 94; *Mortal Coils*, 94, 95; *Venus Vectors*, 99; *Vulva's Morphia*, 97, 99; *War Mop*, 95, 96
Schwob, Lucy, 37, 45, 57. *See also* Cahun, Claude
Schwob, Marcel, 39
Schwob, Maurice, 39
screen memory, 24
secondary revision, 64. *See also* Freud, Sigmund
Segal, Hanna, 70, 176 n. 24
self, 37, 39, 46, 48, 51, 53, 54, 77, 78, 83, 90, 100, 104, 111, 114, 118, 123, 140, 144–46, 150, 158, 161, 164, 165, 169; analysis, 25, 69, 139; artificial-, 164; cohesive-, 37, 39, 41; concealment, 155; consciousness, 111, 135, 145, 151;155; -conscious, 111, 151; -containment, 78; -creation, 45, 50, 158, 161; damaged sense of, 48; decentered-, 130; -definition, 76, 78, 146, 158; -disclosure, 73, discovery, 25; disembodied, 41; disintegration, 78; display, 100; esteem, 77, 111, fabricated, 78; false, 78; feminine-, 85; fictitious-, 46; flawed-, 85; healing, 21; -hood, 37, 42; hybridizations, 159, 163; image, 37, 74, 78, 85, 151, 156; invention, 130, 155; -knowledge, 145, 147, 149; liberation, 163; loss of, 78, 139; -love, 162, -made prison, 41; mutilating, 168; new-, 161; novel, 78; as an object, 18; -ornamentation, 128; and other, 21, 163; *-othering*, 49; perception, 51; pity, 115, pleasure, 104; possession, 167; presence, 111; primitive, 76; recreating the, 169, referential, 140, 173; reflection, 25, 42, 109; reinvention, 172; revelation, 21, sacrifice, 163; sense of, 74, 76, 134;

self (*continued*)
starvation, 135; studies, 39, 42; as a subject, 138; -sufficiency, 107, 111; -torture, 82; true-, 150; unitary, 156
self-object, 48
self-portraiture, 15, 18, 21, 24–25, 30, 33, 37, 39, 41, 42, 46, 48, 51, 53, 54–56, 61–62, 74, 76, 78–80, 83–88, 104, 107–9, 111, 114, 116, 136, 145, 148, 159, 161, 164, 171
self psychology, 48
self-representation, 16, 18, 21–22, 94, 128, 133, 148, 149, 158, 171; art, 18, 171
Selz, Peter, 24
semiotic theory, 97
separation: 109, 121, 123, 128, 130, 136; -individuation, 110; and loss, 173
September 11 disaster, 155
Serrano, Andres, 153
sensuality, 102
sex, 37, 45, 56, 91, 99, 147; -drive, 122; goddess, 113; object, 109; -phobic, 104, 172; "-pictures," 153; third, 37, 45
sexuality, 21, 37, 64, 89, 91, 93, 97, 104, 105, 107, 111–14, 153, 155, 156, 172, 173, feminine-, 89
sexual, 109, 142, 151; desire, 137; difference, 158; dualism, 45; images, 114; object, 104, 111; organs, 153; preference, 163
shaman, 118
Sherman, Cindy: 18–20, 22, 39, 46, 53, 57, 89, 112, 130, 131, 144–56, 162, 173; "artistic play," 145; 153; clowns, 155; doll play, 153–54; dressing up, 146; *enfant terrible*, 153; hide-and-seek, 144; "Hollywood types," 155; masquerade, 148–49, monster beauty, 162; "Olympia from Hell," 154; Peek-a-Boo, 144; play, 145–46, playing house, 152; "sex play," 154; "vomited fantasies," 151
—Works of: "crying girl (#27)," 147; *History Portrait* series, 152–53, 156, *Untitled #15*, 146; *Untitled #56*, 145; *Untitled #82*, 20; *Untitled #90*, 148; *Untitled #96*, 148; *Untitled #125*, 148; *Untitled #133*, 148; *Untitled #138*, 148; *Untitled #197*, 152; *Untitled #216*, 153; *Untitled #222*, 152; *Untitled #250*, 154; *Untitled #258*, 154; *Untitled #263*, 153; *Untitled Film Stills*, 20, 146–49, 151, 152, 154, 155
Siegel, Judy, 179 n. 16, 180 n. 31
silhouette, 118, 127, 173
Siluetas, 88, 124–25, 129–32, *See also* Mendieta, Ana
Simpson, Lorna, 57, 135
Singer, Jerome, 184 n. 55
Smith, Kiki, 162
Smithson, Robert, 122
Social: activism, 27; construction, 137; Realism, 25–27
Socialist revolution, 25
Song of songs, 97
Soutine, Chaim, 62
space, 137; black and white, 137; healing, 143; potential, 45; third, 45; Winnicottian, 48
Spears, Britney, 107
Spence, Jo, 85, 180 n. 52
Spero, Nancy, 122, 132, 180 n. 6, 181 n. 32
Spitz, René, 51, 76
splitting, 139, 140, 173
Stalin, Joseph, 74, 83
standards of beauty, 111, 168
Stein, Gertrude, 41
Steiner, Wendy, 15, 185 n. 21
Stelarc (a.k.a. Stelios Arcadiou), 162
Stettheimer, Florine, 63
Stevens, Mark, 183 n. 22
Stiles, Kristine, 178 n. 22, 178 n. 24
sublimation, 126
suicide, 19, 55–56, 58, 60–62, 63, 66–70, 71–72, 84–85, 132, 172
Surrealism, 37, 39, 41, 42, 46, 48, 55, 56, 87, 154, 171, 172. *See also* Breton, André
Susan Caldwell Gallery, 110
symbiosis, 39, 41, 49, 51, 128, 136, 173; symbiotic: 110, 123; merger, 19

Tabard, Maurice, 42
taboo, 93, 95, 163
Tenney, James, 91
Titian, 152
Toklas, Alice B., 41
Townsend, Chris, 176 n. 6
transference: 76, 77; manifestations, 164
transformational objects of art, 21
transgender, 56
transitional object, 45, 150. *See also* Winnicott, Donald Woods
transsexual, 56, 165; disorders, 161
trauma, 21, 25, 58, 66, 68–69, 70, 120, 124, 127, 172; of birth, 128; of exile, 123
Trotsky, Leon, 74
Turnley, Peter, 142
twinship, 41, 50

Ubac, Raoul, 42; *Mannequin*, 42; *Portrait in a Mirror*, 42
umheimlich, 46, 157. *See also* Freud, Sigmund; uncanny
uncanny, 19, 46, 48, 147, 150, 157, 161, 171. See *umheimlich*
"uncanny double, the," 46
unconscious: 42, 46, 48, 53, 68, 83–85, 94–96, 100, 117, 125, 165, 171; communication, 140; identification, 69; mind, 172
University of Iowa, 19, 121, 125, 131

vagina, 83, 94, 96–98, 102–3, 109, 114, 154
vagina dentata, 162
vagina-phallus motif, 46
vaginal, 104; art, 112; embodiment, 102; forms, 102, 105, 107, 113, 115, 122, iconography, 172; imagery, 112; orgasm, 97; politics, 96; sculptures, 113
Van Gogh, Vincent, 24, 61, 62
Venus, 111, 115, 130, 159, 165; Jewish Venus, 111; Black Venus (Venus Negra), 130; Boticelli's Venus, 159
venus envy, 102, 111
Vienna Aktion, 126
Vigée-Lebrun, Elisabeth, 15
Village Voice, 112
violation, 133, 136, 151, 154, 162
violence, 89, 95; against women, 131, 173
Virgin of Sorrows, The, 79
Viso, Olga M., 181 nn. 25 and 39
voodoo, 125
voyeur, 20, 106, 147; voyeurism, 131; voyeuristic: 109, 162; gaze, 109, 154

vulva, 97, 98, 115, 160, 161; vulvar, 108
vulvic space, 96, 97

Wallace, Michele, 135
Wallach, Amei, 154, 184 n. 42
Walker, Kara, 141
Wanger, Beatrice, 54
Warhol, Andy, 57, 100
Weimar era, the, 27, 33
Weems, Carrie Mae: 135; *Family Pictures and Stories,* 135; *Kitchen Table,* 135
Weldon, Estelle, 176 n. 11
Werefkin, Marianne von, 25, 175 n. 5
West, Cornel, 142
Western art, 134, 157
Western culture, 130, 158, 160
white: female, 141; female body, 133; pathology, 141; privilege, 134, 137; racism, 138
Wichenhaver, Janet, 180 n. 46
Wilde, Oscar, 45
Wilke, Hannah, 18–20, 22, 53, 57, 85, 94, 102–18, 122, 125, 130, 131, 134, 137, 147, 160, 162, 164, 172, 173; "cunt positive art," 102; illness and death, 114–16; "invisible scars, 107; and mother, 112–14; narcissism-exhibitionism, 112–13, 116, performalist art, 107, 110; relational art, 106–7; scarification/starification, 107, 113; "sugargiver," 102; *Support Foundation Comfort* exhibition, 114; vaginal gumfolds, 107; Wilke's nude, 104–6
—Works of: *About Face,* 114; *Advertisements for Living,* 106; *Agreeable Object,* 103; *Appearances,* 111; *Brushstrokes,* 114; *Centerfold,* 103; *C'est La Vie Rose,* 109; *Double Portrait-Mum and I,* 113; *Double Portraits: Name Brand,* 106, *Generation Process Series,* 113; *Gestures,* 114; *Give,* 110; *Handle With Care,* 110, 117; *Hannah Wilke Can: A Living Sculpture Needs to Make a Living,* 110, *Hannah Wilke Super-T-Art,* 107, 110; *His Forced Epistol,* 110; *Intercourse with . . . ,* 106, 109; *Intra-Venus Series,* 114, 115; *Intra-Venus #1,* 116; *Intra-Venus #3,* 115; *I Object:Memoirs of a Sugargiver,* 109, 111, 131; *Needed-Erase-Her,* 112; *Of Relativity Series,* 113; *Pink Champagne,* 102, 103, 109; *Snatch-shots with Ray Guns,* 105, 106; *So Help Me Hannah Series,* 105, 106, 110, 114, 134, *S.O.S., Starification Object Series,* 102, 108, 110, 112; *Stand Up,* 110; *Venus Basin,* 111; *Venus Cushion,* 103, 104, 111; *Venus Envy,* 102, 111; *Venus Pareve,* 102, 109, 111
Williams, Addette, 182 n. 33
Williams, Sue, 162
Wilson, Judith, 133
Winnicott, Donald Woods, 19, 45, 51, 53, 76, 150, 156, 177 n. 6, 185 n. 26; "good enough mothering," 19; *"potential space,"* 45
wish-fulfillment, 135
witchcraft, 97
Wolf, Naomi, 21
Wolfsohn, Alfred (a.k.a. Amadeus Daberlohn), 60–61, 63–68, 71; *Orpheus or the Way of the Mask,* 68
womb, 113, 115, 123, 150, 161; womb/tomb, 163
woman, 25–28, 31, 33, 128, 146, 171; aging, the, 33–36; allegorical, 27; face of, 25, mythic, 28; "the new," 27; nude, 31; as an object, 21; pregnant, 28; proletarian, the, 26–27; to woman transexualism, 165; working, 25, 28. *See* female
women, 91, 150; artists, 90, 112
women's: art, 174; genitals, 79; self-representation, 94
Wood, Thelma, 41
Woodman, Francesca, 39
Woolf, Virginia, 96, 164; Orlando, 164
World Trade Center, 95
World War I, 32–33, 60, 67
World War II, 32–33, 37, 111, 120
wound, 113, 117, 161

X, Malcom, 141
xenophobia, 133, 134, 136, 143, 173

Yoruban religion, 118
Young-Bruehl, Elisabeth, 141

Zapotec stone grave, 124
Zavitzianos, George, 179 n. 33, 183 n. 16
Zedong, Mao, 74, 83